Conversations with Chaim P

Literary Conversations Series

Peggy Whitman Prenshaw
General Editor

12

42

Conversations
with Chaim Potok

Edited by
Daniel Walden

University Press of Mississippi
Jackson

Books by Chaim Potok

The Chosen, 1967
The Promise, 1969
My Name Is Asher Lev, 1972
In the Beginning, 1975
Wanderings: Chaim Potok's History of the Jews, 1978
The Book of Lights, 1981
Davita's Harp, 1985
The Gift of Asher Lev, 1990
I Am the Clay, 1992
The Tree of Here (illustrated by Tony Auth), 1993
The Sky of Now (illustrated by Tony Auth), 1995
The Gates of November: Chronicles of the Slepak Family, 1996
Zebra and Other Stories, 1998

www.upress.state.ms.us

09 08 07 06 05 04 03 02 01   4 3 2 1
⊗
Library of Congress Cataloging-in-Publication Data

Potok, Chaim.
    Conversations with Chaim Potok / edited by Daniel Walden.
        p. cm.—(Literary conversations series)
    Includes index.
    ISBN 1-57806-345-0 (alk. paper)—ISBN 1-57806-346-9 (pbk. : alk. paper)
    1. Potok, Chaim—Interviews.   2. Judaism and literature—United States—History—20th
century.   3. Novelists, American—20th century—Interviews.   4. Fiction—Authorship.   I.
Walden, Daniel, 1922–   II. Title.   III. Series.
    PS3566.O69 Z475   2001
    813'.54—dc21   2001016151

British Library Cataloging-in-Publication Data available

Contents

Introduction

If Chaim Potok had his way, literary critics and casual readers would refer to him simply as a writer, not as an American writer, and certainly not as an American Jewish writer. In 1976, in one of his earliest interviews, he explains, "I'm an American Jewish writer, and I'll accept that definition if you say to me that Updike is an American Protestant writer and [Flannery] O'Connor was an American Catholic writer and Hemingway was an American Midwestern writer. It's much better, I think, just to say whether you are a good writer or a bad writer and leave it at that."

Potok rose to prominence when his first novel, *The Chosen* (1967), became overwhelmingly successful, and he has dealt with the label, "American Jewish writer," ever since. His novels *The Chosen* (1967), *The Promise* (1969), *The Book of Lights* (1981), and *Davita's Harp* (1985) explore the tensions and conflicts within small Orthodox Jewish communities. Yet, they have extended beyond those boundaries and have been translated into German, French, Dutch, and Japanese, and he remains popular among both Jews *and* non-Jews. In interview after interview, Potok argues that although most of his novels take place in a confined section of New York City, the major themes and conflicts of his work are universal. His novels resonate with his large, diverse audience much in the same way that Faulkner's Yoknapatawpha County, while centered on a particular locale in Mississippi, captured the imaginations of readers far beyond the state.

Born in the Bronx in 1929 and raised in a Hasidic Jewish community in New York City much like the one his characters inhabit, Potok grew up absorbing the values and beliefs of his heritage—including rigorous Talmudic scholarship and strict adherence to Jewish laws and rituals—but was also exposed to the ideals of Western art, literature, and philosophy at an early age. As a child, he showed an artistic aptitude and was encouraged to paint. "I started painting when I was about nine years old, but it became a big problem in my family," Potok remarks. "I come from a very fundamentalist Jewish background, and my father would have nothing to do with painting. Painting to him was the preoccupation of the gentile world."

After his *bar mitzvah,* Potok's painting created quarrels and tension in the household, and he eventually shifted his hunger to create from images on canvas to words on paper. When he was sixteen, he read his first serious adult novel, Evelyn Waugh's *Brideshead Revisited.* Its effects were so vivid that Potok reveals its impact on him with incredible detail in nearly every interview presented here. "It absolutely changed my life," Potok explains. "I lived inside that book with more intensity than I lived inside my own world. . . . When I closed the book, I was *overwhelmed* by my relationship to that book. I remember asking myself, 'What did he do to me? How do you do this kind of thing with words?' " Soon after, Potok was deeply affected by another novel—James Joyce's *Portrait of the Artist as a Young Man*—and made a commitment to write. This decision was met with hostility among members of his former Hassidic community, prompting his move to the more liberal Conservative branch of Judaism. This shift to writing and Conservative Judaism and his engagement with the Western world forced Potok to rebuild his world. When he decided to separate from the Hasidic community, he comments that "it wrenched my world entirely. I lost all of my friends. I lost most of my teachers. I had to literally reconstruct my existence."

The conflicts between Orthodox Jewish values with the world of Western secular humanism became central to Potok's work from then on, permeating his literature in what he continually calls a "core-to-core cultural confrontation." Nearly all of the sixteen interviews here feature Potok's reflections on the Western tradition of creating art—of which he is an active participant—and his heritage among people who are often suspicious of artistic endeavors and flights of imagination. Each of his novels have protagonists from the center of Jewish tradition, who are forced to confront and negotiate space with a crucial tenet of Western culture, be it Freudian psychoanalytical theory, text criticism or, most importantly, art.

Whether writing fiction, children's books, or popular histories such as *Wanderings: Chaim Potok's History of the Jews* (1978), Potok tracks the points in which secular culture collides and sometimes fuses with religious faith, in ways that are accessible to Jews and non-Jews alike. This aspect of his literature stems from both his experiences as a painter and his immersion into Western literature.

This collection of interviews, ranging from 1976 to 1999, allows Potok to reflect on these core-to-core confrontations, which have affected his life and literature. An ordained Conservative rabbi and a world-class Judaic scholar, Potok is engaging, articulate, and philosophical, bringing deep insight and consideration into even the most trivial subjects. With a combination of directness and a staggering depth of knowledge, Potok comes across as a calm, almost clinically precise intellectual, even when discussing difficult personal experiences.

In addition to reading *Brideshead Revisited* and studying art such as Pablo Picasso's *Guernica,* a painting he emphasizes had a profound influence on his literature, Potok's life and art were also altered by his stint as an army chaplain during the Korean War. "It was for me, as an individual and a writer, the pivotal experience and remains the lynch pin in everything that has occurred to me in my life," he tells S. Lillian Kremer in 1981. "I went into that world one individual and came out another individual altogether." For the first time, he saw a pagan world that had not been affected by Judaism, and in which non-Jews worshipped and observed as intensely as he had. In several later interviews, he discusses the effect those two years had on his novels, especially *The Book of Lights.*

Whether the subject is his literature, his religious and academic scholarship, or his life, a conversation with Chaim Potok always seems to lead back to cultural conflicts and uneasy fusions. He sees all great art as something that emerges from the tensions between faith and culture, between the individual's beliefs and the cultural systems and ideas that permeate the artist's existence. An interview about Jewish literature will imperceptibly shift into a discussion of Jewish mysticism and kabbalah, as it does in a 1997 interview with Michael J. Cusick. A 1986 conversation about Potok's perceived readers becomes an examination of Jewish and Christian history. A brief talk about his children's books, *The Tree of Here* (1993) and *The Sky of Now* (1994) turns into a discussion about the conflict between a child's wants and fears. Core conflicts rise to the surface in every conversation with Potok, and the surface is analyzed with more depth than originally thought possible.

It's perhaps surprising that, considering the erudite and learned nature of these interviews, Potok's novels are generally quite appreciated and accessible. *The Chosen* was popular enough to be adapted into a film in 1980, and it—as are several of his works—is often assigned to high school students for class reading. The author freely discusses the hard work that goes into his attempts to make his writing as simple, but also as precise, as possible. His writing style is sometimes as intentionally unsophisticated and straightforward as his conversational style is elegant and complex.

Potok's contribution to literature is profound. It introduces the Western world to modern Orthodox Jewish communities, but perhaps more significantly it makes that very particular world seem eerily familiar to non-Jews.

Though his novels are rooted in the past, in the era of his own childhood and adolescence, Chaim Potok as a conversationalist is deeply committed to the tensions of the present and the universal.

As with the other books in the Literary Conversations series, the interviews in this volume are reprinted in the order in which each interview took place. The interviews have not been edited in any significant way. While this form leads to a certain amount of repetition, it also allows the reader to trace the development of Potok's thoughts, as well as revealing ongoing variations on selected themes. These variations add a rich layer of perspective onto a man known for his articulateness and ability to weave seemingly opposing concepts into a cohesive whole.

Chronology

1929	Born Herman Harold to Benjamin Max and Mollie Friedman Potok on 17 February in New York City.
1945	Begins writing fiction.
1950	Receives B.A. in English literature, summa cum laude, from Yeshiva University.
1954	Receives M.H.L. from the Jewish Theological Seminary of America. Becomes National Director of the Leaders Training Fellowship.
1955	Enters the U.S. Army and serves as chaplain in Korean War.
1957	Instructor at University of Judaism in Los Angeles. Director of Camp Ramah in Ojai, California.
1958	Marries Adena Sara Mosevitzsky on 8 June.
1959–63	Scholar-in-residence at Har Zion Temple in Philadelphia.
1964	Managing Editor of *Conservative Judaism*.
1965	Editor-in-chief of Jewish Publication Society of America.
1967	Publishes *The Chosen*, which receives The Edward Lewis Wallant Award.
1969	Publishes *The Promise*, which receives The Athenaeum Prize.
1972	Publishes *My Name Is Asher Lev*.
1975	Publishes *In the Beginning*.
1978	Publishes *Wanderings: Chaim Potok's History of the Jews*.
1981	Publishes *The Book of Lights*.
1985	Publishes *Davita's Harp*.
1990	Publishes *The Gift of Asher Lev*, which wins The National Jewish Book Award for Fiction. Premier of *Out of the Depths* (play) in

Philadelphia in March. Premier of *Sins of the Father* and *The Carnival and the Gallery* (plays) in Philadelphia in May.

1992   Publishes *I Am the Clay.* Premier of *The Play of Lights* in Philadelphia in May.

1993   Publishes first children's book, *The Tree of Here,* illustrated by Tony Auth.

1995   Publishes *The Sky of Now,* illustrated by Tony Auth.

1996   Publishes *The Gates of November.*

1997   Receives an Honorary Doctorate in Humane Letters from La Sierra University. Wins the Jewish Cultural Achievement Award.

1998   Publishes *Zebra and Other Stories.*

1999   Publishes *Isaac Stern: My First 79 Years.* Premier of *The Chosen,* a play adapted from the novel, which wins the Barrymore Award for Outstanding New Play. Wins the O'Henry Award for "Moon."

2000   Receives the Distinguished Arts Award from the Pennsylvania Council on the Arts.

Conversations with Chaim Potok

A Conversation with Chaim Potok

Harold Ribalow / 1976

From *The Tie That Binds: Conversations with Jewish Writers,* Harold Ribalow, Ed., A. S. Barnes and Co., 1980, pp. 110–37.

Chaim Potok's novels are concerned with Hasidic Jews steeped in their pious traditions, with yeshiva students mulling the complicated passages of the Talmud, with young Jews distressed and unbalanced by overt anti-Semitism. These books have won for Potok an enormous and faithful following in the United States and foreign lands. It is surprising and unexpected.

No one is more surprised than Potok himself. A chunky, bearded man of fifty, Potok is a yeshiva product with rabbinical ordination from the Jewish Theological Seminary of America, a Conservative Jewish institution. Potok also has earned a Ph.D. in philosophy from the University of Pennsylvania.

He has taught Hebrew school, has been editor of the Jewish Publication Society of America and is mainly a novelist. After a run of successful works of fiction, he published *Wanderings* (1979), a popular Jewish history, profusely illustrated, a narrative written with many personal asides. It, too, was a bestseller.

When his first novel, *The Chosen,* was published in 1967, it received the Edward Lewis Wallant Book Award (other winners include Hugh Nissenson, Susan Fromberg Schaeffer, and Robert Kotlowitz). More significantly, it became a national bestseller and Potok soon developed into a highly popular novelist. Each of his novels that followed, *The Promise, My Name Is Asher Lev,* and *In the Beginning,* adhered to the same pattern: wide acceptance, paperback reprints, and international acclaim.

We had met socially and casually in Jerusalem some years before we talked about his work and career in New York City on April 8, 1976. Potok has a home in Jerusalem and another in Philadelphia. When he came to the United States on a brief lecture tour, we met at a business office. He had to fit in our conversation between a number of other commitments. Nevertheless, he spoke unhurriedly, in the measured cadence of a man accustomed to lecturing. He is familiar with the professional language of psychoanalysis (as his novels and his personal conversation attest), and, of course, is extremely well versed in Jewish religious, cultural, and social issues.

Potok has a cohesive view of himself as a Jew and he seems completely aware of what he is trying to achieve in the writing of fiction. In the course of our talk, he said—more than once—that he felt himself to be a "freak" in that Orthodox Jews generally do not write fiction or deal with serious Jewish issues through imaginative works. He is, how-

1

ever, quite prepared to continue writing novels and, reflecting on his
success and vast readership, it is no wonder.

Ribalow: Are you surprised that your books have become bestsellers?

Potok: Amazed. I really thought I was writing about a tight little world. I
wondered how many Jews would be interested in that tight little world, let
alone those who are not Jews, people who haven't the remotest notion of
what that world is all about. It's been as much a mystery to me as it has been
to a lot of people. In some circles it has been rather an embarrassment, particularly in some intellectual circles, that is to say, the popularity of these books.
I'm not altogether certain I understand *why* they are popular. The fact that
they are popular is a never-ending source of surprise to me.

Ribalow: You once publicly observed that you questioned the importance
of imaginative writing in the Jewish tradition. What do you think now?

Potok: Well, I think the imagination as such, the faculty of the imagination
and its lonely outpourings, have always been suspect to the intellectual. Maimonides, for example, wrote with great suspicion about the workings of the
imagination. One of the reasons for this is that the intellect has boundaries
and functions in disciplined form. Without discipline, and without boundaries, the intellect cannot maneuver. Even when it maneuvers right up against
its boundaries, and makes attempts to push the boundaries away, there is
always a sense of set configuration, established norms, insofar as intellectual
maneuvering is concerned. One works with ideas that have form. The imagination takes inordinate leaps. One of the characteristics of the imagination is
precisely the fact that it will fight boundaries; it will jump beyond boundaries.
Also, it nourishes from an element of the human being which those who are
very much taken with matters intellectual are very often frightened of. And
that is: the imagination nourishes from the more volcanic aspects of man;
that is to say, his unconscious or his subconscious. That gives rise to very
mercurial material and the intellect is almost by very definition very leery of
that kind of jumping. As a matter of fact, one of the basic problems in modern
philosophy, the one posed by Hume, and possibly by some preceding Hume,
has to do with one element of the imagination that must be utilized if science
is to make any progress. And that is the jump that is made in the process
called induction. It is a jump or a leap of the imagination and a scientific
mind does not quite know how to cope with that inductive leap. It has remained to this day one of the basic problems in epistomology. Now, if that

key element of scientific model-making is a puzzle to the intellectual mind, the whole faculty of the imagination is clearly going to be bewildered to the intellectual mind. Since the Jewish tradition very strongly emphasizes the workings of the intellect, the mind, particularly scholarship, more specifically scholarship in Jewish sources, in the Talmud, the workings of the imagination on that produce creativity bounded by aesthetic norms—that kind of working has always been suspect in traditional Jewish sources. It remains so to this day.

Ribalow: In line with this, I was reading the English novelist Alan Sillitoe, who wrote *The Loneliness of the Long Distance Runner* and *Saturday Night and Sunday Morning.* He is, by the way, deeply involved in Jewish subjects and is a supporter of Israel. I was reading in an autobiographical work called *Raw Material,* and I came across a line I thought I would ask you about, "Everything written is fiction, even nonfiction." Then he adds, "Anything which is not scientific or mathematical fact is colored by the human imagination and feeble opinion."

Potok: The fact of the matter is that even hard scientific data and "mathematical fact" are colored. But the point that he is making is a very important one and that is that we are essentially model-making beings. We don't know what reality is. We take the raw data that impinge upon our consciousness, our perceptions, and when we think that data, we are already giving it structure and configuration. So that even when a mathematician thinks a model, that thinking is a construct. I used to think, when I was doing my doctorate at the University of Pennsylvania, in secular philosophy, that at least logic was the bedrock of human thought. Until I read Quine's *Mathematical Logic.* He makes the point very clearly that it is even possible for models of logic ultimately to be impinged upon to such a degree where we will have to alter even that bedrock itself. There really is nothing that is fixed and permanent in principle insofar as human thought is concerned. By the way, Edward Albee made an interesting remark some years ago when someone asked him what fiction was. He said, fiction is fact distorted into truth.

Ribalow: In how many languages do your novels appear?
Potok: In French, German, Hebrew, Japanese, Portuguese, Danish, Dutch, Swedish. . . . I must have left a few out.

Ribalow: Many in paperbacks, I'm sure.
Potok: As a matter of fact, they are in hardback in virtually all the editions.

There is one country that publishes initially in paperback—France—but, if I remember correctly, *Asher Lev* appeared there in hardback. The first two appeared simply in soft covers.

Ribalow: Is anything of yours being filmed or staged?

Potok: Nothing staged, but there is a production company that has been formed to do *The Chosen* as a movie, and there is an option on *Asher Lev.* [In 1980, *The Chosen* was filmed.]

Ribalow: What kind of mail do you get?

Potok: I get a lot of mail from the hardback readers, and a lot of it runs now all the way back to *The Chosen,* where people pick up the book for the first time. I would say it is easily fifty to sixty percent non-Jewish. Usually, people tell me how warmly they reacted to the book. I suspect that the people who don't like the book don't write.

Ribalow: Why do you think non-Jews read your books?

Potok: I think I have inadvertently stumbled across a cultural dynamic that I didn't quite see clearly myself until sometime toward the end of the writing of *The Chosen.* I think what I am really writing about is culture war. The over-arching culture in which we all live is the culture we call Western secular humanism, the culture that Peter Gay of Columbia University calls modern paganism. Within this culture there is a whole spectrum of subcultures. The basic characteristic of the over-arching culture is what I call the open-ended hypothesis; that is to say, nothing is absolute in any kind of permanent way. A model is a shifting or temporary absolute on the assumption that additional data will be discovered that will impinge upon a given model. That model must be altered. So there is a constant search for new knowledge that is built into the civilization that we live in, this over-arching civilization. But imbedded inside this civilization we have a whole series of cultures which come into this world with *givens,* with models that are fixed absolutes. If they are alterable, they are alterable only under inordinate pressure. What happens is that these subcultures clash in a variety of ways with the over-arching culture, as somebody from this subculture grows up and encounters elements from the outside model.

Ribalow: How does your work fit into this?

Potok: Now, *The Chosen* was about someone from the center of the Jewish tradition clashing with one element from the model of Western secular humanism; that is Freudian psychoanalytic theory. *The Promise* is about a boy from the center of the Jewish tradition clashing with one element from the center of Western secular humanism; and that is text criticism. *Asher Lev* is about a boy from the center of the Jewish tradition clashing with one of the fundamental elements of Western secular civilization; and that is its *art*. And the last book is about a family clashing with the underbelly of Western civilization; that is its anti-Semitism. So what I am trying to present here is a clash of cores of culture, centers of culture. Bellow has his Jews along the periphery of the Jewish tradition, connected emotively to their pasts, but they are in the center of Western secular humanism. Now Western secular humanism has many problems of its own: alienation, dread, the fragmentation of the human being, a hunger for a scaffolding for a particular life. When a person in the center of Western secular humanism encounters the problems of Western secular humanism or modern paganism—if he is still connected emotively to his past—he will see those pagan or secular problems through the tonalities of his particular past. So the Bellow heroes are Western secular humanists but they see the problems of that humanist through Jewish eyes. The Updike people are Protestants so they see the problems of Western secular humanism through Protestant eyes. That is another kind of culture clash. You get the culture clash where people are along the periphery of two cultures. Philip Roth's people are all the periphery of things Jewish. They think Judaism means *kneidlach* and gefilte fish.

Ribalow: *Bauch Judentum.*

Potok: That's right. At the same time, they really don't know the essential nature of the richness and wealth that is at the heart of modern paganism.

Ribalow: Modern paganism?

Potok: Western secular humanism. I use the terms interchangeably. I don't use them in a pejorative sense at all. I'm simply using the term that Peter Gay is using. I think he is using it correctly. He thinks that Western secular humanism is Venetian blinds, wall-to-wall carpeting. When you get a rub up of periphery of cultures, you get cultural monstrosities that are created. That's the world that Roth explored in his Jewish books, *Good-bye, Columbus* and so on. So you get various models, you see, of cultural conflict. *The Portrait of the Artist as a Young Man* by James Joyce was another such model. What I seem to have stumbled across is a kind of core-to-core cultural confrontation. What non-Jews are doing—if I can get it from the letters they are sending me—is that they are simply translating themselves into the particular context of the boys and the fathers and the mothers and the situation that

I'm writing about. So instead of being a Jew, you are a Baptist; instead of being an Orthodox Jew, you are a Catholic; and the dynamic is the *same.* The culture war is the *same.* The particular words or expressions that might be used might be Jewish or what have you, but they are simply putting themselves into the place of the subculture which is clashing core-to-core with the umbrella culture in which we all live.

Ribalow: You were a teacher and a rabbi. How did you happen to turn to the writing of fiction?

Potok: No, I started to write when I was fourteen years old. I've been writing since I really was a kid. I wanted to write the day I finished reading a novel that really changed my life. It was a novel about upper-class British Catholics.

Ribalow: Really?

Potok: You won't believe this story. Evelyn Waugh's *Brideshead Revisited.* It absolutely changed my life. It was an extraordinary encounter with that novel. It was the first serious adult fiction I had ever read. I lived inside that book with more intensity than I lived inside my own world. It was the exact reverse of anything you would think would affect a nice Jewish boy in New York going to a Jewish parochial school. When I closed the book, I was *overwhelmed* by my relationship to that book. I remember asking myself, "What did he do to me? How do you do this kind of thing with words?" That's where my commitment to write began. It was really born—very concretely—out of that encounter, with that *one* book. And it lasted.

Ribalow: Have you read his other work and did any of it have the same effect on you?

Potok: Yes, I've read others, but no, it was that *one* book. It may have been because it was a religious book that it had this effect on me.

Ribalow: I have been working on a literary study of American Jewish writers and I thought I would begin with a definition of a "Jewish" writer. I have read what writers consider a Jewish writer; I have read through symposia on the subject and it really became terribly confusing. The truth is, after you get through reading forty people, all of whom have thought about it, there is no definition. I'll ask you, then, have you a definition of a "Jewish" writer?

Potok: No, but I'll say this. I'm an American Jewish writer, and I'll accept that definition if you say to me that Updike is an American Protestant writer

and O'Connor was an American Catholic writer and Hemingway was an
American Midwestern writer. It's much better, I think, just to say whether
you are a good writer or a bad writer and leave it at that. The most banal kind
of definition would be, "An American Jewish writer is an American Jew who
writes about Jewish subjects." You know, that solves all your problems right
away. Therefore, John Hersey, who wrote *The Wall,* cannot be an American
Jewish writer. Norman Mailer, who is Jewish, isn't an American Jewish
writer because he writes nothing Jewish. But then you have a double problem
when you have an American Jewish writer who sometimes writes about Jewish subjects and sometimes doesn't, or when you have a situation like an
American Orthodox Jew who doesn't write about Jewish subjects at all, like
Herman Wouk. I think that the struggle for the definition is not a profitable
one. No matter what definition it yields, it doesn't really clear up anything. I
suspect that we are much better off if we just move away from that kind of
category.

Ribalow: Graham Greene wrote two kinds of books, one of which he
called "entertainments" and the others were, obviously to him, "serious"
novels. Are you writing "entertainments" or are you trying to be educational,
or are you "giving a message"?

Potok: If you want to give a message, you better write public relations.
I'm really trying to track this core-to-core cultural confrontation in as honest
a way as I can. I'm not interested in writing public relations nor am I particularly interested in writing "entertainments," nor do I regard these novels as
entertainments, to tell you the honest truth. I can't imagine how anyone could
regard them as entertainments.

Ribalow: I read your novels in a special way. I got through reading *In the
Beginning* not long ago, and I see that you and I attended the same yeshiva.
Our backgrounds are somewhat similar. So as I read the novel, I find it a
remarkable achievement that you make dramatic things that one imagines
cannot be made dramatic. A *shiyur,* an intellectual argument between a rebbe
and his student. Theoretically, anything can be made dramatic, but I sometimes think I'm especially intrigued because I've experienced some of it. But
most readers haven't.

Potok: Non-Jews seem to be interested in that, too. I think that is one of
the essential tasks of a novelist, and that is what Henry James and others used
to say, "Dramatize! Dramatize! Dramatize!" Tell the story in a way that
dramatizes what it is you have to say.

Ribalow: Will you write fiction about non-Jews, too?

Potok: The first novel that I wrote, which was almost published and which turned out to be the source for a fight inside a publishing house, had no Jews in it at all. It was all about Americans and Koreans. That novel was ultimately not published. The editor-in-chief of the house accepted it. The publisher did not want it. He didn't feel that it was going to sell. I withdrew it and the editor-in-chief resigned subsequently. I'm glad, in retrospect, that I withdrew it because I know now how to handle the material. I wasn't quite sure how to handle it then.

Ribalow: To jump to another subject. May I ask why you have elected to live in Israel?

Potok: We don't live in Israel, we sort of reside there for part of the year and then come back here. We used to be in the States ten months and in Israel for two months.

Ribalow: Jerusalem.

Potok: Yes, Jerusalem. Then we decided, in '73, to take a crack at Israel for a year. Then the war broke out so we decided maybe we'd better extend it another year so that the children don't get a feeling that Israel is such a depressing place in which to live. We'll probably be back here in a year or so.

Ribalow: Do you plan to write about Israel?

Potok: I think not so much about Israel but about Jerusalem. I want to explain the dimensions of that city in fiction.

Ribalow: Are there any of the modern Hebrew writers who impress you?

Potok: Yes, I'm particularly impressed by two or three. Amos Oz, Aleph Bet Yehoshua, and by Aharon Megged.

Ribalow: Do Israelis know American Jewish novels, stories, writers? I hear complaints by many American Jewish writers who visit Israel that Israelis seem to be oblivious to American Jewish writing.

Potok: That's a fair generalization. They do not particularly care about it; they think it is another world.

Ribalow: What you are writing about, then, is a world twice removed.

Potok: Well, no. As a matter of fact, it's interesting that it is otherwise. A Yemenite came over to me once and said he felt the same experience in terms of culture clash in Israel as one of the characters in the book. This was after I gave a talk about the novels at the University of the Negev in Beersheba. The dynamic is identical. It's going on in Israel just as well as it's going on here, in the same way. You have subcultures inside the overarching culture. Israel is essentially a secular culture. The culture war goes on. The problem in Israel is that it is all subdued beneath the overwhelming effort of the country to stay alive and secure inside that ongoing battle, the war it is having with the Arab nations. But this cultural tension continues.

Ribalow: Do you read contemporary Jewish fiction?

Potok: Yes, I try to keep up. I feel myself very much a part of the stream of novel writing and I try to keep up with it as best I can.

Ribalow: As a Jewish editor—which you have been—what do you think of modern Jewish fiction?

Potok: I think it is one of the most exciting things that has happened in Jewish history in a very long time. We are a people with a long history of culture warfare . . . four thousand years of culture wars. The first was with the culture of the river civilizations in the Near East, particularly its Caananite expression. Out of that culture war came a literature called the Bible. We were then involved in a culture war with Greek and Roman paganism. Out of that culture war came a literature called the Talmud, Midrashic works that were not accepted by the Jewish tradition, and so on. We were then involved with a culture war with Christianity and, for a period of time, with Islam. Out of that came another literature, some of it polemical in nature. The war with Islam was a core-to-core confrontation in Spain and produced an *exquisite* literature. We call that "The Golden Age of Spain." We are now involved in a fourth culture war and that is with secular humanism. I don't know what kind of literature is going to be produced by that culture war. But one aspect of that literature is already becoming discernible, and that is the novel. Some Jewish novelists are tracking aspects of this culture war, whether they know it or not. Bellow is doing the periphery confrontation. I'm trying to track the core-to-core confrontation as best I know how. Others are doing other variations of it. Some may end up doing secular core to secular religion confrontation because the battle goes both ways. It isn't unusual for me to go to a campus today and find a Lubavitcher Hasid who was once brought up in an absolutely secular home but somehow the Hasidim got to him and all of a sudden he's a *baal t'shuvenik*; he's being transformed. So the dynamic functions in many models and in all directions. I think that what is exciting about this American literature is that it is tracking, whether it is aware of it or not, various kinds of cultural confrontation. I have no way of knowing now, no way of guessing, what kind of final shape this literature will take. It's *very* exciting.

Ribalow: As I listen to you, a question comes to mind. You have been editor of the Jewish Publication Society of America, so I would like to address this question to you. Why has the JPS always been backward in publishing creative writing?

Potok: Precisely because the Jewish Publication Society represented a bastion of the Jewish intellectual, the scholarly intellectual. It's exactly in line with what I said before: the novel is a flippancy, a frivolity, and how could you conceivably offer a novel to a serious scholarly audience? If it is good, it is dangerous. If it is poor, it is banal. So why bother with it? That's been changed since I came to the Society. The whole configuration of the Society is quite different today from what it was when I inherited it. It was a publishing house whose basic intent it was to produce scholarly works. The emphasis was, just as it always has been in the Jewish tradition since the close of the Biblical period, on matters of the intellect. So since Sol Grayzel—God bless him, he has just turned eighty—was interested in history, there was a heavy emphasis on historical works. Had a Talmudist been the editor, there probably would have been an emphasis on that aspect. I came in; I was interested in belles lettres and, very slowly, the balance shifted. [Dr. Grayzel died in 1980.]

Ribalow: On Hasidim . . . does your knowledge come from your personal background or from your research?

Potok: It comes from two aspects. First of all, it comes from personal knowledge.

Ribalow: It's in all the novels.

Potok: Except the last one. It's not there because the Hasidim don't teach the Bible. It was impossible to set the last novel in any kind of Hasidic framework. It had to be set in a Galician-Lithuanian framework, as it were.

Ribalow: But your people are still religiously observant.

Potok: Very observant, because I'm talking about the core of a culture in confrontation.

Ribalow: At the very end of *In the Beginning,* the father is just as upset with the son's going into Wellhausen Biblical criticism.

Potok: The novels were arranged, when I planned them. . . .

Ribalow: You planned them?
Potok: Yes.

Ribalow: When you began with *The Chosen,* had you planned the others?
Potok: No, no. But toward the end of *The Chosen,* it became very apparent
to me that the novel I was writing was running away with itself.

Ribalow: Was *The Chosen,* when it was published, the complete book? I
had heard that you had written a book and that it was submitted, that it was
edited and that *half* of the novel was published.
Potok: What happened was . . . this is what I'm trying to say to you . . .
toward the end of *The Chosen,* it became apparent to me that it would be
impossible for me to include within the boundaries of that one book all the
problems I wanted to handle. The novel was suffering from a surfeit of pleni-
tude. It was just an impossible aesthetic situation. Bob Gottlieb, who read it,
sensed that also. I took it home and cut it. I threw out the whole section I
couldn't use anyway. It involved hundreds of pages. What was left of it involved some rewriting. *That* was the novel ultimately published as *The Chosen.* Already in the writing of the last part of *The Chosen,* it became apparent
to me that I could not handle it. Problems that I wanted to handle began to
divide themselves into four basic elements. I set them up in a sort of nebulous
way at first. Then it began to take clearer and clearer shape in a hierarchy, a
kind of rising crescendo of core-to-core cultural confrontations. Danny Saunders in *The Chosen* is able to make some kind of accommodation between
his Orthodoxy and Freudian psychoanalytic theory. Reuven Malter in *The
Promise* is able to make some kind of accommodation between his Orthodoxy and text criticism on the Talmud. Asher Lev sometimes can make an
accommodation between his Orthodoxy and Western art and sometimes cannot. The point to Asher Lev, of course, is that since the Jew has not contributed any aesthetic vessels, as it were, to Western art, his range and
maneuverability in the area of aesthetics is very limited. If ever there is an
experience that will require him to utilize a certain motif that is a horror
aesthetically to the Jew, he will utilize it as an artist because an artist chooses
for his art. Now *Asher Lev* is written purely in the realm of aesthetics. It is
not an halachic problem. Halachically, you can paint all the crucifixions you
want.

Ribalow: Really?
Potok: Yes, you are not violating Jewish law so long as you don't paint

them for purposes of worship. It is *not* an halachic problem that Asher Lev violates.

Ribalow: What is it, then?

Potok: It is an aesthetic line that he crosses. In the eyes of the Jew, the Orthodox Jew, the Crucifixion immediately triggers images of rivers of Jewish blood, because of the deicide charge. For Asher Lev it was a mold. Into that mold he pours Asher Lev just as Picasso also drew a Crucifixion at a critical moment in his life; Chagall puts Russian Jews on crosses and paints Crucifixions. This is, basically, the way the novels were arranged. I began to see that I had a set, as it were, of problems. The final one absolutely cannot be handled within the boundaries of Orthodoxy and that is the problem of text criticism applied to the Bible. And that is bound up with anti-Semitism, certainly in the last century. The last problem is the whole spectrum of traditional Jewish responses to one core element of Western secular humanism—its anti-Semitism.

Ribalow: You mentioned this earlier.

Potok: It is important. Bound up with that anti-Semitism is the way so-called objective scholars handled the Hebrew Bible in the last century. The problem with that is if you just push the anti-Semitism aside and if you come from the core of the Jewish tradition, you discover that despite the anti-Semitism, there are truths to the problems that they posit. You then have to ask yourself, "Do I run away from those truths? Am I in a kind of Jewish tradition that says to me I can't look at the truth? That I can't confront the truth in the marketplace of ideas?" The dilemma here is that it is precisely your love of the Bible that brings you to this kind of scholarship. If you are an honest enough individual, and really hunger for the truth, you are going to have to contend with this scholarship. The irony is that you cannot contend with it within the framework of Jewish Orthodoxy. You've got to leave that boundary.

Ribalow: Your *rebbes* always seem to understand this.

Potok: I am convinced that within Orthodoxy there are minds who fully understand the dilemma of the extraordinary student.

Ribalow: You make that clear.

Potok: They are there. They are willing to take the risks or have their best students take the risks rather than have them stagnate or rather than have them break entirely with Judaism.

Ribalow: You have touched on some of the incidents and themes I have been wanting to ask you about. Nonetheless, let me formulate a few of the ideas that struck me in reading *The Chosen.* Your major young men are Danny Saunders and Reuven Malter. The first is the son of a Hebrew teacher and Reuven is a member of a distinguished Hasidic rabbinical family. Yet Reuven moves from his rabbinical background to clinic psychology and Danny moves to the rabbinate. Isn't that paradoxical?

Potok: There is an underlying symbolic structure to *The Chosen,* which somebody discerned in a piece that he wrote on the novel in a scholarly journal. He sensed it and explored it. I'm talking about the core of the Jewish tradition. I'm talking about it all the time. I decided right off the bat when I was writing *The Chosen* that I had better define what I meant by the core of the Jewish tradition. And that's the reason for the baseball game in the opening scene. In that baseball game you have two aspects of Jewish Orthodoxy in contention. You have the Eastern European aspect, which prefers to turn inward and not confront the outside world. You have the Western European more objective scientific aspect within the core, within Orthodoxy, that is not afraid to look at the outside world that produces scientists. These are in interaction with one another inside the core. That's the baseball game. The way the kids play ball, their styles, the way they think of one another. Then the way David Malter teaches his son Hasidism is an example. I didn't just stick that in there just so that people should learn about Hasidism! There's a point to that! The point was to show you how a Western-oriented, more scientific Orthodox Jew handles historical data. He's very sedate; he's very calm; he'll question this or that aspect of the life of the Baal Shem Tov; he'll talk about the development of Hasidism; he'll talk about the various Hasidic sects. This is his style of teaching as over against the synagogue exhortations of Reb Saunders, which is a more traditional way of teaching, the Eastern European way of teaching. Those two speeches, those set pieces, were my way of defining for myself, and for the reader, what I meant by the *core* of the Jewish tradition. Then, once I had that definition, I take it and confront it with one of the elements from a core of Western secular humanism, that is to say, Freudian psychoanalytic theory, and the book goes on from there.

Ribalow: I've made this point before. In *The Chosen* and, of course, *The Promise,* you use the Talmud as dramatic material. It works very well. How did you conceive using the Talmud this way? When I first read *The Chosen,* I was excited by the very concept of the center of the drama being an intellectual debate on the road to earning a *smicha.*

Potok: First of all, it *is* exciting. If you have experienced it, it really is exciting. My problem was how to make it exciting inside the pages of a book.

Ribalow: I think you succeeded even more with your Reb Kalman.
Potok: Yes, yes.

Ribalow: Because the reader starts to hate him, changes, feels sorry for him. . . .
Potok: Doesn't know how to react to him and finally is ambivalent.

Ribalow: He is sort of. . . .
Potok: Sympathetic, yes.

Ribalow: He ends up a real, living person.
Potok: Yes, I felt that way myself about him as I wrote him.

Ribalow: You did have many problems in writing these novels, didn't you?
Potok: I was confronted with an aesthetic problem that I had to solve in dealing with the Talmudic passages. If I were to do the content of a Talmudic dispute, the whole thing would get bogged down. So I did away with the content and I abstracted the form. So what you are really reading is the interpersonal dynamics of Talmudic disputation—*contentless.* You will note that I almost never insert an actual piece of content inside one of these dramatic Talmudic confrontations. I tried to do that with the last book, *In the Beginning,* with the Bible, but it was impossible. There I had to give very concrete examples of what it was that I meant.

Ribalow: In *The Promise* you have this fourteen-year-old boy, Michael, with his breakdown, and a clinical psychologist trying to bring him out of a catatonic situation. Then you have Reb Kalman, who is rigidly Orthodox, threatened by modern scholarship. He is somehow uncertain about his own situation, not unlike Michael. With Kalman, is this part due to his experiences in the concentration camp?
Potok: Yes, that uncertainty comes from the suffering that he has experienced and leads, in turn, to his certainty. He says to himself, I cannot have gone through what I went through and have lost what I lost if it's all meaningless. Therefore, the very experience serves to reinforce his commitment to the past. The alternative is to say that Hitler succeeded, that everybody really died for nothing. That reinforces his certainty. At the same time, he has lost his whole world. He is in a strange, bewildering world here. He is listening to the music of that past world. And somehow he manages to find it in the

way Reuven Malter studies Talmud. Yet Reuven studies Talmud in a way that is threatening—to Talmud, and threatening to the way that his world studied Talmud, because Reuven Malter takes a Talmudic text and makes it something fluid. That is terrifying to any fundamentalist mind, because the very basic notion of a fundamentalist mind is that the text is a given, it is fixed and our task is to understand it. To reconstruct the text first! That's a terrifying notion to any fundamentalist mind. So here is Reb Kalman in his incredible dilemma finding a boy who has the same love passion for the Talmud and studies it with the same music that Reb Kalman heard his best student studying it back in Europe, but at the same time this boy poses the biggest threat to his, Reb Kalman's, love for the Talmud. That is another piece of the underlying structure of the novel.

Ribalow: What makes it so original is that who else is writing about such things in America today? I don't know if you can undertake to write on such a subject unless you have the discipline and the training for it.

Potok: The experience. . . . Do you know what the ultimate irony in all this is? I heard Maurice Samuel once complain about what it was people like Philip Roth and others were doing with Jewish tradition. And I said to him, "How do you know about the Jewish tradition? The only place you can ever really learn it is if you go to a yeshiva and study it from the inside, from the core." The irony is the longer you go to a yeshiva, the less regard you have for the whole enterprise of writing novels. They look upon it as an utter waste of time, as *bitt'l Torah*. Why are we surprised that yeshivas don't produce novelists? They don't want to produce novelists!

Ribalow: Who is surprised?

Potok: He was. I said, You're not going to get people who understand the core from the core because the core doesn't write about itself because the core denigrates writing. It is only concerned with Talmudic scholarship. I'm a freak! I really am a freak! I had to fight my way up through the yeshiva all the years that I spent there after the time I made my commitment to writing.

Ribalow: It seems clear this is so from the way you create your people. Obviously it is personal. Your Mr. Malter and Mr. Gordon are based on actual people.

Potok: Yes, yes. Michael Gordon's dilemma. . . .

Ribalow: The love-hate conflict.

Potok: Yes, the love-hate is one of the prices you have to pay for a core-to-core cultural confrontation. I don't mean at all to make it sound Pollyannish. There's a terrible price that is paid sometimes for this kind of situation where it can't be handled and the result is a complete paralysis of creativity. You love and hate the same person at the same time—you are absolutely paralyzed. I might add that the isolation experiment that is run in *The Promise* was actually run by a clinical psychologist six or seven times. In two of those instances, the child became catatonic and the therapy was stopped. The catatonic state terminated. The therapy was resumed and in all the instances, the children became amenable to normal therapy and ultimately were returned to normal life.

Ribalow: That's what happens in your novel.
Potok: Yes. That's based on clinical data.

Ribalow: Some critics have complained that you don't deal with love, romance, sex. What do you say to them?
Potok: It all depends on how you deal with it and what you mean by "dealing." If I had to deal with romance in my novels as part of the aesthetics of the novel, that is, if it were really necessary, I would deal with it. If I had to deal with sex—with the sex act—as part of the need, the structural need, for a novel, I would deal with it. I'm not averse to dealing with that kind of material. But I'll be damned if I'm going to put that stuff in just to spice up a book.

Ribalow: In rereading *The Promise,* I found exciting material. The *smicha* exam, for rabbinical ordination, with the questions on the emendations of the texts and the different and varying editions of the Talmud. Is that fiction or reality? The Napoli edition, the Yerushalmi. . . .
Potok: Reality. That all exists. There are editions like that. You can check them.

Ribalow: Are you saying, then, that many of the yeshiva rabbis and scholars are ignorant of them?
Potok: Yes, oh, sure. They may not be ignorant of them but they certainly don't deal with them in the sense of parallel texts the way somebody, let's say in the Jewish Theological Seminary, would deal with them. As far as they are concerned, the text that they have, the Shulsinger Talmud, is *the* text.

Ribalow: Which yeshiva did you attend?
Potok: Yeshiva University, Rabbi Yitzhak Elchanan. And Salanter, the Talmudical Academy, which is the high school of Yitzhak Elchanan.

Ribalow: I also attended the Talmudical Academy, but then I also was a student at the Beth Medrash Lamorim, the nonrabbinical school.

Potok: I went to the yeshiva, not the Beth Medrash Lamorim.

Ribalow: I recognize, of course, the difference. . . . My first question on *My Name Is Asher Lev* is different from what I thought it would be. As I read it, it hit me that you are the only American novelist who has written about Russian Jewry. That is, aside from Arthur Cohen in *A Hero of His Time,* which came out somewhat later. In *Asher Lev,* as well as *In the Beginning,* you do this well: you depict and describe what is happening in the "outside" world as it impinges on your people. In *In the Beginning,* you take the time to deal with Father Coughlan and the emergence of Hitler. Where Asher's father is a *shaliach* of a sort, you introduce the subject of the Russian Jews. No one writes about this in fiction. To a degree, I wonder why. Do you ever reflect on this?

Potok: They don't know that world. A novelist writes about the world that he knows best.

Ribalow: Malamud, in "Man in the Drawer," wrote a short story about a Russian Jew and, of course, there is Cohen's novel. Have you read it?

Potok: No, I haven't seen it yet, but, yes, I know of it. It's about the Russian poet who comes to the United States, yes.

Ribalow: There's very little being done on the subject. Let me get on with Asher Lev. He is from the Crown Heights section of Brooklyn and I assume you are, too.

Potok: My wife is from Crown Heights.

Ribalow: And the Ladover yeshiva in your fiction I assume is the Salanter yeshiva.

Potok: No, the Ladover yeshiva is a Lubavitcher yeshiva.

Ribalow: I see. In line with something I said earlier, the passage of the holidays, the way in which you see everything through Jewish eyes—a woman wears a dress and you call it a *shabbos* dress—these observations, I would think, come instinctively. And, of course, it all gives richness to your stories.

Potok: Right.

Ribalow: You also have the father speak of illegal yeshivas in Russia and throughout Europe and as Asher Lev travels about. . . .

Potok: He sees them. As I said before, the novel is on the level of aesthetics, entirely. The father also has his aesthetic world. The father's aesthetics is *Tsimmes* on *Shabbos*. The father's aesthetic material consists of the Jewish people, which he is trying to remold and rebuild and save. The father's aesthetic world consists of the yeshivas that he is creating; that's also a kind of creativity. Asher Lev is engaged in one sort of artistic creativity. One might say of the Jewish tradition that its real artists were the rabbis, that the raw material of the rabbis were the people and that the goal of creativity was the sanctification of the total people in all its areas of life. That's the last thing in the world you would say about a Western artist. The Western artist's material is his paint, his canvas, his colors, his hues—right? And his goal is to express his own particular vision of the world.

Ribalow: Yes, you make this point throughout the novel.

Potok: There's a whole library of aesthetics in the Western world; there's no library of aesthetics in Jewish writing.

Ribalow: How did you think of writing of a painter?

Potok: I have painted before I was writing.

Ribalow: Have you ever sailed, as one of your heroes does?

Potok: Oh, yes. I love that.

Ribalow: I ask because these are seeming contradictions. I was just wondering whether you simply chose those subjects from out of the blue or drew from your own experiences.

Potok: No, I took them from myself. Also to show that in certain areas one can be inside the secular world or "the world" without necessarily having to be any sort of threat whatsoever to the core of the Jewish religion.

Ribalow: What of the gambling scene in *The Promise*?

Potok: That's something else. You see, the point I'm trying to make is that you can be inside the core of Judaism and at the same time enjoy the world. But, at certain points, particularly the ideational elements of the world, you are going to come into serious conflict. But sailing, playing ball—you can enjoy that. Gambling in *The Promise* is fundamental to the whole structure of the novel. I have in my house in Philadelphia 1,100 pages of typescript that I threw out, that ended up being the first fifty-eight pages of *The Promise*.

Ribalow: You have just answered one of my questions. I was curious to know if you do much rewriting.

Potok: Uh. Over again and over again, to get that very simple style that so many people go crazy about and can't stand. I will strip something down to its barest bones. First of all, I have this feeling that florid prose often covers up obtuseness of ideas. Secondly, I was very much taken, when I was young, with the sonnets of Milton. I remember studying them. My major in college was English Lit. I was tremendously influenced by one particular teacher at Yeshiva University.

Ribalow: What was his name?

Potok: David Fleischer. I'll never forget studying the sonnets of Milton and being awed by the utter simplicity of the language of those sonnets. The language is *so* simple and yet he takes those simple words and he puts them together and makes out of them configurations of exquisite beauty. I never forgot that. I was writing prose at the same time. From that point on, I felt myself beginning to cut down and pare away the prose that I was writing. My notion is that a sentence has to be transparent. You've got to be able to look right through it. If it's somehow thick and unwieldy, it's bad writing and you're hiding something. There's something somehow that you haven't ex-pressed correctly. Some people go crazy over this, because they cannot stand this kind of prose. Now I have a great regard for Updike's prose, for example, and I love reading the good stuff of Nabokov, but I can't write that way. It's a very personal preference on my own part.

Ribalow: I have a reference here to the constant confrontations between Asher Lev and his father on art and Judaism. Asher's mother observes, "Your father sees the Jewish people as one body and one soul. When a head hurts in the Ukraine, your father suffers in Brooklyn."

Potok: Yes, that's the Jewish concept of "all Jews are responsible to one another."

Ribalow: You include a passage in *The Promise,* of which I'm not sure of the source, whether it's from the Midrash or whether it's your own. You say there are three kinds of Jews in the world. . . .

Potok: That's from the *Taanya.*

Ribalow: The *Rosho,* the one who sins and has evil thoughts. The *Benoni,* the one whose acts are without fault but cannot control his thinking. . . .

Potok: And the *Tzaddik,* the righteous man.

Ribalow: And the *Tzaddik;* only *Tzaddikim* have control over their hearts.

Potok: Their hearts and their actions. That comes from the *Taanya,* which is, I would say, the central book in Lubovitch Hasidism.

Ribalow: Jacob Kahn, the old master artist and teacher of Asher Lev, is also a very interesting character. There is a tendency to try to guess who these people are, but we have to assume they are imagined characters. Kahn says, "Art is not for people who want to make the world holy."

Potok: *Absolutely not.* Correct.

Ribalow: It is a sentence that struck me when I read it. Again, Kahn says, "Art is a religion" and calls it a tradition of goyim and pagans, and its values as goyish and pagan.

Potok: By goyish, of course, he means Christian and pagan.

Ribalow: Your Asher Lev is in a dilemma. Right in the middle. But he does feel responsible for his people.

Potok: He has a tremendous sense of responsibility and that's the anguish.

Ribalow: And Kahn says that the responsibility of the artist is to his art.

Potok: Right, to his art.

Ribalow: Yet Asher Lev's mother seems to understand this to a greater degree than Asher's father. I'm not sure whether it is understanding or whether she wants to encourage her son.

Potok: Part of the reason that the mother understands it is that she is able to stand away from both of them simultaneously. The father is involved in his work; he is always running around. She is alone standing by the window. Asher Lev is suddenly involved with his work and he is gone. She stands at the window and can think. Can you imagine what the mother is thinking of as she stands all those hours and all those days by the window? She is able to achieve a distance, some kind of perspective on both of these people. She is also doing her own work, you see. It is not that she is a vacuous individual. She is a significant person and is able to think. It is because of that that she is able to sympathize both with the husband and with the son. At the same time, she is torn by the two of them.

Ribalow: You seem to know a good deal about the techniques of art. You have painted, as you said a while back.

Potok: Yes.

Ribalow: There is the slow realization that the attraction of Michelangelo's Pieta motivates Asher Lev to begin to think in terms of the Crucifixion. No doubt you have been to Italy.

Potok: I saw the Pieta and I had the same reaction to it.

Ribalow: How did you arrive at the concept of the observant Jew identifying with the Christ image?

Potok: That was one of the longest, most agonizing processes I've ever lived through in my life. The reason for it is that I kept fighting it.

Ribalow: Just like Asher Lev.

Potok: I absolutely kept fighting it. In the back of my mind, I knew it was something that was going to happen.

Ribalow: I've made a note here, saying, "agonizes over Crucifixion." So it was not only Asher Lev. It also was you.

Potok: I wrote the book and kept living it as I was writing it. It was the strangest kind of experience because I kept saying to myself, "There's going to be another way out of it." And I kept checking it with people—what would you do? What would you do? What would you do?

Ribalow: I remember that a few years ago, when I was in Jerusalem and we met in Professor Moshe Davis's home, you were in the midst of the novel and you did raise this question.

Potok: Yes, I was always asking. I kept checking with people. It seemed inconceivable to me that I had stumbled across an idea that led to such an absolute blank wall. There is no other form in Western art other than the Crucifixion that a Jew can use to depict ultimate, solitary suffering? There has to be! Well, there isn't. Now, on the assumption that this Jew is committed to his people—he comes from the core of the Jewish tradition and is at the same time committed to Western art, which is what Asher Lev is—when he is confronted with the particular dilemma that *he* is confronted with, he will choose for his art. And the only vessel available to him at that point in his life by means of which he can express his feelings of his mother's protracted solitary torment, the only aesthetic mold available to him, is the Crucifixion. Jews haven't participated in Western art. Religious Jews haven't participated in Western art. There are no Jewish molds in Western art. So he turns to the Crucifixion. Again, he is not violating Jewish law. What he is violating is an aesthetic line he is crossing.

Ribalow: It is the same thing when he draws the nudes.

Potok: Exactly. But the nudes are containable, you see. But the Crucifixion evokes images of rivers of Jewish blood. Jews were slaughtered for that. So the *rebbe* cannot excuse that kind of thing. He has a revolution on his hands in the terms of the community. The *rebbe* cannot answer his people any more, and so he sends Asher Lev away.

Ribalow: What has been the "Jewish" reaction?

Potok: I get it in the head—constantly. Every time I speak, somebody says, "Why did you *do* that?"

Ribalow: They do?

Potok: Yes. They ask, "Why that?" or "Pick the Holocaust." I said that, first of all, the Holocaust is not a theme in Western art yet. It's not a mold. Nobody knows what to do with the Holocaust. On the assumption that it will become a mold in a hundred years, the last thing in the world it is going to be is an aesthetic mold for ultimate faith. There is no other mold in Western art than the Crucifixion to depict that particular feeling.

Ribalow: When I started reading *In the Beginning,* I recalled a few lines by A. E. Housman, who was a favorite of my youth: "I am a stranger and afraid, in a world I never made." James T. Farrell used these lines for the titles of two of his novels. I thought of these lines in connection with your work because your novel, in a way, deals with Jews in "a world full of goyim." This did not hit me when I read your earlier novels. But here there is a special quality in your descriptions of anti-Semitism, the street hoods, of whom one is Polish and one is Jewish.

Potok: That's right.

Ribalow: How did you come up with the image of a Jewish hood, one who attends the same Hebrew school that David Lurie goes to?

Potok: There are bullies all over. I picked a Jewish bully, first, to show that bullying is something endemic to growing up; secondly, to show the difference in quality between a goyish bully, whose bullying is based on anti-Semitism, which is something inexplicable. The Jewish bully's actions are based on envy. He doesn't evoke the kind of terror that the Polish boy evokes. His reasons are comprehensible. The other one—bewildering! Also he has a thousand years of hate behind him. He represents something.

Ribalow: You have David Lurie growing up in the Bronx. Your earlier books are set in Brooklyn. Where are you from?

Potok: I was raised in the Bronx, right where I wrote that book.

Ribalow: Again, you bring many current events into your work: The Hebron pogroms in 1929 and the Depression and the Wellhausen Bible criticism.

Potok: They called it higher anti-Semitism.

Ribalow: These Bible critics weren't Jews, were they?
Potok: No, they were Protestants.

Ribalow: One reviewer of *In the Beginning* comments on the constant ailments afflicting David. He gets colds frequently. He has a leg infection. He undergoes surgery. Why do you make him sickly?
Potok: First of all, he was. Second, one of the things I wanted to do with this boy is put him into a world filled with bewildering accidents. One of the most bewildering of accidents is anti-Semitism to the Jew. That is to say, one never knows where and how it is going to strike. The accident, plus the photograph, form the basic controlling metaphors of *In the Beginning*. The concept of accident, and how the Jew handles it—what do you do after an "accident"?—by accident I can mean anything from killing an animal to a major catastrophe. What do you do the Monday after the Sunday of the accident? How do you lead your life? That, plus the controlling metaphor of David Lurie's relationship to the photograph, to what went on before the photograph, what's in the photograph and what came out of the photograph— those two poles comprise the controlling metaphors of that book. And I'll let others figure out how those two poles work.

Ribalow: There are constant references to contemporary history: to Father Coughlin and his anti-Semitism, to Vladimir Jabotinsky, the father. . . .
Potok: Of Revisionism.

Ribalow: And the concentration camps. The camps enter your story with great impact. It wasn't what I expected to find as the novel was going along.
Potok: That's the greatest accident of all.

Ribalow: The half-dozen pages on the impact of looking at the photograph. . . .
Potok: You see how the two metaphors finally are joined at the end?

Ribalow: The pictures?
Potok: It is the pictures of the concentration camps. It is the photographs of the greatest accident of all. You see how the book is structured. It is the photographs of the greatest accident of them all that the Jewish people has experienced. Fused together, they take David Lurie out of his Orthodoxy and tell him, "I've got to dedicate my life to fighting what it is that these accident-

makers are doing with something that I take to be the most beautiful photograph of all; that is to say, the picture of my people as given in the Bible."

Ribalow: There is a hint of that in the earlier photograph taken of a group of Jews, posing with knives and guns in Poland, ready to fight for their own survival and identity.

Potok: Exactly. That's one of the basic elements of the way the book is structured.

Ribalow: You also list a lot of the books one should be familiar with.

Potok: You can do your own course of Bible criticism by just reading this material.

Ribalow: Let's return for a moment to the two photographs. The first shows a group of European Jews—armed. And David Lurie is admonished to forget it because it was illegal at the time for Jews to carry weapons. The second depicts death camp agonies, with bodies piled on bodies. That's what motivates David to move to the side of the secularists.

Potok: Right. Very good. It's the union of the two metaphors that run all the way through the book that finally turns him away in an attempt to really understand, by entering the world that caused the accident to his people, that is to say, the secular world. As a result of the fusion of these two metaphors, he leaves his Orthodoxy, enters one of the metaphors: the secular world, in order to understand better the other metaphor: the photograph, the Bible, which is the picture of his people at a certain period of time. He has got to use secular instrumentalities on a sacred book, secularize that book in order to get out of the book what it is that is truly unique about his people. In other words, what were their beginnings really like?

Ribalow: Yet the father cannot forgive him for what he calls "going to the goyim." This father is not a *rebbe*. He is removed from the Jews you wrote about in your previous novels. Yet he is just as rigid and adamant as they are.

Potok: He suffered at the hands of the goyim, remember. How can any father let his son go to the goyim and let him use their instrumentalities on the *Chumash*? It's incredible.

Ribalow: That's an echo of what happened earlier, when Rav Kalman went to the Talmud to examine different texts.

Potok: The difference there is the rabbi's son can make his accommodation with Freudian psychoanalytic theory. He drops the Freudian anthropology, he drops the sociology and he uses the therapeutic process to heal human beings. That's an accommodation. You can quarrel with that accommodation, but it is valid and he says to you, I'm helping people. Reuven Malter takes scientific text criticism and uses it on the Talmud. He won't use it on the Bible, because for him the Bible is a divine work, whereas the Talmud, we can see, is the creation of man, we know when it was edited and so on, and people debate it. So he will not take it into the boundaries of the Bible. Once you do so, the Biblical text becomes fluid and the Orthodox Jewish tradition cannot contain the notion of the fluidity of the Biblical text because all of Orthodox Jewish law is based upon the fixity of the Biblical texts, particularly the first five books of Moses. So you cannot apply this methodology to the fundamentalist text.

Ribalow: What of the Higher Biblical criticism?

Potok: The Higher Biblical criticism is even worse than text criticism. It talks about sources and editors, so you end up not knowing what comes from where. It's a very powerful and dangerous instrumentality as far as the Orthodox Jew is concerned. In order to do it, you have got to leave Orthodoxy.

Ribalow: I have a question I have been wanting to pose to you. Cynthia Ozick has a new book called *Bloodshed and Three Novellas.* She has an introduction to the book in which she goes to some lengths to explain one of the stories, because she struggled to make the story particularly clear and one non-Jewish critic didn't understand what she was writing about. In this introduction, she writes, "English is a Christian language. When I write English, I live in Christendom." She makes the point that had that particular tale been written in Hebrew or in Yiddish, no Yiddish or Hebrew reader would have had trouble with it; it would have been crystal clear to that reader. Because the critic was a goy, *naturally* he didn't understand it. So let me ask you: Is English a Christian language?

Potok: English is not a Christian language, although there are Christian elements in the English language. English is an amalgam of I don't know how many languages. There are whole elements of English borrowed from pagan culture as well and borrowed from Mediterranean paganism and borrowed from Teutonic paganism. . . .

Ribalow: Do you think she means that if you are writing like Yehezkel Kaufmann for Jews in a Jewish language, only the Jews know what he is saying when he is being critical? This way, if she is writing in English, somehow or other, things she is trying to say Jewishly get blocked?

Potok: Well, then, the problem in a situation of that kind is for the writer somehow to abstract from his material the particularist elements in such a way that the dynamic of what it is that he is trying to express is capable of being communicated. It isn't only language that has this problem. Art has it as well. There are artists who are transcultural; there are artists who can only talk to their particular region. This is not a problem unique to language. It is a problem that any artist has: How to jump from *your* particular to all the particulars of all the readers who might one day encounter you? How did Evelyn Waugh jump across his world to me? He did it somehow. Evelyn Waugh was not writing *Jewish.* He was writing *English.* I'm a Jew. I read him as a Jew. How did he jump across to me? My problem as a Jew, when I write English, is not as a Jew. I don't have a Jewish problem. I have a problem as an artist. My problem is how to create a particular world in such a way that, first of all, it is crystal clear to me and to my eyes, what it is that I am saying. The boundaries have got to be sharp.

Ribalow: Isn't it the failure of some of the Jewish writers that they are uncertain as to what they want to say?

Potok: They are murky. They don't really understand what it is they are writing about. And if you are murky and don't understand what you are writing about, a Christian won't understand what you are writing about. It has absolutely nothing to do with the fact that the English language is Christian. It is not Christian. There are Christian elements in it, there are Greek elements, there are German elements, there are Jewish elements, Middle English. . . . How can anyone say the English language is Christian? It is not! Its beauty lies precisely in the fact that it has absorbed the language systems of so many cultures. That is its richness. And I rather suspect that somebody who says that the English language is Christian is really saying that what he is writing is murky and cannot be understood.

Ribalow: I'm bothered when I see certain writers become successful and I think little of them. It happens very infrequently that I read someone like you and enjoy both the work and your success.

Potok: Thank you.

Ribalow: And yet I'm not alone. Having been raised to some extent in your world, I think I'm closer to your books than other readers are. I can't help wondering—when I see your novels become bestsellers—"Who are all these readers; where do they come from?" But it is happening and it is a very fine thing.

Potok: Yes, and I also try not to think about it too much. Because when you begin to write for people, you are through. I'm grateful for it. I accept it for what it is. I'm constantly mystified by it. And when I'm in my room, doing my work, I'm writing for myself.

Chaim Potok

Elaine Lindsay / 1978

From *Literature in North Queensland,* Volume 6, Number 3, English
Language and Literature Association, 1978, pp. 68–71. Reprinted by
permission of *Literature in North Queensland,* English Language and
Literature Association, University of New England, Australia.

EL: Why do you write?

CP: For the same reason that I breathe—there's not much choice in the
matter. The fundamental task that I set myself when very young was to attempt to clarify my own personal experiences by utilising the medium of
serious storytelling, to mould, to give shape to and to probe the nature of
what it is that we do with our lives, human experience. I do not intend to use
the novels to teach or to convey messages . . . the only thing I want to do
with the novels is to explore human relationships and my own place in this
very big and often very lonely universe.

EL: You're passing on personal experience rather than the experience of
the race?

CP: I don't think that personal experience can be divorced from the experience of whatever particularity an individual is embedded in. The experience
that a novelist explores might be his own personal one, but he's probably
going to find that he is in some very deep way related to other people around
him. In my own instance the people are the Jewish people and so an exploration of the nature of Asher Lev and his conflict became an exploration into
the nature of the Jewish people and their relationship to this extraordinary
adventure we call western art.

EL: This relationship or conflict seems peculiarly intense within the Jewish situation . . .

CP: Because the choices are rather agonizing. My own personal experience was not the kind of polarization that's typical of heroes in the modern
novel—generally they're polarized against the world that gave them life and
so at a point they will break with that world and it might perhaps be easier
for them. Certainly painful but perhaps a bit easier for them than it is for
some of my people to break with their world because they really continue to
love their world.

What I am confronted with in these novels is an exploration of the dimensions of antagonistic loves. These boys love the particular world from which they came and in which they are still embedded. At the same time they have come across components from the umbrella civilization in which we all live, that is to say, the secular world, western civilization, and have fallen in love with those elements of secular civilization.

So what you have is a situation where two loves are in conflict within the same individual. Two loves can live side by side but when they really clash as is the case with Asher Lev there's no way of winning—whichever love it is which you choose, the other love is gong to be hurt by it.

EL: Is it a conflict between moral and aesthetic blindness?

CP: I think that the Jewish tradition has its own aesthetics and its own sense of morality . . . its aesthetics have very little to do with the aesthetics of the western world. I don't know that it's a matter of blindness—I really think it's a matter of having a different sense of the aesthetic nature of reality. The Jew's aesthetics are in the service of morality, the service of man and the service of the commandments. But the aesthetics of Asher Lev are just aesthetics for the sake of beauty itself, for the sake of enhancing the world so that it becomes a prettier place to live in.

Sooner or later these two different senses of aesthetics are going to clash, as they do when Asher Lev confronts the problem of painting the crucifixion. There isn't anything legally wrong in the Jewish tradition with painting the crucifixion—you can paint all the crucifixions you want as long as you don't paint them for purposes of worship. What the crucifixion does to the eyes of a Jew is that it evokes pictures of rivers of Jewish blood, because of all the hundreds upon thousands of Jews who have been slain for the deicide charge through the centuries. What Asher Lev violates is an unwritten moral aesthetic code, and he violates it because he has no choice; an artist must choose for his art by definition, no matter who's going to be hurt as a result.

EL: Why is there no Jewish tradition in art?

CP: It's an inordinately complex problem but I might be able to sum it up in this way. In the ancient world all art was inextricably linked with paganism, with the gods—you made images of the gods and you wrote dramas for the gods. The Jew, the Israelite, came into the world with an alternative reading of reality. His was a world not bound by the nature-deities and he loathed the image-making activity of man. Since all of drama and all of graphic creativity was involved with the gods the Jew backed away from that and funnelled all of his creative energy into the one area of human expression where image-making was not three-dimensional—words.

Once image-making became stripped of its relationship to the gods, the Jew began to enter that arena of creativity as well, but that has happened relatively recently in human history because of the connection of the graphic arts to pagan reality. Jewish civilization came into the world at war with the nature cycle to which pagan reality was bound and it broke the cyclical grip that nature had on human experience—the gods live, the gods die, the gods are resurrected, they live, die . . . that is what man participated in and it was with this that the Jew broke, making God as he saw it beyond the nature cycle, freeing man so that he could create a new world, a new reality with a dream for the future rather than nothing but this endless cyclical trap in which pagan man found himself and the ancient world.

EL: In *Asher Lev* you suggested that if the Jew becomes an artist it is incumbent upon him to become a great artist, this being the only way to justify what he's done to everybody else's life. Is this applicable also to the writer?

CP: I think that writers pay a terrible price for what they do; they pay it in loneliness, and very often they pay it in the harm that they do to other people by opening up images of reality that people would prefer not to see. I think the only justification for this kind of activity on the part of the writer is that he do it as honestly as he can, and that he try to do it better each time, with greater skill or for a greater purpose.

I don't want to make it sound as though life is all gloom and doom for an artist—there are great moments of joy, a kind of soaring that one rarely feels in normal life. But the artist feels that not very frequently—most of it is hard, gritty work. The only compensation for the hard work, for the pain that he sometimes causes people is the truth that indeed there are people who are grateful for the honest mirrors that they are shown of themselves. That makes the hard work of the artist, a person like Asher Lev, more than worth-while—if he can create a really beautiful work of aesthetics that can at the same time be a truth.

An Interview with Chaim Potok

S. Lillian Kremer / 1981

From *Studies in American Jewish Literature*, Volume 4, 1985, pp. 84–99. Reprinted by permission of *Studies in American Jewish Literature*, Dan Walden, Editor.

Kremer: Like your nineteenth-century European counterparts, you have a dual career as rabbi-scholar and creative writer. Few American novelists have been involved as you have in non-literary scholarship. Certainly your Hebraic erudition is evident in the fiction's Yeshiva scenes. Would you comment on the integration of translation, scholarship, and imaginative literature in your life and work? Did you intend to integrate the three from the beginning of your career?

Potok: Yes, looking back, that was probably the reason I chose to go to the Jewish Theological Seminary. I know that I really never wanted to be a pulpit rabbi. When I was finished with Yeshiva University, I had a choice I could have made at that point, either to go on to Columbia or Harvard to do a doctorate in English literature. I knew that I wanted to write fiction and I knew that my subject was going to be, in one way or another, Jews and Judaism and its interplay with the twentieth century. I decided at that point to go to the seminary to get a broader and deeper understanding of the nature of things Jewish. I had lived a life thus far inside an ancient tradition and I decided to see if there was anything deeper to it, broader to it, that I could begin to utilize and that is really the fundamental reason I went to the seminary. Always, whenever I chose to do something it was, and still is, to utilize it in fiction. That is one of the things that ends up happening to someone who thinks of the world through fiction. It seems to me to be absolutely impossible not to end up having fiction became a Kantian category of thought. In a very strict technical sense almost, just as time and space and modality and causality are categories of thought. You cannot think the world outside of cause and effect or outside of time and space. Someone who is serious about writing fiction cannot think of the world outside the categories of fiction. My whole world has been an effort to utilize the sophisticated learning at the seminary for fiction, the very sophisticated learning at the University of Pennsylvania, where I got my doctorate in secular philosophy, very deliberately chosen to

see what the center of the Western World was really like, for fiction. All that
for the purpose of seeing whether somehow those aspects could be fused,
and not to be overly romantic about it, to see in an honest way what aspects
of the two cultures really could not be fused, were absolutely impossible in
terms of blending.

Kremer: How successful do you think this fusion can be?

Potok: The mechanism of fusion is an interesting one. It is what I call a
selective affinity. From inside one culture you take a look at another culture
and you select out of that culture those elements that you feel some affinity
with and those are the elements that you attempt to blend. Now, why you feel
an affinity to this or that aspect of another culture is a function of tempera-
ment, training, rebellion, and millions of encounters that go into the creation
of a human being at that point in time. We fuse with those elements that we
feel good about in another culture. Sometimes those elements fusing with us
spark tremendous creativity. But there are aspects of secularism that I think
no Western religious thought can easily fuse with and as the novels progress
what I try to do is present increasingly greater difficulties of fusion. My
subject in all my books is the interplay of the Jewish tradition with the secular
twentieth century. My subject is the attempt to fuse the cores of two cultures,
because the Jews that I write about are at the very heart of their Judaism and
at the same time they are encountering elements that are at the very heart of
the umbrella civilization. Danny Saunders encounters Freud right from the
heart of western secular humanism. Obviously, it is very easy to fuse with
Freud. Just ignore Freud's anthropology. Reuven Malter encounters text criticism right from the universities of western secular humanism. It is easy to
fuse with scientific textual criticism. Ignore its application to the Bible. Asher
Lev encounters western art. What is more central to the western adventure
than its art? It gets very sticky to a certain point to fuse with western art
because Jews have no real experience with western art until the modern period. So Asher Lev has a problem. In western civilization the only aesthetic
vessel available to us for the depiction of a long solitary torment is the crucifixion. Asher Lev paints a crucifixion because as a painter he has to express
his feelings and the only vessel available to him is the crucifixion. David
Lurie encounters scientific Bible criticism right from the center of Western
civilization, the universities of Germany in the last century. And he encounters also its anti-Semitism, right from the heart of Western civilization. And
it is impossible to fuse with scientific biblical criticism from a fundamentalist

stance and David Lurie cannot do it and has to leave his fundamentalism. So these are core-to-core culture encounters. Those confrontations are the invisible scaffolding of the novel. What I'm really writing about is the feelings of people involved in those confrontations because a novel is not only time and character, but is also feelings. Whether the feelings are suppressed as they are in Hemingway, or dealt with openly the way Jews would deal with them.

Kremer: In light of your interest in core-to-core conflict, I wonder if you plan an Israeli novel and whether you plan to explore the core-to-core encounter between Jewish émigrés from European and Arab backgrounds. Have you considered that subject for a future novel?

Potok: Absolutely. That Jew will have his core-to-core confrontation in Israel along the same cultural dynamic lines that a Jew here in the United States might have his or her cultural encounter *vis-à-vis* the umbrella culture here which is western secular humanism. The umbrella civilization in Israel is Jewish-western-secular-European. I call it a WASH culture, white, anglo-Saxon, Hebrew culture. The Sephardic Jew coming from an oriental country will have a culture encounter with that umbrella civilization. I certainly want to write about Israel, or more specifically about Jerusalem, and you couldn't possibly write a novel about Jerusalem or Israel and not have that as one of the major problems to deal with.

Kremer: When we talked last, I asked you about the sparse treatment of women in your novels and you indicated that you thought a woman might play a more significant role in the Jerusalem novel. I presume that is because the women have taken a more productive and assertive role in Israeli society than their Hasidic counterparts have in Orthodox communities.

Potok: That may be so, but there is another important aspect to the role of the women in the novels and why I feel they will probably play more significant roles in the future and that is why I'm slowly moving away from that nineteenth-century world I talked about, that close, family-centered, tightly structured Jewish world, where indeed the woman does play secondary and tertiary roles. As you move more and more away from the rabbinic tradition, enter more and more into the secular world, the secular Jewish world, the secular world generally, you have to deal more with the role of women.

Kremer: As we sit before your bookcase, which contains many examples of traditional Judaic sources, the books of the Talmud, *Pirke Avot,* and copies of your own novels, I am eager to get some clarification on the sacred and secular in your fiction. Some critics discuss the flight of your protagonists from the religious to the secular world in autobiographical terms. You are successful in both worlds, as a scholar and novelist. How do you integrate the two?

Potok: I grew up in both worlds simultaneously. I was reading English books when I was a kid. At the same time, I was reading Hebrew books. I was studying Talmud at the same time I was reading Stephen Crane and mastered a passage of Talmud at the same time I was trying to master a passage of English prose. I would study the chapter of a novel that I liked in exactly the same way I studied a text of Talmud. I don't know any other way to study. You take the text apart and try to figure out the way it was put together.

Kremer: New Criticism is not so modern after all, is it?

Potok: Not as far as I'm concerned. I wasn't terribly interested in what the author intended. Nor was I terribly interested in what the author was. Had I really been interested in what the author was, I could never have gone to Ernest Hemingway, because I regard Ernest Hemingway as a not very pleasant human being. But the first ten years of his prose, that is to say from *In Our Time* to *A Farewell to Arms,* is really splendid. I have always been a part of both worlds. The problem has always been, for me, how to fuse core elements of both worlds and how far you can go with fusion before you lose the essential nature of one's identity. As I said earlier, there are lines that you might think you cannot cross. You cannot cross toward Judaism as a secularist; you cannot cross toward secularism as a participating Jew. But having said that, the ability to maneuver between the two cultures is so enormous and so potentially enriching that there is a lot to talk about before you draw the lines. Even if you leave Judaism's fundamentalism, you do not necessarily leave it. You have a community and a history that you can relate to.

Kremer: Would you speak to the use of your autobiographical references in the fiction? How much does David Malter's portrait owe to your father-in-law and to what degree is Max Lurie's character based on your father's Polish experience?

Potok: My father-in-law was a Labor-Zionist; he was a very learned Jew, modest, traditional. He was not a Talmud scholar. That aspect of Malter's personality came from someone else. The character of David Malter, his humanity, was very much the humanity of my father-in-law, when I came to know him. As far as my own father was concerned, yes, he served in a Polish unit of the Austrian army; and yes, he was tough; and yes, he was a Revisionist; and yes, he saw the world as sharply divided between Jews and non-Jews; and yes, he didn't care very much for non-Jews because he thought their main job was to kill Jews; and he had some very bitter experiences in the Polish army. He had fought in the Polish army against the Russians for between three and four years and his reward was a pogrom when he returned. So the fathers were borrowed from the core characters of real people. Certain aspects of both fathers are either creations of the imagination or taken from other individuals, but the cores of both fathers are substantially the cores of people who once lived and are now dead.

Kremer: Is young David Lurie's experience with Eddie Kolansky analogous to your own experience growing up in New York?

Potok: The bicycle episode was invented. The experience of anti-Semitism is very real and very vivid and anyone who grew up in any of the urban areas in the United States, whether it was New York or Boston, any of the big cities, will have experienced that or some similar instance of anti-Semitism. I experienced instances of anti-Semitism in New York on more than one occasion and had occasion to defend myself a number of times. The illness of David Lurie is in part mine and in part my brother's. The world of the imagination and the accidents of David Lurie are partly mine and partly the imagination. But that was a very real world and some of it is still there. The streets, the zoo, a good deal of it is still there. The people are no longer there. The people are gone. The schools are gone.

Kremer: To what degree is the Brooklyn world you write of your own? Did you travel in Williamsburg Hasidic circles?

Potok: My wife grew up in Crown Heights. As a matter of fact, she grew up about a block and a half from the international center of Lubavitch. She grew up on Eastern Parkway and I lived in Brooklyn for a couple of years. I did not live in Williamsburg, but I know that area very well. Friends of mine lived there so it wasn't too difficult to do the research. Once you know the people, once you know the insides of the people, where they live can be very easily researched. Hemingway researched virtually all of *A Farewell to Arms* because he wasn't in Italy during the Caperetto retreat which occurred much earlier, much before he got there. Hemingway knew the Italian army to a certain extent. *A Farewell to Arms* is a research novel, much in the same way Stephen Crane's *The Red Badge of Courage* is a research novel. What is important is that you have an organizing vision so that the research forms a tapestry and isn't chaotic.

Kremer: Have you had Hasidic response to your novels?

Potok: Yes, and it is mixed. They are not monolithic, as *The Chosen* makes clear. Hasidim have different views of the novels. Some regard them highly; some would rather that they had never been written. Even within the same Hasidic group, there will be differences of opinion. Some Lubavitchers think *Asher Lev* is an abomination and others think *Asher Lev* is great and so on.

Kremer: Toward the conclusion of *In the Beginning* David Lurie rebukes his brother Alex with the observation that turning from sacred literature to fiction is a lower order of human endeavor. Did you experience similar judgment when you turned from the rabbinate and Judaic scholarship to fiction?

Potok: There was anger. There was rage. I still experience it. There is something in the Jewish tradition which casts a very definite denigrating eye upon the whole enterprise of fiction. Somehow it just doesn't seem to be very high on the scale of important things the Jew would dedicate his or her life to. Scholarship is what counts in the Jewish tradition, Talmudic scholarship, not the product of the imagination. That was always frowned upon because it was a menace. The imagination is boundless. It knows no rules and regulations. It is outside the pale of the rational. Rabbinic Judaism of the Talmud is rational; it is bound by the mind and is suspicious of the imagination. Imagination is pagan; imagination is Greek.

Kremer: Is Alex Lurie an autobiographical character?

Potok: One aspect of that character is autobiographical and that is the revolt into aesthetics. There are a number of ways that a person backs off from his or her own heritage and chooses his or her own road to travel, if there are problems with the heritage. For a long time, my revolt was an internalized one and, looking back on it now, it was not too difficult for me to realize that I took one of the safest ways out. Rather than break up the family and create all kinds of havoc outwardly by breaking with the forms of the religion, I internalized the rebellion and by moving into the world of the novel, I entered into an aesthetic rebellion.

Kremer: If I may take you back for a moment to an earlier comment, you said you never intended to have a pulpit. Yet, I understand that you were in the United States Army Chaplaincy in Korea. Did you function from the pulpit in that instance in the traditional sense?

Potok: Oh, yes. I was an army chaplain and, of course, this was a require-
ment for graduation and ordination from the seminary. We were volunteered,
as it were, to serve in the United States armed forces because there were, at
that point, an insufficient number of Jewish chaplains.

Kremer: I read in *Wanderings* that you believe the Korean experience to
be a crucial one in terms of the encounter of a Jew with Oriental culture and
that it caused you to examine your faith in a different way than you had
before. What was the significance of that experience to your writing career
as a whole and to *The Book of Lights* in particular?

Potok: It was for me, as an individual and a writer, the pivotal experience
and remains the lynch pin in everything that has occurred to me in my life. I
went into that world one individual and came out another individual altogether—not so much changed outwardly in the sense of observance, but profoundly changed inwardly so that everything that I saw had altered radically.
I was taught all the time, as I was growing up, that paganism is an abomination. If you read the Bible carefully and take it seriously and study some
passages in the Talmud seriously, you realize quickly enough the attitude of
Judaism toward paganism, its forms, its values. Judaism is a counter-culture,
a radical counter-culture to the pagan world. I found things that were extraordinarily beautiful and in an ironic way I began to really discover beauty in
the world through a pagan culture, the beauty of God's world through paganism, an intriguing bit of irony. I discovered another paradox. I had been
brought up to believe that Judaism made a fundamental difference in the
world and I ended up in a world in which Judaism meant nothing. It was a
rich culture, an alluring culture that had ugliness in it, and it had horror in it,
and it had beauty in it. It was certainly no more savage than our own Western
culture and in many ways a lot more structured, with a more profound sense
of the unity of things. It required a lot of rethinking and it took me a long
time before the rethinking even began. And what I started to do was work
backwards. What I decided to do was go back and find out who it really was
who went there. And the different kids I've written about are probably different aspects of my own being. So you have Danny Saunders, Reuven Malter,
Asher Lev, David Lurie, their various worlds and various families, teachers,
and so on. *Wanderings* was written so that I could clear up in my own head
the cultural package that I carried with me to that country. And this last book
was written to attempt to cope with the encounter itself. How can one possibly respond to a century in which all the dreams that we dreamed in the first

fifteen years of the century, have been reduced to dust. Nothing of the golden dreams with which the century began really materialized in any significant way. In the final analysis, the most crucial encounter I experienced when I was in the Far East took place when I stood at Hiroshima. And I knew, in the most mind-boggling way, that if it hadn't been for certain Jewish physicists, that bomb would never have been developed. And, it was dropped on the wrong enemy. If you care about things Jewish, and if you care about being a human being, some sort of response has to be worked out toward a paradox of that kind. The whole century is full of paradox of this kind, where somehow things just did not work out. How do you go on to the next century knowing this? When are we going to have a greater time? When are we going to give ourselves better gifts from our own species than we have given ourselves in the early decades of this century? All this was triggered at the moment when I stood at the center of the bomb blast.

Kremer: Clearly the horrible events of Hiroshima have influenced your thinking and your creative efforts. I remember reading that you believe that a Jewish writer writes from the framework of the Holocaust, with the blood of the Holocaust always somewhere in the background of his mind. I think that has been evident in all your novels and most forcefully in *In the Beginning,* where I think the historic currents of the pogrom find inevitable resurgence in the Holocaust. Is that how you interpret the Holocaust? Do you view it as an ever-present element in the American Jewish consciousness? We are not physical survivors, but we are psychological survivors; are we not?

Potok: Yes, I think that the whole people feels that and probably the American Jew feels it in a special way; he is quite guilt-ridden in all probability. For whatever reason, he never did enough at a crucial point in time by way of an effort to get the thing stopped, or to protest it. Wrong or right, spoken or unspoken, that is the general feeling. And that sense of guilt is triggered from time to time, especially when Israel is involved in a war, and you get that extraordinary reaction on the part of the American Jewish public in defense of that country. A good deal of that reaction comes from a sense of the guilt we all have regarding the Holocaust. I don't see how it is possible to think the world through Jewish eyes without having the blood-screen of the Holocaust in front of your eyes as part of the filtering. I'll go even further and say that for thinking people, Jew or non-Jew, I don't think it is possible to think the world anymore in this century without thinking Holocaust. As a matter of fact, I would go further and say as far as the species is concerned, those of us who think and are sensitive, who care, have already made the concept Holocaust into a Kantian category. Certain human experiences are seen through that concept; we talk about the Cambodian holocaust, the Vietnamese holocaust, the holocausts in Africa. They are mini-holocausts, holocausts with small *h*s rather than upper case *H*. But it is intriguing to me that the term is used so that the Holocaust has now become a kind of measuring stick for the horrors that we perpetrate on one another.

Kremer: Most American writers who treat the Holocaust approach it reluctantly, presumably because they did not suffer directly; they were nonparticipants. Like other American treatment of this subject, yours resists graphic recreation of the concentration camp universe. In *The Chosen,* the Holocaust remains in the background. You use documentary references such as the name of an infamous camp or the newspaper photographs that were released shortly after the camp liberations, or allusion to camp atrocities in *The Promise.* Do you have any plans for Holocaust fiction set in the European context of the Nazi era?

Potok: I've been very hesitant to write a novel about the Holocaust because I don't know how to handle that material. I wasn't involved with it in terms of my own flesh, although we lost the whole European branch of the family. I don't know whether or not I can write a Holocaust novel. I don't know whether I can get the distance needed to handle it aesthetically. It seems to me to be so a-aesthetic an experience that I don't quite know what thread of it to grab hold of so that I could weave it into some sort of aesthetics. I'm not altogether certain whether I want it to be a separate novel, if I do write a Holocaust work, or whether I want it to be a part of the Jerusalem novel I want to write. As a matter of fact, one of the things I want to do with Asher Lev is show how he will make a serious first effort to depict the Holocaust in serious Western art, which will probably ruin his career, but he is going to try to do it. That's a novel I really want to write. It's a serious question and I don't have an adequate response for it at this point.

Kremer: In light of all the terrible human events we have been discussing, how is an affirmative stance possible in Jewish-American fiction?

Potok: I think that goes back to the essential nature of the Jewish tradition. After all, there aren't many more people on this planet with a higher record of battering than Jews. And somehow what we do is rethink the past. I would almost say that we poetize the past. We're constantly re-poetizing the past and its disasters in an effort to climb the scales of new visions toward newer dreams. This is basically the collective temperament of the Jewish people. The concept that the world could be at the base of things essentially meaningless is a concept that the Jew cannot come to terms with. It is in itself a meaningless concept. At worst, what the Jew will say is if the world is meaningless, then it becomes the task of the human being to pump meaning into it through his actions. That's the very last resort of the Jew who might be backed up against the wall and will throw up his hands and say there's really nothing ontologically out there.

Kremer: Certainly your characters are idealistic despite their history of suffering. Unlike most survivor figures, those in your novels do not focus on bitterness. Rather they are determined to make a new beginning, whether it be in America in a life dedicated to Jewish culture in Abraham Gordon's case or as a fervent Zionist as seen in David Malter's situation. Is that attitude reflective of your own upbringing? In *Wanderings,* you refer to your father's support of Jabotinsky and the Irgunists and I realize that you spend considerable time in Israel. To what degree is the influence of past family support and current personal commitment to Israel reflected in your literary emphasis on moving from the ashes to renewal and rebirth in Zionist terms?

Potok: It's founded upon everything that I was taught and led to believe as a child. My family suffered a great deal as a result of the Holocaust. We lost everybody in Europe and it was a fairly large family. And my father's response was to work all the harder to rebuild the people, the land itself. Why? You would get varying answers from him, depending upon his frame of mind. Sometimes he would say to stop working would mean that Hitler won, which is one kind of answer. Another kind of answer would be because it is intrinsically worthwhile, the Jewish tradition still has something worthwhile to contribute to the world. The bottom line to all of this would be that somehow out of the ashes something new has to be built. The Hasidic response to suffering and evil was to transfer suffering and evil into joy. And suffering and evil became the raw material out of which the Hasidic temperament created dance and song. But there is no question at all that the notion of the inherent meaningfulness of things came to me from my father. And the potential meaningfulness of things came to me from the world of my own experiences.

Kremer: Many Jewish-American writers have turned to the comedic tone. Do you feel the comic is an inauthentic voice in which to render twentieth-century experience or does it hold no appeal for you?

Potok: No, it isn't that the comedic doesn't appeal to me. I've thought about this often because people have pointed out to me that the comedic tone really is not the way I write and I've come to the conclusion that the reason for that is that I was brought up in a yeshiva, and things are very, very heavy in Jewish parochial schools. Your friends might have certain interesting and strange senses of humor, but the models, the teachers and rabbis, really don't. If you go to yeshivot from the time you are five or six years old until the time you are twenty-one, which was my span of yeshiva education, and you retain any sense of humor at all, that has to border on the miraculous. I think for many the comedic tone may be the only way to handle the twentieth century, because to handle the twentieth century seriously may lead one to lose one's mind. Humor is essentially one of the ways the secular humanist responds to an essentially impossible world. He doesn't have the heaviness of sanctity to fall back on, or the heaviness of mystery. There are no mysteries to the secular humanist. Something is either potentially capable of being explored and answered or of no interest whatsoever. There are no mysteries to a logical positivist. Now, in this new book, *The Book of Lights,* there are comedic tonalities, especially in one of the characters. The reason for that is that for him not to resort to the comedic would be for him to be incapable of handling the particular dilemma that confronts him. That is precisely the dilemma of the twentieth century. How do you live with the insanities that we have created? This particular character can only live with it through a screen of the comedic.

Kremer: Until the *Book of Lights,* your protagonists were all young men. How has the shift to an adult central consciousness affected your writing? Have you experimented with form in the new work?

Potok: First of all, the new novel is in the third person. The form is quite different. There are some technical problems in this novel in that parts of it deal with visions and one had to decide early on what sort of prose to use for the visions, how to represent the interplay of people in the vision, and how to describe what is going on. There is a great deal of travelling in this novel. I did not want the book to become a travelogue. I wanted to have the travelling reflect the personality of the traveler. Each sentence has to tell me what the individual is seeing and experiencing. My hope is that the thing works.

Kremer: A maturing of your craftsmanship is evident in *Asher Lev* and *In the Beginning.* In the first instance, the authorial voice gives way somewhat to character revelation and action; in the second, the progression is to a fine integration of history, religion, and myth within the narrative context. I was particularly taken with the windowshade stream of consciousness imaginings of the youngster in *In the Beginning*.

Potok: One of the things I tried to do in my new book is integrate technical scholarship with the novel form. That has never been done before—highly technical scholarship with character development, the development of consciousness. Another thing that has occurred through the novels is that I moved away from the set piece. *The Chosen* starts with a baseball game, which is a set piece. It then goes on to the hospital, which is another set piece. It goes on to his home, which is a third set piece, then to Danny's home, which is a fourth set piece. Long protracted set pieces don't occur in the new novel. Often, events that occur to an individual aren't exhausted when they first occur, but are constantly referred back to as different aspects of events are remembered because another event triggers another aspect. That is happening constantly in the new one because I really don't think that people fully register an event as it occurs. What they will do is register one aspect of it or they will register an unconscious leap. They will remember one aspect of it and then remember different aspects of it as they encounter different events days, months, even years later. Those are things you learn as you continue to write.

Kremer: Are you using time as *durée* here, in the manner Joyce and Woolf do?

Potok: Yes, exactly right. Two fundamental things about the novel continue to intrigue me and I think this is our gift to ourselves as far as this form is concerned. One is the handling of character, people. No other form can handle people in significant depth over long periods of time. No other form can move back and forth, in and out, nothing can move the way the novel can in terms of the dimension of time. People and time are what I think the novel is really all about and I think they are limitless.

Kremer: Where in the spectrum of American Jewish literature would you place your work?

Potok: I see myself as occupying a set of one, and by that I mean my subject matter is Judaism in its confrontation with the twentieth century and I don't know anybody else who really handles that.

Kremer: Don't you feel any affinity exists between your work and some of the issues treated by Bellow, Malamud, and Roth, the Roth of "Eli, the Fanatic"?

Potok: I don't feel myself terribly close to Roth because Roth is dealing with peripheries. That is to say, his Jews are peripheral Jews and even his secularists are peripheral secularists. Even his professors are not terribly professorial. One of the ways to handle encounters of the peripheries of culture is through the comic mode. I don't feel very much akin to that sort of novel-making. Bellow's people are peripherally Jewish and right at the heart of the secular world. That's another kind of model. In the final analysis, a writer, any artist, is trapped by his own particular experiences and his own vision of things. My experience is so entirely different from that of Roth's. While we write about Jews, even the Jews that we write about are different, conceptually different. I don't know that Roth would know how to talk to a Jew he might encounter in one of my novels if he were to encounter him on the street, beyond a few Yiddishisms. Once the superficial contact is made that would be it as far as the conversation is concerned. Bellow would be able to talk to them in some depth because Bellow is cultured Jewishly. Bellow really knows Yiddish literature. But it would stop there; he wouldn't be able to go beyond the Yiddish into the rabbinic, the heavy content of rabbinic tradition. So, I do feel myself much closer to Bellow in terms of the Jews than I feel myself to Roth, although the Roth Jews are all over the place. Wherever I go, I see them and I can talk to them, again superficially. Interestingly enough, I feel closer to someone like Joyce who really did, in terms of models, precisely what I'm trying to do. Joyce was right at the heart of the Catholic world and at the same time at the heart of western secular humanism. And his confrontation, both as an artist and as a human being in the twentieth century was a core-to-core confrontation. As a human being, he fused his Catholicism with his secularism and produced a Catholic-secular way of writing, if such a thing is possible. His epiphanies, his sacrament of language, the way he structures and sees things are all Catholic, Jesuitical, and he went the secular route through his Catholicism. That didn't happen to me. I stayed inside the Jewish tradition and took the secular into it. He took the Catholic into secularism and I took the secular into Judaism.

Kremer: Do you feel a similar kind of kinship to Flannery O'Connor?

Potok: To O'Connor, and interestingly enough, in no small measure, to Greene, who grapples with the problem of evil in a strange Catholicism. There are models, in this century, for what it is I'm trying to do with my work, but they aren't people like Roth.

Kremer: How do you feel about I. B. Singer's fictional world?

Potok: I. B. Singer's quaint, exotic, erotic Polish mysticism, with its overwhelming preoccupation with evil and the demonic just isn't my world. It may be Isaac Bashevis Singer's world, but it certainly isn't the way I would respond to the realities of the twentieth century. It simply isn't my experience.

Kremer: Do you think that your work has freed the American novelist to write of the Jewish tradition with greater erudition, with greater emphasis on Jewish thought, theology, philosophy, scholarship, than was hitherto the case?

Potok: It has shown the possibility of writing about that material creatively, the potentiality of using that material for fiction. No one tackled this material before. Or if someone tackled it, it was presented in some arcane fashion, as the ultimate in exotica. One of the reasons no one tackled it is that this world itself, the Talmudic world itself, produced no novelists willing to write about it in a positive way. The reason for that is that it generally denigrates the creation of fiction. Therefore, if someone comes out of it and writes fiction, he is not going to write about it in any particularly positive way. Also, you have to know about it very well to write about it. You have to know the dynamics of a page of Talmud if you are going to write about it in such a way that you are really not writing the content. You are writing the dynamics and somebody's feelings about being involved in the dynamics when someone finishes reading that passage, he thinks he has suddenly mastered a passage of Talmud. And what it is, is an abstraction, the abstractive dynamic of Talmud. The trick was to give the illusion of having mastered the content without getting bogged down in the content. That was very difficult to do. I worked at it and worked at it. That is impossible for me to do in this new book because this new book deals with Kabbalah. You cannot present a page of Kabbalah the same way, because Kabbalah, if it is anything, is content. Therefore the technical problem became how to present a page of Kabbalah and at the same time utilize the aesthetics of fiction. I don't know if I solved the problem. It was an interesting aesthetic challenge.

Kremer: When you decided to become a novelist, Jewish-American writers had neither establishment acceptance, and consequent audience popularity, nor the critical acclaim they enjoy today. Saul Bellow, for example, claims to have adopted Flaubertian restraint in the early novels to prove purity of style before releasing the authentic voice in *Augie March.* Have you felt similar constraints?

Potok: Yes, he does talk about that and he explodes in the first sentence of *Augie March.* I always felt it was necessary for me to master a good English sentence. I was not interested in the kind of English writing that I had trained on. That is to say, the writing of the eighteenth and nineteenth centuries. I realized that for all intents and purposes my subject was going to be a nineteenth-century subject. I was really still dealing with coherent groupings that were confronting the outside world, as a solid group rather than shattered groups, with the focus being on individualism alone which is essentially the nature of the second half of the twentieth-century novel. I did not want to deal with that subject in nineteenth-century prose. I was concerned that stylistically the subject was exotic enough. If I made the prose exotic, then I think that everything would have just been too top heavy. That's why *The Chosen* is in a kind of talky prose, the sort of prose that someone like Reuven Malter would talk. It is an effort to do a literary job, as it were, on the sort of talky Brooklynese that you might hear from a more less erudite kid growing up on the streets of Brooklyn. I never had the urge to present my credentials along the lines of Flaubert and James. My major concern was to be as up to date as possible in terms of prose with an essentially nineteenth-century subject.

Kremer: The values and symbolism of most British and American writing are Christian and secular. How did you, as the child of a devout Jewish family, respond to that literature and determine to become a part of that heritage?

Potok: What was interesting to me was the fact that I could be moved by it. This meant that there was something very compelling about that literature. That aspect of the compelling is what really intrigued me and drew me into the literature. When I was fourteen or fifteen, I read *Brideshead Revisited* by Evelyn Waugh. I was at that time a student in a parochial Jewish school in New York and nothing could have been further from my mind, and my imagination, and my feelings than the upper-class British Catholic world Evelyn Waugh writes about in that novel. And yet, the novel was an overwhelming experience for me. It posed some questions to me. What is it about this form that makes it possible for strangers to meet on the page? What is it about this strange world that I plunge into every time I open a really good novel, that lures me into it and keeps me turning the pages? Early on it became clear to me that essentially three ingredients were involved here. One was the play of the imagination; the second was the exotica of the world that I was entering; the third was the style, the writing itself, the language with which that world is being presented. It was the use of words and rhythms to weave patterns of private imagination, all of which somehow created strange worlds that drew me into them.

Odyssey Through Literature: An Interview with Chaim Potok on "The Kabbalah," in His Novel, *The Book of Lights*

Leonard Rubinstein / 1982

From *Odyssey Through Literature* 29: "The Kabbalah," Leonard Rubinstein host, November 7, 1982. Reprinted by permission of Nancy Marie Brown and Leonard Rubinstein, WPSX, Penn State University.

Rubinstein: My name is Leonard Rubinstein, and I am with Chaim Potok, author of *The Chosen, My Name Is Asher Lev, The Wanderers, The Book of Lights,* and other novels. Dr. Potok, I was reading in *The Book of Lights* about the Kabbalah, which is a very dangerous subject evidently in Judaism because it speaks of the irrational. You say in the book that it's a method of understanding by intuition and image rather than by reason. Can understanding by image be understood in words?

Potok: Well, nothing is capable of being understood except through words. Clearly the only way we can communicate is through words.

Rubinstein: Understanding and communicating are the same thing?

Potok: Yes. Kabbalah is dangerous, and yet for the longest time, it was very much a part of the Jewish tradition. Many of the rabbis of the Talmud were mystics, but the mysticism of the Rabbinic tradition is not what we normally regard as mystical experience. No rabbi is known to have experienced God in the sense of his self being dissolved into the being of God.

Rubinstein: You mean that epiphany is not part of the Kabbalah?

Potok: Classical Rabbinic Mysticism was characterized by an attempt on the part of certain rabbis to ascend through the celestial spheres, to attain a vision of the throne of God. The poetry that the rabbis used to describe that was their way of capturing in language what they took to be real experiences. And the experiences consisted literally of ascents through a series of celestial spheres, to an encounter with the radiant presence of God's throne or of God seated on the throne.

Rubinstein: This is an experience which has about it the nature of a sequential event?

Potok: Yes. It is called Merkabah, or Throne, and it may have its beginnings in the first chapter of the book of Ezekiel.

Rubinstein: This is still rational, still ordered, however supernatural it may be. It obeys the laws of cause and effect, the laws of time . . .

Potok: . . . and the laws of logic, to some extent . . .

Rubinstein: . . . and it can be communicated . . .

Potok: . . . and is communicated.

Rubinstein: Now whatever it is that we're talking about when we talk about the phenomenon of epiphany, epiphany can be experienced, but by definition cannot be communicated . . .

Potok: . . . cannot be communicated. That's right. We don't quite have that in Rabbinic Merkabah, or Throne, mysticism.

Rubinstein: As differentiated from the Kabbalah.

Potok: That's right. Kabbalah, which means received tradition, is the name given to Jewish mysticism that began early in the Middle Ages. It was studied and practiced by small, elitist groups that wished to engage in contemplation of God's inner nature. We call that Theosophy, knowledge of God. There were small circles of Kabbalists in Spain and in southern France. According to the same scholars the expulsion of the Jews from Spain in 1492 was a traumatic event throughout all Jewry. How could a just God permit that to happen to an entire Jewish community that had been obeying the covenant? One response to that question was worked out by a young rabbi, whose name was Isaac Luria, in a very small community of Jews in the Hill Country of the Galilee, in a town called Safed. Interestingly enough, it was mostly a community of Jews who were silk merchants, but whose spiritual life often involved them in contemplation of the Being of God and the nature of evil. I'm going to try to give you a kind of capsule presentation on his thinking.

How do you explain evil in general and the expulsion in particular? Well, at the very beginning of things, something went wrong with the creation. There is a creator God. The world is filled with the light of this God. God begins the act of creation by withdrawing the light. In the areas from which the light is withdrawn, matter begins to take shape.

Rubinstein: Matter is the absence of light.

Potok: Now, between the light of God and the corporeality of matter there is some kind of borderland. In this borderland, the vessels of light are mixed with and contain gross matter. The borderland is the arena of creation.

Rubinstein: Now, matter is absence of light. So we have light at one pole, we have matter, which is the absence of light, at the other pole, and in between are containers?

Potok: . . . are vessels of the thinnest degree of light, the light is gradually attenuating itself, so that matter can come forth in its place.

Rubinstein: The vessels of light broke.

Potok: And the light tumbled into the darkness. And what you have is the elements of light of the divine trapped inside the grossest of matter. So that from the very beginning of things, this creator God did something fundamentally wrong. This is a very startling idea. You see why Kabbalah is very, very daring.

Rubinstein: It's heresy already.

Potok: Well, it was saved from heresy by its next bold step. Once you understand that creation went awry from the very beginning, you can then begin to understand why there is so much evil. Our world is inevitably linked to what went wrong from the very inception of the creative process.

Rubinstein: This trouble is the agony of light trapped here?

Potok: The agony of light trapped, yes, which translated morally into the agony of the human being caught up in a corrupt world.

Rubinstein: Now this light is not God because God made the light, but the light is a divine quality.

Potok: The light is divine. You'll have some Kabbalists who—well, I don't know if they will go so far as to say it is actually God, but it is certainly divine.

Rubinstein: All right, now rescue us from heresy.

Potok: Here is where Lurianic Kabbalah—the Mysticism of Rabbi Luria—is rescued from heresy. The task of the Jew, and this is an audacious leap, is to free the trapped divine sparks from their encapsulation of matter. This tension between the divine light, the sparks of God, and the grossness of matter is what is causing the corruption of the world. How does one free the divine sparks? Because if we could free all the sparks, we would restore the original act of creation.

Rubinstein: We would no longer have this grotesque distortion.

Potok: We free the light through the observance of the commandments. The commandments of God, when performed by us, act upon the gross matter and penetrate it. They break shells, set sparks free. We have to understand that Kabbalists didn't conceive the world as the result of cause and effect, but as sustained on an ongoing basis by God.

Rubinstein: By an act of God's law.

Potok: By God's law and God's will. Therefore, man's task in all of this is to augment the work of God, and in that area where God, for whatever reason, went wrong with the act of creation, man's task is to help right that wrong.

Rubinstein: God's troubleshooters.

Potok: That's exactly correct. That's what I meant when I said an audacious step.

Rubinstein: I have two questions. We began with the discussions of the Kabbalah, right, as an effort to answer the terrible question, how can a just God commit apparently unjust acts? This explanation ultimately makes man responsible for cleaning up after a God that made a mistake. Is the expulsion of the Jews from Spain and the result and the horrors of that, not so much an example of the injustice of God, as of the incompetence of God?

Potok: God's incompetence, and the warp in the cosmos as a result of the error in the initial process of creation. There are passages in the Zohar, the central text of Kabbalah, where you will find a very daring understanding of the nature of God. One passage interprets the first verse of Genesis in the following way. "In the beginning God began . . ." and so on. The Zohar takes the Hebrew word for "in the beginning" as a reference to the God who is absolutely unknowable, the Infinite One who no one could even begin to approach. That God, in order to begin the process of creation, created Elohim, the God we know. And it was Elohim who then began the process of creation, and in one way or another brought on the cosmic disaster.

Rubinstein: Now that's perfectly Greek, if you examine the Greek gallery of gods. Behind every level of god, of divinity, is another lever of divinity that parented this.

Potok: One can possibly argue that the first one in the Bible to do this was the author of Job. If you experience injustice, and you have a belief in God, what you might do is say, I don't understand what's going on in this world, but on a level higher than human understanding things do make sense.

Rubinstein: Of all the works of the Bible, I love Job the best. And I love Job very simply for what he says to other men. Other men come to him to explain, as we are explaining to each other. He says, Whatever you can say, I can say, whatever you know, I know. I want to talk to God. And he succeeds in talking to God, who tells him to shut up.

Potok: Well, not quite.

Rubinstein: He consents to speak to him even if he says only to shut up.

Potok: Job's argument against the people who come to talk to him is that their conventional wisdom simply is wrong. Their conventional wisdom says that if you hold the commandments, you will be rewarded. Job's contention is that it doesn't work. The concept of reward and punishment, as handed down by conventional wisdom, simply does not hold.

Rubinstein: Do you want to know what audacity is, my arguing with you because I don't think that's the way. . . . It seems to me that what he is saying is that you don't enlarge God by diminishing man. God speaks to him. God says, Gird up thy loins like a man. All of his friends are saying you are being punished for your sins. He says, How do you know I sinned? They say, Because you're being punished, right? He says, It wouldn't do any good, it wouldn't be respect for God to lack respect for myself. Of course the whole thing starts with the devil saying that people are good because they are rewarded. The story of Job is out to prove that people are not good because they are rewarded, because that's not good, that's only cupidity, right? The story of Job is about a man who will be good though punished for being good.

Potok: Or a man who was good, and was punished anyway for some inexplicable reason.

Rubinstein: But the story of Job explains it to us, if not to Job. That is the section in which the devil and God make this pact.

Potok: What kind of just God lets a devil make a pact like that just to prove a point?

Rubinstein: What kind of man is going to judge the morality of God?
Potok: That is the point of the book of Job.

Rubinstein: That's the point of the book? To say that God is understandable is already to refute the definition of God.

Potok: Biblical faith meant faith in the faithfulness of God, and vindication in the Bible means a belief that God is just, and Job's contention is that he cannot get justice from God because he can't bring God to court. Who is going to bring God to court, and blame him for punishing a just man? I am a just man, says Job.

Rubinstein: What I don't understand, if we're saying that God must be just, then justice is a concept higher than God. We have people who don't believe in God, and yet everybody believes in justice, but justice is a bigger abstraction than God is, this insistence, this conviction in even the smallest of children that something ought to be fair. Is justice a quality of God, or is justice the name of God, or is justice just simply the limitation of man's understanding of the universe?

Potok: It is clearly an attribute of God that's most fundamental, because the God of Israel is inconceivable apart from the quality of justice. That's one of the fundamental differences, by the way, between the Israelite God and the pagan deities. There was a whimsical quality about pagan deities, a flippant disregard about essential justice, which is entirely absent from the Israelite God.

Rubinstein: Are you saying that the power, and the will, and the act of God are all constrained by the concept of justice?

Potok: Abraham said that in his argument with God over the fate of Sodom and Gemorah.

Rubinstein: If this is true, then God is constantly on trial.

Potok: He is, indeed, constantly on trial. Certainly from the time of Job on.

Rubinstein: But the story of Job is that God wants us to question Him because we are His creation, and self-respect for man is respect for God.

Potok: Yes. But Job's radical stance comes at the end of biblical history.

Rubinstein: But that question to me characterizes the Jew. If the question did not exist before, then the Jew did not exist before, as I understand the Jew.

Potok: It characterizes the Jew from the early second-temple period and on.

Rubinstein: What was his contribution before then?

Potok: A notion of the one God, of meaning in human events of history, and of the covenant, of the possibility of redemption, and many others, all found in the Hebrew Bible.

Rubinstein: But these are not invested with the concept of justice.

Potok: They're full of the concept of justice. And apparently up until the period of Job, the covenant was seen as working. If the Israelite people are punished, it's the people's fault. It's never contemplated that it might possibly be God's fault.

Rubinstein: But that's Job. Job's point is that punishment is not proof of sin. Up to that moment, proof of sin was the punishment, which is circular and unfair.

Potok: But remember that the author of Job writes a thousand or more years after the beginning of the biblical period.

Rubinstein: All right.

Potok: So you have a thousand years of Jewish history without that idea.

Rubinstein: So what happened in Jewish history that led up to this kind of stance?

Potok: Probably the Maccabean revolution, where the covenant seemed to have been dissolved. About the year 130, before the common era, pious Jews were fighting Syrian Greeks and were being slaughtered.

Rubinstein: Do you realize we are talking about an approach to humanism within religion, aren't we?

Potok: That's quite true.

Rubinstein: Placing a responsibility upon the person rather than upon the God.

Potok: This is one response, by the way, to the problem of what to do with the covenant relationship when it doesn't seem to be working anymore. The response of Job is that it doesn't seem to be working here, but in some higher sphere clearly it functions in a way that we don't entirely perceive. Another response is reward deferred. That's the Messianic response.

Rubinstein: The concept of reward is a very primitive and childlike religious concept.

Potok: But it's fundamental to the covenant. You obey my commandments, I reward you.

Rubinstein: These are not mutually exclusive, are they?

Potok: No.

Rubinstein: But religion more fully understood would say that the reward for doing good is being good.

Potok: That's already a Rabbinic concept. I'm still at the end of the biblical period.

Rubinstein: When man is still subject.

Potok: We're still functioning with biblical concepts. The third response is the apocalyptic one, the notion that at the end of time, in some strange and terrible way, God is going to put things right in a mighty act that we can't quite foresee.

Rubinstein: Is that the day of judgment?

Potok: Yes. You have these three responses developed out by Judaism when the covenant idea ceased functioning adequately. Then comes the Rabbinic period, with a very sophisticated play on the notion of the covenant. But that's a few hundred years later.

Rubinstein: But we're moving toward the assertion that the fate of man lies in man's hands primarily, that man must act, and that whatever happens to him will be the consequences of his acts.

Potok: We have a lot of that in the Rabbinic period.

Rubinstein: It's also existential, it's also humanism, it's also all of the things it's not supposed to be.

Potok: You have Rabbis saying that the Torah has been given already, now it is up to us to decide what to do. You have Rabbis saying that we don't listen to voices from heaven anymore, we need to worry about our destiny here on earth. All kinds of daring things are said.

Rubinstein: Are all of these compatible?

Potok: They don't have to be made compatible as far as I'm concerned, because if you're talking about a thousand years of Rabbinic literature, you're going to find the entire spectrum of human thought, and you can pick and choose whichever is compatible with your own feeling.

Rubinstein: The only thing that's attractive about being educated in the Jewish tradition is that it does have language, it does have terminologies which will accommodate almost every body of thought.

Potok: Well, remember that Judaism is four thousand years old. It has tried and tested a lot of ideas. Western secular humanism is two or three hundred years old. Chances are that you are going to find a lot of Western secular ideas in an old civilization like Judaism.

Rubinstein: You're being very generous about this. My question really is perhaps even more bold: Were many of these ideas generated by the Jewish religion?

Potok: It may very well be, through Christianity. Yes, it may very well be. My feeling is that they probably were.

Rubinstein: My name is Leonard Rubinstein, and I have been talking with great delight to Chaim Potok about matters religious and matters literary and matters most puzzling indeed. Thank you.

Potok: Thank you.

When Culture Confronts Faith

Doug Morgan / 1983

From *College People,* October 1983, pp. 8–13. Reprinted by permission of Union College, Lincoln, Nebraska.

What happens when one's faith clashes head-on with a dominant idea in secular culture? How does an intellectually honest believer relate to the theory of evolution, higher criticism of the Bible, relativistic morality and all the other components of the modern Western outlook on life which are at odds with traditional faith?

Chaim Potok, a best-selling Jewish writer, deals with such questions in a way that is artistic, authentic, and compelling. Artistic because Potok expresses his ideas primarily by telling stories. He's written five highly acclaimed novels in the past fifteen years, and is currently working on another. Authentic because Potok writes from his own rich heritage of Orthodox Judaism. In each book the beliefs, customs, struggles, and complex psyche of twentieth-century American Judaism come alive in fascinating detail. Compelling because one who has grown up in a deeply religious subculture finds it easy to say "I've experienced that, too," while reading about the challenges and conflicts faced by Potok's leading characters.

The novels speak to Christian as well as Jewish readers because, as Potok puts it, he has "stumbled quite inadvertently upon the central problem of any system of faith in the secular culture."

In addition to his novels, Potok has written an interpretation of Jewish history entitled *Wanderings.* A recent film version of his first book, *The Chosen,* has brought Potok's work to the attention of an even wider audience.

Raised in strict Orthodox Judaism, Potok broke with his fundamentalist past when he graduated from college, and entered the Western, more liberal element of the Jewish tradition. He completed rabbinic training at Jewish Theological Seminary and was ordained in 1954. He also holds a Ph.D. in philosophy from the University of Pennsylvania.

Recently Chaim Potok granted an interview to CP's editorial director, Doug Morgan, and following are excerpts. Few CP readers will agree with everything Potok has to say, but we believe his perspective is valuable in helping to clarify how a believer should relate to modern culture.

You've said that each of your novels deals with a "core-to-core culture confrontation." What do you mean by that?

Well, at the heart of each culture is a very special way that it sees the world, a way that it thinks the human experience. Western civilization, for example, has as its core ideas generated by Descartes, Spinoza, Kant, Hume, Hegel, Nietzsche, Darwin, Freud, Picasso, Stravinsky, Kafka, and of course many others.

Now inside Western civilization are a number of other ways of seeing the world that are not secular readings of the human experience. You might have various kinds of Christian ways of thinking the world, various kinds of Jewish ways of thinking the world, ethnic ways and so on. All of us grow up in particular realities—a home, family, a clan, a small town, a neighborhood. Depending upon how we're brought up, we are either deeply aware of the particular reading of reality into which we are born, or we are peripherally aware of it.

Two hundred or more years ago most people on the planet were never aware of any reality other than the one into which they were brought up. But today we become aware of other readings of the human experience very quickly because of the media and the speed with which people travel the planet. And what ends up occurring today is that very early on ideas begin to clash inside people. You will turn on the television set and an idea that is very strange to you floats in toward you from the tube. That's a culture confrontation.

Various kinds of culture confrontations are possible. What I'm writing about are what I call core-to-core confrontations. That is to say, an individual brought up in the very heart of his own particular reading of the world encounters ideas from the very heart of the secular umbrella civilization in which all of us live today.

Can you give some examples from your books?

Well, in *The Chosen,* Danny Saunders, from the heart of his religious reading of the world, encounters an element in the very heart of the secular reading of the world—Freudian psychoanalytic theory. And these two elements are at odds with one another because Freud is utterly adversary to almost all the ways of structuring the human experience found in Western religions. No Western religion can countenance Freud's view of man. And yet there are some magnificent things from Freud, profound insights into the nature of man. The question that confronts an individual like Danny Saunders is, How do you come to terms with the good things in Freud and what do you do with the things that cause you tremendous stress? That's a culture confrontation; that is essentially what I'm trying to track.

Would you say either side wins this kind of confrontation in the lives of your chief characters?

In culture fusion something is yielded by both sides. The ideal would be that out of the fusion something new would result. You hope when you give something up that you gain something back. It is impossible to fuse totally with a culture for which you feel a measure of antagonism. The problem always arises when there is something in an alien body of ideas that attracts you. If nothing attracts you to it then you simply walk away from it.

As you are engaged in that kind of confrontation, trying to sort out how the fusion would take place, how do you decide what to discard and what to retain? Are there principles to guide you in that process?

Well, one hopes that if you're really related to the core of your particular culture, you have profound commitments to it, and that you are aware of how much you can strain it before you do violence to its essential nature. I'm dealing with individuals who are really familiar with the worlds in which they live.

The principles to use are the principles of one's own heart and mind.

Your latest novel, The Book of Lights, *suggests a sort of ironic contrast between a well-educated twentieth-century Jew who studies the Kabbalah, an ancient source of light, and the "death light" from nuclear weapons which some Jews helped to create. Could you comment on that?*

Yes. There is considerable irony in that, bitter irony. As a species we are always hungry for new knowledge. And here is this extraordinary gift that has been given to us by individuals in this century, the gift that finally unlocks the source of the energy of the universe. And what do we do with it? We make a bomb with it to destroy. I don't know any greater irony than that. And it is even more ironic in that the bomb was ultimately dropped on the wrong enemy.

The references to Kabbalah in The Book of Lights *reminded me of apocalyptic writings. Are there similarities between the two types of literature?*

There are, you're absolutely correct. Kabbalah essentially nourishes from apocalyptic literature. In the second and first centuries before Jesus, there were a variety of responses to the breakdown of the covenantal relationship. The covenant between God and Israel clearly stipulated that if you observe the commandments, you will be rewarded, if you don't you will be punished.

That's the treaty relationship. In the period of the Maccabean revolution it was precisely those who were observing the commandments who were being slaughtered. So, an enormous tension grew up—the Maccabean revolution against the Syrian Hellenizers which took place in the second century.

An enormous tension also grew up with regard to the essential nature of the covenant, because the covenant seemed not to be working. But three responses grew out of that tension. One was the response of the author of the book of Job, who claimed that though the covenant relationship doesn't seem to be working here on earth, it does work on a cosmic level—we just can't fully understand it. And since we can't understand it fully on a cosmic level, why don't we simply assume that we can't understand it fully here, even though it really does work.

The second response is the apocalyptic response which has its beginning in the book of Daniel, and states that God is going to enter history very soon and offer us a new revelation. We will then be afforded all sorts of visions of what it is the future is all about. We will be able to walk with God, as it were, seeing the essential nature of creation. What we have to do is hold fast to the faith because soon, soon in a great explosion of war and traumatic action, God and His angels will enter history and resolve all the difficulties of man. That's another response of the covenantal relationship's breakdown. We call it the revelatory response.

The third response was to say, Well, it's not working too well now, let's defer the concept of reward to a later time. Let's do God's work on a day-to-day basis, try to make the small things of the world holy, and *wait*. By doing the small things on a day-to-day basis or a week-to-week basis and not expecting God to enter history tomorrow, thus deferring the covenantal reward to some nebulous future time, we might help bring that reward to us. That's the Messianic approach.

The Jobian response was easily absorbed into Rabbinic Judaism. The apocalyptic response became Christianity and to a very great extent fed into Kabbalistic literature, which picked up on the notion of the apocalypse and said, "If God is entering history I would like to know what God is. What is God all about? How do I experience God?" The third response became what we call Rabbinic or Talmudic Judaism.

But you're quite right in sensing significant apocalyptic moments in Kabbalah. I think that what you are sensing are those elements consisting of gnostic thought that entered both Judaism and to a very great extent Christianity in the first couple of centuries after Jesus.

What struck me was that Kabbalah became significant for a twentieth-century individual like Gershon Loran. Perhaps apocalyptic literature has lasting significance, too, even though not every generation of believers relates to it in identical ways.

Sure. It's meaningful to Gershon Loran in *The Book of Lights* because all the other categories that he has used as a possible source for meaning in his life just don't seem to work for him anymore. This is a very battered young man. Every time something good happens to him it's wrenched out of his life. Every time he forms a relationship it is destroyed. His first visionary experience on the roof of his apartment house takes place on the day that the atomic bomb is dropped on Japan.

My feeling is that when normal systems no longer work effectively for a religious individual, that individual will resort often enough to the apocalyptic dimension of the religious experience, to the expectation that very quickly the horrors of the world must be resolved, and will be resolved by God. I think it is a fall-back system. Apocalyptic versions are fall-back systems when the normal systems cease to offer effective answers to the dilemmas of existence.

In an interview with Christianity Today *a few years ago, you said you viewed the universe as meaningful, though there are pockets of apparent meaninglessness. From a traditional Christian standpoint, history has meaning because it is moving towards a goal—a time when all things will be made new. What makes history meaningful for you?*

Well, I *do* believe that it isn't a blind swirl of absurd forces. I cannot see history in that fashion at all. It is meaningful to me in the sense that it is a record of my species and I can look at it and learn from it. Learn both from the terrible things that we have done and from the magnificent things we have done.

I think that to a very great extent we are partners with the divine in this enterprise called history. That is an ongoing relationship, and there is absolutely no guarantee that things will automatically work out to our best advantage. We will have to have very serious efforts put into the making of good history in order for us to benefit from it. I do not believe that grace is automatically extended to Homo sapiens by a benevolent deity. We have to earn that grace. And by grace I simply mean no act of unearned kindness is granted to a deliberately malevolent species. In other words, Judaism is not Calvinism.

So, the significance of one's actions now are how they contribute to what the world is for subsequent generations?

That's right.

You worked for several years on the Jewish Publication Society of America's translation of the Hebrew Bible. How did your work on that project affect your view of the Bible?

It gave me the opportunity to see the Bible from a vantage point of the many periods in which the Bible was created. Generally these days we have a tendency to see the Bible from our own perspective. Jews will see it through the perspective of Rabbinic Judaism, which has its own rather special way of interpreting the Bible. Christians will see it through the perspective of Pauline Christianity, to a very great extent. What my work on the translation offered me was the opportunity to see the Bible through the Bible itself. I began to get a sense of what the words really meant in their original sense. I also began to see the rather sophisticated artistry that went into the creation of the texts of the Bible. Whoever the people were who put the final touches to it, they were artists. And they enjoyed, they loved, what they were doing.

When you laboriously translate the Bible word for word over a period of sixteen years, you become highly sensitive to the words. And I became aware of the extraordinary artistry that was part of the tapestry of the text. As a writer, this filled me with another dimension of attachment to that text.

Yet your work in biblical scholarship has led you away from a literalist/ fundamentalist view of the Bible. Would you call the Bible inspired in any sense?

Oh, yes. Profoundly inspired. It's an attempt on the part of one people to link itself with that dimension in the universe which is divine, immaterial, the goal for the best of human striving, the source of whatever wisdom and intelligence and compassion we have.

Was there a particular reason why you decided to make a film out of The Chosen*? Were you pleased with the way it turned out?*

Interestingly enough the film initially was acquired by a Methodist fundamentalist from New Orleans named Roger Harrison. He wanted the world to see that there were American boys who were serious about their studies and about how to relate to their families and the world and that not every American teenager was into drugs and sex and hot rods, as he put it.

He was the one who got the initial seed money together to acquire the property and get a screenplay written. The film was his dream for about seven years. I trusted him. Ultimately when it went into production the people we chose had an absolutely fine track record, they had made some extremely high-quality films in the past. Again it was on the basis of trust and I was very satisfied with the results.

Are there more films planned on your subsequent novels?

Yes, there is some thought about making a film of *My Name Is Asher Lev.*

One practice very prominent in the Bible which has to a great extent been lost sight of by Christians is Sabbath observance. Do you see any significance in the Sabbath for individuals in our modern society?

I think it is a very important day. It's a crucial human experience. One of the unfortunate tendencies of modern society is the false sense of dominance it often gives man. The feeling that anything we want we can have. In the final analysis that feeling leads to profound dissatisfaction. It seems to be the nature of things that the more you have the more you want, the more you want the more you have, the more you have the more you want, and so on. And there is no real happiness to be had from all that wanting.

The Sabbath serves as a balancing act for the rest of the week. It is a day that situates man in his proper place as one more element of totality of things. It is a day for nourishment, reflection, for family, for the replenishment of spent human resources. I find it a crucial day in my own life.

Many Christian groups have experienced and are experiencing internal controversies which I find very similar in principle to those that are dealt with in The Promise. *Do you think it is possible for a religious group to be tolerant and allow for plurality of views and still maintain a clear identity and sense of purpose? If so, how do you do that?*

That's a very serious problem. Within Judaism itself you will find a significant spectrum of difference in terms of responses to your question. For example, Jewish fundamentalists, the very orthodox, will say, "No, it is not possible. There is one reading of the Jewish tradition; all other readings are wrong."

To the extent to which a Christian group is a fundamentalist group, I would suspect that it would have to respond in the same way. But Judaism has a complex variety of readings, especially in the modern period. Rabbinic Judaism is much more than its specific orthodox or fundamentalist component. And this permits the Jew to maneuver with a very richly textured tradition that is more than 3,000 years old.

I can see where the problem would come into very serious play with specific Christian fundamentalisms. I would suspect, though, that if a Christian
fundamentalism looks deeply inside itself, it will find a spectrum of readings.
It is inconceivable to me that a million or three million or half a million
human beings will think and feel precisely the same way on any single subject. I think that we all finally ought to admit that while a system of thought
has boundaries, the boundaries can be narrow or wide. Even the most fundamentalist of fundamentalisms, if it really looks, will find fairly wide boundaries.

The trick then is: How do you respect one another? The alternative is
disruption of a planet. It is no longer just burning people at the stake, throwing people out, excommunicating people or fighting wars. Either the species
learns to listen—*to listen*—or we will simply disappear as a species. Now I
submit that the price you pay for listening is far less than the price you pay
for not listening and disappearing.

I'm not altogether certain that a fundamentalism of necessity has to argue
that it is the only reading of the human experience in order to stay alive.
There has got to be another way of articulating one's commitment to a body
of ideas—a way other than saying, "I'm right and everybody else is wrong."
And that's what we have to learn in the next half a century to a century,
otherwise we are just not going to be around to talk to ourselves anymore.

An Interview with Chaim Potok

Elaine M. Kauvar / 1986

From *Contemporary Literature*, 27:3 1986, pp. 291–317. Reprinted by
permission of the University of Wisconsin Press.

The interview took place over brunch at the St. Regis Hotel in Manhattan,
which, as Chaim Potok remarked, was the "New York thing to do." That
sense of the fashionable in contemporary urban life is characteristic of the
complexity of Potok's personal stance. Philosopher, rabbi, historian, and novelist—Potok has chosen his imaginative materials from the generation immediately preceding our own, and his novels provide access to a past that
enables us to deepen our understanding of the present. It was an especially
propitious time to have this interview, for Potok's most recent novel, *Davita's
Harp,* has established a new direction for the writer. The conflicts and rewards inherent in religious belief are central to all of his novels from *The
Chosen* to *The Book of Lights,* yet none of those novels has a woman as its
central character. In Davita, Potok has created a sensitive young girl who is
drawn to Orthodox Judaism despite the fact that her mother has turned away
from it. Through Davita's eyes, the reader witnesses the dilemmas now facing contemporary Judaism and indeed all religions within which women are
struggling in their desires to play active and meaningful roles. Beginning in
the thirties, *Davita's Harp* brings together the religious and artistic themes
in Potok's earlier novels. The first of a planned trilogy, it examines issues at
the core of American Jewish life, and through Potok's creation of a central
female sensibility, his concerns are given wider significance and an entirely
new dimension.

The moment in his career when an artist changes his direction is always
exciting. As he moves toward the realization of his plans, the critical reader
follows, questioning and discovering. Chaim Potok's discussion of these matters produces a literary as well as a philosophical event.

Q: Since many contemporary writers and critics think that the relationship
between writers and readers is a problematic one, I thought we might begin
with a question about your imagined audience, if you have one.

A: I don't have an audience that I conjure up. I didn't think about an audience at the beginning because, of course, I didn't have one. And then with the publication of *The Chosen,* the audience immediately became so large that it's very difficult to put a face to it. If I could put a face to my audience, I think I would go out of my way to blank out that face. I think it's very dangerous to imagine that you're writing for an audience because what happens is that you begin to tailor your intuition toward that audience without realizing it. A writer should follows his or her own intuition and hope that the audience will follow the writing, rather than the other way around. To cater to an audience is invariably to cater to its lowest common denominator. When an artist follows his intuition, in some interesting way he has tapped into the highest common denominator of an audience, and that's what I think a serious writer really ought to be doing.

I don't know who my audience is, but I'll tell you whom I write for. First of all, I write for myself in order to clear things up in my own mind. There are certain problems I have set for myself that I try to clarify. I try to do that with simple sentences because I have a kind of built-in prejudice against obfuscation and fancy sentences. The second person I write for, interestingly enough, is the first person who reads what I write on a daily basis, and that's my wife, who has an uncanny literary intuition. I figure if what I write can get to her, then I have more or less made my point. The third person I write for, if I write for anyone, is my editor Bob Gottlieb at Knopf, and that's it.

Q: I'm very interested in your views on the question of audience because the relationship between the reader and the writer has become such an issue. Some critics and writers think contemporary literature has as one of its programs the destruction of the relationship between the reader and the writer. And speaking of contemporary writing, what do you think of self-referential novels?

A: Well, it depends upon how good they are. Some of them can be enjoyed for their sheer aesthetic pleasure. Nabokov, for example, is exquisite. But for the most part, novels of that kind are exercises in aesthetics that are, in the final analysis, just another form of onanism.

Q: Do you think it is essential for a text to have meaning?

A: You know, there's a very important epistemological issue in all of this, and I don't know how to resolve the issue. I don't think it's capable of resolution. I think you take a stand one way or the other. If the novel is an attempt to mirror or to give configuration to reality, then what right does the novelist have to do it in story form, since reality is intrinsically not a story?

There is no real configuration to reality; we know that now. There's no beginning, middle, or end; if yours is to be an honest artistic endeavor, what you must try to do is somehow represent reality as structureless. Now, if that isn't a difficult task, I don't know what is; it's almost a contradiction in terms. You've got to build a structure that conveys structurelessness. But the one thing that you must never do is to convey the notion that reality has the configuration of a tale. That's the essential epistemological stance of the nonstructuralists, that is to say, the storyless storytellers. On the other side, you have those who say—and I side with them—that the fundamental endeavor of the story is to create a model. The storyteller who's serious about his or her art in the twentieth century never makes the claim that his or her novel is *the* model of reality. It is a private model of reality, a personal vision of things. That's another epistemological stance. However, having said that, I must say immediately that I regard the story as a necessary but insufficient element of novel-making. In other words, if a novel is all story and nothing else, then it is not what I would regard as a serious novel.

Q: It's very difficult to define what a novel is these days.

A: Of course, and those difficulties are a result of what's happening in the twentieth century. One of the casualties of self-knowledge has been the self-novel. We gained a great deal from Freud; we know a lot about ourselves. We were once in the position of thinking that the more we knew about ourselves, the happier we would be. However, by knowing so much about ourselves and our place in the universe, what we've suddenly discovered is that we're very tiny and quite possibly utterly insignificant. That's a terrible thing to know.

Q: Yes, Freud dealt our narcissism a very sharp blow indeed.

A: That's exactly right. Now along comes the novelist and says, "If you start building up reality in terms of stories and their beginnings, middles, and ends, you'll end up with pre-Freudian illusions." So the only thing left for the novelist to do is to use words with the full knowledge that all that's being talked about are words. Words become the aesthetic of the novel, and the subject of the novel is the arrangement of words. This aesthetic is also true for much of modern painting: paint is the aesthetic of painting, and the subject of painting is paint and spatial arrangement.

Q: Do you find that position sufficient or sustaining?

A: Well, it's an aesthetic experience that you don't really retain for too long a period of time. But while you're engaged in it, it can be exquisite.

Nabokov is magnificent. Nabokov can spin words like a magician. Barth doesn't quite have that quality, but he is marvelous. Both Barth and Gass are extraordinary wordsmiths. But many contemporary novelists are a lot of sound and fury and loveliness; in the final analysis, they signify nothing, and I think a novel must signify.

Q: Which modern novelists have been significant to your development as a writer?

A: Joyce was seminal because *A Portrait of the Artist as a Young Man* is a core encounter. When I read *Portrait*, I was about nineteen, and I would suspect that I absorbed whole components of that novel into the deepest recesses of my being; they simply remain there. Joyce has a storyteller's way of structuring a certain kind of confrontation that makes a lot of sense to me. In *Portrait* he deals with an individual at the heart of his Catholicism encountering elements from the very heart of Western civilization.

Q: And that encounter is the reason for your attraction to that book?

A: That's precisely my attraction to *Portrait*. Joyce was very close to what I'm trying to do. Interestingly enough, when I was young, the book that really started me writing was *Brideshead Revisited,* because Waugh utilizes this form also. He shows somebody at the heart of one culture encountering elements from the heart of another culture, and we find out what happens when parts of the cultures come into confrontation. When I read Mann's *The Magic Mountain,* it was a transforming experience because, for the first time, I realized that you could handle ideas inside the novelistic framework and not have the framework collapse.

Q: Have those novelists contributed in any way to your choice of historical time, the time in which you set your novels?

A: You mean the time in which we live. Well, I think that for the most part, serious novelists, and I can think of very few exceptions, really use their own lives and/or what they know best as raw material for their creativity. My work is set in the time that I experienced, the time I know best, the time that's problematic to me. I'm trying to record a certain aspect of what I experienced. First of all, I'm trying to record it because I want to straighten it out inside my own mind: I'm trying to understand what it is that happened to me. Originally, I thought that just a few people might be interested in this setting. No one could have anticipated the reaction to the novels.

The central problem of our time, I think, is how people confront ideas different from their own. We tend to forget that two hundred and more years ago, most people grew up, lived, and died within a twenty-five-mile radius of where they were born. Most people never encountered a new idea or, indeed, never encountered a stranger in an entire lifetime. We encounter new ideas and strangers all the time today. We think it's a normal way to live, and we automatically set up a mechanism to deal with this encounter. We still don't like to meet a stranger: we're on our guard, but we anticipate that, sooner or later, there is going to be a stranger with whom we're going to have to cope. That's new in the history of the species. We meet new ideas and new people in a variety of ways, and what I'm trying to explore is one such way.

Q: I see. But none of your novels is set in the late twentieth century, and I'm curious about why you've made that choice.

A: What I'm doing is setting the groundwork, and I'm finished with that now. I have in my cast of characters a psychologist, Danny Saunders; a talmudist, Reuven Malter; I also have a Bible scholar, David Lurie; an artist, Asher Lev; a mystic, Gershon Loran. Now I have a feminist writer; that's what Davita's going to be.

Q: Oh, so there will be a sequel to *Davita's Harp*? Does Reuven Malter's appearance at the end of *Davita's Harp* mean that he will play a part in the sequel?

A: Absolutely! All of these people are going to be brought into the contemporary period, and the first one who will be brought into this part of the century will be Davita. As a matter of fact, she is going to be brought right into the eighties on a journey that she makes to the Soviet Union. That's the point to the whole Communist background in the first of the Davita novels.

Q: One structural similarity in your novels is the scenes with which you open your novels—the baseball game in *The Chosen,* the birth of the pups on the roof in *The Book of Lights,* and the harp and the picture of the three stallions in *Davita's Harp,* for example. How are these seminal scenes related to the way you begin writing a novel?

A: I use the openings to make the statement concerning the central metaphor of the novels. The central metaphor of *The Chosen* is combat of various kinds, combat on the baseball field, combat in Europe, and then what happens when the combat in Europe is actually brought home to Brooklyn because of the Holocaust and the subsequent hunger to create the State of Israel. The central metaphor in *The Promise* is people gambling and winning or losing.

The central metaphor in *The Book of Lights* is the mystery and the awe that some of us sense in the grittiness of reality. Sooner or later, somewhere at the beginning of the novels, you're going to find the central metaphor treated in one way or another.

Q: Those central metaphors are visual. I understand that you paint; and I'm interested in whether you visualize these scenes, whether they appear in your mind like paintings.

A: Yes, and the imagery may very well come from the fact that I do see the world the way a painter does. I started painting when I was about nine years old, but it became a big problem in my family. I come from a very fundamentalist Jewish background, and my father would have nothing to do with painting. Painting to him was the preoccupation of the gentile world.

Q: He thought painting was idolatrous?

A: Absolutely. It was all right as long as I was a child, but once I became a *bar mitzvah,* my painting turned into a very difficult problem in the house. There were quarrels, and I think what happened was that sometime around the age of fifteen, I simply shifted the hunger to create from images on canvas to words on paper.

Q: Was writing acceptable to your family?

A: It was more acceptable than painting because you didn't smell up the house with turpentine and you weren't so visible. It was certainly more acceptable ideologically because the Jewish tradition has always been far more comfortable with words than with iconography. Words and texts, after all, are the stock-in-trade of the Jewish tradition. Images are, for the traditional Jew, the stock-in-trade of the gentile world. The Jewish tradition simply has not participated in Western art: there hasn't been a single instance in the history of Western art of a Jew participating in art in a seminal way. Not one instance! I'm talking about a religious Jew. Even in the modern period, no religious Jews participated in Western art. Chagall was not a religious Jew.

Q: What does Picasso's work mean to you? And why is *Guernica* so important?

A: Well, Picasso's *Guernica* is a central element in my life. I don't remember the first time I saw it. All I know is that every time I came into New York, I used to go to see *Guernica* as one goes on a pilgrimage. I've read about *Guernica,* and I almost know its creation step by step as well as what came out of it, the work that Picasso did after he finished *Guernica. Guernica* is just one vast element in a whole series of things that Picasso did by way of reacting to that bombardment. I also have studied that event, and I've written about it in *Davita's Harp* exactly the way the event happened, so far as historians have been able to record it. It's inconceivable to me that anybody who's serious about art can ignore Picasso. That's like being serious about Renaissance art and ignoring Michelangelo. I think it'll take two or three hundred years before the Western world absorbs what Picasso did with art, but certainly he changed the way we look at the world.

Q: Did Picasso change the way you look at the world?

A: Oh, yes. The ability to restructure reality in terms of a single individual's vision of it and have that change people's eyes is what the artist's power is all about.

Q: And that power is what makes art such a problem for Jews?

A: Exactly. That's why people are afraid of artists, because artists possess the power to create metaphoric visions of reality. Reality is, for our species, the sum total of all the ways that we see reality, and even that doesn't begin to tap into what reality is. But for an artist like Asher Lev, Picasso is the beginning and the end because Picasso is the possibility of creating truth.

Q: Why is Picasso important for Davita Chandal, the writer?

A: *Davita's Harp* is about the human imagination. The aboutness of the novels is one of the things that I always think of as I structure a novel in terms of its central metaphor. I would say that *The Chosen* is about two components in the core of Judaism or the core of any tradition, one component looking inward and one component looking outward to solve its problems. Both of those elements are in confrontation with an element from the core of Western civilization. *The Promise* is about the confrontation with text criticism. *My Name is Asher Lev* is about a confrontation with Western art. *Davita's Harp* is about the utilization of the human imagination as a way of coming to terms with unbearable reality. Every time Davita confronts something unbearable, she restructures it through the power of her imagination. Finally at the end of the novel when she suffers this terrible indignity, she restructures the graduation ceremony by having her uncle, her father, and her aunt there along with everything that she has imagined. All the metaphors of her imagination are present in that last scene—the birds, the horses, the sea, the cabin. So you have this seesawing back-and-forth between reality that's unbearable and the imagination that tries to rethink reality. One of the people who has powerfully restructured reality in our time is Picasso, and the metaphor par excellence for that restructuring is *Guernica*. Guernica is the prime example, the first example in modern Western civilization of the destruction of an entire civilian area solely for psychological purposes. It's a horror, isn't it? Would you visit a Guernica during its bombardment?

Q: No.

A: Would you go and see Picasso's *Guernica*?

Q: Yes, of course, I would.

A: Why?

Q: There is truth in it even if it's about a horror.

A: That's the point. That's the redemptive power of art. The artist, in strange fashion, redeems the horror of reality through the power of his or her art. For me, Picasso's *Guernica* has become the most significant achievement in this century of the redemptive power of the artist.

Q: Is that redemptive power part of what you refer to at the end of *Wanderings*—the sense of renewal?

A: Absolutely. That's why *Guernica* appears again and again in my work, and it will continue to appear. But there is another way to deal with reality that the new Davita novel will explore, and that is not to run away from reality by restructuring it through the imagination but to sink into it and reveal it in infinite detail.

Q: Will Davita's art cause her the difficulties Asher Lev encounters in his community? In other words, is there a core conflict between art and Judaism?

A: I don't think there's a conflict between art and Judaism alone. I think there's a conflict between art and any established institution, because in the modern world, for the most part, the artist is antagonistic to established institutions. This is a manifestation of the Enlightenment and post-Enlightenment periods for a whole series of reasons, which George Steiner and others have explored. The artist is, to some extent, the prophetic voice of secular humanism, and nobody likes prophets. The artist is the outsider par excellence. There are court prophets, and there are literary prophets. The court prophet is your public relations man who says everything is fine and I'll write your publicity for you. The literary prophet says many things are really in terrible shape, and I'm going to show you how bad it is. The modern artist's voice is really an antagonistic one.

Q: So the modern artist has to remain a creature apart?

A: Well, the bourgeois world handles him in a very simple way. For ten or twenty years, they will attack him; and then they buy him out. That's why capitalism seems to be unconquerable. I think Marx made that point in *The Manifesto* somewhere.

Q: Would you say Philip Roth has an antagonistic voice? The response to his work has often been one of outrage in the Jewish community. What do you think accounts for the difficulties Roth encounters when he writes about Jews?

A: I think that what Roth is doing is writing about the Judaism and the Jews he knows, and what he knows is essentially a peripheral kind of Judaism and Jewry which is very often in confrontation with peripheral elements of Western civilization. The Jews, especially in Roth's early work, know very little about things Jewish, and not too much about the Western world. Zuckerman knows very little about Judaism. Zuckerman is a writer, so Zuckerman, one might say, is inside Western civilization; but Zuckerman is a later manifestation of Roth. By the way, I think the Zuckerman novels are quite good. But the early Roth, the Roth of *Goodbye, Columbus* and *Portnoy's Complaint,* is a Roth who utilizes the comic mode to deal with individuals along the periphery of one culture encountering elements from the periphery of another culture. When peripheral elements of cultures meet, the result is nearly always grotesque. You handle the grotesque in the comic mode, because to handle the grotesque seriously is unbearable. I don't have to handle my material in a comic way because there's nothing grotesque about my subject.

Q: Is Roth's comical mode another reason why he has had so much trouble with the Jewish community?

A: I think many people don't understand what Roth is doing. I don't think people are saying that those things don't exist; what I think the Jewish people are saying is that they wish Roth wrote in Yiddish so that the gentiles wouldn't be able to understand what he was writing.

Q: Roth might answer that his humor is intended to dissipate the current sentimentality about Jews. In his essay, "Some New Jewish Stereotypes," he argues that the Jew has become a kind of cultural hero and that new Jewish stereotypes have appeared in the work of Jewish novelists, as a result. Do you think there is a new Jewish stereotype?

A: I think that there's a new Jewish stereotype in the American novel, yes, indeed. If you write about the same kind of person over and over again, that person will become a stereotype. In other words, you already know what to expect from page one. All you have to do is hear the voice, and there are going to be very few surprises. The *schlemiel* is a stereotype by now. You put a *schlemiel* on page one of a story and you can spin it out by yourself; all the novelist is giving you are a few variations on a basic theme.

But there's a fundamental difference, I think, between what I'm trying to do and what Roth is trying to do. Roth, for the most part, places his cultural world on the periphery of things Jewish. Roth either doesn't know, or isn't interested in, the heart of things Jewish in America or in general. What I'm interested in are individuals right at the core of the general civilization in which we live and to which Jews contribute in a fundamental way. For the first time in history, Jews participate in a seminal and central way in the umbrella civilization in which they find themselves. It's a very different scene today from whatever it was in the past, and that's what I'm trying to explore, that kind of confrontation.

It's virtually impossible, by definition, to have stereotypes once you begin this kind of probing in depth because no stereotype can possibly contain all that you have to say. But if you write about the peripheries of culture, stereotypes are inevitable. The perfect example is the stereotypical Jew who is written about in the last century's American literature. What did they know about the Jew? They knew the peripheral elements of the Jew, the stereotypes. When you start with the core elements of any culture—not only Jewish ones—the stereotypes will fall away.

Q: What is your reaction to being called a Jewish writer?

A: If the categories remain consistent, it doesn't bother me. By consistent I mean that if you call John Updike a Protestant writer or if you call Flannery O'Connor a Catholic writer, then I don't mind being called a Jewish writer. Academicians need these categories in order to teach coherently, but all I ask is that the categories be consistent. I think the proper way to categorize, if I were to do it, is to say that all of us are American writers with different kinds of subjects and territories. Updike, for example, is an American writer whose territory often is small-town Pennsylvania and New England, and I'm an American writer whose territory is a small section of New York.

Q: Another way of looking at this categorizing appeared in an article Alan Lelchuk wrote last year for *The Times* (Sept. 25, 1984). He argues that it is

time for the Jewish writer to become just the writer, a writer. Lelchuk maintains that it's a disservice to call someone like Henry Roth, for example, an
ethnic writer. Lelchuk wants to call Henry Roth a "writer, period." Do you
agree with Lelchuk?

A: Yes, I agree. I think those are old categories. I think they were used at
a time when Jewish writing began to move on to center-stage in American
literature so they had to categorize Jewish writing somewhat. They didn't
quite want to categorize it as American literature because Jewish writing was
too new. I think only the most provincial of minds would regard the Jewish
writer as too new today because he or she is clearly center-stage in American
literature.

My first novel, which was almost published, was entirely about Americans
and Koreans. There were no Jews in it at all. It was taken by the editor-in-
chief of a New York house, but the publisher didn't want it: he thought it
wouldn't sell because it was too artistic. So he agreed to publish it and then
warehouse it because he didn't want to upset his editor. I didn't like that, and
the editor didn't like that; so I withdrew my manuscript. I was told that the
editor quit in part as a result of that fracas, and I went on to write *The Chosen.*
My first novel has never been published; it became the paragraph or so in
The Book of Lights which deals with moving the Korean grave. It isn't necessary, you see, for a Jewish novelist to write only about things Jewish. Indeed,
the first half of *Davita's Harp* doesn't have all that much Jewishness.

Q: No, it certainly doesn't, and your point is especially interesting in light
of Murray Baumgarten's recent book *City Scriptures,* in which Baumgarten
maintains that Jewish writing is at an end because the Jew now symbolizes
marginality—the modern situation. For that reason, Baumgarten argues that
Jewish writing will be both Jewish and universal at the same time. What do
you think of his conclusion?

A: Well, I don't know. Jewish writing always was both Jewish and universal. What is more Jewish and universal than the Book of Isaiah? What is
more Jewish and universal than Maimonides who was read, understood, and
used by Aquinas?

Q: Baumgarten thinks that assimilation has virtually wiped out the distinction between being Jewish and being American.

A: I understand, but I think that is an echo of a time prior to the decades
in which we're living today, because the fact of the matter is that we're living
through a different kind of phenomenon. There's an intensification of things

Jewish that doesn't negate an intensification of things American. The two
seem to be either in an overlap configuration or, for many, identical. That's
very different from what Baumgarten says. Who would have envisaged the
kind of situation that we have today? Who would have envisaged a book like
Silberman's *A Certain People,* a book that is very different from *City Scriptures?*

Q: Do you think Silberman is correct?

A: Oh, yes! He's correct, no matter what the Israelis say or the American
Zionists say. Something unique in Jewish history is happening in America.
Unfortunately, Jews have too many doomsters in their midst. At the same
time, I'm not blind to the reality of black anti-Semitism. However, I think
we're living now through an extraordinarily fortunate time in Jewish history,
a time with enormous potential for creativity.

Q: Does this potential for creativity in any way lessen the struggle against
paganism the Jewish artist and writer face or is that struggle an inevitable
one? Your characters, Asher Lev and Gershon Loran among them, certainly
struggle with paganism.

A: Sooner or later, you have to come across that problem, especially as an
artist. An artist deals in images, and the Jewish tradition has a very serious
problem with images. It's had a serious problem with images from the very
beginning because in the ancient, pagan world, images were intimately connected to modes of worship. The Second Commandment is against image-
making because image-making was part of ancient worship. The tools with
which the sculptor sculpted his idols were sacred; the stone was sacred, and
the quarry was sacred. There were blessings that were made all through the
process. Anything connected with that process, therefore, was anathema to
the ancient Israelite.

All through the Middle Ages and into the Renaissance, Jewish law regarded Christendom as essentially an idolatrous civilization. Therefore, Jews
did not participate in Western art. As a result, there are no Jewish motifs in
Western art. The few that are there were introduced by Rembrandt and some
others. In the modern period, Christendom has been replaced by secular humanism, and the religious Jewish artist feels capable, at least potentially, of
entering this civilization, because virtually all of the christological artistic
elements have now become attenuated. The Crucifixion, for example, as a
salvationist artistic motif becomes a motif for suffering and loses its salvationist tonality.

Asher Lev typifies what might happen to a religious Jew who wants to enter the mainstream of Western art. First, everyone in his immediate community will try to talk him out of it. If he has a mother who wants to go along with him, the two of them will have to fight off everybody else. Let's say the child is tenacious and there are no choices involved: he must enter the mainstream of Western art. Strangely enough, the problem will become more serious if he continues to be an observer of the Commandments. Remaining observant is a crucial element in all of my books, because once you make the break with that, no Orthodox Jew will consider you a problem anymore. They would rather have you out of the camp and on your own than inside the camp and an observer of the Commandments who does all the other things that they can't understand. That's the problem.

Q: But isn't there as great a problem with writing literature and remaining observant?

A: Well, yes, because writing novels is considered a frivolity, and it becomes upsetting when the subjects that you write about are subjects like the ones in *Asher Lev*. I have been consistently and viciously attacked in the Orthodox press because of my books, especially since *Asher Lev*. If you're writing honestly, it is indeed a problem; if you're writing to entertain, then there's no issue. But if you're writing seriously about fundamental issues that involve Jews committed to the Jewish tradition and, at the same time, trying to make their way seriously with core ideas of secularism, then you're going to have problems from the Orthodox.

Q: Are those problems part of the reason that *Asher Lev* is your darkest novel?

A: It's the darkest novel because essentially it is a metaphor for how far a writer can take his material.

Q: At the end of the novel, the rebbe tells Asher that he's crossed a boundary and that he's alone.

A: And that's, I think, ultimately what's going to happen to most writers who are serious both about their Jewishness and about their writing. Sooner or later, they're going to cross a boundary and they're going to be alone.

Q: You suggest in *Asher Lev* that a balance between the Master of the Universe and the Other Side can be attained and that the balance can be achieved in art, but not without anguish.

A: That's correct, and the anguish comes from crossing the boundary. My point is that if you have to cross the boundary as an artist, at least create great art. Don't do it over frivolous things. Great art is the only way to make that anguish worthwhile.

Q: Asher's father asks Asher if there were a choice between "aesthetic blindness" and "moral blindness," what he would choose. Does the artist have to make such a choice?

A: Asher Lev made his choice. The artist will choose for his art.

Q: So the choice for the artist is an aesthetic one?

A: He will choose for the aesthetic, no matter who might be hurt. Indeed, that's what separates the modern artist from the artists of the past centuries who rarely, if ever, made a choice like that.

Q: Then art doesn't necessarily have a moral purpose.

A: It can have. But the moral quotient of the artistic endeavor is, at times, necessary and never sufficient; the aesthetic element, however, is at all times necessary and sometimes sufficient.

Q: Has Asher found a balance between being an artist and being Jewish?

A: He has found a tenuous balance; in the end, he sacrifices his relationship to his parents and his community, and he's going to pay for that sacrifice by trying to become a greater artist. He will find his own "play of forms," as he puts it. In the next novel in which Asher Lev will appear, his "play of forms" will have to do with how to attempt to render the Holocaust artistically. Nobody knows yet how to handle the Holocaust as a motif in Western art. That's what Asher Lev is going to be preoccupied with.

Q: Are there other reasons besides idolatry for problems with creativity among Jews? I'm thinking about David Lurie's brother in *In the Beginning* and what you say there about Maimonides's mistrust of the imagination.

A: Jews tend to mistrust the imagination because the imagination is mercurial; it doesn't seem to be controllable and it defies reason. Maimonides, for example, took creations of the imagination like mysticism and made them creations of reason like physics. The imagination is a very sticky problem in Judaism. With all of that, there has been in the Jewish tradition enormous creativity born out of the imagination. Religious Jews don't seem to realize that Kabbalah is a product of the human imagination.

Q: What do you think of Harold Bloom making Kabbalah a basis for literary criticism?

A: I think it's indicative of the power of kabbalistic thought. When categories of law and normal reason seem to collapse, there will take place forays into the world of the imagination. Lurianic Kabbalah is in part a response to the expulsion from Spain. The categories of response yielded up by *Halakhah,* Jewish law, simply collapsed in the face of that tragedy. Those categories state—and Maimonides says this over and over again; so does the Talmud, and so do the rabbis—that if a community is destroyed, it's because it sinned. If a man is ill, it's because he's sinned. Apparently, they weren't quite ready to say that about Spanish Jewry. What Lurianic Kabbalah ended up explaining was that the entire universe was awry: somehow God had erred in the very process of creation. And it's the task of the Jew to set it right through the performance of the Commandments.

This gnosticism, as Gershom Scholem pointed out, entered through the back door of Judaism, without the Jews knowing where it was from. The drama of creation gone wrong is essentially first-, second-, and third-century gnostic thought; but by the time it comes into Judaism, nobody remembers its origins. It is a perfect explanation in kabbalistic terms; and the reason it's perfect is that it fuses together two essential elements—one, it explains the evil of the expulsion from Spain and, two, it makes sense of the fundamental need of the Jew to perform the Commandments. That is an awesome concept, the notion that, by obeying the Law, you force the coming of the Messiah because the doing is quantitative. And at a certain point, you tip the scales and make creation right again.

Q: Kabbalah has been powerful for you both as a novelist and as a Jew?

A: Oh, yes, because once you open up all these categories of the imagination, you can begin to use them for literary creativity as well as for literary criticism. You can handle good and evil, the demonic, and categories like the "Other Side." What it offers you is a realm of metaphors that the *Halakhah* simply doesn't contain. No legal system possesses this spectrum of metaphors, and metaphors are what novelists use to give life to their writing.

Q: From what you've just said about the difficulties associated with the imagination, I wonder whether your characters are isolated because they're imaginative. David Lurie, for example, has words instead of friends.

A: Yes. And another thing that isolates them is the fact that they're located so much in the core of their tradition. Almost by definition, that position is going to isolate you from a lot of people. My characters tend to be loners, and they tend to be alienated intellectually. To be entirely candid about it, they are extensions of my own being, because I grew up very much involved in the world of the mind, and in the worlds of art and literature. Each of these characters, with the exception of Davita, is really, I suppose, a different aspect of myself and a reflection of my fundamental interests.

Q: Then are your characters isolated by their intellectual interests?

A: Yes. Except that one of the things that I was very careful about from the beginning was not to use the intellectual problem as the focus, but the feelings resulting from it. In other words, the intellectual problem is only the beginning. I'm specifically interested in the things that come out of the intellectual problem, how they affect relationships, how they affect how you feel. What I want to show is that the life of the intellect has powerful ramifications in the normal routine of daily existence, that it isn't merely something abstract.

Q: Isolation seems to be related to the many meanings of silence in your novels; for example, the pervasive silence in the Saunders home and David Lurie's refusal to talk for a while. What has silence meant to you? Is it mystical, psychological, or both?

A: That's hard to pin down. I'm not altogether certain I know myself what the tonalities are of that strange form of human communication. It means, I guess, the terrible frustration that all of us feel on occasion at not being able to communicate properly, even with the people we deeply love. We ask ourselves sometimes how we can ever communicate with anybody and understand anybody when we can barely understand or fully communicate with ourselves. That's the meaning of silence on a human level. On the cultural level, it's difficult to penetrate into another mind-set, into another culture's way of thinking about the universe. Then there are many silences in the world that have to be penetrated on the ontological level or on the theological level, especially in our century, with the Holocaust and the silence of God. So I would suspect that the silence in *The Chosen* and the silences that appear here and there throughout the novels are manifestations of the silences that all of us experience, most of the time without being fully aware of it. Perhaps we experience them as just breaks in communication or as nonverbal communication. Most of us think that communication is verbal; but a lot of communication is nonverbal, like the silence in *The Chosen*.

Q: Yes, and despite Danny Saunders's rebellion from silence, he comes back to it, in a way, with Michael Gordon.

A: Then he goes ahead and pragmatizes silence: he uses it in a psychological experiment.

Q: And one begins to wonder what that experiment was really all about.

A: Yes, you begin to think that perhaps it's not because he loves Michael so much; it's because Danny might really be terrified of what Michael represents. Michael represents an attempt at culture-fusion that ends in some significant measure of creativity. Danny looks at Michael, and it's not too difficult to conjure up in your imagination the possibility of Danny saying to himself, "This is what I might have become. I hate looking at this situation, and I'm going to treat this kid the same way I was treated."

Q: I guess there's a dark side to all of your novels.

A: My characters are not intended to be nice heroes. They sound decent and caring. But on a number of occasions Asher Lev, for example, reports the bed that his parents sleep in. Why is that information so terribly important? Of all the things that he had to report about in his home, he had to pick out the bed his parents slept in? Asher makes the point, at least twice, that they sleep in a double bed. That's highly improper for those people. First of all, if it's really a double bed, then out of respect to your parents, don't say so, because your religious parents are not supposed to sleep in a double bed; and if it isn't a double bed, why do you say it is?

Q: So Asher's aesthetic rebellion has got a very dark side to it, a hostile side.

A: Absolutely.

Q: If silence is nonverbal teaching, and mysticism by its very essence is silence, what is the role of language in revelation? Is revelation attained linguistically or silently?

A: Revelation is always attained linguistically. In other words, the content of revelation is words, and words contain the essence of the revelation. You can't get away from that in the Jewish tradition.

Q: So you would agree with Gershom Scholem and Walter Benjamin's belief in the efficacy of language rather than with Buber's "mysticism of silence"?

A: Completely. I'm talking about the Jewish legal tradition, which Buber didn't fully understand. The tradition emphasizes words and commandments as the content of revelation. In the Jewish tradition, you put the equivalent sign between words and commandments.

Q: Then silence and words aren't really in conflict.

A: They are not in conflict, provided that there is some measure of communication going on. After all, there is communication going on in *The Chosen* because Danny and his father study Talmud. The fact that they study Talmud means that some verbal communication is taking place, that Danny can then sort of half-spill over into nonverbal communication, which he tacitly interprets. It's not that there's no communication; it's that there's hostility, indifference. There's something going on that Danny doesn't understand, and it's the metaphor for precisely what it is that the religious person does in terms of his relationship to God in the twentieth century. Something is going on, and we don't understand it. There's a silence between the Jewish people, or indeed all religious people, and God in this century. But whatever it is—and I don't understand it—the silence is not a break in communication. It's a communication of a different kind, and what we try to do is tap into it and see what it's all about. It's very difficult to grasp the notion that silence can be another aspect of the verbal.

Q: Then silence and words are not in conflict; but certainly, there's a conflict in your characters with the demonic side of life. You write about it very movingly: Asher Lev struggles with the Other Side; Gershon Loran finds a way to life through it, and the story of the evil witch Baba Yaga haunts Davita Chandal's imagination.

A: I think we all struggle with that side of life. There's a dark side to man. We are a killer species. There's no question about that. As a novelist, you have to cope honestly with that killer side. Religions have a way of handling it. Rabbinic Judaism, for example, regards the evil inclination as the motor energy for human endeavor. The Commandments are a check against unbridled human evil. But Kabbalah understood that there are times when neat categories aren't enough, and what it did was ground that evil inclination in man as in close an ontological reality as you can get without creating a dualistic universe. The dark side is a force that we have to cope with.

Q: The dark side seems to mean a great deal to you both as a novelist and as a human being.

A: The dark side is man's powerful ability to destroy and to create at the expense of other people, to do the most magnificent things at the cost of lives. Peter built St. Petersburg, but thousands of human beings died during the construction. That's the strange mixture in man.

Q: The dark side recalls the conclusion Freud reached in *Civilization and Its Discontents*—and Reuven Malter wonders how the "Talmud and Freud can live side by side." Can they?

A: You have to do a lot of reinterpreting of Freud and the Talmud in order for them to live side by side, because Freud's is entirely a secular system. Freud was very much involved in the dark side. I would regard Freud as the prophet of the Other Side, a man whose life's work was to elucidate the workings of those dark primal elements that drive us to hurt, to destroy, and to create.

Q: In his new book, *Freud for Historians,* Peter Gay argues that Freud is indispensable to the work of uncovering and interpreting historical events. As a Jewish historian, do you think there is anything to be gained by applying Freudian methodology to Jewish history?

A: I don't think it's possible to look at the world and ignore Freud, because he tapped into something truly elemental. One of the ways you make use of Freudian thought, I suppose, is by trying to understand the dark forces of history. You certainly can apply it to an individual like Sabbatai Ṣevi. Of course, one of the problems of using Freud in connection with Jewish history is that so many of the sources are lost to us, and we don't have accurate pictures of individuals. But I'm wondering whether it's possible to use Freudian analysis on some of the individuals in the Talmud. I would love to have someone do a Freudian study of the one excommunicated rabbi in the talmudic period. But we don't have enough material on that rabbi.

Q: If that material were available, how do you think Jewish historians would react to using Freud?

A: Well, first of all, the historians who are writing today are almost all secularists, so it depends upon what you mean by "using Freud." If you're talking about using Freud to explain the Holocaust, that boggles the mind; but to use Freud to explain Sabbatai Ṣevi is very acceptable. Jewish historians don't use Freud in their work, not because they may have an intrinsic objection to Freud, but because of their Wissenschaft training. That training is very suspicious of the insides of hidden motivations; it emphasizes the outsides, that is to say, facts, givens, records, and chronicles. Once you start engaging in psychological interpretations, you're in the realm of literature. That has to do, not with Jewish historians alone, but with the modern discipline of history per se and the nature of contemporary historiography.

Certainly, I don't see how it's possible for a novelist to avoid using Freud,

and I say this in spite of Nabokov, who disliked Freud and in whose work
you can find resonances of Freud everywhere. My feeling is that the whole
Western twentieth century sees the world through the models of Freudian
thought. We see it that way, whether we know it or not; it's part of the
eyeglasses through which we frame reality. The reason that the artist taps
into this more than anybody else is that the artist is working very much with
his unconscious, and it is the unconscious element in the human being that is
fed by those primal forces. That's why traditions are very fearful of the imagination: because it is fed by primal, mercurial forces that are very difficult
for traditions with their staid, moral, and legal systems to control.

Q: Yet with all the use Davita makes of her imagination, she is powerfully
attracted to those traditions. In fact, *Davita's Harp* is unique among your
novels: for the first time, the main character is a young girl who on her own
turns to Judaism for comfort. How did you come to write about a young girl?

A: I needed Davita for a number of reasons, some of them technical and
some of them very deep and personal. I'll begin with the deeper, personal
reasons. I have known Davita's story now for about twenty-five years, because Davita is my wife, and what happens to Davita at the end of the novel
actually happened to my wife, except that it wasn't the Akiva Award that was
taken away from her because she was a girl; it was the class valedictory. She
knew she deserved the valedictory, and when it was given to a boy, she asked
the head teacher what happened, and he told her exactly what it is that the
teacher tells Davita in the novel. My wife has never fully gotten over that
experience. It's one of those scars that just stay with you for the rest of your
life, and my wife was thirteen years old at the time. Her family was leftist,
Labor Zionists and socialists. Because I wanted to explore Marxism as one
of the other core elements of Western civilization, *Davita's Harp* became the
Marxist exploration. For novelistic reasons, I needed a woman. You know
this, but I'll say it anyway. Artists are basically very egocentric, selfish people, maniacally devoted to their craft, whether they know it or not. They
don't like to talk about their art, for the most part. I am among the more
articulate of novelists. Most novelists write and don't fully understand what
they're doing. I've gone through a doctorate in philosophy as well as rabbinic
training, so I've been trained to look at things. If you study analytical philosophy and epistemology long enough, you look at everything. I invented Davita
because I needed a writer as one of the cast of characters that I'm developing.

Q: I wondered why you hadn't written about a girl earlier.

A: I had to make sure all my boys were out of the way before I tackled the girl. With each of the novels, I set up what I regarded at the beginning as an insurmountable technical obstacle to myself, and then I bemoan my fate by saying I'll never be able to do it. In *The Promise,* for example, the challenge was the double climax. In *Asher Lev,* I wanted to handle the Crucifixion theme without it being a cliché. That, by the way, is one of the reasons that there is a double crucifixion at the end. Each of the books had different kinds of technical problems that I set up for myself; that's the only way I can get up the energy to write. *Davita's Harp* was an especially interesting challenge. Could I convincingly do a girl's voice? I must say that it helped to have my wife and two daughters around. But for the most part, when I was through the first seventy-five to one hundred pages, I really had it straight.

Q: How did it feel to write about a woman?

A: It was an incredible experience to recognize a very powerful feminine element inside myself. There were times when it was really scary, because I regard myself as very masculine. I was very athletic when I was young.

Q: Do you think that the strong emphasis Judaism places on the male role may have contributed to your uneasiness when you discovered you could identify with a woman?

A: Yes, it's a Jewish cultural thing, but it's also an American cultural thing, a Western cultural thing, and probably a species cultural thing. The male does not like to discover feminine sensibilities inside himself, and I discovered them when I was writing *Davita's Harp.* I discovered a certain way of feeling the world, a certain way of reacting, a certain softness, and a certain toughness because Davita is also a tough cookie. But she has a feminine kind of toughness and a certain kind of wiliness that's almost matriarchal. The biblical period admired the matriarchs' tribal cunning. If it hadn't been admired, they would have written it out of the Bible, believe me. It's the rabbis, not the Bible, who had a problem with matriarchal cunning, and the rabbis sought all kinds of ways of explaining what Sarah did, what Rebecca did, what Leah did, and what Rachel did. Davita's wiles are almost biblical, and it was fascinating to get inside her.

Q: She's certainly a budding feminist, as she demonstrates when she says *Kaddish* (the prayer for the dead) for her father. Actually, Davita's experience is like the one Sara Reguer describes in her essay, *"Kaddish* from the 'Wrong' Side of the *Mehitzah,"* in which she calls *Kaddish* an "unlucky *mitzvah"* ("commandment") because it provides great comfort and women aren't allowed to participate in it. [*On Being a Jewish Feminist,* ed. Susannah Heschel (New York: Schocken Books, 1983.] Reguer argues that Jewish women need to rebel within Judaism. Would you agree with her?

A: I agree with her, though I haven't read that essay. I find it difficult, at times, to understand why women like Cynthia Ozick and others remain inside the Orthodox camp. At the same time, I can understand why they remain because there's an element of significant texturing there that they can react to, that resonates inside them. So they would rather remain Orthodox Jews and do the changing inside than step outside.

Q: Is it possible to change the *Halakhah*?

A: With regard to women? Orthodox *Halakhah,* you mean. No. It will not change.

Q: So you think Judaism and feminism cannot be reconciled?

A: Not Orthodox Judaism. What they're going to end up doing is finding all sorts of ways to accommodate the women, but never on equal terms. They'll put window or glass in front of the *mehitzah* (the partition separating men from women in synagogues). They'll make the *mehitzah* on the same level without anything in front of it. They'll give the women their own *minyan* (a quorum of ten men required for communal prayer service); they'll let them dance with the Torah by themselves on *Simhat Torah* (the holiday which celebrates the annual conclusion of the reading of the entire Pentateuch), though most Orthodox Jews will not do even those things. All kinds of things will happen, but there can never possibly be equal status among men and women in Orthodox Judaism.

Q: Is the issue of Jewish feminism a theological one and not a sociological one?

A: It's a powerful sociological issue that borders on the theological. Orthodox Jewish law is grounded in God—hence all law is theological, no matter what its sociological origins.

Q: Then is Davita's desire to be a Jewish woman scholar and remain within Orthodox Judaism impossible?

A: It's not going to work. It doesn't work; and what Davita ends up doing is becoming a writer while remaining a traditional non-Orthodox Jewess. She has a really radical break with fundamentalism in her early twenties.

Q: I'd like to ask you one more question about *Davita's Harp.* Why does Dos Passos play such an important part in the novel?

A: I remember reading Dos Passos for the first time early in college. His novels brought me into the socialist world, which is one of the reasons that Dos Passos appears in *Davita's Harp*: that's my homage to him. I learned a great deal about the reality of the twenties and thirties in the United States from reading Dos Passos.

Q: It's interesting to hear that an historian once learned history from a novelist. In *Zakhor: Jewish History and Jewish Memory,* Yosef Yerushalmi discusses the current, tarnished image of the historian and claims that the image of the Holocaust is "being shaped, not at the historian's anvil, but in the novelist's crucible." Do you agree with Yerushalmi?

A: Absolutely. I think that his point is certainly valid. But it's not the novelist in the modern sense as much as it is the storyteller; although today, stories are told mostly in novel form. The storyteller has always been the first one to grapple with reality, and by storyteller, I don't mean a professional. I mean the member of the family who told stories as they all sat mending the nets, or making wool, or sewing. They needed something to transform the monotony of those long evenings so somebody told stories.

Q: Yerushalmi also thinks Jews "await a new, meta-historical myth" because they aren't prepared to confront history directly, and that the novel provides a "temporary surrogate."

A: Well, clearly the storyteller is the first one who tries to organize reality and to give it a configuration, and myths are made through the telling of stories. We *Homo sapiens* love a story because it is the initial way that we give configuration to the chaos that surrounds us and terrifies us. When the metaphors in a tale take on the quality of heightened truth and spin off other metaphors in their wake, that's the beginning of myth-making. The more powerful the mythic metaphor, the more its staying power. Then the historian comes along and talks about the effect and the meaning of these metaphors. Metaphors have a profound effect on human history, as we know all too well.

Q: In a way, the novelist is more crucial in shaping people's reactions to history than the historian.

A: Well, the novelist is nothing more than the storyteller of Western secular humanism. The original storyteller was the one who spun the folk tale, the one who organized reality around the hearth. We organize reality in terms of causal relationships. To that extent, I think Yerushalmi is correct, because it's our metaphor-making power that creates myth and, ultimately, enables the historian to do his work.

Q: Yerushalmi argues that modern Jewish historiography can't even begin to address itself to those Jews who have never fallen because Jewish historians must attend to historicism and not to theology. Is his argument an acceptable one?

A: Of course. It goes back to what I said before with regard to Freud. The training of historians in this time of Wissenschaft is by definition scientific. The scientist deals with elements of existence that are tangible and recordable; if he's going to deal with attitudes, he wants them recorded somewhere. If he's going to make interpretive leaps of models that are outside history, then he will become suspect in the eyes of his fellow historians. Yerushalmi is absolutely right if by "fallen," he means Jews who are no longer observant and not Jews who aren't committed to the Jewish people or to its destiny. That's the irony of the modern period—that Jewish history has been reclaimed by nonobservant Jews.

Q: At the end of *Wanderings,* your own history of the Jews, you describe a "sense of renewal, a foresharpening of self-identity, a feeling of approaching some distant fertile plain." Does your sense of renewal come from within Judaism?

A: My sense of renewal comes from what I regard as the inherent ability of the Jewish tradition to confront new civilizations and to renew itself as a result and also from the ability of the Jewish tradition to pull back when it realizes that it's about to give up too much. I think there is a real possibility for the creation of something quite extraordinary, a third Jewish civilization. Indeed, the Jewish tradition may be one of the ways that Western civilization will save itself because I think Western civilization is in very serious danger of utilizing the dark side of its seminal thrusts for self-destruction. The concept of personal freedom is the central notion of Western civilization just as the concept of covenantal relationships was the central notion of biblical civilization. The concept of messianism, that is to say, reward deferred to a future time, is the central concept of rabbinic civilization. Now, there's a dark side to the concept of personal freedom, and that's hedonism. Hedonism will destroy any civilization; it's going to destroy Western civilization. I think the Jewish ethos is a very sharp check to hedonism because the Jewish ethos offers the human being an alternate way of living in this world. It doesn't offer a future world because it's salvation-oriented in this pragmatic, gritty world; that orientation is the best check to hedonism that I know. But it's touch and go.

Q: Does that third civilization you're hopeful about explain why at the end of *Wanderings* you describe our situation as being "between worlds"? And many of your characters, from Reuven Malter to Jacob Daw, are preoccupied with their "in-between existence." Is their preoccupation a result of the modern condition or their religious struggles?

A: It's a result of being in the cores of two cultures simultaneously and having to fight the battle of how to fuse them. It's also "between" in the sense that I think Jewish history is now in a between phase. We've had two civilizations so far: one was biblical and the other was rabbinic. The rabbinic civilization came to an end with the Holocaust. No one has any illusions that we're in the rabbinic period today, except maybe the Orthodox. But a civilization that can't say something to its total people or that isn't in a seminal phase of creativity really doesn't speak in a significant way to the world or to itself. Rabbinic Judaism is not in a seminal phase of creativity. What it really wants is simply to repeat the past. So we're in a between period today. What will happen in the future is very difficult to discern, though there are some outlines of it. But it is something that will come out of our fusion with the best of Western humanism unless we're inundated by the periphery of things Jewish and things secular. That's also very possible.

Q: Perhaps that "between" period and your sense of renewal account for the vital part beginnings play in your novels. David Lurie, for example, begins his story with the *midrash*, "All beginnings are hard." At the end of your recent novel, Davita decides to leave the yeshiva and enter a public school. In fact, your novels end with beginnings. Have beginnings played an important part in your life?

A: Very significant parts. The first beginning was in starting school and entering the world of yeshivot. Then there was a long period of anguish when I knew that I had to leave that world, and there was another beginning with the Seminary. When I left the Seminary and went to Korea, I brought with me a very lovely cultural package: what my Americanism was all about and what my Judaism was all about. It was very tidy, and it all fell to pieces in Korea; and so there had to be another beginning. I had to reconstruct everything from the start. There was yet another beginning when *The Chosen* was published and I was suddenly a serious novelist. I think if life for a writer isn't a series of beginnings, that writer is in a lot of trouble.

An Interview with Chaim Potok

Lynn Hinds / 1986

From WPSX-TV, April 7, 1986. Reprinted by permission of Penn State University.

Hinds: Chances are that many of you have read some of Mr. Potok's novels, goodness knows lots of people have. *The Chosen* I believe was the first, then *The Promise, The Book of Lights, In the Beginning,* and *Davita's Harp* is the last one. You're not just a novelist, you're a scholar, which is unusual, I think for a novelist.

Potok: There have been novelists who've really known scholarship and done considerable research into the worlds that they write about. Thomas Mann comes to mind. I entered the world of scholarship because I wanted to know the world that I was writing about, and I wanted to know it thoroughly. I was writing about the hearts of two civilizations that in one way or another were coming into confrontation. My own particular world, the Jewish world, and the general civilization in which all of us live today, the world we call Western humanism. And the best way to learn about the Jewish world was to enter its world of scholarship. I entered the Jewish Theological Seminary of America. As a result of the training that I received there, I became an ordained rabbi. I went for the scholarship, but when you graduated, you automatically received rabbinical ordination. And subsequent to that, I went to the University of Pennsylvania for a Ph.D. in secular philosophy so that the world of scholarship is central to what it is that I try to do as a novelist.

Hinds: Now there are others who have this sort of dichotomy between religious study, whatever religion it is, and a modern secular Ph.D. kind of studies. But, many of them become teachers, or become ministers, or priests or rabbis, but not many of them become novelists. Why a novel, as it were?

Potok: I decided to be a writer. I decided I was a writer. Everything I've done since then had, as its fundamental purpose, to teach me to be a better writer and to teach me that subject that I wanted to write about. But, from the very beginning, it's always been the writing that has been the focus.

Hinds: I guess what I'm asking about is that I don't want to be critical of it or I don't want to flaw it, I got interested in so much through novels;

history, philosophy . . . And the novel is a great way to go, I think. And I think that it is a great way for more young people to get better educated. Judaism has come up against Greece, against Egypt, against Rome, against Christianity, and against Islam. And today we talk about Western humanism, secular humanism. That's what you write about primarily. Is that different from the others?

Potok: It is in a very fundamental way. In the past, no matter how close Jews might have been to the core of civilization, they never affected the essential nature of that civilization.

Hinds: Something of an outsider.

Potok: That's right. For about three or four hundred years, for example, when Islam ruled southern Spain, the Jews were very much a part of that civilization, but never affected it in a fundamental way. Today is the first time in the history of the Jewish people that the Jews actually constitute a fundamental element of our umbrella civilization. And to a great extent Jews have reacted to that umbrella civilization. Whole components of the civilization have come out of the Jewish experience. Freud, Kafka, Karl Marx, Einstein, artists, novelists, filmmakers, songwriters, and so on. For the first time in their history, Jews are confronted with a situation in which they contribute massively to the general civilization, and at the same time are central to that civilization. You have a situation that is ripe with enormous possibilities for Jewish creativity and at the same time dangerously leaning in the direction of assimilation and disappearance.

Hinds: You talk, for example, of a protagonist in one of your books who becomes a clinical psychologist and you call that a sort of secular version of the Rebbe, the Hasidic leader.

Potok: That's precisely what it is. In *The Chosen,* Danny's father tells him that he is going to be a kind of TZADDIK for the world. That is to say, a secular version of a spiritual leader. A pre-modern psychoanalyst, one might say, is the secular counterpart of the spiritual leader, to whom people would come with their problems.

Hinds: Except that I once heard someone criticize psychiatry because it relates a man only to their own psyche, and not to something outside them, a god, Yahweh.

Potok: That's the secular element. The secular world's faith is in humankind. We can and must somehow manage by ourselves. There is no sin, no salvation, no priest, no rabbi, no sense of connectedness to ultimate mysteries. If something is intrinsically insoluble, immeasureable, unquantifiable, then nothing can be said about it. This general way of thinking is only about three hundred years old.

Hinds: Is it the case then, the one that has its root in the supernatural, in its absolutes and values, serves as a way to question the other, the culture of secular humanism?

Potok: It serves as a balance to it. It serves as a counter to the hubris, the overweening pride that so many feel when they regard humankind as intrinsically capable of solving problems on its own. This has been a bloody century. The present culture of celebrity—worship and pervasive cynicism are symptomatic of our problems. No secular solutions are as yet in sight.

Hinds: Your novel, *The Book of Lights* has as its theme the Jew who is into mysticism versus the Jewish scientists who were involved in creating modern physics and the atomic bomb. Is that the paradigm you were after?

Potok: *The Book of Lights* is about the tension between my particular tradition and the only pagan, or idolatrous, civilization left on this planet, which is the world of Asia. When the world begins to break apart and normative religious responses don't make sense anymore, there are a number of ways you can proceed. One is in the direction of cynicism. You abandon the world you were brought up in, you become a hedonist, you live for the moment. Or, you go enter a monastery—a commune of sorts—you close off the world. Or you attempt to reach beyond the material world, you leap into the mystical. And that is the response of one of the individuals in the novel. Because of an experience he had on a rooftop in New York one day, when he witnessed a dog whelping her pups. He saw life come into the world. He spends his young life waiting for a repetition of that moment of creation, of contact with the mystery and the sublime; he believes that this will give him the answer to the chaos he perceives in the life all around him. We live now in a time when all the hopes, all the dreams, all the optimism of the beginning of the century really didn't materialize, save in the realm of technology. The protagonist in the novel is aware of that. One of his closest friends, the son of an atomic physicist, is riddled with guilt over the fact that his father played a major role in the creation of the atomic bomb. These two individuals end up in Korea, in the United States Army, and they find themselves in confrontation with overwhelming questions: the effect of the bomb on the exquisite beauty of a pagan world they have been taught to abominate; the incomprehensible suffering in that world; the idolaters worshipping idols with the same intensity as Jews worshipping on the Day of Atonement. They find a world in which there is no anti-Semitism of the poisonous European variety; a world in which Judaism really doesn't figure as a cultural component. As a result, their own world of values, their Americanism, their Judaism, their role in Western civilization, are relativized and become ambiguous. They have an answer to the question: How can one make commitments in an utterly ambiguous world? That is what the novel tries to explore.

Hinds: I find, I hope you don't mind my saying this, that the diversity and variety within Judaism is not dissimilar to what you find in Protestant Christianity, for example. There are all these great varieties, and as you struggle with your novels, whether you're Jewish or not, you find a great deal of resonance in your own life and experience. And I appreciate that.

Potok: Judaism is a world religion and has an enormous spectrum of responses to the human situation, and the responses are not unlike the responses that any group of people has toward the human experience. People who read my books who aren't Jews struggle with those same resonances.

The Prime of Chaim Potok

Marcia Zoslaw Siegal / 1992

From *Inside: The Quarterly of Jewish Life and Style,* Winter 1992, pp. 60–63, 84, 86. Reprinted by permission of *Inside,* Jewish Federation of Greater Philadelphia.

Chaim Potok—professor, scholar, historian, rabbi, editor, playwright, and popular author of eight best-selling novels—might be a superstar in some circles, but at Hymie's, the deli not far from his Main Line home, he's just another customer. Ever since he was a kid growing up in the Bronx, Potok has loved delicatessens, which is why he often chooses them as the setting for business meetings and interviews.

On a recent weekday morning, Potok and I sit face to face across a table in a quiet booth and discuss his life and work. After the waitress brings the author eggs, English muffins and coffee, I serve him an unexpected question:

"If you were a fictional character, how would you describe yourself?"

Potok flashes a bemused smile and considers his response before answering:

"A man in his early '60s, of middling height and balding, brooding, I would say. Intense. On guard. Antennae open constantly to the world. A lover of literature, of the oceans and of traveling. I do not lose my temper easily, but there are things which annoy me very much: disorganization, shallowness, when people don't keep their word."

Some might describe him as an egoist. And Potok is the first to admit that his novels are primarily a means of self-exploration. He makes no apology for being, in one form or another, the central character in most of his books.

An intensely private man, Potok nevertheless has opened his heart and exposed his innermost conflicts to millions of readers. His writings have been translated into every major language, including Norwegian, Chinese, Dutch, and Hebrew. The author has no idea how many millions of books he has sold, but offers the fact that *The Chosen,* published in 1967, is now in its sixty-sixth paperback printing.

But those who think they know Chaim Potok through his semi-autobiographical novels may be surprised to discover another significant part of his past—one revealed in his latest work of fiction, *I Am the Clay,* the tale of three Korean refugees.

A departure from the Orthodox Jewish world about which he has written so eloquently, the novel is set in Korea, where Potok served as a U.S. Army chaplain in the 1950s. Although *I Am the Clay* did not make the bestseller list when it was published this past spring, Potok says it confronts, for the first time, the Asian experience that irrevocably changed his life.

Ever since *The Chosen,* Potok has put his quest for self-discovery into print. With the story of Reuven Malter and Danny Saunders—two young, observant Jews searching for self-realization—the author captured the hearts and minds of readers on several continents. It was nominated for a National Book Award and made into a popular film starring Robbie Benson, Maximillian Schell, and Rod Steiger. The novel was also turned into an off-Broadway musical.

Potok received the Athenaeum Prize for his second book, *The Promise,* the sequel to *The Chosen;* more recently, he won the National Jewish Book Award for *The Gift of Asher Lev,* the story of an artist who breaks his Hasidic ties in order to pursue his art. (Potok is an accomplished painter.)

"My novels have been a progression," explains Potok, "each more complex than its predecessor, as my own inner conflicts have evolved."

If his books are so personal, what makes them so universally admired?

"They're about culture choices one makes, and we're all going through culture conflicts," he states. "Each of us comes from one world and then encounters other worlds that present alternative ways of thinking about the human experience. Everybody goes through this. Each of my books is a different facet of this confrontation."

Although there will be Jewish characters in his future work, Potok insists they will be very different from those in his previous books. It is unlikely, the author emphasizes with a shake of his head, that he will be revisiting the Orthodox landscape of his beginnings.

"If you want to know about my early life," he tells me," read *In the Beginning.* That's what it was like to play the street games. That's what it was like to fight with the gentile kids and endure their anti-Semitism. That's the world of the Great Depression."

Here's how Potok writes it in the book: "The street we lived on, before our world fell to pieces and we plunged into the decade of the Depression, was wide and tree-lined and lovely. It was a quiet, sunny, cobblestone street filled with well-to-do families who owned cars, went to their synagogues and churches, spoke English civilly to one another—the seniors in the heavy accents of their European lands of origin—and who felt that, at least for them, the immigrant's dream had been realized, they had been right to abandon the blight of Europe and gamble on golden America."

Born in 1929, Chaim Potok was the oldest of four children. His parents, Benjamin and Mollie Potok, were both descendants of Eastern European Hasidic dynasties. The author likes to reminisce about his childhood neighborhood in the Bronx with its small, one-room synagogue lit by naked light bulbs and warmed by clanking radiators; his frequent illnesses; his dreams and nightmares. Potok easily summons to memory his Hebrew teachers and his rigorous studies at Orthodox yeshivas where he learned to husband his time in order to accomplish all he had to do.

"I see myself running through the streets playing Dick Tracy and Terry-and-the-Pirates, and afterward, sitting in my class in yeshiva and then going home and doing my homework," he recalls. "I think whatever it was I did at the moment, I did very intensely. That, I suspect, was part of my home ambience, which was very religious. Everything that was done was completed with tremendous intensity."

Because he grew up during the Great Depression, Potok's youth was touched with somberness. "There was a period when we were on welfare. My father had been quite wealthy in the 1920s—he had been in real estate before the crash—and he spent the next decade rebuilding his life—by opening a jewelry and watch repair store."

Potok also recalls the anti-Jewish sentiments of the time: "You had Father Coughlin from Detroit yelling anti-Semitic diatribes at you from the radio on Sunday afternoons. Did I listen to him? Absolutely! You wanted to know what the enemy was saying so you could respond. And if you didn't listen, the anti-Semitic neighbors would turn up their radios so you would hear him when you walked down the street.

"And then, of course, there was the ranting and raving of Hitler, which I would get on the radio—with a lot of static—from time to time."

He recounts the sense of lunacy abroad and, at home, the overwhelming feeling of precariousness: "I wanted to milk everything for what it was worth, because you never knew if there would be another minute."

But the Depression was nothing compared to the revelations of the death camps following World War II. The entire European branch of the Potok family was destroyed by the Nazis. Potok still remembers the day his father received a letter from Europe telling him that not one relative had survived. "He sat down and told my mother, and she just fell to pieces. She kept saying, 'Nobody? *Nobody?* I can't believe *nobody.*' "

Although the family never spoke of the Holocaust, the horror of it surfaced in Potok's recurring nightmares, and he privately wondered how God could have allowed such a thing. "Once I talked about the Holocaust with my father," he says. "He told me that we had lost 103 aunts, uncles, second cousins, whole families. Then he turned away."

The only other time Potok questioned God when he was growing up was when the old city of Jerusalem fell during Israel's 1947 War of Independence. "I remember going into my father's store and blurting out, 'Why did God *do* something like this?' " Potok's father got so angry in response to his impertinence that the young man ran out of the store. "There were things one just didn't question," the author observes.

In a household too poor to afford toys, Potok turned to books: "They were my toys. Books were my escape." Amidst the poverty of the surrounding Bronx neighborhood, with the towering steel girders of the elevated train and the permeating stench of a nearby brewery, the marbled sanctuary of the New York Public Library branch on 170th Street rose up high and white "like a Greek temple."

In an essay published last spring in *TriQuarterly,* a literary journal, Potok describes a seminal experience he had at age sixteen: "I had never read a difficult contemporary novel before. In my school we read only classics. I decided to read a serious adult novel. To this day, I don't know why I decided to do that."

He found his passion for literature awakened by Evelyn Waugh. "I will never forget the experience of reading *Brideshead Revisited,*" Potok continues. "The world of that book—how other than my own it was!"

As a student at Yeshiva University in Manhattan, Potok continued reading books by Trollope, Fielding, Dostoevsky, and Kafka, all of whom were outside the school's sanctioned curriculum. He also read literary criticism.

"The guys in my class would notice these books, and I would get interesting looks from some of them," Potok says. "In my world, you were really eyeballed if you were reading outside the curriculum."

Out of the conflict between his Orthodox upbringing and his love of literature, Potok began composing essays, poetry, and short stories—at night. In his world, fiction writing was considered a frivolous pursuit. The only person who knew what he was doing was his closest and dearest friend, Aaron Landes, now a rabbi in Elkins Park, a Philadelphia suburb.

"I didn't want to tell anybody else," says Potok. "My feeling was, 'Keep a lid on it, because you'll only antagonize a lot of people.' "

After college, Potok enrolled in the Jewish Theological Seminary of America—not because he intended to be a pulpit rabbi, but because he wanted a deeper understanding of Judaism. Responding to a sense of destiny, the future author felt he wanted to write about things Jewish. "What else did I know at that point in my life?" he shrugs.

After Potok was ordained and had received a master's degree in Hebrew literature in 1954, he was required, as were all graduates, to spend time in the military chaplaincy. Potok was pleased because he thought it would be his ticket to Europe: "I wanted to be in Paris, to go to Germany as a conqueror—and I wanted to absorb the European experience because it would help me as a writer. Of course, 'Man plans and God laughs,' as the Yiddish saying goes."

Instead of Europe, twenty-five-year-old Potok was sent to Korea, where he served for sixteen months. "My whole life was changed as a result," he says. "Nothing was simple after Korea."

Asia was a world totally outside his frame of reference. Taught by his yeshiva teachers to have contempt for idolatrous cultures, Potok was surprised to discover in the Orient a world beautiful beyond all imagination.

"I remember standing in a Shinto shrine in a marketplace in Tokyo and seeing an old man there. He was in front of an idol of a female goddess, swaying back and forth like the Jews on Yom Kippur night in the little synagogue where I grew up. I remember asking myself if the God I prayed to every day was listening to *this* man's prayer? And if not, why not? I asked myself, 'Where are you ever going to see greater devotion in a moment of prayer?' And if the God that I prayed to *was* listening, then what were Judaism and Christianity all about?"

Just like his protagonist in *I Am the Clay,* Potok would from then on view life from a radically changed perspective.

In 1958, Potok married Adena, whom he had first met when they were both counselors at Camp Ramah in the Poconos. Shortly after the wedding, the couple settled in Los Angeles, where Potok headed the local Camp Ramah organization and taught at the University of Judaism. Two years later, they moved to Philadelphia so Potok could pursue a doctorate in philosophy at the University of Pennsylvania and serve as scholar-in-residence at Har Zion Temple.

Wanderers by nature, Potok and his wife then moved to Jerusalem where he worked on his thesis—the theory of knowledge in the Kantian and post-Kantian period—as well as his first novel.

He returned to Philadelphia in 1966, this time as editor-in-chief of the Jewish Publication Society (JPS), a prestigious position he held for the next nine years. It was Potok who was responsible for JPS's 1973 publication of *The Jewish Catalog,* a contemporary manual on Jewish life that was considered revolutionary for the staid publishing house. The *Catalog* embodied the spirit of the Jewish counterculture with its social and political concerns. It not only became the best-selling JPS book after the Bible, but it also showed that JPS could meet the challenges of a new generation.

In 1979, after yet another extended sojourn in Jerusalem, the Potoks settled into a comfortable Tudor home in Merion, where they have resided for the past thirteen years. It is the longest period of time Potok has ever lived in one place.

Though he has traveled great distances, Potok is indelibly marked by his Orthodox origins. "It is woven into the fibers of my being," he remarks, tapping his heart with his strong fingers. "There is a great deal of passion and beauty in that sort of faith."

However, among the Orthodox community, Potok remains a controversial figure. "I have offended them," he says, "writing about them when they don't like to be written about"—and, in their view, maligning them with his portrayals of their insularity and infighting. Many Orthodox Jews maintain he has given credence to what they consider heretical: modern criticism of the sacred talmudic and biblical texts.

In his own Main Line neighborhood, reminders of Potok's past are very much present: conservatively dressed men in traditional black hats and long black coats walk to and from synagogue; women with long-sleeved dresses and covered heads pass by with broods of children in tow. It moves him, Potok admits.

"When I see the kids go by from the Talmudical Yeshiva of Philadelphia, I sometimes wonder what my life might have been had I not become a writer," he says thoughtfully. "I know the closed worlds they live in. I might have remained a very traditional Jew. I might be teaching Talmud at some yeshiva, but it wasn't to be."

The Potoks raised their three children in a kosher home, prayed with them and sent them to Jewish schools. (Today, thirty-year-old Rena is a doctoral student in comparative literature; Naama, twenty-seven, is a graduate student in theater; and twenty-four-year-old Akiva is a professional photographer.) While Potok says he may switch on a light or drive on Saturday, he adds,

"Shabbes is Shabbes, as far as I'm concerned. It's the day of rest. I don't work on my Shabbes."

The couple belongs to a *chavurah* (a small group of people who regularly study and pray together) at Temple Beth Hillel-Beth El in Wynnewood. "The service is very Orthodox in that we omit nothing," explains Potok, "but women participate in everything. We're very lucky to have a place like this. It's one of the great attractions of Philadelphia for us." Potok, along with his wife, still studies Talmud, just as he did in his youth.

"It's an ongoing exploration," says Potok of his talmudic studies. "I don't understand fully what my relationship is to the universe and to God. At times, it's an open and full relationship. At times, it's silent and withdrawn. I believe that we live in an imperfect world created by an errant God, and our task is to try to perfect it."

If Potok hasn't yet perfected the world, he strives to perfect his writing. He is now at work on a major piece of nonfiction, which he expects to complete next summer.

The book revolves around the family of Soviet refusenik Vladimir Slepak, whose father was an ardent Bolshevik. Vladimir, by contrast, rejected Communism in order to embrace his ancient Jewish heritage. Potok says the book is rich in the kind of conflicts that fascinate him: parents and children moving in different directions, the confrontation of disparate cultures.

"If you assume, as I assume, that what was going on with one family was going on with tens of thousands of other families in the Soviet Union, what you have is a microcosm that might help to explain, to some extent, the dissolution of Soviet ideology. That's the journey I'm on."

Potok recently made a side trip: he wrote a children's book, which is illustrated by *Philadelphia Inquirer* editorial cartoonist Tony Auth. Told from the point of view of a ten-year-old, *The Tree of Here* is the story of a boy, not unlike the young Potok, who is constantly being uprooted.

Adena is the only person with whom Potok shares his creative process. She reads his work-in-progress on a daily basis. A psychiatric social worker and Jewish communal leader (she is currently the president of the Auerbach Central Agency for Jewish Education), Adena is, by her husband's description, "very calming, very people-oriented. I find her reaction is always very honest, very sharp and keen."

Acknowledging the tendency of the artist to be monomaniacal and self-centered, Potok says, "Adena keeps me human. In that regard, I consider myself fortunate."

Has success perhaps spoiled Chaim Potok?

"Look, I've been writing for so long, and it hasn't spoiled me yet," he claims, noting that he's grateful that fame did not come to him too early in life when he might not have been able to handle it.

For Potok, there is always a lingering fear of losing the gift. "I don't like to think about that," he remarks. "It's lasted a long time. But, isn't it possible that I'll wake up one morning to find it's suddenly gone?"

When all is said and done, how does Chaim Potok want to be remembered? The author repeats the question, his brown eyes intent behind silver, wire-rimmed glasses.

"As having written some serious books," he replies. "Books that deal with living human beings. Books that affect lives.

"As a decent person."

Potok Has Chosen to Create Worlds from Words

Mike Field / 1994

From *The Johns Hopkins University Gazette,* Vol. 24, No. 11, November 14, 1994. Reprinted by permission of Johns Hopkins University.

Born in the Bronx to Polish immigrants just months before the start of the Great Depression, Chaim Potok grew up in an Orthodox Jewish home where his businessman father, "a great admirer of the capitalist system," discouraged his son's early aptitude for painting in favor of a more practical occupation. Potok received rabbinic ordination in 1954 and a doctorate in Western philosophy in 1965, but, other than a two-year stint as a chaplain on the front lines in Korea, he chose not to make religion his avocation.

Instead, he turned his talents to writing. In 1967 he published *The Chosen,* a novel that examined value systems in conflict and won Potok a worldwide audience. Seven other major novels have followed, including *The Promise* and *My Name Is Asher Lev.*

This fall, Potok joined the Writing Seminars program as a visiting professor, where he teaches an undergraduate course in fiction writing.

Q: I've read that in 1945 at the age of fifteen or sixteen you read Evelyn Waugh's *Brideshead Revisited* and decided to become a writer. Is this story true?

Potok: It was after I read *Brideshead Revisited* and soon afterwards read *A Portrait of the Artist as a Young Man.* Those two did it for me.

Q: *Brideshead Revisited* was not the novel I would have initially thought would have propelled you to commence writing.

Potok: I think it was the writing. I think it was also the realization that you could really create the world out of language. I was a very orthodox Jewish boy. I figured if these writers could get me to be interested in two different Catholic worlds that there was something about this form of communication that I wanted to be part of. That it captivated me the way it did, that it worked its magic on me, made me realize how powerful this medium is. And I wanted to become part of it.

Q: Can you teach writing?

Potok: Somebody who does not have basic talent cannot be taught writing. Somebody who has talent can have his or her writing improved through the learning of technique.

Q: When you say technique, are you talking basic mechanics?

Potok: Structuring.

Q: Was teaching in the back of your mind always, or was it something you came to?

Potok: It was never in the back of my mind. I never wanted just to teach. I got a rabbinic ordination so that I could know my own tradition better because I knew I wanted to write about it. And I went and got a doctorate in secular philosophy because I wanted to know Western civilization better, because I knew I wanted to write about that. I taught school all along, until it was possible for me to then concentrate solely on the writing. I do this now, this teaching, to keep myself in touch with younger people and with the newer thinking that's going on, which you can find in academic circles, much easier, probably, than you can anywhere else.

Q: You actually wrote your first published novel, *The Chosen,* in Jerusalem.

Potok: That's right. I was working on my doctorate, finishing it in Jerusalem because two of the people I needed to work with were at the Hebrew University. And that same year that I was working on my doctorate I wrote *The Chosen.*

Q: Back and forth? You'd set one down and you'd pick the other up?

Potok: I wrote *The Chosen* in the morning and my doctorate in the afternoon.

Q: Did you prefer writing one to the other?

Potok: Actually no, I thought they were two very interesting and very different experiences.

Q: You said the reason you went to rabbinical school was to find out about yourself. Was the thought in your mind that you were going to be writing about this?

Potok: I knew that I was going to write. What else did I know to write about? I knew I was going to write about something Jewish and something American. I mean that's what I was. I wanted to know my subject better. I learned a lot about the gritty side of life in the Army. I wanted to learn about the creative, the core of Western culture, and I did that by doing a doctorate in philosophy.

Q: Are there certain issues that you are trying to figure out when you write, or is the writing more just an innate process and these issues come to the surface?

Potok: *The Chosen* was an intuitive process. I was dealing with something that troubled me a great deal, and that is, what happens when two idea systems collide inside human beings? Both seem at times to be inherently valid. And both are at times contradictory. It was only after I finished and published *The Chosen* and got reaction to it—letters from everywhere and all kinds of people—that I began to realize that I was not the only one going through these experiences. What I'm trying to explore is how people react when things that are very dear to them are challenged by alternate ways of structuring the human experience.

Q: You paint as well as write.

Potok: Actually, I began to paint when I was about nine or ten years old. It really became a problem in my family, especially with my father, who detested it.

Q: Why?

Potok: He thought it was a gentile enterprise. He couldn't connect to it. He was very religious.

Q: Did you have to paint on the sly?

Potok: Oh no, there was no sly to paint on in our apartment in New York, and it became increasingly problematic as I was growing up. And then I think what I did was I shifted the hunger to create from painting to writing, which is much more accepted in the Jewish tradition.

Q: Do the results differ from what you expected at the beginning?

Potok: You dream of the accidents. You pray for them. You hope for the accidents. In other words, the unanticipated moves: Because what that means is that the piece that you're creating is alive, it's like a child full of surprises. If it's not suddenly making its own demands and is only lying there inert, your best bet is to walk away from it and start something else.

Q: The last two books you've written are children's books.

Potok: I think it is very important to deal with the fears of children. In so many ways that's where our problems begin. One of the primary terrors in our society is the terror that results from the very nature of our society. We are a mobile society. The dream of America is to move up the economic ladder. Every move vertically involves a move horizontally, because if you get a better job and you move up that vertical ladder economically, you're going to trade your house for another house—horizontally. You're going to move from one kind of house to another kind to match the economic move. Your child is moving too. Nearly every move to a child is a terrifying time. It's by the way also very stressful for adults. *The Tree of Here* is about that fear. The next book for children, *The Sky of Now,* is about the terror of falling.

Q: Literally, like falling down steps?

Potok: From heights. It's a sort of metaphor for what happens when Americans become failed Americans. What do you then do about flying? Children's literature has always fascinated me from the time that I myself was a child. I see it as a great opportunity to communicate with young people.

Radio Curious: Chaim Potok

Barry Vogel / 1997

From "Fresh Air," Radio Curious, February 1997. Reprinted by permission of Barry Vogel.

I: Chaim Potok's novels address the conflicts between Jewish religious and secular ways of looking at and living in the world. His novels include *The Chosen, My Name Is Asher Lev,* and *The Book of Lights.* He is also the author of the nonfiction book *Wanderings: The History of the Jews.* Chaim Potok grew up in an Orthodox Jewish family in New York. He left Orthodox Judaism for the Conservative branch of Judaism, where he was ordained as a rabbi. He's never been a practicing rabbi in the sense of having a congregation, but his religious concerns have always motivated his art. For nine years he served as the editor of the Jewish Publication Society in Philadelphia. When he left that position, he continued to work with them on the Society's translation of the Hebrew Bible. He was the secretary of the translation committee that translated the third book of the Hebrew Bible. What they did was go back to the original text and translate it into contemporary English. All three volumes that they worked on, the Torah, the Prophets, and Writings, will be published together in September. Chaim Potok divides his time between a home in Philadelphia and an apartment in Israel. He lives just outside of Philadelphia, and his new novel, *Davita's Harp,* is published by Knopf. Welcome back to Fresno, it's a great pleasure to see you again.

CP: Thank you.

I: Can you tell us a little bit about the story of your new novel?

CP: It's a story about the imagination of a young girl, how she sees a certain aspect of the history of the twentieth century, how she reconstructs that history through her imagination—that history being on one hand, the Depression, through which she lived with her family, her mother and father. Her mother a non-observant Jew, her father a non-observant Episcopalian from New England, her mother from Poland. And at the same time, how she sees their tremendous commitment to and preoccupation with what was in the thirties a very important part of the American scene, the fight for social justice, particularly as it was expressed through the ranks of the Communist

Party. The mother was very high up in the party, on an intellectual level; the father is very high up in the party on an action level. Her father is a reporter for one of the major newspapers, Communist newspapers in the United States, and how she sees their vision of things. And how she experiences their bitter disappointment with that vision as a result of the Hitler-Stalin pact. How, in turn, she is attracted to another vision of things, a religious one, and in turn is bitterly disappointed with that. What she does with those disappointments is the harp of the story.

I: It's almost a reversal in a way in that in this story the daughter goes from a kind of secular world into a religious world. And her parents are fervent Communists. And it's as if you were comparing ardent political beliefs to ardent religious beliefs in a way that someone would wholeheartedly throw themselves into it and how it would conform their world view and all their motivations.

CP: That's indeed what I'm doing, and I was really doing this, for the first time. It's an effort to explore the extent to which people are caught up in the systems of thought that are unbending. And what happens when you have an individual caught up in those systems of thought that can't go along with the final steps in either of those systems, especially when those systems of thought hurt that individual terribly. And that system of thought still demands that individual's loyalty. In the instance of communism, the mother simply cannot come to terms with that ultimate step that occurred with the Hitler-Stalin pact, and in terms of the daughter, she cannot come to terms with that ultimate step that occurred to her purely because she was a girl. Those are terrible wounds. These are individuals who are trying to make sense out of the wilderness of our lives. And in both instances they are terribly hurt.

I: I was surprised, I think, to find that you're as interested as you obviously must be in the Spanish Civil War and the Communist activism of that period in America.

CP: Well, I think it's very hard to grow up in the United States, to have grown up here in the 1930s and not be terribly interested and quite concerned with what was, I think, the central thrust of the '30s, that is to say the effort on the part of the entire country to instill or to institutionalize measures of social justice in the country. When we realized that we entered the '30s without unemployment insurance, without social security, without any way of taking care of the poor, the indigent, except through the somewhat disorganized private means. When we realized that this was what the shape of the

'30s was like and when we realized what is in place today, in terms of how we care for ourselves, we ought to be curious about how all this came into place, and one of the pivotal elements that brought it into place, one of the thrusts that was a force in its institutionalization, were these leftist groups that sort of forced us to see the world in a certain way. It's interesting in that I myself have no sympathy whatsoever with the Communist Party of this country or any country—it's utterly the reverse of how it is that I think and construct the world for myself. At the same time, I would be the last one to deny that they had some significant effect on the American scene, especially in the '30s. Anybody who was intellectual, anybody who thought, anybody who cared had to in one way or another come to terms with what it was that left wing socialist Communist ideology was all about.

I: One of the things that happens to the main character in the book, the young girl, is that she is really cheated out of something that she deserves from her religion, from her yeshiva, really, her Jewish school, because she's a female. Did you have any direct encounters with that in your life that you observed that helped form that part of the story?

CP: Yes, shortly after I was married, my wife told me that when she was thirteen, she attended a Jewish parochial elementary school in New York City in the Crown Heights Section of Brooklyn and she was first in her class, both in Hebrew and in English. And she deserved to become the valedictorian and it was given to a boy, and she inquired of the principal or the head teacher why and was told straight out that it was because she was a girl. How would it look in the eyes of the other Jewish parochial schools in the area if the best student in the graduating class was a girl? How would the boys look in the eyes of the other schools? What would the quality of the school be like in the eyes of the other schools? She was profoundly hurt by this. I would say deeply scarred—that's not the sort of thing you forget about in a lifetime. The story remained with me and grew in the strange fashion as stories grow inside novelists. They take on a life of their own and when the time comes and they're ready to be written about, they get written about, and I guess this was the time for the writing. Also, my wife's family was very much involved in Socialist Zionist causes, and my side of the family was very capitalist and revisionist, very anti-Socialist. My wife's side of the family was quite Social-ist. As a matter of fact, there was a cousin here or there on my wife's side of the family apparently, who flirted even with the extreme left part of the Socialist spectrum, the Communist party and so on. These ingredients were rich enough or similar enough for me to want to explore them in terms of a novel. And *Davita's Harp* is the result of that. That amalgam of elements yielded ultimately, *Davita's Harp*.

I: Do you think that Judaism is any more sexist than any, than most other religions are? Do you think of it as a sexist religion?

CP: All the major religions on the planet, as far as I know, and this probably includes Asia, but certainly in the Western World and certainly in that part of the world that bridges East and West—Islam, all the major religions in the historical period are patriarchal in nature. The reasons are probably complex and this isn't the place to go into them, although I rather suspect we can figure them out without too much difficulty. What happened before the historical period, we really don't know, that is to say before writing, we really don't know. There are some theories that religion, especially in the area of Greece, may have been matriarchal, but we really don't know and there isn't much point in conjecturing. It isn't so much a matter of sexist, which is a kind of deliberate, almost vindictive way of looking at things, as it is simply a way that the species developed its existence and carved out certain areas in which it behaved in certain ways. Sexist, I think, is a deliberate way of behaving in a kind of malevolent or quasi-malevolent way. I don't think there was anything sexist involved in this sort of behavior. It becomes sexist when alternatives are possible and you deny the alternatives. And to that extent, yes, in the modern period there is no question whatsoever in my mind that there are certain elements of the Jewish tradition, indeed all traditions that are quite deliberately moved into the male area, because there is a male feeling that power will be lost, domination will be lost, something significant will be yielded to the female side of the species, and they don't want that yielded.

I: When did you start becoming aware of the double standard in Judaism in terms of how it treats men and women?

CP: Well, I became aware of the way women feel about this when we lived in Jerusalem from 1973–1977. At a certain point in that period of time, I was, and my wife, both of us were involved in the building of a new synagogue. And the question was, where do you put the women? And the women, it was all agreed, would be put on the balcony. And the rabbi wanted, he was of the old school, European rabbi, he wanted a wall of some kind built on the balcony to divide the women from the rest of the synagogue so that they couldn't even be looked at. And in terms of custom—there are no real laws about this in Judaism, but in terms of custom and tradition, once the women are off the floor with you, you don't really need a separating wall. If they're on the balcony, then the balcony is separation enough. In any event, the rabbi tried to prevail and the women sort of let themselves be known and heard, and there was some sort of strike and my wife and the wife of a very good friend of ours kind of found themselves in a leadership position and that strike, that was the first time I had ever encountered an instance of that kind, where women actually expressed themselves quite vocally in terms of how they felt in terms of their position in the synagogue. And the women won, the women won. When I returned to the States in '77, I became increasingly aware of what was happening. It also helps when you have two daughters that are growing up and who let themselves in no uncertain terms be known in so far as their feelings with regard to their being women is concerned. There is no question at all that the rising tide of feminism sensitized me in the past I would say decade, decade and a half, to how it is that women feel. There is no question at all. I would, in all candor, have to say that prior to this, indeed I was not sensitive to it. I used to give a lecture where I talked about people growing up and rebelling against the society in which they grew up, and I always used he. A woman once came up to me and said, "don't you think women rebel?" And from that point on I say he and/or she. I'm very sensitive to the situation now, and indeed am very grateful to the women who point these things out to me.

I: Are there any theological rationalizations of the different ways of treating men and women that still make you wonder? You know, that still sound like justifiable reasons to you for differences that some women still object to, that some women would object to.

CP: There is a strong tendency in the Jewish tradition to very carefully make separations—it isn't always male and female. The Jewish tradition, especially that part of the tradition that we would call the priestly tradition, sees the world as structured, very hierarchically, and very sharply. That, by the way is one of the fundamental reasons that Jews look with horror upon blurring of the lines of species. That's one of the fundamental reasons why Jews won't eat non-Kosher foods. Those foods seem to be between the boundaries of certain kinds of seafood, certain kinds of animal food seem not to fall very strongly on one side or the other of the dividing line. And those are the things that are looked upon as sort of, how would I put it, errors in the process of creation, things that you stay away from because their place in the order of creation isn't clear cut. So, from that point of view, I would suspect that the Jewish tradition intrinsically looks upon the dividing between male and female in a very strong way. And that has all sorts of implications. One of the fundamental implications basic to the Jewish tradition is the notion that women simply don't have to observe most of the commandments. It's not incumbent upon women to observe most of the commandments. If it's not incumbent upon a woman to pray and it is incumbent upon a man to pray, then a woman really shouldn't participate with the man inside the actual dynamic of the prayer service. Also in the temple, there was a separate section for men, a separate section for women. When the temple was destroyed and it came to construct a synagogue, they simply copied that basic structure and duplicated it in the world of the synagogue. So, there's no question that in the classical Jewish tradition, there is this separation, just as there is in all the major religions. The question that faces us now, is of course, how do you revise this, what do you do with it, what kinds of commitments do you make to the tradition for the next hundred, five hundred, thousand years, which includes the woman in the dynamics of the tradition and at the same time not raze the tradition and distort it entirely. That's what everyone is struggling with today.

I: I don't think we've ever had the chance on the air to talk about your impressions of the movie *The Chosen*, which was adapted from your novel, your first novel. So, I'd love to hear what you thought of the movie.

CP: Well, I thought they did a very fine thing with the book; I thought they retained the quality of the world of the book. Now I especially liked that they didn't turn it into a Second Avenue Yiddish theater with all the false sentimentality that pervaded that world, and I especially also liked the fact that they didn't turn it into Catskill mountain jokes. It's a story that is told with tremendous integrity; it simply takes you into that world without any apology for what that world is all about, and I rather enjoyed very much what it is they did with it.

I: You had a little cameo in the movie too, right?

CP: I did my Alfred Hitchcock thing. I was the Talmud professor there.

I: That's a pretty autobiographical story for you, isn't it?

CP: It's the world that I grew up in. The Chassidic world was my mother's world. She's the descendant of a long line of Chassidic Rebbes, Chassidic leaders. She's a descendant of the Reizener dynasty, one of the great dynasties of Europe, and my father's was a Chassid, came from one of the great

Chassidic groups in Europe. So, although I didn't grow up deeply inside that world, in the sense that I didn't wear the side curls, and so on, the home was very, very religious, the prayerbook was a Chassidic prayerbook, and I grew up inside one of these very small synagogues, a stible, we call them. And that was my world, until I began to go to, well late high school and college.

I: Were there things you weren't allowed to do as a child that you really wanted to do, that you saw other kids your age doing?

CP: There were things that I wondered what others were doing, for example, on Saturday morning, when people went off to the movies and saw the Flash Gordon Series and things of that kind, and we went off to synagogue. There were things that were forbidden to us that I saw others doing and was curious about. But, in essence, as long as I got the grades my father wanted me to get, he pretty much left me alone. The one problem that I had with my father, who was a very religious Jew, had to do with painting and drawing. Because I began to paint when I was about nine years old and that was okay up until my bar mitzvah, when I was about thirteen, and afterwards it became a problem in the house. For him, painting and drawing were really expressions of what it was the Gentile world did, and no Jew should seriously spend time doing that sort of thing. And, it became increasingly difficult for me to do this kind of thing at home. And I think what happened was that at about the age of fourteen-and-a-half or fifteen, I moved that hunger to create into the world of writing as a result of reading a novel. That overwhelmed me. The novel was *Brideshead Revisited* by Evelyn Waugh. And, I began to write, and I stopped painting and drawing, indeed until *The Chosen* was published. My father was very annoyed even that I was writing, but writing was closer to the Jewish tradition than painting. It has to do with words; it's also very quiet. You sit in your corner and do it. When I was about seventeen I got a letter from an editor of the *Atlantic Monthly,* to whom I had sent a story, and the editor invited me to send them a novel, if I was writing one, because they liked the story. And I showed the letter to my father, and he was angry at the editor for encouraging me. That's the kind of world I grew up in.

I: What makes painting and drawing outside of the Jewish tradition?

CP: It has to do with image-making. It's not anything that anyone who was a religious Jew really bothered with for 2000 years. Its iconography is very much connected to Christianity. There is of course the problem of commandment that forbids the making of images.

I: Now I thought that commandment was more literal, that it prevented the making of images of God . . .

CP: Sculpture.

I: Yeah, but I mean that if you were doing a sculpture of a friend or of an animal that wasn't meant to be worshipped, that that would be fine.

CP: That's correct, except it has been so interpreted over the ages that, what it really is trying to say is that anything connected to the umbrella civilization, that in any way at all has to do with its mode of worship, is forbidden to you. Now, we ought to thank the Lord that the Canaanites only depicted their gods in human form, their high gods in human form, because if they had depicted them in animal form, which is what the Egyptians did, then there would have been no decorations at all in the Solomonic Temple. As it was, the walls there were filled with grapes and fruit and animals and so on and so forth. Indeed there are animals in synagogues in Europe, but no depiction of human beings. All through the Middle Ages, the umbrella civilization in which Jews lived in Western Europe was Christianity, and Christianity was regarded by the tradition essentially as an idolatrist tradition because of its iconography, its images, its statuary and so on. Therefore, no religious Jew ever had anything to do with this extraordinary adventure of Western civilization we call art, until the modern period, when Christendom is no longer the umbrella civilization, but it's Western humanism. Western humanism Jews can begin to enter, even religious Jews. And indeed, you have the phenomenon now of religious Jews painting.

I: Well, did you know any Jews who were in the art world when you were young and your father was forbidding you from painting and drawing?

CP: None whatsoever. As a matter of fact, the only religious Jew I knew who was a writer, and I once appealed to him when one of my Talmud teachers took me to task for wanting to be a writer. The only religious Jew I knew who was a writer was Agnon and I mentioned Agnon to this Talmud teacher, and he looked at me and said, "He will fall upon evil ways one day." He didn't think that he would make it as a religious Jew. How could you conceivably remain in any way at all dedicated to God and spend your life writing stories, it seems, when what you are supposed to do with your life is study, study the word of God, not write stories. It seems such a frivolity.

I: It's hard to defy your father, isn't it, when he's not only the authority figure of being your father, but he also claims to have God on his side, to have the whole Jewish tradition on his side?

CP: It's very hard. The only way you can do it is if in some way or another you are possessed by the dream that you have. It is very, very hard to do it. It has got to be some kind of inexplicable calling, and that's what happened to me when I read *Brideshead Revisited*. The book possessed me, and really everything that I've done with my life from that point on has been for the writing. I went to Jewish Theological Seminary because I knew that I was going to write about Jews. What else was I going to write about? And I wanted to know my subject, so I went to get a really good Jewish education, a kind of Western-oriented Jewish education, and the degree that they gave you then was rabbinical ordination when you were finished at that school. Later I went to the University of Pennsylvania for a Ph.D. in Western philosophy because I wanted to know the essential nature of the umbrella civilization, western civilization in which we all lived. Everything that I've done has been for the writing.

I: What was it about *Brideshead Revisited* that so changed your life?

CP: I think it had to do with the essential nature of somebody investigating or coming up against a closed world, that Catholic world. This is a book about an upper class, British Catholic family, and I was a member of a very closed, very Orthodox Jewish world. And you can imagine that I knew a great deal about upper class British Catholics. I was overwhelmed by that story. I was utterly caught up in it. In the personality, a strange being of the mother of that family. The wavering personality of the daughter, the disintegrating personality of the son, that whole strange English world. I was fifteen years old, a little Jewish boy in New York and found myself, after about 70–80 pages, so inside the world of that book. That was the first time in my life that I was actually inside the feelings of people. I had read all my life. I can't remember a time when I wasn't reading. But always the book was a distance from me, and I knew that I was reading, no matter how caught up I was in the story. This was the first time when I was actually inside the people and their feelings and I remember closing that book and looking down at it and sensing the power of this form of expression. And the question then became for me, how do you use words to create this kind of magic. There seems to be something magical about this kind of power, and I wanted to find out what this magic was all about, what this power was all about, and that's what I've been doing all my life.

I: How come when you decided to leave the Orthodox tradition, you didn't leave the Jewish religion altogether and just become secular?

CP: Well, if I had had the sort of situation that James Joyce was in, I probably would have left it altogether. In other words, if there were no alternatives inside the Jewish tradition for me, I probably would have left it entirely. It was an intolerable situation for me. Orthodoxy for me meant someone always looking over my shoulder, or me having to look over my shoulder. Orthodoxy for me meant somebody always judging what it was that I was doing. Now a fundamentalism for me meant at that point that I really couldn't do the kind of art that I wanted to do with my life. I couldn't criticize whoever I wanted to, I couldn't write with a sense of freedom that I wanted to. I wanted to create my own vision of things, and any fundamentalism has its vision of things. Fundamentalism almost always precludes the concept of the individual and his/her own private vision of things. It offers you its vision, you take it or you're out. And that is simply impossible in so far as serious creativity is concerned. It's good for public relations, or it's good for someone who isn't writing about fundamentalism or things that have to do with the world in which he/she finds himself. But, if you want to write about that world, you want to explore, you can't do it inside a fundamentalism. Now, if I had not had a non-fundamentalist alternative inside the Jewish tradition, there is no question at all in my mind that I would have left the Jewish tradition entirely. As it was, there were two non-fundamentalist traditions inside the Jewish tradition. One was the Conservative Jewish alternative, the other was the Reform Jewish alternative. The Reform Jewish alternative was simply too far for me. The Conservative Jewish alternative was very close to my way of thinking, without the fundamentalist commitment. And that's why I went to the Jewish Theological Seminary.

I: And you studied to become a rabbi, as opposed to, you know, majoring in journalism or writing or literary criticism. Why did you want to become a rabbi? You never really practiced as a rabbi.

CP: Nor did I ever want to. For the same reason that when I decided to do a doctorate at the University of Pennsylvania, I didn't do it in English literature. The last thing in the world that I wanted to do was become conscious of the process of writing, or self-conscious about the process of writing. I'm very conscious of it. But, I didn't want to learn about the history of the Jewish language, its long development, its twists and turns, because there is so much that's intuitive in the writing process, so much that you have to get out of your unconscious, your subconscious, elements that you really ought not to be fully aware of as you do the digging. And that's one of the fundamental reasons I didn't do it in English literature and didn't do it in journalism and didn't do it in writing.

I: Did you find yourself getting into major disputes with the rabbis who you were studying with when you were studying to become a rabbi yourself?

CP: Constantly, but that was one of the glories of the Seminary. Unlike the parochial school that I attended, and I attended parochial schools from the time I was about five-and-a-half to the time I was about twenty or twenty-one, where you really couldn't open up your mouth and open up your mind and voice things that were outside the parameters of fundamentalism. In the Seminary, you could say almost anything you wanted. And that was one of the glories of that particular school. It was a mind-opening experience. Plus the fact that it was in the Seminary that I discovered not only Talmud, which I had studied all my life, but poetry, philosophy, theology, writing, love poems written by rabbis in the Middle Ages. A whole spectrum of literature that simply was unavailable to anybody going to an Orthodox parochial school.

I: Did your father ever threaten to disown you?

CP: Well, at that point, though he was very unhappy with my choice to go to the Seminary, there wasn't very much he could do about it, because I was twenty-one years old. And, he knew by that time that it was either Seminary or nothing. And, he settled for the Seminary, although I must say he was very unhappy about it, because what he really wanted was for me to become an Orthodox rabbi and teach Talmud in a parochial school or an academy of leaning somewhere.

I: Did you ever reconcile that?
CP: No

I: You refer to Orthodox Judaism as fundamentalist, and fundamentalism literally refers to a form of Christianity. In what way do you feel that Chassidism, or Orthodox Judaism is a form of fundamentalism?

CP: Well, I use it in its normal sense today, that is to say, the notion that scriptures isn't, the book that we call scriptures, is entirely divine, God given, unalterable, frozen in time, that in the Jewish tradition, that really looks in horror at the notion of altering itself in any profound way, or even in any shallow way, although it does alter, it does change. They look askance at the very concept of tampering with the tradition. A tradition that really sort of stands outside of history, is unaffected by the stream of things, regards outside cultures as passing fancy, some of them as fads, regards feminism with horror, by the way, regards it as the most outspoken element of the fads of the twentieth century, something that it doesn't want to have anything to do with, something that it sees as a basic threat to its existence. That's essentially what I mean by fundamentalism—that's what everyone means by fundamentalism, and any Orthodoxy is certainly fundamentalist.

I: Just as in Christianity, there are some groups of people who have headed toward a more fundamentalistic, more fundamental view, in Judaism, there's a younger generation of people from outside Chassidism or Orthodoxy who is going into that. And I wonder if you have any ideas why that's happening?

CP: Oh, yes, there are, with all the problems of fundamentalism, there are powerful attractions and tremendous pluses that it has. One of its most important pluses is the fact that it offers you stability, and this is anything but a stable world in which we live. It offers you truths that have lasted 2000 and more years. It offers you history; it offers you a sense of connection to the past. And it offers you something else that people are really hungry for today, and that secularism simply has been unable to fashion for itself—it offers you community. For whatever reason, the secular world has really been unable to create for itself the concept of community as we generally understand it—people collected together with a common history, common goals, shared systems of thought, whereas religious communities do indeed offer you that. There is power in that feeling of community; there is enormous solace in the notion that in times of great travail, people will collect together, share the travail with you, help you out, a community of joy, a community of suffering. A common base of understanding. That is a powerful attraction in these very querulous times in which we live, and it isn't only Judaism, it's the whole world that's experiencing this turn now to fundamentalism. It's Christianity, Protestant Christianity, Catholic Christianity, it's Islam. Everywhere you turn in the world today, you've got this movement toward security. People are hungry to feel themselves part of a kind of grand scheme of things, and there's nothing more grand than religious thought.

I: There's another interesting phenomenon, I think, happening in many religions, I guess and also in Judaism, which is a return to religion by the children of parents who have become very secularized themselves. And, I think in Judaism, it tends to be the second-generation Americans in families that came from Eastern Europe, and it seems to me that there are some first-generation Americans who regarded their parents' form of religion, Eastern

European Jews' form of religion as being superstition, and because of that, they rejected it. I wonder what you think of that?

CP: They regarded it as superstition and they regarded it as out of place in America, because the idea then was that everybody should be an American. And one of the things you did very quickly when you came to this country was you went to night school and you learned English. And you forgot as quickly as you could the world from which you came. Also, this is a country where you can advance, certainly during the period of the first immigration, where you could advance economically if you were fortunate enough, cunning enough, clever enough, sharp enough and opportunistic enough. And that first generation was the sacrificial generation. The children advanced economically; they understood the power of education. Their children, that is to say the second generation of Americans, had all the material wealth they needed, and in the '60s, began to look around and hunger for something else. Tremendous dissatisfaction with the materialism in this society, when you have all the materialism. When you don't have it, you want it. But, when you grow up with it, at one point or another in your life, you begin to be dissatisfied with it, not everybody, but enough were dissatisfied with it to go in a number of directions. Some of them formed the cadre that caused the trouble in the '60s and early '70s in the United States; the trouble, of course for some people it wasn't trouble, it was glorious idealism. Others began to look around to see if they could express themselves in different ways, and those were the individuals who began to move towards religious values, spiritual values. As I said before, the world is a very perilous place to live, especially with the specter of the bomb hovering over us, and whenever you have a situation like that, whenever you have a society in a breakdown position, which is what we are now, we're in a post-modernist phase today, all the dreams that we started the century with seem not to have materialized, and we're really living at the brink of potential destruction. Whenever you have a situation of this kind, people will hunger for old truths. By the way, it's an interesting phenomena that you raised. In Babylonia, with the first exile, 586, or thereabouts, after the destruction of the first temple, the first generation of Babylonian Jews almost entirely had Babylonian names. The second generation, and we have these from contracts and so on, the second generation began to have Hebrew names, and increasingly, as Babylonian Jewry continued, you have an increasing number, so the phenomena that you talked about a moment ago, is not a new one in the history of things Jewish.

I: That's interesting, do you see that as being a positive thing, that people in many religions are returning to their religion, either in a conservative way or in an Orthodox way?

CP: Yes, I think it's a very positive phenomenon, as long as one remains open minded as one is, as long as one is willing to accept the notion that there are no ultimate answers to any of the human problems, that each genera-tion finds its own answers. And as long as you accept the idea that fanaticism of any kind, *any kind,* is wrong and ultimately self-destructive and destructive of others.

I: How threatened do you feel by the group in America of Christian funda-mentalists of the Right, who would like to see America be a Christian state, who talk of America as a Christian state?

CP: Well, anyone who wants to bridge the very wise gap between church and state that was established by our founding fathers frightens me. There's no question that this is a secular country, with the tonality of Christendom. There's no question about that. Just as Israel is a secular country with the tonalities of the Bible and the Talmud of Judaism. And that's fine. I have no argument with that and I can live with that. Once you begin to plug funda-mentalist ideas into the secularism of the land and try to alter the essential secular structure of the society, I begin to be very, very concerned, because it isn't only a matter of the Jews. It's a matter of secularists too. They have a place in this world; they have a place in this society. There are many people who don't believe at all. What do we do with them? Do we make them Christians too? So it isn't only a matter of concern from the point of view of my being Jewish about this move toward Christianizing the land.

I: Let me ask you, I know that Philadelphia recently hosted a gathering of American Holocaust survivors, and actually people from around the world, I think, came to Philadelphia for it. And remember the Holocaust has been the bywords of survivors. It appears to me sometimes as if there's a kind of almost Holocaust-like industry growing up, and I don't mean to sound crass about this, but there have been like books galore written about the Holocaust, photograph books, and exhibits and this and that, and sometimes I wonder, maybe we want to be careful of how we remember it. I mean, do you think there's any point where you start to trivialize the memory by constantly packaging it and repackaging it, then, I was just wondering what you think about that?

CP: Well, we do that all the time as a species, with the traumatic moments of the past. I mean, how many novels were written about the First World War after the First World War? A lot of them were great novels, a lot of them were absurd and trivial. How many novels were written about the Second World War, the Spanish Civil War? Some of the novels were great, as I said, some of the novels were simply trivial. The Holocaust is one of the central traumatic events in the whole history of the species. The species is going to deal with these events, one way or another, because that's how we handle these events, we've been doing this ever since writing was invented. Well, you're right, it could become trivialized. But, that's the price you pay for trying to come to grips with the faculty of the imagination, with a horror of this kind. Some of the greatest art in the world has used that as its theme—horror, and horrible events, for example, Picasso's *Guernica*. The event Guernica was a horror. The painting *Guernica* is one of the glorious creations of our species, and I'm sure there were depictions of Guernica that were trivial, that were nonsensical. I have no question at all with, about the nature of the handling of the Holocaust. I think it is going to continue to be handled, it's going to continue to be a subject in art; I think that memory is one of the most profound ways that the human species reacts against horror. Art is one of the ways we transform horror. We make it something that we can live with, that we can remember, that make it more or less bearable so that we can keep it in memory and try very hard never to do it again. The most horrible thing that we can do with horror is forget it.

I: I know that you followed closely a few weeks ago, the President's visit to Bitburg, to the cemetery where SS troops were buried. And there have been a lot of interpretations of it, and to some people it's just a kind of strategic blunder in public relations, people just weren't thinking, and they didn't realize how many SS were buried there, and other people see it as a more deeply rooted, perhaps anti-Semitic expression, where the insensitivity runs so deep that they were blinded to what they were doing. What's your interpretation of that plan?

CP: Oh, I don't think it was an anti-Semitic statement at all. If you want to do something anti-Semitic, you can do things that will cost you much less than this Bitburg thing cost the Reagan administration. I just think it was somebody's casual indifference to what it was that was going on there and what it was that it could potentially all be about. It's also almost a Greek tragedy in the sense that here is a President who, of all the presidents in recent history is the most public relations conscious, the most image-conscious president that we've had, and on this one public relations thing, he stumbles and stumbles badly. Indeed, I just read the other day in the *New York Times* that soon after President Reagan and Herr Kohl left the cemetery, somebody placed very close to their wreaths, wreaths to the SS troops. I also read in a recent article in the *New Republic,* the German army that was supposed to be blameless in the Holocaust indeed played a major role in the Holocaust, so a lot of the things that simply had been laid to rest in the past forty years since the end of the Second World War have suddenly come out exactly the reverse of what was intended is now happening. And it's going to take a long time before the German American relations achieve their reconciliation that some people seem to have wanted from this laying of wreaths. I just think it was a very unfortunate blunder all around.

I: The last time that you visited with us on "Fresh Air," we talked about the translation that you had worked on of the Hebrew Bible in which you went back to the original text and translated that into contemporary English, and that was, I guess, a couple of years ago. How has that book caught on so far? What kinds of places or people are using it?

CP: The publication of the last of the three volumes signaled a major cultural moment in the history of the country. It was very widely reviewed. There was a whole page on the translation in *Time* magazine. The singular element in this translation is the fact that the Hebrew Bible was translated by Jewish scholars, utilizing the most sophisticated modern knowledge. All of them superbly trained, and most of them trained in the United States. Many of them trained in the United States, and it's in American English, that's what's great about this translation; it's in our English. It's our language. And, it has been very quickly adopted by synagogues throughout the English-speaking world; it is now used in Jewish and Christian seminaries throughout the United States, and it's wherever you go into a Jewish home, both non-Orthodox and Orthodox. Because, you see, while Orthodox Jews will pray in Orthodox synagogues and will be fundamentalists in terms of how they look at the sacred works of the tradition, the fact is that many of them are very sophisticated people in terms of Western education. And are very much curious about and interested in what it is that non-fundamentalist scholars that are Jews do with the text, and so you will find this translation in many Orthodox homes. I don't ever want to give the impression that modern Orthodox Jews are people that are entirely out of the cultural mainstream. Chassidic Orthodox Jews, Jews who don't care for modernism, see even in Orthodox, you have a spectrum; you have modern Orthodox who really send their children for example to universities, who are very much involved in the modern world and you have Orthodox Jews very much to the right of that, who will have absolutely nothing to do with modernism, who are contemptuous of it, who will not send their children to any secular institutions. Those Orthodox Jews probably will not have anything to do with this Bible translation.

I: Do you miss not working on it anymore after working on it for so many years?

CP: It was an extraordinary experience for me. Yes, there are times when I miss it, although it took so much time away from me and from my family, because we used to work during the academic holidays, since the translators were all academicians, which meant that no holidays for me and my family and my wife and our children for about sixteen years, and that was a pretty high price to pay for that translation, so from that point of view, I'm glad that it's done and I'm glad that we succeeded in doing what it was that we set out to do. But, from the point of view of the camaraderie, the knowledge, the minds that were put to work on this, the electric excitement that was generated every time we sat around a table translating, that sort of thing I miss very much.

I: You just completed a new book; it's just been published, *Davita's Harp,* are you working on another novel now?

CP: I am beginning to go through the normal novelist sleeplessness and staring-out-the-window kind of time, where a new novel is in the process of gestation. What I now think I want to do is take Davita into the Soviet Union of today—that's what I'm playing with now.

I: That should be interesting. Do you ever go through those fearful periods that I know some novelists do that they're not sure that there's another novel in them and they panic for a while until they actually get a coherent idea of what their next book's going to be?

CP: Oh yes, that's part of the business of being a novelist. You do that not only from novel to novel, but you also do that from page to page sometimes. You're not sure you can get another page out.

I: But you always do.

CP: Somehow, so far I always have managed to get the other page out.

I: Well good luck with your new novel, and I want to thank you for visiting with us again.

CP: It's a pleasure.

I: And my guest has been Chaim Potok, who has written a new novel. It's titled *Davita's Harp*. It's published by Knopf. And Chaim Potok lives in Philadelphia. He also lives part of the year in Israel. His other books include *The Chosen, My Name Is Asher Lev, The Book of Lights,* and a nonfiction book called *Wanderings: The History of the Jews*. And, thank you again for being with us.

CP: Thank you.

Giving Shape to Turmoil: A Conversation with Chaim Potok

Michael J. Cusick / 1997

From *Mars Hill Review*, No. 7, Winter/Spring 1997, pp. 64–83. Reprinted by permission of Michael J. Cusick and *Mars Hill Review*.

It would strike some as odd that an ordained rabbi who served a chaplaincy in the Korean War, later earned a Ph.D. in philosophy from an Ivy League university, earned a reputation as a world-class Judaic scholar, and wrote several best-selling novels along the way, would be known for his mapmaking abilities. But Chaim Potok has spent the majority of his life doing just that—mapping out the terrain of his Jewish past in novels which have transported both Jew and non-Jew into fictional worlds that transcend religious boundaries.

Perhaps best known as the author of *The Chosen*—which in 1981 was made into a movie starring Robby Benson and Rod Steiger—Potok is the author of eleven novels, two children's books, and several works of nonfiction including the critically acclaimed *Wanderings: Chaim Potok's History of the Jews*. "Long ago, in *The Chosen*," he writes, "I set out to draw a map of the New York world through which I once journeyed. It was to be a map not only of broken streets, menacing alleys, concrete-surfaced backyards, neighborhood schools and stores . . . a map not only of the physical elements of my early life, but of the spiritual ones as well."[1]

The result of such mapmaking has been an insider's look into opposing world-views—conservative Jewish-American culture and twentieth-century secularism: clashing values, beliefs, ideas, and dreams. This has been the underlying tension in all of Potok's writing. And it has also been the story of his life. Born in Brooklyn in 1929 to Polish immigrant parents, Chaim spent his early years in an Orthodox Jewish home and was educated at parochial schools. At sixteen, he encountered serious literature and his life was forever changed.

"Here was someone trying to give shape to turmoil I myself was experiencing," he writes. "A growing sense of a world outside my own; pulsing sexuality; questions about God and the nature of my own self. Here was an author shaping his deepest thoughts and feelings with language, exploring an interior human terrain I had never thought possible to configure with words."[2]

Deeply touched, he began to read ravenously and to write. At eighteen, after having a story accepted by the *Atlantic Monthly,* he received a letter from the editor, who inquired if he was writing a novel. His father—who had planned on his son's becoming a teacher of Talmud—was less than enthusiastic about the younger Potok's newfound career choice. In their conservative Jewish world, writers of fiction were looked upon with suspicion. Thankfully, Chaim continued to write, and he has not stopped.

My first encounter with Potok occurred at a used bookstore where I found a mint first-edition copy of *My Name Is Asher Lev.* Our most recent encounter took place in Philadelphia, where he graciously invited me to his home. As we met in person for nearly two hours, I was struck by this man's kindness and his staggering depth of knowledge.

In the room where we met, the author's own expressionist paintings hang in contrast to walls of scholarly books—illuminating once more the tensions of his life and work: creativity and canon, progress and tradition, faith and reason. As is evidenced by his writing, such tensions are not easily manageable, though for the person of faith they are an essential part of finding one's way in the world. As Potok himself might say, "Such tensions are an essential part of the mapmaking process."

Mars Hill Review: Tell me about the transforming encounter you had with literature at the age of sixteen.

Chaim Potok: My first major encounter with contemporary serious literature was Evelyn Waugh's *Brideshead Revisited.* It happened in high school one term, when I was reading the established canon of literature—the classics, especially the nineteenth century. I was done with my exams, and I decided for a reason that is not clear to me to this day, to read a contemporary adult novel. I went to the public library and browsed around for a while and by sheer chance found *Brideshead Revisited* by Evelyn Waugh. I have no idea what attracted me to it. Maybe it was the fact that it was about upper-class English Catholics.

I took the book home and at first found it difficult to get into. But once I grew accustomed to the prose I became utterly enchanted by that world, and by the prose. It was really the first time in my life that I understood the importance of language in the writing of a story. Most of the time I wouldn't want the language to interfere with the story. I preferred language that was transparent and didn't call attention to itself. But reading that novel gave me a very vivid sense of the rhythms of the English language, its texture, its cadences, the way sentences can be constructed to obtain certain effects.

I remember that as I was reading it I found myself thinking about the characters during the times I was away from the book. I would try to anticipate what their thoughts and feelings might be when I returned to the book. I was utterly taken by the character of the mother—her tenacity, her odd personality, her faith. I remember closing the book when I finished reading it and feeling bereaved because all the people I had read about were gone. I remember sitting there saying to myself, "What power there is in this kind of creativity."

Very soon afterward I read *A Portrait of the Artist as a Young Man* by James Joyce. Here was a picture of a middle-class Irish Catholic family. And Joyce was telling a story about ideas—confusions of the head and the heart— that I myself was experiencing and couldn't put into words. I was only sixteen at the time, but here was a man mapping all that dark territory with the power of words and the imagination. Those two books did it for me.

MHR: And it was then that you knew you wanted to write stories?

CP: Yes. When I was done with Joyce, I said to myself, "This is what I want to spend my life doing—writing stories." I was only a kid, so I had no idea whether I would succeed or fail. I didn't even have an idea as to how to go about doing it. I just knew that I wanted to write stories. It unlocked something very deep inside of me and transformed me, no question about that. And writing stories is what I've done ever since that time.

MHR: As you began writing from your Orthodox Jewish background, you discovered that your culture collided with others. And you've described this as a "culture confrontation."

CP: My first culture confrontation was with literature. Later on in my twenties it was with the core ideas of western culture, because I went ahead and got a doctorate in philosophy at the University of Pennsylvania. I didn't want a doctorate in literature because I was afraid it would make me too self-conscious about my writing. But I did want to know what western culture was all about at its core, so I chose philosophy. I thought western culture would be something I would want to write about, and I wanted to know it well.

MHR: You didn't set out to confront cultures, but it naturally happened?

CP: My particular natural life experience has been that of cultures clashing in a certain way—confrontation of core elements. From my Jewish culture to literature, for example. I grew up at the heart, at the core, of one culture. And then I encountered an element from the core of the general culture in which I was living, and that element was modern secular literature.

That confrontation of cultures, from the heart of one culture to the heart of another culture, is what I have been calling a "core-to-core culture confrontation." There are many ways in which we encounter other cultures. We can encounter the periphery of another culture—its noise, its passing fads, its pop culture, superstitious elements, and so on. Those are—without sounding too elitist—more or less peripheral elements of a culture in the sense that they are the easiest elements of a culture to acquire. They demand the least of the person acquiring them. They are interchangeable elements which come and go. They don't effect the essential direction of a culture in any profound way.

All cultures have these elements. And yes, it is an elitist view of culture. But the fact of the matter is that cultures are really made by the more creative elements in their midst. Those creative elements drag everyone else along willy-nilly in their wake. Unless, of course, there is a cultural inundation from the periphery, which is what some people think we may be suffering from these days, especially in the United States.

Others had other kinds of culture confrontations. Friends of mine encountered the world of science that they found stunning, and to no small degree overwhelming. Others encountered Sigmund Freud. I remember one of my friends reading Darwin, and that was the end of his view of Genesis.

That was the world that I grew up in. And the subject of my writing then became this confrontation: What happens? How do you feel? What do you think? What are your dreams? How do you relate to human beings around you? What are the dimensions of this confrontation? How does it affect families? It's my feeling that in the modern period we're all going through this sort of confrontation one way or another.

MHR: And this is regardless of religious background—believer or unbeliever?

CP: Absolutely. And now in a major way the Islamic world is going through this kind of confrontation. But they are resisting it mightily, just as

Judaism and Christendom did—and as many Christians and many Jews still do.

MHR: You wrote your first novel, *The Chosen,* to come to terms with your past. What elements of your religious upbringing did you need to come to terms with?

CP: The fundamentalism. The very structured way of seeing the world. The "givenness" of tradition. The inability to maneuver and question. The legacy of the past that you are expected to absorb, master, and give back to the coming generation untouched, unaltered.

That was pretty much my beginning. And the first crack in that wall was literature. Literature presents you with alternate mappings of the human experience. You see that the experiences of other people and other cultures are as rich, coherent, and troubled as you own experiences. They are as beset with suffering as yours. Literature is a kind of legitimate voyeurism through the keyhole of language where you really come to know other people's lives—their anguish, their loves, their passions. Often you discover that once you dive into those lives and get below the surface, the veneer, there is a real closeness.

MHR: Is this the idea that underneath the differing beliefs, religions, and cultures, there is a sense of underlying basic humanity?

CP: Right, and that was astonishing to me. It was astonishing because I had always been taught, and therefore believed, that Jews were different in kind. We had a very unique destiny. And yes, Jews are different. But, at the same time, what I was coming to learn was that we all are very much the same in our passions, in our lusts, in our loves, in our drives, in our fears. The differences are interesting because they lend texture and richness to the human experience, but it's the similarities that might just save us as a species.

MHR: Save us?

CP: We are in a race with our own worst selves. We've always been both a killer species and a cooperating species. There have always been these two sides to our being. And we now have the capacity to kill ourselves with consummate ease. It's touch and go as to whether we will survive as a species on this planet. So, my hope is that we can learn more and more about the similarities.

I think that this is one of the happy by-products of literature. I'm not sure that literature aims for that. I think that serious literature aims for good sentences, good writing, and more or less serious subject matter—not filled with frivolity. But a by-product of that is the effective making of maps—of other paths of life that I as a reader can then walk. That brings me closer to another world, and I then say, "That's interesting, I can relate to that."

MHR: Does that explain why your novels have such a broad appeal, though limited to Jewish culture?

CP: James Joyce was once asked why he only wrote about Dublin. Even though he wrote about other places, we know Joyce as the writer of Dublin in the same way we know Dostoyevsky as the writer of Saint Petersburg, and Kafka as the write of Prague. So when he was asked why he only wrote about Dublin, Joyce responded by saying, "For myself I always write about Dublin, because if I can get to the heart of Dublin I can get to the heart of all the cities in the world. In the particular is contained the universal."

The greatness of the novel is that you are taken into the specifics of other worlds by the mapmaking abilities and the language abilities of another human being. So that if I spell out my particularities and you're reading them, and if the language is okay, and the story is interesting, what you end up doing inside yourself is taking those particularities and linking them to your own. And those two generate a universal. You as the reader can then function inside that universal.

MHR: That reminds me of a sentence from *The Gift of Asher Lev*: "Art happens when what is seen is mixed with what is on the inside of the artist."

CP: That's exactly right. It's a relational experience. Art happens somewhere along a relational arc, between what you are and the object of creation. And that's why art is very often a different experience for each and every person. I am convinced that the readers who come to my books experience them differently because they are not sitting back as passive individuals with this thing called a book being pumped into them, filling their empty reservoir. That's not the way it works. They're coming to a book with a whole life. And it's the relationship between their life and the life inside the book that forms the experience of reading—the arc.

MHR: There's something very mystical about that.

CP: Yes, but then there's something very mystical about gravity too, which we can't quite see [laughing]. True, you can do mathematics on gravity, and it's harder to do mathematics on the relationship between a work of art and the person experiencing it. Both are invisible and both are very real.

MHR: Throughout your work there is a strong thread of autobiography. As a Jew, what has been the role of remembering?

CP: I think Judaism is a memory religion par excellence. We are told to remember. Americans generally don't remember much beyond five years in the past. Who remembers the Persian Gulf War today?

MHR: I think Christians struggle with forgetting our past. Will you say more about the idea that Judaism is a memory religion?

CP: We have about four thousand years of history to remember. And what you are really bidden to do as an intelligent Jew is to remember and incorporate that history into your essential being. The biblical images of Abraham and Jacob are real. The story of the binding of Isaac is real. The story of Joseph is real. The story of David and Solomon, that's a real story. It all becomes a part of the way you think about the world.

A cartographer doesn't make maps out of the imagination. He surveys, he looks at previous maps, he checks the roads, he gets information, he uses tools. An individual who makes maps of the human experience—and we all do that consciously or unconsciously—makes it with information, or with tools. What Judaism wants Jews to do is to map the world with certain kinds of information. And that information consists of the value systems, the tensions, the successes and the failures, the dreams and the terrors of the Jewish past.

Now, I have to be very careful with all of this, because you can be so freighted with history that you can become paralyzed. That's the tension that we all live under—how to use the history and not get weighted down to such a degree that you can't function.

MHR: You've talked about the past on the collective level, but what about on the individual level? Is it important to have a knowledge of your own story?

CP: I think that in one way or another all of us have a story. And people who don't know their story are devastated individuals. Narrative is what holds life together. But narrative ought to be flexible enough so that you can insert new sentences here and there. And sometimes we begin the serious process of rewriting at certain points of our lives. A person who doesn't have a narrative is a sorry person indeed.

MHR: Do you mean they don't know where they have come from or where they are going?

CP: They have no map. They are stumbling around, and they are terrified. And terror ultimately leads to rage—either rage at yourself with an inclination toward self-destruction, or rage at the outside world, and you hurt somebody.

MHR: We've touched on art somewhat. What are your views on the distinction between sacred and secular?

CP: Sacred art depicts meta-historical moments by and large. It is fixed. It is an expression of the core of the church, its doctrines, its transcendent history. Nothing much changes in this art through the centuries.

In the modern period anything is possible, even with a crucifixion. That's the nature of a modern secular world. The individual makes his or own paradigms. And my feeling is that the richer the individual's awareness of the tensions of the past, the richer the modern paradigm he or she is going to present to us.

MHR: So the more an individual is aware of the past, the richer the art?

CP: The deeper one's awareness of one's roots in the past, the richer will be the tensions of the present, and the way one presents any particular art.

For example, there is a texturing to Dostoyevsky that you just don't find in most modern writing—especially American writing, because Dostoyevsky has this enormous tension with the past of Russian religion and history. I might not care for his anti-Semitism, or his passion for Russian glory, or the sense he had that Russia was the greatest culture in the world and that he didn't need the west. But that's not the issue here, the issue is what it did for his work. It added to it immeasurably.

MHR: Dostoyevsky spent years in prison. Asher Lev, David Lurie, Danny Saunders, and several other characters of yours suffered and went on to enormous creativity. How does suffering affect one's output of creativity and art?

CP: Well, it will either mature you or destroy you. If it destroys you, we won't hear about you anymore. But if it matures you, then you might make a contribution. All of us, at one point or another in our lives, have suffered—if not in our own flesh, then in the flesh of those we love. We will experience suffering.

It's the task of the artist to take that experience and map it through her or his own way of seeing the world. That's what I tried to do with the individuals I was writing about.

MHR: What would you say about the idea of encountering the sacred in the midst of the secular?

CP: My sense of it is that the sacred is everywhere. And by that I mean we are surrounded by mystery, we are surrounded by beauty. A child is born and it's a mystery. A person dies and that's a mystery. What are we doing here? That's a mystery. I have to respond to that one way or another. And that's what I mean by the sacred—things that are given, yet oddly given. I have to respond to that and ask myself, "What map do I make of this? What relationship do I have to this?" I'm a writer, and I have to deal with such givens.

You might tell me that the smile of a child is biologically and genetically driven, and I will say, "Fine." But even that statement is in many ways a mystery. Man's propensity toward killing is a mystery to me. Those aspects of ourselves that tend to drive us up and out of ourselves in a search for realms of being beyond our mere mortality—those are what I call the sacred. The constructive, the cooperative, the creative—those are the sacred.

The destructive—that is the demonic. As I said earlier, we are in a race with our own selves. And we have no guarantee as to which of those two elements of our selves is going to win. That's why those of us concerned with the sacred have to work hard. We have to lobby for it, because we can be sure of one thing: those taken up by the demonic are very good at what they do.

MHR: When you talk about what could be, is there a sense of the original "image of God"?

CP: Yes, absolutely—there is a sense of an origin to things. And my feeling is that the biblical image is a magnificent metaphor of that feeling or sense that we have of the mysterious origin of things. That is the quintessential mapmaking. It's so rich that it has forever changed the mindset of our species.

Is it ontologically true? Well, the fundamentalists will say yes. Someone who knows a great deal about the history of Jewish thought will probably say that it has profound value in the way it has set the human mind in a certain direction—that that is its truth. And for me that's truth enough.

MHR: Whether or not the ontological reality is there?
CP: That's right.

MHR: Are you saying that whether or not the existence of it all is real isn't as important as the metaphor that guides your life?
CP: It's the richness of it. That is an awesome reality. I can't step beyond

the richness of that and move to the other side. Do you know that in the Hebrew Bible there isn't a single mention of God as he, or she, or it truly is? There is only the mention of the creator God who is constantly trying out new plans and failing. He creates the world and fails. He creates Adam and Eve and fails. He creates the Garden of Eden and that doesn't work. He creates a human species and fails, so he brings the flood. He saves a human being whose first act is to get drunk. He chooses a people with whom He constantly quarrels. That's the creator God.

The God utterly infinite, utterly unapproachable, utterly spiritual—we don't hear of that God. That God won't turn to us. It is inconceivable that he would ever turn to us. That God is all that ever was and is and will be, into infinity and eternity. How could that God conceivably relate to us? It is the God of the Bible that we relate to!

So I can't make the step beyond creation to the infinite God. But I can certainly relate to the God of the Bible. I talk to him all the time and complain all the time.

MHR: What do you mean by "God failed" at these different steps?

CP: He creates the world and then he has to destroy it by flood. He gives Adam and Eve a garden to till, and they ruin things—and in many ways that's his failure too. He sends a flood and saves a family, but in the aftermath there is the horrible scene between the sons, the grandson, and the father. Then he chooses a people and they are constantly at odds with him.

That's the role of God in history—making plans and seeing plans foiled. There's constant tension between God and the human beings he has created. That's not a terribly glorious picture of a deity, is it? Well, that's the God that we relate to, the Jews anyway. Beyond that God, there's got to be some infinite being. The Bible doesn't talk about it, although Jewish mysticism does. Kabbalah—oh, yes.

MHR: In *The Book of Lights,* where you deal with Kabbalah, the mentor of the main character Gershon says, "You do not care to know of the great rabbis who were filled with poetry and contradictions." What kind of poetry and contradictions does he mean?

CP: The rabbis of the Talmud were filled with poetry and contradictions. They had a very open-eyed, hard-nosed way of looking at the world. They were not fundamentalists. They were open to all kinds of ideas. And they said things that would upset us today. One of the great things about learning the Jewish tradition is that you come to understand the notion of maximum flexibility inside a closed world. The daring of some of those rabbis is really astonishing.

The poetry has to do with flights of the imagination and how they interpreted the Bible in the broadest way conceivable. There is an enormous spectrum of thought in rabbinic literature, from absolutely literalist readings of the text to the most imaginative readings. It's a very rich system of ideas, filled with contradicting views, which is very exciting for a writer.

It all fell to pieces in the modern period when it faced secularism. And in the wake of Darwin and Nietzsche came Jewish fundamentalism, which didn't exist in the premodern period. Newton and Darwin did it to Judaism just as they did it to Christianity. Fundamentalism is a western religious reaction to Darwin. The text freezes, ideas freeze, because the alternative is a real terror, the terror that we are not the center of the universe and that it's all a series of odd accidents.

MHR: Because for it to be a series of odd accidents contradicts the entire history of Judaism.

CP: Absolutely . . . absolutely. Therefore, you have the development of Jewish fundamentalism. It comes along and says, "This isn't a series of odd accidents. Just read the first chapter of Genesis."

Then the modernist says, "The first chapter of Genesis is a metaphor." And the Jewish fundamentalist answers, "It's not a metaphor, it's the word of God. A metaphor means that somebody else can come and write another metaphor, but the word of God you can't change."

This is one major discourse in contemporary Judaism.

MHR: Is that part of the reason you named your history of the Jews *Wanderings*?

CP: Yes, we have wandered a great deal and been in contact with most of the great cultures of the world in a variety of ways. I also wrote *Wanderings* before I wrote *The Book of Lights* because I wanted to know who I was when I got to Korea—that's what *The Book of Lights* is all about. It's my encounter with another culture—a nonwestern culture. It's also my encounter with the horrible event that western culture dropped on eastern culture, the atomic bomb. I did all that exploring for *Wanderings* before I wrote *The Book of Lights* because I needed to know who I was.

MHR: How did your two years in Korea shape you?

CP: It transformed me totally. Totally. I'm still trying to figure out what that was all about.

I know when I went to Korea I was a very coherent human being in the sense that I had a model of what I was—I had a map. I knew who I was as a Jew. I had been through Jewish Theological Seminary and was ordained. I knew who I was as a member of western culture. And I knew who I was as an American. I had a passion for America; when I was in high school history I was one of the winners of the Hearst National American History Contest— about thirty thousand kids participating, with nine winners.

When I went to Asia—Japan, Korea, and the other parts of Asia I visited as an American soldier—it all came unglued. It all became relativized. Everything turned upside down. And that "upside down" is what I explored in *The Book of Lights*, which was written from an American point of view. The next book about Asia, *I Am the Clay*, was written from an Asian point of view. Those two books so far are my explorations of that world. My time in Asia utterly transformed me and left me with nothing but questions for which I'm still struggling to find answers.

MHR: What are some of the questions?

CP: Let me give you an example. I remember realizing one day in Japan, after just having gone through some of the temples in Kyoto, that I was in a world that didn't hate Jews. Even today with all the anti-Semitic books that are in bookstores, the Japanese don't hate Jews. It was a very exhilarating experience to find myself in a world where I wasn't being judged for what I was. I was only another white face. The irony was that this was a pagan world. It was a world that my scriptures told me to avoid, to condemn.

MHR: So, in one sense, the named enemy was the one who embraced you the most?

CP: Exactly. I remember a scene where I was visiting a temple and I saw an old Japanese man praying. He had a long white beard and a fedora hat, and a long brown coat. He was praying with such intensity that the first thing I recalled were the old men in the synagogue I grew up in. On the night of Yom Kippur, the most sacred night of the year they would pray this way with the same intensity. I remember saying to myself at the time, "What am I seeing here? Is this man praying to an idol? And what is the God that I pray to doing at this moment? Is he answering his prayers? If not, why not? When are you ever going to see greater devotion in prayer? And if the God I pray to is listening to this old pagan's prayer, then what are Judaism and Christianity all about?"

I had dozens of experiences like that every week—cultural encounters.

The Koreans had lost over a million people during the war, which is staggering. I remember saying to myself, "Why did these people suffer? They were
just in the way of empires." It's one thing to read about it in the newspapers,
but it's another thing to actually stand there and see it.

I remember my father once saying, "Jews suffer because they decided they
were different. You're going to be different, people are going to point at you,
and they are going to make you pay the price for it." He believed we were
different, and though he didn't like to pay the price, he said he would pay the
price if he had to. That's the sort of thing that happened to me again and
again for the sixteen months I was in Asia. I was totally transformed by it.

It not only relativized my Jewishness, it relativized my Americanness and
my westernness simultaneously. It set everything into specific culture con-
texts and at the same time taught me that my culture could be viewed from
outside its perimeters by another culture, and be seen in an altogether different way. What happened was that I began to see my culture from the outside.
When that happens to your head, you are never the same again.

MHR: Once you were outside your culture with a different perspective,
what did you learn?

CP: You have to get outside of your culture for a significant period of time
and get inside the culture that has brought you outside of your own culture. I
did just that. I read, I talked to Asians, I befriended them, I listened to them.
Once you cut through the veneer of the politeness, and their own hesitations,
you get close to them and see the sameness, even though it's another world.

MHR: You spoke of complaining to God, and in your writings there are
characters who shout at God. It seems to be more acceptable for Jews to do
this than for non-Jews.

CP: The tone is set immediately in the Bible with Abraham. He has a long
talk with God and tries to change God's mind regarding Sodom and Gomor-
rah. "Suppose there are some decent people there. What are you going to
do—kill them all?" Well that's pretty audacious, I think. After all, it's God
he's bargaining with. It may be the creator God who doesn't get his or her
way all the time, but it's still God.

Of course, the first grave lament—the one that sets the tone for all the
laments in Jewish history—is the Book of Job. Now, the Book of Job is about
one thousand years into Israelite history. That's quite a note to strike, the
Book of Job. It was struck because there was a sense that the covenant relationship wasn't working. At least it certainly wasn't working in this world.

MHR: Not working in terms of reciprocity?

CP: That's what covenantal relationships are all about. I do something, you do something. If I do something and you don't, you've broken the covenant. It's as blunt as that. It's a treaty—I keep my end, you keep your end. If you don't, the treaty is broken.

By the time of the Book of Job, there was a sense that the covenant was not working. Much of it had to do with the Maccabean Wars and the awful suffering that Jews went through. But for whatever the reason, the writer of the Book of Job said, "The covenant isn't working."

It is one long complaint. It amounts to Job taking God to court. In the Jewish worldview, the metaphor for complaint to God is the idea of taking God to court because Judaism is a legal system. "Now I know I'm going to lose this case, because you're God and I'm a simple human being. But I'm going to take you to court anyway, and I'm going to let the judges know how I feel and what the charges are. I'll lose, but it's what I'm going to do anyway."

Remember, the book was canonized, which already tells you that this attitude is acceptable to the rabbis of the Talmud. To canonize a book in the ancient world was to guarantee its permanent existence. Not to have it canonized was to virtually guarantee its oblivion. We've had complaints like this all through Jewish history. Books of complaint were written in the wake of the Crusades, the massacres in the 1600s in eastern Europe and the Ukraine. This is now part of the Jewish tradition, complaining against God.

I once talked about this to Norwegian clergy. They invited me to a conference, and I told them about this tradition of Jewish complaint. Some of them were aghast over it. But then they said, "I wish we had done this a year or so ago." They had an awfully tragic ferry accident where hundreds of Norwegians perished, and when their parishioners came to them, they didn't quite know how to handle it. My response, and the Jewish response, is to yell at God.

There used to be a tradition, which may still be in existence in some Jewish communities, where if you had a complaint against God you stopped the service on Saturday. You went up to the ark, you opened the ark, and you stood there shouting at God until the rabbi finally led you away.

MHR: The thing that's so fascinating about this is that it happens inside a system of faith. If you're going to rage against the master of the universe, you had better have some kind of faith as to what he is essentially like.

CP: You shout out of faith, not because you don't have any faith. If you don't have faith, you don't have anyone to shout at.

MHR: There's so much richness to the Jewish traditions. I'm fascinated by it.

CP: Yes, well, remember how old it is!

MHR: As you think about the big picture of the Book of Job, is there anything else you glean from it, other than the court-docket concept?

CP: The Book of Job is a metaphor par excellence of the Jewish tradition of complaint against God. A poet—a great poet—must have suffered terribly. And he took one of the oldest stories known to him and used it for his own purposes.

The story was about a man who was tested by the gods. The author of the Book of Job made that ancient story the framing device for his poem. Here's a man of faith. God destroys his family, and virtually destroys him, but the man of faith doesn't lose his faith. He is restored by God, lives on, enjoys a new family and new wealth. That's the epic.

Between those two elements of the story the poet inserts what we call the Book of Job. Job is sitting in torment, comforted by his friends, lamenting his sorry state, hoping to die. He pours his heart out. And the response of the poet was, "You're right, the covenant isn't working—not visibly, and not on this earth. But it's working in some cosmic fashion, and we don't fully understand it."

That was not the biblical view. The biblical view was that the covenant was working visibly. In the time of David, in the time of Solomon, in the time of the kings, if you disobeyed you were punished, and if you obeyed you expected to be rewarded. The Book of Job insists that covenant was not working anymore, that it was no longer effective for some reason on the earthly scheme of things, though it was working in some cosmic fashion.

First of all, that's not terribly satisfying to the earthling. And second of all, it's very intellectual; it satisfies the head but not the heart. That's the answer of the writer of the Book of Job. That's one answer to the breakdown of the covenant.

The second answer was the rabbinic one. And that is, "The covenant may not be working, but it's going to work again in the future, and we have to live our lives in the meantime in accordance with God's laws."

MHR: That's the idea of the messiah?

CP: Yes, redemption was deferred to some future time. The third answer was an apocalyptic one. That is, "It's not working, but it's going to work next week, because God is sending somebody to get it to work right." That's what I call "hot messianism." The rabbinic version is cooled down messianism, deferred messianism. Hot messianism became Christianity. There is no such idea as loss of faith because you complain against God.

MHR: What do you mean that there's no such thing as a loss of faith?

CP: As far as I can recall, there's only one instance in all of Talmudic literature of a rabbi who lost faith in God. That's seven hundred years of Talmudic literature! The rabbi was Elisha Ben-Abuyah. He once saw a man send his son up a ladder to chase away a mother bird so he could get the fledglings. He did this because the biblical law is that you are not allowed to catch both the fledglings and the mother bird at the same time. As the boy did this, he fell and broke his head and died.

Now, the problem in this particular instance is that in the biblical verse you are promised that if you do this you will have long life. Elisha Ben-Abuyah was with another rabbi when he saw this. The other rabbi was aghast, but said nothing and ran away crying. Elisha Ben-Abuyah shouted out, "There is no judge, and there is no justice"—which was his way of saying God doesn't work the way he claims. He maintained that attitude, and he was excommunicated. But even so, some of his students still followed him.

There is no such thing in the ancient world as not believing in God, or the gods, unless you were a member of one of the Greek intellectual societies. Even Socrates believed in some form of a deity. He didn't believe in the statuary of Athens, but he had his own notion of what a deity was and how it functioned. To believe that there isn't any deity is a modern idea.

MHR: I read the Old Testament and there are images of sacrifice, ritual, slaughter, law-keeping to the minutiae. Then through the centuries, the most conservative branches of Judaism tried to follow that. What do you do with the idea of sacrifice and the law-keeping?

CP: Maimonides was a twelfth-century rabbi and philosopher who was born in Spain and lived in Egypt. He was very uncomfortable with all the rules of the sacrificial system. He said it was just a stage in Israelite development. The fact of the matter is that Maimonides probably didn't grasp the notion that there was no other way to worship God in the ancient world. You worshiped God through giving gifts, and the gift was something precious to you. One of the most precious of possessions was the cattle you owned. If you felt you had sinned, you offered God a gift by way of propitiation.

That was the notion behind the sacrificial system. Blood in the ancient world was considered a cleansing liquid because it was the liquid of life. They saw that if you lost blood, you died. Therefore, it was the blood of life, and it was used to purify.

As far as we can gather, that was the notion behind the sacrificial system. It was part of the way Jews worshiped until the destruction of the second temple. I know Jews who are sophisticated scholars and very religious, who want to see the sacrificial system reestablished. I don't.

MHR: What does it mean, then, for you to worship?

CP: To ask, to remember, to lament, to complain, to seek one's own self and that which is beyond the self. Prayer is the trajectory and the perspective, enabling you to locate your own sense of self in this trajectory. If you don't have a sense of where you are from, you don't know where you are at! And if you don't know where you are at, you have no sense of self. And if you have no sense of self, you are a very frightened human being.

MHR: For you, worship involves prayer and Jewish tradition. But is worship bigger than that? Is it part of your everyday living—your writing, for example?

CP: Yes! Absolutely. Writing is an act of worship too. And learning. For some Jews, learning is more of an act of worship than worship itself. There is an issue in Jewish law as to whether or not you may interrupt someone for prayers when they are learning. Some rabbis say yes, some say no.

MHR: You said writing is an act of worship. You have also written that nothing is sacred to the writer save the act of writing. Is that a paradox?

CP: Well, there is a difference between worship and sanctity. In worship you enter into a relationship with somebody or something. The worship is in the relationship. I don't think there is something objectively sacred about anything that I write, but the act of creating has an aura of sanctity to me. The moments when I lose myself—that's what I dream of, to get lost in the writing—those relational moments, that arc of relationship between my being and the writing, the thing being created, is as close as I can get to the essence of worship. I feel the same way, for example, when I'm in a synagogue and I'm lost in prayer. I don't think there is any intrinsic sanctity to the particular words, because if circumstances dictate, I would have no objection to changing the words.

There is a major discussion going on in my synagogue right now as to whether to change the words in a prayer that is 2,000 years old. That prayer only mentions the patriarchs. Well, what about the matriarchs? The discussion is whether to include not only Abraham, Isaac, and Jacob, but also Sarah, Rebekah, Leah, and Rachel. Now that's a major change. But there is no frozen sanctity for me in that old formula; the sanctity lies in the relationship between myself as a human being and the text in the act of worship. That arc, again, that trajectory—that is the sacred moment.

The same thing occurs to the writer. That is the mystery. That's the lone moment of awe. That's where we somehow come out of our mortal self. That's the moment of the transcendent.

MHR: In *Davita's Harp,* Jacob Daw says to Davita, "A writer is a strange instrument of our species, a harp of sorts, fine tuned to the dark contradictions of life. . . ."

CP: That's what I'm talking about. A harp is a bunch of strings, and it is nothing unless someone is playing it. It is the melody of the harp that is the mystery. Sometimes if you leave a harp out in a strong wind, the wind will make the melody.

In Los Angeles somewhere, there is a harp that is a sculpture which reacts to winds. The harp is physical, the wind is physical, even though we can't see it. The music—what's the music? The music is the relationship between the harp and the wind. The writing is the relationship between the writer and the piece of paper. Worship is the relationship between the worshiper and the text.

MHR: Can a writer such as yourself ever retire?

CP: I don't know how writers retire. You see, I don't know how writers are made. Somebody who is in a profession and transfers at a certain point and climbs the ladder, gets to the top. The profession dictates the time frame.

Writing doesn't dictate a time frame. There can be long periods of time when you are not writing at all and you are sitting there looking out a window and thinking. It's as mysterious to me now as it was when I was sixteen, seventeen years old.

I don't know what retirement means, because there is no time frame for a writer. I may decide I don't want to write anymore—so, okay, I'm finished writing. But that doesn't mean it's going to turn off. All it means is I'm going to lie there and toss and turn, and sentences are going to go through my head as they always do, and sooner or later I'm going to pick up the pen and write.

I have no illusions about writing. It's not something I do, it's something I'm driven to do. I don't understand it.

MHR: Writing seems to be more than just writing on a pad of paper, or typing at a keyboard. When you are looking out the window and imagining, that's part of writing too.

CP: Yes, and it's the fact that anytime you encounter anything, you are always looking to see if you can use it or rephrase it or restructure it. The head works constantly in terms of structure, creating form. I don't know that anyone who is a writer can get out of that. If you wake up one day and you don't have that anymore—that's the time that you retire.

MHR: What do you see on the horizon for humanity as we approach the end of the twentieth century?

CP: Well, it's generally our fate as human beings that as we approach the end of a century, we go collectively mad. And as we approach the end of a millennium, we grow collectively even madder. That is what is happening to us today: More fundamentalism. More visions, more insecurities, more madness. And you can see it all over the planet.

We just have to get over this hurdle of the next few years. What's interesting to me is that these calendrical cycles are entirely artificial. Nature knows no calendar. Nature simply hums along. We are the ones who have created the calendar, and we react to it. So we think some enormous event is about to occur, because of some map we've imposed on it.

In all candor, what I'm hoping is that we make it to the end of the century and turn the corner. The last century has been the most awful century in the history of the millennium. I hope and I pray that we are at the beginning of the end of that awfulness as we turn into the next millennium.

Notes

1. Chaim Potok, "The Invisible Map of Meaning: A Writer's Confrontation," *Triquarterly,* Spring 1992.
2. Potok, "The Invisible Map of Meaning."

Response Interview with Chaim Potok

Jennifer Gilnett / 1997

From *Response,* Seattle Pacific University, October 29, 1997. Reprinted by permission of Seattle Pacific University.

Response: Many of your writings deal with characters who are "coming of age." Why has that been such an important theme for you?

Potok: I think that those are the ages where individuals from any given culture are profoundly affected by ideas that might come to them from other cultures. Those are the vulnerable ages.

Response: How well do you think American higher education today is assisting students in this formative time of their lives?

Potok: I teach at an Ivy League school and I doubt that's representative of what is going on generally in the United States. My impression is that in many areas universities are wanting. And it's very difficult to pinpoint exactly what it is that's going wrong, why and where. I think a lot of people are quite concerned, and rightly so, and are attempting to reevaluate the educational process.

Response: In the courses you teach, what are some of the questions that students are asking today?

Potok: Universal questions like: Who am I? What do I owe my community? What am I learning about my past? What am I preparing to give to the future? What sort of commitments am I going to make? Students are involved in the search for meaning. They're very concerned about what place they're going to find in this culture in the next century—what the real world is going to be like for them.

Response: At Seattle Pacific, we use your novels *The Chosen* and *My Name Is Asher Lev* in our freshman core classes. What attitudes do you hope that we would bring to an exploration of your works?

Potok: An openness to discuss all sorts of ideas. The conviction that no idea should be foreign to us. A willingness to debate without fear of consequences. At the same time, an acknowledgment that, as a civilization, in the end there have to be limitations; there have to be borders; there has to be some measure of what most of us will agree is the deviant in our culture. There has to be some way of living a day-to-day life in spite of the fact that the discussion remains fluid.

I think that's the fundamental purpose of the university: to teach the student how to create a balance between an ongoing, fluid discussion about the nature of a culture, and the reality that when the student wakes up Monday morning he or she has to commit himself or herself to something. It's one thing to discuss; it's another thing to live.

Response: That's reminiscent of the character Danny Saunders in your book *The Chosen.* Here is someone steeped in both religious readings and psychoanalytic theory. His efforts to reconcile the two push him to a deeper understanding of himself and the world, don't they?

Potok: Yes, I think that really can happen—and that would be the ideal for me. And you know, you don't have to be overly brilliant to achieve that sort of understanding. The character Asher Lev isn't especially smart academically. He's gifted as an artist. But, he certainly doesn't have significant academic prowess. Not all kids are geniuses at the level of Danny Saunders. All of us can achieve this at our own level, if properly directed.

It's important to confront ideas from outside our cultures and somehow come to grips with them and not be overwhelmed by them. The best way for that to happen is to be firmly grounded in whatever culture you come from so that you confront the world from a base of knowledge and commitment, rather than from a base of ignorance.

Response: In *My Name Is Asher Lev,* you write that "one man is no better than another because he's a doctor while the other is a shoemaker. One is no better than the other because he's a lawyer while the other's a painter. A life is measured by how it is lived for the sake of heaven." What does it mean to live a life for the sake of heaven?

Potok: That's a very strong strain of thought in Judaism, and my guess is in Christianity as well. There's this great Hasidic story of a shepherd who came to the synagogue on the Day of Atonement and couldn't read the prayers. And the Hasidic master told him to do whatever it was that he could do the best. And the shepherd whistled. And the Hasidic master said to his followers, who were sort of aghast at this, that that whistle meant more to God than all their prayers together, because that whistle really came from the very soul of that shepherd. It's the depth of a life lived. That's what touches the transcendent. And everybody's capable of that.

Response: The characters in your books often suffer real trauma in the course of their lives. And that seems to bring on a reckoning, a sense of calling to use their individual gifts in the culture. What role do you think suffering has for us as people?

Potok: If we live, we're going to suffer sooner or later—especially in this century. It's inconceivable to me that anybody could have lived through any significant part of this century and not encountered major trauma of one kind or another. It makes little difference where you're from or what your background is. And sooner or later we have to come to terms with that suffering. It affects our lives and our commitments in profound ways.

Response: For the characters in your books, one way of expressing themselves is through art. Do you see this as something that's becoming lost in a technological culture?

Potok: I don't think it's going to become lost because I think the hunger for art is fundamental to human expression. It's one of the essential means of human communication. It's one of the fundamental ways that we give meaning to our existence. It can be put on the back burner for a while by benighted individuals and by technology, although people sophisticated about technology know that technology, too, has its aesthetics. It's not anything we can set aside.

Response: In *Davita's Harp,* the character Jacob Daws said that "a writer is a strange instrument of our species, a harp of sorts, finely tuned to the dark contradictions of life." Would you agree with that description of your vocation?

Potok: Oh, yes, oh yes. I do, indeed, believe that. It's through the writer that the world and its winds are heard. But, remember that the harp is an instrument and the winds that go through it, that hit it, are not the same as the music or winds that come from it. Transformations take place as a result of the contact with the harp.

The harp is capable of angelic music and also capable of some very heavy strumming. And I think it's the fundamental responsibility of a writer to deal with both the angelic and the darkness. No one else is going to do it. The politician sure isn't going to do it.

Response: I think of Asher Lev's choice to paint the crucifixion as a metaphor for the pain experienced by his parents. As a Jewish writer, what kind of response did you receive within your own culture about this choice?

Potok: It was not received well at all. The echoes of it continue to this day. I paid a high price for that book. But that's the job of a writer. You pay the price, but you have to be honest. If you're not, no one's going to pay any attention to you. And I made that decision when I was sixteen, seventeen years old: that I would do it to the best of my ability. And I've been paying the price ever since. I mean I've paid other prices since the Asher Lev book, but that was a particularly steep price.

Response: The religious establishment is a figure of authority in many of your writings. How have you been affected as a writer who writes about questions of faith within a religious subculture where art may not be valued?

Potok: For me, in my culture, it was an uphill struggle. The only worse kind of struggle that one can envisage is if one enters into the doing of art—painting, sculpture and so on. There is still significant respect for the word in Judaism, so that if you're sitting and writing, and if you're standing before a canvas trying to make pictures. And that's of course a problem that Asher Lev had.

Response: There is a line in *My Name Is Asher Lev:* "The master of the universe gives us glimpses, only glimpses. It is for us to open our eyes wide." Do you think that as human beings we tend to squint at the realities around us rather than keep our eyes wide open?

Potok: Actually, squinting gives you a sharper image than just keeping your eyes wide. But we tend to blink and cut pieces of the world out, or we tend to turn away from them. Of things we don't understand, or that frighten us, or bore us, we do get only glimpses.

We go about creating constructs or "maps" of reality and mostly what we're making maps of are these glimpses. We are map-making animals, meaning-making creatures. That may very well be the human partnership with the universe and with God—to make maps out of glimpses. Certainly we cannot see the universe the way God sees it.

Response: Where do you see the intersection of those "maps" today between the Christian and the Jewish cultures in America?

Potok: Well, connections can be made along very broad lines. In many ways, we speak the same language of meaning, of response to mystery. The dimension of the spirit is what we try to acknowledge, to tap into, and make sense out of. Science is interested, and rightly so, in particles, in the world of physics, and the world of nature, and the world of matter. Our commitment is to another realm, the realm that cannot be measured and quantified.

Because both Judaism and Christianity come from the same mountain and the same city ultimately, we can pretty much speak the same language once we get past the ideological sparring about origins and beginnings. And that's becoming increasingly invaluable in the world in which we live, which is more and more technological, and more and more materialistic, and more and more hedonistic.

Response: What do you think is the most important question we should be asking for the future in a community like Seattle Pacific?

Potok: Well, the fundamental theme that we have to address for the next century is how to create thinking, moral beings in the face of what will most definitely be a supreme technological age.

I think people are asking this question in the deepest recesses of their being. I think that what they want, whether they can articulate it with an unremitting expansion of technology. I think everyone is profoundly concerned about what sorts of commitments we make in a society where values have been rendered virtually entirely relativistic and instrumentalist by the findings of science and by the technologies that we've created.

Response: Is that what you meant in *The Gift of Asher Lev* where you said, "And without God, what is man? Everyone needs the help of someone to create the work of creation that is never truly created."

Potok: Exactly right.

Chaim Potok: *The Gates of November*

Mike Cuthbert / 1998

From AARP Prime Time Radio, Washington, 1998. Reprinted by permission of Mike Cuthbert, AARP Prime Time Radio.

MC: Hi everybody, I'm Mike Cuthbert in Washington. Welcome back to Prime Time Radio. Not too many weeks ago on this show we discussed the dissolution of the Soviet Union and the reasons for it. We discovered that it's likely that the facade the Soviet citizens learned to live behind cracked. And once, openly admitting to the lies and distortions they had lived with, the same people could not and would not go back to the system of deceptions that had become habit . . . habit in order to survive. Chaim Potok, famed novelist, had questions about the Soviet Union and its people. Rather than study the whole society, he looked at one family with two basic questions in mind: What can cause a person or a family to overthrow a fairly decent life in order to intentionally and willingly crack and rend the fabric of the society they live in, and can that family be used successfully as a model for understanding how an entire governmental and philosophical system can unravel? Well, you have to read *The Gates of November* for yourself to determine the answers to those questions, but in the meantime, we have Chaim Potok with us to talk about the Slaypek family and what happened to them. Welcome, good to see you.

CP: It's good to be here. Thank you.

MC: Of all the dissident families you could have focused on for answers to your questions, why did you pick the Slaypeks?

CP: In part it was chance, and in part it was because they were the major players in the dissent movement in the Soviet Union during the sixties and seventies. Now, he in particular, his wife too, had been in refusal letters, to say their exit visas had been refused them by the Soviet government for close to eighteen years by the time they finally left. I began to hear about the Slaypeks in the sixties and seventies, friends of mine would go there, meet with them, were told that they were reading some of my books. They would send their regards back through my friends. And, in the early eighties, my

146

wife started to say maybe we should go and meet some of these dissidents
and see what's going on. And, finally, in January 1985, we landed in a snow-
storm in Moscow, and we met with the Slaypeks, and it was instantaneous
bonding of human beings. Now, they were, at that time, after the five-year
period they had spent in exile in Siberia, near the Mongolian border, and they
were absolutely certain they would never get out. And, when we left them
that night, we were reasonably certain we'd never see them again. It was a
sad evening. And then they were out.

MC: A sad evening except for (laugh) a very funny incident in which
Vilotja said, you're from Philadelphia, do you know Chaim Potok?

CP: Well, yes, he didn't know who we were, because when you call them
on the telephone, even if you called from outside your hotel, you never gave
them your name. One never knew whether or not the phones were bugged.
We knew who they were, my wife was setting up a meeting with them. So
when we finally got to the apartment, after walking from the subway through
the snow to the apartment, one of the first things he said was, "Do you know
the writer Chaim Potok?" And I said, I'm the writer Chaim Potok. And, he
said, no, no, no, no, no, maybe my English isn't so good, I meant do you
know the writer Chaim Potok. And then, we had been briefed in Philadelphia
to bring with us calling cards, you know that quintessential bourgeois label
of identity, so I showed it to him and well, it was an embrace and it was just
a lovely night from that point on, and a melancholy night when we parted.

MC: We've been speaking about the Slaypeks as if it's just Vilotja and his
wife Masha, but of course, this would hardly be a story, just a couple. This
is a story of generations as well, particularly the older generation, represented
by Solomon Slaypek, the most mysterious and perhaps, I don't know if vile
is the word, but he certainly got my blood boiling several times. He was
known as Sam, at one point, and I suppose one of the most cogent things
said about him was said when he came back to Moscow. Whenever people
heard the name Sam, they thought only about cruelty to the enemies of the
revolution, about wiping out opponents without mercy. The waters of the
river turned red from the blood of the corpses. That was Solomon Slaypek,
the father of this wonderful Vilotja.

CP: Yes, he was no doubt the killer for the Bolshevik cause. He became
the head of a ten thousand man army, fighting the cause of the Communist
Revolution in China, of all places, in the Asian theatre of operations.

MC: Where he was known as Sam?

CP: And, he was known as Sam, and he had quite a bloody reputation. For the cause of Bolshevism, he would kill, and killed indeed. And, as Vilotja was growing up, he began to hear stories from individuals who would suddenly pop up out of his father's past. And, those stories were rather upsetting, and finally all of this came to a head when Vilotja and Masha themselves decided to break with the system.

MC: And, of course they broke with the system, but they also then had to break with Sam, who represented the system.

CP: And, when they told Sam that they were planning to apply for exit visas, there was an explosion that night in the family. He called them enemies of the people, the worst thing you can call a Soviet citizen. He said to them, from now on, you and I will be on opposite sides of the barricade. And indeed, there is the strong probability that he was one of the more potent instruments in keeping them inside the Soviet Union for as long as they were there. He had tremendous influence, apparently, with the party, and he didn't want his son to leave.

MC: Which is one of the peculiar parts of this whole story. We have Solomon Slaypek, who at one time was known as Simon Vitavech, I believe, it was not right to appear to be Jewish or to be Jewish in the Bolshevik Revolution, and yet he was, he turned his back on his faith, and eventually on his family, to serve a Revolution he had to know was corrupt. Did you ever solve the mystery of Solomon Slaypek entirely to your satisfaction?

CP: There are numerous mysteries about this individual. First of all, how he got radicalized in New York, what that was all about, and radicalized he was, to the extent that when he was in New York after fleeing from Russia, because he didn't want to be conscripted into the army of the czar, he wanted to come back to the motherland to participate in what he thought would be, and correctly so, the Communist Revolution, 1917. And they wouldn't let him back in, so he ended up going through Canada, through Vancouver, through Bladevostek, into the Asian mainland, and that's how he ended up as Commander in Chief of an army of partisans. That's one mystery—how that transformation took place in New York. Another mystery is how he avoided being arrested during all the purges. And, I don't know the answer to that second mystery. The first I could conjecture—lonely person, caught up in the meetings and ideals, he was young, and so on. I don't know how he avoided all those purges. Everyone around him was picked up and shot.

And he was in a very visible and important position. He was head of the Foreign Correspondent Desk of the Soviet telegraphic agency. He was the one preparing the briefing books for Stalin and the members of the Policy Bureau of all the information coming in from outside the Soviet Union. Why wasn't he picked up, why wasn't he, I don't know to this day. I'm trying to get into his files. I've been trying to get into his files, all through the many years of writing this book, so far without success. I'm still trying. If I succeed, I'll add a piece to a future edition of the book, and we'll see if we can solve that mystery.

MC: Chaim Potok is our guest. His latest book is nonfiction, *The Gates of November,* chronicles of the Slaypek family. We have the family on the front, pictured. I'm assuming this is Solomon.
CP: That's correct.

MC: And, on the back, we have not only Vilotja, but also Masha and their two sons, Leonid and Sonja, as I recall.
CP: That's correct.

MC: But, there's other subtexts going under here. We mentioned Solomon turns his back on his faith. That was not always easy for Jews in Russia or anywhere else. If you were Jewish, you were Jewish, no matter what your position. And the book traces some of the more incredible twists and turns of first Russian, and then Soviet policy toward Jews. A policy, in which, to be Jewish was to be automatically an enemy of the state. It was continuous. And yet Solomon escaped that as well.
CP: And that's another of the mysteries in connection with that individual. It's mystery after mystery, and I'm still trying to probe it. But, an end had to be made to this book (laughter). I didn't want to spend the rest of my life writing it. So, I simply leave it as a mystery.

MC: But I guess what puzzled me was how he was able to escape, but Vilotja was not. He was, he did not get jobs because he was Jewish. He had difficulty because he was Jewish, and yet his father did not. It just didn't make sense.
CP: His father was in on the very first level of the Revolution. The first level of the Revolution, those early years after 1917, the new Soviet Union seemed to have turned a corner in terms of its relationship with its Jews. And indeed there was the feeling that a new world was dawning, so far as the Jews of the new Soviet Union were concerned. They were equal citizens. And, for

those first ten years, a good case can be made out that if you were willing to participate in the activities of this new party and this new world, yes, you were regarded as an equal citizen. Those that wanted to stay religious were hounded, hounded, terribly hounded. But, so were Christians who wanted to stay religious, hounded. If you wanted to join with this new adventure, you were part and parcel of the new adventure. It was with Stalin, especially after the Second World War, that there was a return to old-style Russian anti-Semitism that had been part and parcel of the fabric of the Russian culture for many, many centuries.

MC: Given their background, with their father's position, how do you explain that fact that Vilotja and Masha kept enough of their faith to want to, eventually want to emigrate to Israel, to the point that their sons decided to go to the United States, and they said no, we're going to Israel.

CP: I think it wasn't so much a matter of keeping the faith, because they had no faith in any normal sense of the term. These were areligious people; they were individuals with no religion whatsoever in any formal sense, in any informal sense. Religion was not a category of thought in so far as they were concerned. What they had was a national identity. In the Soviet Union, on your internal passport, there was a a line that says national identity: so, you're a Georgian, you're this, you're that, and one of the nationalities is Jewish. And, that's what they had on their internal passports. Their connection to Israel came about as a result of primarily, the Six Day War and their sudden realization that this was a strong country, a proud country, a country that could defend itself, and here was a land in which they could live as free citizens and as Jews. Secular Jews, individuals who wouldn't be bothered, and told what to do by an overriding state. They made their commitment to Israel, and they stuck with that commitment. Their children did not like Israel, and both of their sons now live in the United States. In many ways this is a melancholy story, it's a mixed success that they've experienced. They live in Israel, the sons are in the United States, grandchildren are in the United States; they paid a significant price for that freedom.

MC: And they will not move?
CP: No, they are committed to living in Israel. They quite love it there.

MC: They are committed to living in Israel, but they neither of them, of course, moving there in the late eighties as they did, neither of them lived there long enough to get any retirement. How do they live?

CP: Well, with some difficulty, my guess is that one or the other of the sons sends them some money, and perhaps friends help them out. They live with some difficulty. Because they've only got partial pension. They didn't live in Israel long enough, or work there long enough to get full retirement pensions. And now, they're both retired, and Vilotja is ill, he's had his first heart attack, a telephone call from the other side, as he puts it. Masha has had some eye surgery.

MC: At one point in 1976, Vilotja and Masha, who up to this point seemed like a dedicated husband and wife, get a divorce. Explain why they had to do that?

CP: They divorced because Vilotja thought that the reason that Masha and the remaining son weren't being permitted to leave was because they were connected to him, and he was a major security risk, since he had been instrumental in the development of the air defense system of the Soviet Union. And, the Soviets were furious at him for wanting to leave. He had been really, a tough operator in that developing system. Indeed, second-level security clearance, security clearance right below Stalin and the members of the Policy Bureau. And, Vilotja and Masha thought that if they divorced, then Masha and the boy would get an exit visa and they would be able to leave, and Vilotja would stay behind. They were quite willing to do that, but the government would have nothing to do with that. The government said we don't believe in this divorce, it's a phony divorce, and it didn't help.

MC: And for once, the government was right.
CP: Yes. Of course, yes.

MC: As you mentioned, they had to endure five years of exile. What was the ostensible reason for that exile? What was the spark that got them sentenced?

CP: The spark that got them sentenced was a demonstration that took place outside their home. They hung, I think, a placard from their home from a balcony of their apartment on Gorky Street, and the placard said: let us join our children in the United States. Let us join our children. That was it. That was all they did. KGB broke into the apartment, water was poured on Vilotja's head from the apartment above, scalding water, there was a real fracus with sticks and so on, and the two of them were arrested. Vilotja was sentenced to five years in exile in Siberia. Masha was sentenced and then given probation. She was free to go, and she volunteered to join her husband in this little collective farm a few kilometers away from the border of Mongolia, a miserable spot of earth. And there they endured for five long years. She had to go back periodically to Moscow, otherwise they would have lost their apartment, so every four months or so, she took a week-long trip back to Moscow from that Mongolian border. Buses, little planes, big planes, it was a horrendous trip in the winters, in the summers, whatever it was. And she was the lifeline of that family. And indeed Vilotja once told me that if it hadn't been for her—she was a physician, she was his physician. If it hadn't been for her he would have died.

MC: There were so many peculiar things that in our previous conversation about the dissolution of the empire that we talked about in the opening. We found Catch-22 is so normal in the Soviet Union, or was so normal, that you just didn't bring it up. But there was a classic, I thought, when Vilotja returned from exile. They had lifted his internal passport, and if you don't have an internal passport, you can't work, you can't get a work permit. Now, he was being threatened, after five years of being in exile, with going back to prison for parasitism, because he couldn't get a, . . . he wouldn't work. In other wor . . . , he wouldn't work because the very police station that was going to arrest him, to throw him in jail had lifted the permit that allowed him to work. This almost sounds funny. It's so bizarre and so impossible, that you almost have to laugh. What does Vilotja Slaypek do when he talks about those things?

CP: He laughs. (laughter) You're quite right, the alternative is to go mad. And he shrugs it off, and he says, "Well that's the system, and that's the system that we had to live under and fight." He once told me that during a questioning session on the part of the KGB, they said to him: "You know too much, we're not going to let you go." And he said, "What are you talking about, I've been out of engineering now for more than ten years. There's no way that I can possibly catch up in engineering. I know nothing that's of significance in terms of being a state secret. And not only that, but even when I started, we were ten, fifteen years or more behind the United States in engineering. How could I possibly know an important secret?" and their response was: "We were ten years behind?" He says, "Yes." Their response was, "That's a secret." (laughter).

MC: I'm Mike Cuthbert in Washington. This is Prime Time Radio. In fact, he turned out to be right; one of the sad things about his life is when he was finally able to work in Israel, he's so far behind in his field he can't get a job in it.

CP: He was unable to catch up. He did some sort of work in the engineering laboratory at the University of Tel Aviv, but it's impossible to catch up after you're out of engineering for fifteen, eighteen years or so, and he knew it when he went to Israel. And he did the best he could with the life that he had.

MC: They were at one time heroes to thousands of people. There were synagogues all over the country here in the United States that paid attention to what was happening to the refusniks, supported them in every way possible. It turns out that in some cases, I could not doubt the Slaypeks' case, their livelihood was supplemented by gifts and money from outside. They are not heroes now, except in your book. Do they resent the fact that at one time they were world famous and now they are so obscure they can't even get a full-time pension?

CP: I don't get any sense of resentment from them at all. And, I just saw them a couple of months ago; they were inside our home outside of Philadelphia. I get a sense of quiet; I get a sense of sadness out of them, that they're separated from their sons and their grandchildren. I get a sense of acceptance of what it is that's happened to them, and I get a determined sense of absolute certainty from them that they did the right thing. Even though they paid a high price for it, they did the right thing. Even though the Soviet Union is gone, even though things may be different for Jews in the Soviet Union today from what they were when they lived there, they are convinced that they did the right thing for themselves and for their children.

MC: Are they and/or their children now highly, moderately, or not much religious?

CP: They are not religious at all, in any formal sense of that word, in any observing sense of that word. I get no sense at all that they're practicing. They are deeply committed, the two of them, Masha and Vilotja, deeply committed to the state of Israel. My guess is that their politics are along Likud lines, that, I never asked them how they voted; it's really not my business. I may ask them one day, but my guess is that they voted for Netanyahu and that they are very suspicious of giving away too much, although they want peace, they want peace very much, they don't want to give away too much too fast. That's pretty much what their politics involve today. They're very caring of the new Russian immigrants that come in; they deal with them. And, he himself is active in the New Russian Party in Israel.

MC: Vilotja has gone back to Russia since locating. What are his impressions of his old home on Gorky Street now?

CP: Well, it's sad. He has met with dear old friends who live in the apartment house where he grew up and where he spent much of his active life. One of his friends asked him, "Are you sorry that you left the Soviet Union, because of the changes that took place?" He said, "No." She said to him, "But there's no anti-Semitism now." His response was, "That's correct, there's none now, but there may very well be a resurgence of anti-Semitism sometime in the future, and I don't want to involve myself anymore in the life of Russia. I've lived that life and I've cut that cord entirely." When I asked him, "What would your father be doing now if he were alive in Russia?" he said, "My father would be in the front ranks of the Communists carrying the banners in their demonstrations and trying to reestablish the Communist party for another go, for another try at the Bolshevik dream."

MC: An unreconstructed Bolshevik.
CP: Absolutely.

MC: Chaim Potok, we're going to leave our audience with the question that you ask at one point in your book, and that's whether that could ever happen here. That's another reason to read *The Gates of November;* that echo is with us as well, that kind of fervent willing suspension of belief could happen anywhere, I suppose. But, we're glad that the Slaypeks escaped and that you told their story. And, thanks for telling it again on Prime Time Radio.

CP: Thank you for having me.

Chaim Potok

Tony Auth / 1998

From *Philadelphia Inquirer Online,* March 1, 1998, http://www.phil-
lynews.com/Inquirer/98/Mar/01/opinion/POTO01.htm Reprinted by
permission of Tony Auth.

Question: What motivates you to write stories for children?
Answer: The look in the eyes of a child when he or she reads or hears a
good story. There's such a light and a dancing in those eyes. Getting that
light is worth all the effort it takes to make a good story.

Q: What makes a good story for kids?
A: One of the things that fascinates and challenges kids is their sense of
entering into a very serious contest of sorts, which the heroine or the hero of
the story experiences. That contest can be physical, or it can be totally imagi-
nary. Sometimes the contest is between two parts of yourself hitting against
each other. The child senses him- or herself participating in the contest and
tries to figure out what he or she would do—and then the delight when somehow in the story the child prevails!

Q: Do these stories help kids?
A: It's a bit of a crazy world for children, this adult world we live in, and
they can use all the help they can get. A good story in which a child overcomes a difficulty is a help indeed.

At the same time, you don't want the difficulty to be trivial. In my first
book for young people, *The Tree of Here,* the difficulty is that an eight-year-
old child has just been told by his parents that the family is moving for the
third time. In *The Sky of Now,* a boy of nine realizes that he is terrified of
heights, but he wants to be a pilot when he grows up, like his uncle. And the
surprise comes when the uncle, as a birthday present, gives the boy glider
lessons. And that becomes his first lesson as a pilot. Most of the book takes
place inside the glider.

Q: Which is harder—writing for adults or writing for children?
A: Each is a different realm, and each has its difficulties. But I'll tell you:
I just finished a book of short stories for young adults, and for each of the

stories I wrote, I must have written six other stories. A novel for each story, in other words.

Q: Are there enough good stories for kids?

A: For me, there are—I just love writing them. They're all over the place.

Q: Should adults read works in this genre?

A: Adults should read kids' stories constantly. The imagination, the soaring of the mind and the spirit that you find in stories for children—it's all simply astonishing and in the end profoundly satisfying.

Q: Is it art?

A: It certainly can be. Look at Maurice Sendak's *Where the Wild Things Are*. Look at Dr. Seuss. I think that what he has accomplished is to raise the genre of the children's book to an art form.

HARDtalk: Chaim Potok

Tim Sebastian / 1999

From "HARDtalk," BBC Radio, June 25, 1999. Reprinted by permission of BBC Television, London.

T: Chaim Potok, a very warm welcome to the program.

C: : It's good to be here.

T: If life is about choices, you seem to have had very few in your childhood. Do you resent that looking back?

C: That's very interesting. The fact of the matter is that things were chosen for me for a long time and probably as an artist, writer, they're still being chosen for me. We live in a choosey world, that's the great pride that we have in ourselves for the first time in our history. As a species. There is a sense of the self and a self that can choose its destiny. My world was chosen for me when I was very young and then finally enough when I was sixteen I read *Brideshead Revisited* and *Portrait of the Artist as a Young Man* and those two books chose for me the fact that I would be a writer for the rest of my life.

T: Gave you an insight into a world that you never knew even existed.

C: A miraculous insight into the process of creating through the imagination and interestingly they were two Catholic worlds, and I came from a very religious Jewish background. One was an upper class English Catholic world and the other was a middle class Irish Catholic world. You can imagine I knew a lot about upper class English Catholics when I read *Brideshead Revisited*. What an extraordinary experience that was.

T: And when you got to the end of the book you felt bereaved.

C: That I have lost these people, they were gone. I had been so involved in their lives, and this was such a strange world for me and yet by the time I was 70–80 pages into it, for the first time in my life I found myself anticipating their feelings, their thinking, wondering what they were going to do with the particular problem that they were having. I lost track of my own reality for the length of time it took me to read of evil and war's reality.

T: You saw the way worlds are created out of words?

C: That's correct and I realized how words can bridge chasms across worlds. The power of the imagination, and the power of words on paper. How you could bring others into your own life, others that you would regard as bizarre, unestranged. That was the beginning for me, of my life as a writer, and you're quite right that was chosen for me by history, by chance, by events, by whatever.

T: Let's talk a bit about the life that your parents initially chose for you because you said you were locked in. How rigid was your upbringing?

C: Very, very Orthodox. They wanted me to remain inside the Orthodox Jewish world. My father wanted me to teach Talmud in a Jewish academy of higher learning. He wanted me to be a rabbi.

T: You are a rabbi.

C: Yes, but . . .

T: But not quite the kind that he wanted?

C: In a nonfundamentalist Jewish reading of the tradition.

T: Now this was a world where study was fine and scholarship was fine but dissent and questioning, they weren't on the agenda were they?

C: No, there was a limit to the kind of question you could ask. You are encouraged to ask questions but you learned very early on that you couldn't step outside a certain boundary. You couldn't ask questions involving principle. You could ask questions about how we do a thing, is this proper, is that proper, but you could never ask why we do a thing, in the sense of attempting to undermine the principle underlying the action. You learned quickly what the boundary was by a gesture from your father, by a raised elbow; these are aspects of culture that are more caught than taught.

T: Like a cold.

C: Exactly, exactly, and I learned that, but when you become a writer, serious writer and you want to do the exploring that you feel language bids you do, you're questioning everything. You're standing outside the world that you're describing.

T: As a serious writer, as a serious novelist, let me put it that way, I think you said you cannot remain within a fundamentalist sect, can you?

C: I couldn't. I found myself worrying about who was going to read it and what rabbi is looking over my shoulder and I was going to upset people.

T: You did?

C: I did but I did it from the outside. It's very different when you accept people from the outside because you're not there to see them undergoing the tumult of the upset and my sense of it is that if you're going to write seriously you're going to upset people.

T: Your first act of rebellion was to paint, wasn't it? It wasn't to write at the age of eight.

C: I didn't realize that I was rebelling although of course I was; about the age of eight or nine I started to draw and paint and I was told that I was rather good at it, but my father didn't want me to do that sort of thing.

T: Why not?

C: He felt that it was first of all a waste of time, that was at the least.

T: Because no religious Jew ever gets involved in Western painting?

C: At the worst it was a Gentile enterprise.

T: And a sin.

C: And therefore potentially leading one to sin and when I became thirteen, which is the age when you adopt the commandments, and so on, you enter adulthood, as it were, he really was upset and my guess is as I look back on all of this, that when I read *Brideshead Revisited,* what I did was shift the urge to create from painting to writing. I think that was the way it went, and in the Jewish tradition words on paper are far more acceptable than paint on canvas.

T: Why is that?

C: They also didn't smell up the apartment with turpentine. Judaism is a word world and from the very beginning there has been a suspicion of the icon in the Jewish tradition of the image and a concentration on the creating of the world through words. That's the emphasis of the Jewish religion. It's a text world from the very beginning of Judaism and so as long as I got my As my father left me alone.

T: Your parents were reasonably well off to start with but then the recession hit, didn't it, and hit them badly?

C: That devastated the family. One of the bleakest moments of my life which I remember so vividly as I'm sitting here talking to you is the day the social worker or the investigator or the inspector came in for the welfare department of New York, looked around our house, and asked my father all kinds of questions because we were destitute. My father was very well to do; he was in the real estate business all through the '20s and was wiped out. He lost his work in '29 and he lost all his money in '33 with the bank crash. So we were really destitute.

T: What's the lasting effect of that on you?

C: I think I worry all the time about money, about spending money, about where the money will come from, about poverty, about taking care of my children, about the future. You can't get over terms of that kind.

T: Still hangs over you?

C: Oh yes, it is part of the cortex of your being.

T: When you started writing and reading in earnest, your own writings produced some derision, didn't they, from those around you?

C: They produced derision and when I started publishing they produced a lot of anger. There's a school about a block and a half away from where I live where my books are forbidden.

T: How does that make you feel?

C: That makes me feel not very pleasant, but I understand where they come from. Not only are the books forbidden to be read, but they're not even in the school library.

T: You may understand but you don't sympathize, do you?

C: No.

T: This is narrow-minded, isn't it?

C: It's narrow-minded, I also think it's harmful. It's part of an attitude that sees the rest of the world as a threat to your world and because it's a threat you won't engage it. And you feel that the only way that you can secure your own existence is by sealing yourself off from the outside world, and my sense of life is that if this is the price you have to pay to sustain your own culture, I don't want to participate in that kind of culture.

T: By 1950 you were certain, weren't you, that you didn't want to live in a Hasidic community?

C: Yes.

T: That involved rebuilding your world from zero.

C: It wrenched my world entirely. I lost all of my friends, I lost most of my teachers, I had to literally reconstruct my existence.

T: No help from the family?

C: My mother was sympathetic; my father, I don't think he could get over it till the day he died.

T: What did your mother say to you when you told her you were going to write stories?

C: My mother was interesting. My mother was more sophisticated than my father because she attended a gymnasium in Vienna during the First World War. So while she was very, very religious, I remember her saying to me, you want to write stories, she said you'll be a brain surgeon and on the side you'll write stories. She understood what it was I was trying to do and indeed when the stories started to come out she was very proud. My father died before *The Chosen* was published, before the first novel was published, but my guess is that had he read it and seen all the fuss that was made of it, he would not have been impressed. To him I stepped outside the boundary.

T: What kind of Judaism did you find then to replace the Hasidic?

C: A traditional Judaism that is not fundamentalist.

T: So it's broader?

C: It's broader, but it's different than being broader, it's a new way of reading text. It's a way of reading text against a historical background with an understanding of where Jews come from, how they're part of the world in which biblical and Rabbinic Judaism developed. The interface between Judaism and the worlds around it all through the centuries, and non-literalist, that's the word I wanted before, a nonliteralist reading of the traditional text of the Jewish religion.

T: So it's more open-minded in every way?

C: Open-minded and it simply explodes the background and the dimensions of Judaism and from my reading of it enriches it to a tremendous degree.

T: So it was a huge relief for you wasn't it?

C: Yes, it was a relief, it was exciting, and it was threatening because you had to rethink the fundamentalist base of your tradition and where it's gone in all of this.

T: At the same time as you were rethinking and rebuilding your world.

C: Exactly.

T: Hard to do.

C: Very hard.

T: I think so much of your life is how hard beginnings are, isn't it?

C: All beginnings are hard.

T: Especially when you have to make them rein in yourself.

C: And especially when you have to make them everyday, sometimes.

T: Why do you think that you went on to train as a rabbi when you were questioning so deeply your faith and your religion and where you were going?

C: I actually went to train as a rabbi because the school that I went to was the only school available to me for the broader understanding of my tradition that I was getting in my fundamentalist world. I knew that there was another reading of the Jewish tradition. There had to be, and I was not getting its literature, its philosophy, its poetry. I was not getting that in the closed yeshiva world in which I was being raised. So where was it? Where was this other reading? And it was in this school; I attended that school in order to become a better writer, I knew I would write about things Jewish. What else did I know to write about? And if I was going to write about things Jewish I wanted to write about them from a base of knowledge. Now when you went to that school and graduated you were a rabbi whether you wanted to be or not because that was the point of that school.

T: Did you ever question that through a period that you actually wanted to be a rabbi?

C: No, I never wanted to be a rabbi. That is to say, I never wanted to be a pulpit rabbi. I never wanted to officiate at a pulpit. I knew that I would spend my life writing. Succeed. Fail. Irrelevant. I knew that I would spend my life writing.

T: You talked about expanding your base of knowledge. Your base of knowledge expanded enormously when you volunteered to serve in Korea in 1956.

C: Yes, I thought that was the right thing to do.

T: Why?

C: Well, the kids there needed chaplains and the seminary asked the students to volunteer and the students volunteered, and it became part of your being in the seminary.

T: Asked or told?

C: They were asked because some people refused and felt it necessary to leave the seminary. They wouldn't go on with that. It was for a while a condition of being in the seminary but you have the option of not taking it on, of leaving.

T: This was a huge leap for you away from your world, the world that you knew, wasn't it?

C: It was a mind-transforming experience; in sophisticated postmodern terms it was said that it was a paradigm shift. The world that I brought with me to Korea, which was a very coherent American, Western, Jewish world, was utterly transformed by the sixteen months that I spent there.

T: Into what?

C: Into a relativizing experience, an experience where I saw sufferings the likes of which I could never imagine in my life, that forced me to ask myself whether the God that I approached was listening to the pagan. The intensity of the worship that I experienced in pagan shrines and asking myself, wait a minute, is the merciful God that I speak to not listening? Why not, and if that God is listening, then what are Judaism and Christianity all about, because Judaism and Christianity came into the world as iconoclastic-condition counter cultures to Paganism. It was one experience after another living there.

T: It didn't matter who you were, did it?

C: I was a white face; it made no difference if you were dead, it made no difference who you were, and not only that, you were simply another white face in a culture in which Jews were of no significance whatsoever. I was always taught that Jews played a major role in the development of western culture. No, you have a whole side of the planet in which Judaism plays no role whatsoever, utterly insignificant, and in addition to that no anti-Semitism. It's a pagan world that the Bible teaches us to be contemptuous of, read Deuteronomy, and it's the only place on the planet where there's absolutely no anti-Semitism.

T: So you came back with your world shattered?

C: And wrote about it to a very great extent in *The Book of Lights*. Tried to rebuild the world that I took with me, having it rear another face. I'm still struggling with it.

T: But the struggle is good for you, the struggle is your fuel isn't it?

C: The struggling is what feeds the writing.

T: But if you didn't have the struggle then you wouldn't have anything to write about.

C: Absolutely correct.

T: A struggle between modernity and tradition, a struggle between Judaism for its own sake and Judaism in the wider world. What is it? Can you define your struggle?

C: The fundamentalist struggle is the place of my sense of self. What am I as an individual trying to achieve, my goals, my sense of authenticity, my sense of self, vis-à-vis my place in community. That's the essential struggle.

T: : In all your books.

C: And in all of Western culture today. That's the modern struggle because we have no sense of self until the modern period. You are an individual but your destiny was determined for you by the group into which you were born. But the sense that you can create your own destiny apart from community is a very modern idea. Those four letters S-E-L-F are intrinsic to the modern adventure and that tension is what I am trying to explore in the books. Now my books wear a Jewish garb, as it were, because they came out of my own personal experience, but when I read *Portrait of the Artist as a Young Man,* that identical experience, self and community, wears a Catholic garb, and that identical dynamic wears another kind of Catholic garb in *Brideshead Revisited,* and most of modern literature explores that tension between self and community from Jane Austen on.

T: Why was *The Chosen,* do you think, such a big hit, because it looked inside the Hasidic community for the first time? It brought out the tensions that were in there?

C: I'm not sure. I think that it was the success that it was because there was an exotic quality to it. I think that it was the success that it was because I wrote it in a very special way. I decided not to use exotic language. I wanted people to get into it and not define any obfuscation in the way the book was being written, and also I think that young people read it today. They read it all over the planet today including Australia, New Zealand, South Africa and so on because they find in it issues that are pertinent to their relationship, betrayal.

T: You did this through the two students?

C: That is correct, and their fathers.

T: Who came from different sects.

C: And the rivalry that turned into friendships.

T: There is so much of your journey in that, isn't there?

C: I think there is in serious modern literature so much of the writers inside most of those great books that we've created in the Western world.

T: How do you define yourself, as a writer, as a rabbi, as a teacher?

C: I define myself as a writer, as a rabbi, and as a teacher, or I flip it around and say writer, teacher, rabbi.

T: But you don't want to have too much to do with rabbis you said before we came on air.

C: Not too much, not too much, although I have rabbis in my family. I'd rather keep my head clear so that I can do the writing.

T: You've said that Judaism is at a turning point, a crossroads now, why?

C: There's no question about that. It's caught up in the identical dynamic that we are all caught up in. All religions, all peoples are caught up in the modern world of trying to define themselves, vis-à-vis this powerful technology that we are facing.

T: Is it worse now than any time in history? A lot of people look at their time in history; this was a defining moment, this was a turning point.

C: I think what's different now is that we have a different set of answers for the old questions.

T: I thought that you just had more questions as time went by.

C: It may be more questions but we at least today perceive the questions as having been answered far more definitively than they have been in the past and that's in the wake of Newtonian physics and everything that sabotages the modern world.

T: But Judaism isn't the problem now, but how to preserve the integrity of the faith and yet integrate it into society and be a part of the wider society, that more than ever.

C: Absolutely and not only that, but for Judaism today, we are part of the mainstream society, of wider society. I mean whole components of Western culture in the past couple of hundred of years are the creations of Jews, and we have never had an experience like this before. We've always been on the sidelines. Jews have participated as a power, but never were they able to affect the essential nature of the culture in which they live.

T: So it is time to come out of the sidelines?

C: We are out of the sidelines. We are fundamental in Western culture today.

T: But you still have an exclusive club, don't you? It is a very exclusive club, which a lot of people fear.

C: Oh, yes. Nobody wants to give up his or her sense of self and what everyone is trying to do today is calibrate to the best of one's ability that sense of self with community and that's a new experience. That we're all trying to do that dance, that calibration dance, as it were. How do you retain a sense of self, which is the source of Jewish creativity?

T: Intermarriage is a big problem, you've faced that in your own family, haven't you?

C: No intermarriage; intermarriage is when one of the partners does not convert to Judaism. Once the conversion takes place it is not considered intermarriage.

T: Because one of your daughters, she married a Christian who then converted. What if he hadn't converted, how would you have felt?

C: I don't want to face that problem and I told her that would not be a problem because I couldn't countenance that.

T: You couldn't countenance your daughter marrying a non-Jew?
C: That is correct.

T: And if I said I didn't want my daughter to marry a Jew that would be discrimination, wouldn't it? It would be seen as discrimination?
C: Oh yes, but on the contrary I would understand perfectly.

T: And a lot wouldn't, would they?
C: Absolutely and that is the problem that we face with the modern world. How you create these boundaries, how you chalk across these boundaries, how you respect the boundaries, how far you're willing to go beyond that boundary, do you dissolve totally as a self? Those are the new issues and we are all grappling with those issues.

T: Do you enjoy asking these questions?
C: Profoundly, and responding to them, and more than that I enjoy being asked the questions because they force me to think.

T: The debate is so far away from your childhood, isn't it? You couldn't be further away from your childhood.
C: Galaxies away.

T: Chaim Potok, we're glad you dropped into this galaxy at least temporarily. Thank you very much.
C: Thank you.

A Visit with Chaim Potok

David L. Vanderwerken / 2000

Reprinted by permission of David L. Vanderwerken.

This interview took place on Friday, April 28, 2000, at Dr. Potok's home in Lower Merion Township, a section of the greater Philadelphia metropolitan area. His gracious and lovely wife, Adena, welcomed me into their sprawling Tudor residence. We sat in his study amid several of his paintings adorning the walls. We spoke for two hours. The transcript of our encounter will serve as an appendix in my critical study in progress on Potok's work.

DLV: You began painting as a youngster, turned to fiction, to history, and in the nineties you became involved in stagecraft, children's literature, adolescent fiction with the *Zebra* collection, filmmaking with the Golem video. You're always surprising your audience. Is this pattern of versatility continuing? Are you taking art photographs, sculpting?

CP: No, I'm not sculpting or taking art photographs. I began as a painter when I was about nine years old. Some person came off the street into the school I was attending, and he volunteered to teach the students art for a summer to keep them off the street and out of trouble. And for a buck or so an hour. A number of us got together, and he coached us, and he discovered that I had some talent, and he urged me to draw and paint. And I began to draw and paint. Now in my world, which was a very religious world, you didn't waste time drawing and painting. But my father let me alone til I was about thirteen, and then he began to get annoyed, *increasingly* annoyed. And by the time I was fifteen or sixteen I switched the hunger to create from drawing and painting to literature. And literature—well, it's words on paper rather than images. And words on paper my father could make some sort of peace with, and as long as I got my marks in school, he left me alone. That's the way it started. I've been writing ever since I was sixteen or seventeen. From time to time I would go back to drawing and painting. These works on the walls are mine.

DLV: Do you still paint?
CP: I do occasionally.

DLV: What is the impetus for your turning to the stage—dramatizing high-light scenes from *The Promise* [*The Carnival,* 1990], *My Name Is Asher Lev* [*The Gallery,* 1990], *The Book of Lights* [*The Play of Lights,* 1992], and the original composition *Out of the Depths* [1990]—different technical chal-lenges, sheer pleasure in trying something new?

CP: It's a pleasure in trying something new; it's people in the theater world who are asking me to write for the theater. Some have been very successful; some have not been so terribly successful. This recent one, *The Chosen* [drama version, 1999], which was done here in Philadelphia and in Pittsburgh, won the Barrymore Award for best new play. This was done last year.

DLV: A few years ago, when asked when would you retire, you gently replied that writers have no expiration date. Faulkner was always threatening to "break the pencil," but he never did. Bellow has produced a daughter and a new novel [*Ravelstein,* 2000] at age eighty-four. Singer and Malamud wrote to the end. Roth [*The Human Stain,* 2000] in his later sixties has turned into Joyce Carol Oates in productivity. Mailer rolls along [*The Gospel According to the Son,* 1997]. You're certainly not slowing down. Where does the energy, the drive, come from?

CP: It comes from the original drive that starts you going. I don't know what it means to retire. Somebody retires from a job. One day he's in the office, the other day he isn't. A writer writes out of experience, and as long as experience continues, he has stuff to write about. So I'm not sure I under-stand the concept of retirement when it comes to a writer.

DLV: Faulkner always talked about artmaking as a demonic activity, ruth-less, selfish—echoing Melville—that the artist is married to his/her art first. So God help the artist's spouse or significant other. Is the artistic tempera-ment from the *sitra achra,* the "other side"?

CP: Yes, that is a fundamental question, and the first Asher Lev book [*My Name Is Asher Lev,* 1972] deals with that. I think that art is from the "other side" but given to us to use with wisdom, beneficently, so that we can judge "this side." There is nothing in the world that is as powerful an instrumental-ity as art; we can bring it to bear on the foolishness, the mendacity, the hypocrisy, and the hunger we have to create meaning for ourselves. So the artist has an enormous responsibility. I would agree with Asher Lev that he has the responsibility to do the best that he can within the realm of the "other side" in order to make "this side" a better place in which to live. But you've got to plumb the "other side."

DLV: Now you and Adena have a collaborative relationship in that she is your first critical reader—she vets everything—and you have spoken of it as fruitful, supportive, unlike Scott and Zelda Fitzgerald, let us say. How do you make that work?

CP: One makes that work by sheer luck. Pick the right mate from the beginning. And I picked the right mate. It's two people inside the same soul. I was just very lucky.

DLV: How did the ghosting of Isaac Stern's *My First 79 Years* [1999], another surprise for your readers, come about? Or is "ghost" the wrong word. Would "edit" be more accurate?

CP: It's not a ghost and it's not an edit; it's a new idea, and I'm not sure exactly how the thing works. Let me tell you how it happened. My editor, Bob Gottlieb, called me, and he said "How would you like to write Isaac Stern's memoirs?" I knew of Isaac Stern, of course, everybody does, and I said let me meet him. We met for about a minute and a half out of a two-hour meeting. The rest of the two hours we talked about this and that, but that minute and a half was what made me decide to do it. He asked me, "Why do you want to do it?" *He* asked *me*! I said I don't know anything about music including the professionalism of music. He said, "I'll teach you" and that was the end of the conversation. It took us about two years of meetings, questions, answers, and going through his archive. It worked out very well. It's a peculiar kind of writing. I structured the book. I gave it its beginning, its middle, its end, its paragraphs and chapters. But the material of the book is his. The book is a "written with" but in a peculiarly vibrant way.

DLV: Your children's books, *The Tree of Here* [1993] and *The Sky of Now* [1995], collaborations with illustrator Tony Auth, haven't been particularly well received by educational professionals who review for *School Library Journal* and the like. Did something go wrong or did these reviewers get it wrong? They must have sold well since I had trouble acquiring copies.

CP: I'm not sure I know what went wrong with those books. I'm not sure if anything went wrong. I'm not sure I know what that audience demands. I gave them a quiet book with a gentle buildup with no big explosion in the end. What both those books taught me was how to write that kind of story for other kinds of audiences. And that became *Zebra*.

DLV: Yes, *Zebra and Other Stories* [1998] has fared well with those who review adolescent literature. Is this because you were on more familiar ground, in that the sensibility of early and middle teenagers is at the heart of your canon?

CP: That's an interesting question and I don't know what the answer is. In both of those children's stories is a moral core that's very close to my heart. But I don't know if I got the imagination and that core to mix together. I'm going to let time judge those stories. Interestingly enough, of all the stories I have written, *Zebra,* is the least Jewish. *Zebra* is about middle-class children. There is a hard moral core in *Zebra* that somehow I was able to mix perfectly together with the imagination.

DLV: In the *Zebra* collection, you try to update the Potok teenager from the thirties and forties to the eighties and nineties. Still there are no piercings, purple hair, tongue studs, hip hop clothes—the kinds of youthful attire I saw on the streets coming to your home. Are you still getting "with it"?

CP: There is the boy with the blue hair, remember. Those are kids with real problems. Those other problems are surface problems.

DLV: Is *Zebra and Other Stories* intended to be your most extended "secular" fiction? Actually, I discern a lot of spirituality at work in those stories.

CP: You're getting it. Let me point out to you that the first story, "Zebra," has the boy crossing an intersection where he gets hurt, and the last story has a crossing in it too. Those stories are a series of crossings. I'll leave the specifics to the reader. That book is carefully constructed.

DLV: You and your literary contemporaries bristle at the reductive "American Jewish Novelist" label that we academics have tagged you with for our own convenience. Do you find being lumped into the "Children's Literature/ Adolescent Literature" grouping equally confining? Tim Podell's *Good Conversations!* [1997] video series, one of which features you, focus on young people's writers, like Robert Cormier for example, and aim at the huge urban public school market.

CP: I don't find myself confined by any category as long as it enables children to read what I've done. If academicians need labels, fine. As long as we're in the schools and being read.

DLV: Any movie projects in the works, either adaptations of your texts or other involvements like *Myths, Mysteries, and Mysticism: The Golem* [1996]? The rights to *My Name Is Asher Lev* were sold years ago. I remember your cameo in the film of *The Chosen* [1982]. You seem comfortable in front of the camera.

CP: There's constantly been interest in *My Name Is Asher Lev.*

DLV: I'm thinking that *The Gates of November: Chronicles of the Slepak Family* [1996] would make a terrific feature film or at least an HBO original production. Solomon Slepak, the "Old Bolshevik" survivor, is easily the most colorful and interesting character in the story.

CP: Somebody has approached me—I don't know who it was—or approached my agent, I should say. They are talking about a picture of it, of that impossible Bolshevik, who would still be a Bolshevik today.

DLV: Any desire to "trod the boards" yourself like the King and the Duke in *Huck Finn*?

CP: [Loud laugh]. Oh no, my daughter does that very well, but I don't have any desire to "trod the boards."

DLV: In the Podell video interview, you mention a book you're contemplating about senior citizens. Are you going anywhere with that?

CP: In that I'm writing about some of my characters as elders. In my next book I'm taking Davita Chandal into her early seventies.

DLV: From previous interviews, I've sensed that you feel underappreciated critically compared to Bellow, Morrison, et al. Do you also feel that this neglect may be changing? At least fourteen theses and dissertations were devoted to your work in the nineties. I see a reevaluation of your work afoot, led by S. Lillian Kremer, sparked by the innovative paths your work has taken since the special issue of *Studies in American Jewish Literature* in 1985 and Edward A. Abramson's Twayne series book on you in 1986. Isn't it time to re-read you from newer critical perspectives, such as gender theory, postcolonial theory, culture studies?

CP: I think so, but I'm going to leave that to the future. I just want to make one comment and that's very important: when I started, I made a deliberate attempt to cast my work along the most elemental structures of the English language. I can write long sentences. Read *Wanderings* [1978] for proof. I decided, from the point of view of my craft, to deliberately fashion a style that would run counter to the exotica of the world in which I live. It would rub against the exotica. Now that has a tendency to take the material down a bit and simplify it, and it's wrong to think you can do that. So *The Chosen* [1967] and *The Promise* [1969] and *My Name Is Asher Lev* [1972] and all the other books have as their firm foundation the commitment to tell the story, but tell the story simply. On the other hand, underneath all that story-telling is another level of storytelling that has to be gotten at. And that's for the future.

DLV: Over time, critics, especially reviewers for *Commentary,* have pounded away at your style. An *I Am the Clay* reviewer [Ray Olson] called it "bad Pearl Buck." You're "Dreiserian," ouch, the unkindest cut of all. You've said a number of times that your style is a matter of choice and appropriateness. Of course, critics also get after Updike for being too stylish, but they love the ornate rhythms and textures of Morrison. What are they missing with you?

CP: They're missing the essential nature of the story. The story is the important thing. As for *I Am the Clay,* British critics loved its style—and they invented the language.

DLV: Some critics seem to think that, judging from your novels, both your libido and your sense of humor have been surgically removed. Not a fair or true assertion? Actually, both humor and sexuality exist in your work, but in an understated way.

CP: I would agree with that entirely. Especially in my world. The libido is concealed. We did not engage in that kind of open conversation when I was going to school. So it's not overtly in the books. But it's there all right. It's there. You can find it.

DLV: In her review of *The Promise* [1969] in good old *Commentary,* Dorothy Rabinowitz describes your sensibility, with some disdain, as "Jewish American Genteel." Besides throwing up your hands, how else would you respond to that comment?

CP: I don't know what she means. I'm not dealing with the ribald, I'm not dealing with the flesh. I'm dealing with a whole dimension of human activity that has to do with the brain and I'm trying to deal with it honestly. If it isn't fashionable, if it's too brainy—well, let it be fashionable in fifty years.

DLV: Do you feel you get honest reviewing responses or do reviewers push the "Potok button" and go on automatic pilot. Not even the courtesy of a fresh look. I'm thinking of the reception of *The Gift of Asher Lev* [1990].

CP: I don't read all the reviews, so I don't really know what's going on. *The Gift of Asher Lev,* I'm told, got very serious reviews.

DLV: Unlike many of your contemporaries, your work is a "schlemiel-free zone," so to speak. Why no "Gimpel the Fool" [Isaac Bashevis Singer, 1953] and such?

CP: My world is totally different. Others have done the schlemiel thing. I have another take altogether.

DLV: You've had ethnic, religious, doctrinal, and political confrontations in your work, but what about race? Can we expect anything on the order of Malamud's *The Tenants* [1971] from you?

CP: Nothing that's anticipated, right now.

DLV: Sheldon Grebstein, in his piece on *The Chosen* and its popularity,[1] suggests that you "caught a wave," as it were, in 1967 with the Six-Day War, Jewish kids in sometimes violent rebellion against the elders, and the exotic appeal of Hasidim. Any merit to his rationale?

CP: Well I don't know, the original impetus may have been some of that, but the Six-Day War was awhile ago and the book is now an acknowledged classic. I don't know what makes a book a *book*.

DLV: You're very open and accessible, unlike Pynchon and Cormac McCarthy. Even Bellow and Roth largely detest interviews and presenting lectures. Are you a man on a mission like Elie Wiesel? What core message or messages do you hope to communicate to humankind?

CP: The core message is the value of literature. Wherever I speak, I speak about the value of literature: its power, its explosiveness, its fearsomeness, its necessity to grate on the nerve. If there is a core message, that's the core message. To speak about literature as a conveyance, as a means, does two things: one, as much as possible tell the truth; two, as much as possible tell the truth with love. I don't know anyone else who does that.

DLV: Although the conventional wisdom on your work is that it's ultimately affirmative, I see a lot of sadness and darkness in the fiction. Your characters are insomniacs, haunted by hallucinations, or when they do sleep, they are tormented by disturbing dreams. I see your affirmations as more muted, subdued, than Bellow's in *Humboldt's Gift* [1976], for example. Am I misreading you?

CP: No you are not. You are absolutely correct. The haunting is there, the dreams are there, the necessity to balance the dark and the light is there. There is no getting around the fact that we are mortal. Shades haunt us.

History haunts us. And the artist is the one who is the most open to this kind of haunting.

DLV: Can readers expect more variations on the mystical turn we see in *The Book of Lights* [1981], *I Am the Clay* [1992], and some of the recent shorter pieces?
CP: Absolutely.

DLV: You've spoken in some detail in other venues of the profound impact of your time in Korea and the Far East as a chaplain. I see affinities between you and your Asian experiences and Vonnegut's prisoner of war experiences in Dresden as a watershed moment that essentially redesigned your sense of yourself. Have the traumas of Israel had a similar kind of effect on you?
CP: Korea was on my flesh. I experienced Israel from America, and while I experienced it keenly during the formation of the state, I still experienced it differently in the sense that there was distance. I go back and forth to Israel all the time, but Korea was lived intensely. Nothing's been the same since. It's on my flesh.

DLV: After nearly fifty years, reports are just now coming out acknowledging atrocities in the early days of the Korean conflict. Both *The Book of Lights* and *I Am the Clay* imply that Korean massacres weren't all that hidden. Do these developments dredge up some unpleasant memories for you?
CP: They do. We knew about those things—on both sides.

DLV: You've mentioned enjoying Andaatje's work, especially *The English Patient* [1992]. Are you also a Salman Rushdie fan? Some serious core-core conflicts there.
CP: I have mixed feelings about Rushdie. I read the last book [*The Ground Beneath Her Feet,* 2000] and it just went on and on and on. *Midnight's Children* [1980] is a good book.

DLV: What's your Dutch connection? You have some pieces published in the Netherlands that haven't been published here. And *I Am the Clay* is dedicated to your Dutch publisher, Phil Muysson.
CP: He was the one who suggested that I might write something about Korea. There are two or three books in Dutch that haven't come out in the United States. Also *TriQuarterly* is publishing a new short story of mine in the millennial issue they're doing.

DLV: How much Western philosophy, or Eastern for that matter, seeps into your work? After all, you did a Ph.D. in philosophy with a dissertation on Solomon Maimon, among others.

CP: The Ph.D. dissertation was on Kantian epistemology and modern philosophy, and all through *The Chosen* and *The Promise* you see that. I went to the University of Pennsylvania to learn philosophy and Western culture and to think about clashing cultures. That's all I knew to write about. That was going to be my subject. I didn't know how I was going to do it, but that was going to be my subject. I went to Jewish Theological Seminary, not to become a rabbi, but to become an educated Western Jew, not an Eastern European Jew, a Western Jew in the sense of a deep scientific base of knowledge in traditional texts.

DLV: Since culture confrontation is your central theme, and you live so close to the heart of the Amish world, "Christian Hasidim," have you ever thought of fictional treatment of that world?

CP: I have so much to do in my own world that I can't get involved in someone else's, but they are very interesting people.

DLV: What would Franklin think of Philadelphia today? Where have the Quakers gone?

CP: It's not just where the Quakers have gone, it's where has the whole city gone. The grid is gone. And yet you know we are somehow preserving the grid. There is an integrity to Philadelphia. It took Philadelphia a long time to wake up. A major force has been the University of Pennsylvania.

DLV: You've done synagogue class lesson plans and study guides for moral education. Where are today's young people getting moral education if not at home or the public school system? MTV? Comedy Central?

CP: All of the above. There is stuff that's coming out in synagogues and other sources. It's a terrific competition in values. Many of my younger friends who have young children position themselves against the common pop culture. It was very different when I was growing up. But at the same time you have to pick and choose in our common culture because some of it is good. So you're constantly at odds with the world.

DLV: What attracted you to Theo Tobiasse's work so much that you wrote the introduction to his coffee table book [*Tobiasse: Artist in Exile,* 1986]?

CP: My interest in Tobiasse is twofold. One, he provided me with a place where I could write in Southern France, and two, he's a colorist and I love colorists. I like less what he does with it than the fact that he does it. And he's very popular among certain elements in France and Japan. He's never quite made it into the museums. I wrote the introduction for one particular reason that interested me and that is that he was an Anne Frank who succeeded. He was a hidden survivor. He made it.

DLV: Are you comfortable with the electronic revolution? You have a fax machine, e-mail. Do you compose onscreen?

CP: I write it out, then I put it into a computer. I think I'm beginning to learn to write directly on the screen.

DLV: A number of goyische writers you admire were overtly, blatantly, anti-Semitic: Hemingway, Fitzgerald. Do you compartmentalize when it comes to Robert Cohn or Meyer Wolfshiem?

CP: Let me give you a take on Robert Cohn. But first let me talk about Hemingway. Hemingway and Fitzgerald and some of the others were of a category of anti-Semitism that was midwestern anti-Semitic, clichéd, and didn't really understand what they were talking about. Hemingway had very good, close friends who were Jewish. Not only could Hemingway be an anti-Semite, but an anti-Protestant, an anti-Catholic. He was of that mental set. Hemingway is, was, and will forever be a certain category of midwestern American who is anti-everything. And anti-nothing. That's the important thing. And so is Fitzgerald. This does not entail demonic anti-Semitism, however.

Robert Cohn, while he is not inside Hemingway's world of values, is really an interesting person. He worries about the bulls, he worries about human relationships, he worries about Brett. He represents an aspect of human values that, if you shift the focus, says to you maybe he's a pretty good guy. Who says that Hemingway's point of view is the right point of view? And as for Meyer Wolfshiem, he's a Jewish rogue—and there are Jewish rogues.

DLV: You and Douglas Coupland echo each other in your belief that a human life has to have a narrative line, a story. According to Coupland, Generation X members have no master narrative. What about Generation X Jews? Edward Margolies, writing [in *Yiddish,* 1987] on *The Book of Lights,* suggests that American Jewry is so comfy and assimilated that no creative tensions exist any more; hence, no plot. Does he have a point?

CP: It's impossible to tell. The minute we say that along comes somebody with a whole new take on something. I don't think any generation is so comfortable that they can't find something that rubs them the wrong way. I would leave that open. God knows there's a lot of tension in American Jewry but it's of a different kind. Assimilation, how to discover one another, how to live with different aspects of the Jewish tradition and blend them all simultaneously. It's a very different kind of Judaism from the Judaism that's going on in Israel. They don't understand what we're doing here; they have no clue as to what's going on in America. Because this is a new kind of Judaism altogether. A lot of it is made up of non-Jews coming to Judaism who are changing the face of Judaism. So I think we're going to need another generation of this kind of Judaism before we see what the culture mix is going to be. There's no predicting what it's going to be. But somebody will write of it.

DLV: Part of Jewish belief is that species humankind must complete creation. Environmental scientists tell us that we are quite rapidly trashing creation, so we'll destroy ourselves long before Earth is an iceball circling a fried sun. Dr. Potok, give us some cosmology here. Where are homo sapiens headed?

CP: That's the big question. I don't know what the answer is. Forever, we have been at odds with ourselves. We're not on this planet for a long time. For the longest time of that not long time we have been constantly killing each other. I don't know what the answer is, but clearly the hope is, the dream is, that somehow we create a balance between what our needs and wants are, and what we have to achieve on this planet. We are jungle animals brought recently into civilization and still trying to deal with our jungle natures.

DLV: As an old college ballplayer, I was struck by a comment you made in a 1986 interview with Elaine M. Kauvar that you were quite athletic in your youth. Reminisce, please.

CP: I loved play and sports. Ringalevio, stickball, sandlot baseball. I played all the time. Then I started high school and I had less time for sports. But up until college I loved sports. And then in the summer when we were away at camp, I loved tennis, rowing. I fished. Those were glorious years. And then came the seminary and instead of fishing, I worked.

DLV: Whatever happened to Herman Harold [Chaim Tzvi]? Is he still around somewhere the way James Gatz was within Jay Gatsby?

CP: That's a good question. I haven't been Herman Harold since high school. I want to think about that. I don't know where he's living.

DLV: Tell us about the next Davita Chandal book, the one in progress. We have two Chandal stories since *Davita's Harp* [1985]: "The Seven of the Address";[2] and "The Trope Teacher."[3]

CP: It's about one-third completed. I'm working now on a section in which a Holocaust survivor, an architect, is asked to design a Holocaust memorial, and he simply cannot bring himself to design it.

DLV: Dr. Potok, thank you for your time and graciousness.

CP: You're welcome. My pleasure.

Notes

1. "The Phenomenon of the Really Jewish Best-Seller: Potok's *The Chosen.*" *Studies in American Jewish Literature* 1.1 (1975): 23–31.

2. *Winter's Tales.* New Series 8. Ed. Robin Baird-Smith. New York: St. Martin's, 1993. 77–99.

3. 1992 in Holland; *TriQuarterly* 101 (1997–98): 15–83.

Index

OBSES

The
Obsession
Duet

1

*P*aranoia skates down my spine as I walk a little bit faster down the sidewalk. The cold night air fills my lungs, and my heartbeat thuds loudly in my ears. All I can see and feel is that creeper from the party coming up to me and grabbing my wrist. His fingers biting into my flesh. The smell of alcohol on his breath as he spoke into my face.

"Dance with me..." He didn't ask, he demanded, and there was no way I was going anywhere with him, so I kicked him in the nuts and left the party. But now I can't help but feel like he's following me.

Reaching the end of the sidewalk, I chance looking over my shoulder. My gaze falls on nothing but darkness. The light pole above my head does very little to illuminate the street, and when I look back again before crossing the street, I find someone walking toward me.

Panic bubbles up inside of me, and this time, I start running. The air rips through my hair, and my lungs burn as fear implants itself deep in my gut.

Run. Don't look back. Just keep running.

Cutting down a side street, I hope to throw the guy off, but as I continue running, I can still hear his footfalls behind me. This has to be a nightmare, something I'll wake up from any second now.

Glancing over my shoulder, I realize it's anything but a dream. My eyes catch on the plaid pattern of the man's shirt. Instantly, I know this is the creep from the party. *Shit.* Instinct tells me to run, but deep in my gut, I know what I should do.

My hands shake as I try and pull my phone out to dial 9-1-1, but my fingers slip over the sleek device, and I keep putting the wrong passcode in. Panting, I make it underneath an illuminating streetlamp and force shallow breaths into my lungs.

A grunting sound meets my ears, and when I look over my shoulder again, the man is gone. Just gone, vanished like he wasn't there at all.

Dazed, I stare at the exact spot he was in, fearing he'll reappear any second, but he doesn't. A strange calmness washes over me. It makes zero sense, but I don't dwell on it long enough to digest it. Instead, I shove my phone back into my pocket and run the rest of the way home.

By the time I reach my apartment, the exertion is evident, I'm gasping, and a sheen of sweat has formed against my forehead. I fumble with my keys, almost dropping them before finally getting the damn door open. Once inside, I slam the door closed and lock it before turning and sagging against the door.

A moment later, Max is by my side. The eleven-year-old cat I rescued from being euthanized last year has been my most trusted friend. I sink my fingers into his long fur and let his low purring calm me.

You're okay, everything is okay... I repeat to myself.

It's been years since I'd felt fear like that, not since I was a little girl living in foster care. My skin crawls, and I suppress the thought.

All that matters is that I'm safe. That I'm in my apartment and nothing happened to me.

Everything is going to be okay...

2

Slamming my fist into the fucker's face, I watch with glee as agony overtakes his features. He should've known he would die, especially after touching what was mine.

An image of *my* beautiful Dove fighting to get away from him. Her big, blue eyes brimmed with fear, her plump bottom lip trembling. Clenching my fist, I let the anger from that memory sink deep into my bones.

"What were you planning to do when you got her alone? Huh? Why were you following her?" I growl, my patience withering away with every passing second. Part of me doesn't want to know what he had planned, but the other, bigger part does. I want to hear the words, want them to fuel my anger even more.

"I don't know what the fuck you're talking about," the bastard sneers, playing stupid.

I cock my head to the side and give him a bemused expression. "You must think I'm a fucking idiot, huh? That I didn't see her tell you no. That she didn't push you away? Or that I didn't watch her run out of the house and down the street? That I didn't see you follow a short while later."

If it wasn't for me, he would've hurt her, but I *was* there, just as I've always been. And just like all the others who have tried to hurt Dove, he too will die at my hands.

"You're fucking crazy!" he spits. Blood drips down his lip from the punch I landed against it, and all I can do is stare at it. I can't stop the cruel smile that splits across my face. My blood sings with joy, and the dark beast inside me cheers with elation at the sight of his blood.

Grabbing him by the hair, I tip his head back, reveling in the scream that pierces the air. *Ahhh, there is nothing like when they scream or beg for me to let them go.* The hope that shows in their faces before all is lost. Before I snuff the light out of their eyes with my hands.

"Crazy? You haven't seen anything yet," I sneer.

Clenching my fist a little tighter, I pull back my arm and land another punch, this time, my knuckles meet the bridge of his nose and the satisfying crunch of bone cracking fills my ears.

The monster inside me is terrifying, real, and it consumes me. I don't stop as his screams continue to echo through the warehouse. They all cry and beg, but at the end of the day, it's their own fault. Had they made a better choice, they wouldn't be here.

By the time I'm done, his face is unrecognizable, and he's slumped over in the chair I've tied him to. Turning, I grab a knife and lift his chin, or what's left of it. Then I slice him from ear to ear. I feel nothing as I do this, no that's not true. I feel something. Joy, happiness, relief. His death makes the weight on my chest a little lighter.

Dove is safer now that I've extinguished him. Safer now that another worthless person is gone from her life. Another person wanting to hurt her that won't ever get the chance.

I was put on this Earth to protect her, to ensure her safety as long as I lived.

I might never have her in the way I want, but at least I can always make certain no one hurts her. She will forever be mine, even if she doesn't know it.

Walking away from the body, I head to the sink and wash the blood from my hands. I spend way too long watching the reddened water swirl down the drain. When it finally runs clear, I scrub my hands with soap, rinse, and dry them. Pulling out my cell, I text Rob to tell him to get the cleanup crew together.

Most people would probably feel guilt or at least some type of emotion after doing what I just did, but I don't feel anything.

Not that I can't feel at all, because I can, I just chose not to. Feeling all the time would make it hard for me to kill people for the mob, on top of protecting Dove.

My phone chimes and I see Rob's name flash across the screen, letting me know that he's gotten my message. When he arrives, I walk out to my car like nothing ever happened. I consider just driving home, but at the last second turn onto the street to Dove's place.

She lives in a relatively safe area, but that didn't stop me from putting cameras and motion sensors in her house. I would go to any length to ensure her complete safety. Even in the safest neighborhood in the country, no one knows what happens behind closed doors.

Parking on the street a few houses down, I shut the car off, and look up at the apartment building. *How much longer can I do this?*

Subject myself to her sweet scent, soft murmurs, and beautiful face. How much longer can I go on before I'm forced to claim her? My need for her is starting to consume me, eating away at every single rational thought that I have. Every day I'm forced to tamp it down, but I'm not a saint, and soon enough, I'll break.

Forcing the thoughts away before they take root, I exit the car and walk across the street at a leisurely pace. It's quiet, and if you look hard enough, you might see a few stars hanging in the night sky. When I reach the door to the apartment building, I slide my keycard into the door, waiting for the click to push it open. No one even glances my way as I walk inside. I've been here so many times most people probably think I live here.

In fact, I know one of Dove's neighbors actually thinks I do. Of course, I don't correct her. What would be the fun in that? I use the walk upstairs to clear my mind, and by the time I reach Dove's door, I'm a little more composed. Pulling out my phone, I check the surveillance feed in her bedroom one last time. The image confirms that she's sound asleep, tucked nicely into her bed. Unlocking her door, I enter her apartment slowly. I've done this so many times it's like riding a bike to me.

Quietly, I close the door behind me. I'm welcomed by the darkness of the apartment, feeling at home in more than one way. The dark is where I thrive and the shadows my best friend. It's the only place I can be myself. But Dove, she is light, pure, vibrant, and innocent. My darkness threatens to taint that light, to snuff it out... and that reminder alone keeps me away, but never too far.

I've only taken one small step inside, but Max is right there, curling his fury body around my leg, purring loud enough to wake the dead. He, too, thinks I live here. Bending down, I pat the top of his head before shushing him away.

The soles of my shoes make little noise as I move through the house like a ghost. I know where every corner, every creak, and every piece of furniture is. I know about every window and every door, and even what's hidden in each cupboard. I know how she likes her coffee, what her favorite books are, and what time she gets up every morning.

There isn't one thing about Dove that I don't know about. I know her inside and out, maybe even better than I know myself.

Standing just outside her half-open door, I clench my jaw. Her sweet scent of vanilla and sugar surrounds me. The scent stirs a deep primal need within me. One that urges me to go to her and claim her completely, without mercy or care. It slams into me, gripping me by the balls and urging me forward. I don't want her to be mine. I need her to be mine.

Swallowing thickly, I grapple for control. The beast wanting to be set free so he can mark her. Barely containing myself, I sneak into the bedroom. There's a tightening in my stomach when I first see her. It's like butterflies taking flight, like riding a roller coaster. She's lying partly on her stomach, her cheek resting against the sheets.

Dark brown locks of hair shield most of her face, and I'm forced to suppress a laugh, realizing she's kicked most of her blanket to the edge of the bed. Parts of her are still the same, while others have changed. Drinking in the view before me, I become mesmerized by her perfect legs that lead up to a plump ass. Her firm globes are covered by a pair of sleep shorts that leave very little to the imagination. Saliva fills my mouth at the thought of parting those thighs and licking her virgin pussy, feasting on it, eating until I've had my fill.

Fuck, I wonder what she would taste like; if she would beg me to stop or beg me to keep going? My muscles clench, and my cock presses against the zipper of my jeans painfully. It'd be so easy to take her right now, to cover her mouth and take what I want, to sink deep inside of her and let her innocence coat my cock... Taking a step toward the bed, I almost give in to the urge, but at the last second, I pause and curl my hands into fists to stop myself from touching her.

One taste would never be enough. I could never give her up, so I'll refuse myself while I still have the strength. Letting my gaze wander, I move to her heart-shaped face. Long lashes fanning out like crescent moons against high cheeks. Soft, pink lips that are slightly parted, and an adorable button nose. *My angel.*

I don't know how long I stand staring at her, watching as her forehead wrinkles, and she rolls over, tossing her leg over a pillow.

Every inch of me is being pulled toward her, and when I can't withstand the burn any longer, when the pain in my chest becomes too much, I pick up the blanket and cover her back up. She murmurs something inaudible in her sleep, and I force myself to walk away even when everything inside me is screaming to go back there.

This is something I put myself through almost every night. Loving Dove is my greatest weakness, but I won't give it up... I can't. No matter what I do, no matter how many people I kill, she will always be mine. The devil already owns too much of my soul for me to allow myself to let her go.

The love I have for her is the only good thing left in my life, the only thing pure, and that's why I won't ever take from her. I won't ever hurt her because if I ever do, then there would be no light left in me, and the darkness would swallow me whole.

Without a sound, I leave her apartment and walk back out to my car. Each step is heavier than the last. *When will I stop putting us both through this pain? Never.*

Maybe I would have an easier life if she wasn't in it. If I would just let her go and stop watching her. But I will never stop because Dove deserves a happy life. She needs to be safe, and someone needs to protect her from the monster who lurks in the dark.

And who is better to protect her from them than one of them?

3

No matter what I do. I can't shake the strange feeling that I'm being watched, it's been like this for years. Going to the grocery store, on the drive to work, even in my apartment. It always feels like there are eyes on me, but every time I look up, there's nothing there. No one is watching, at least not that I can see. I do my best to brush off the feelings, but it's a lot harder than you'd think.

I'm pretty sure no one is actually watching me. I mean, why would someone do that? I'm no one. It makes more sense that I've imagined all of this, especially after the incident with the creeper the other night.

This is my body's way of staying guarded after having a shitty childhood. At least that's what the therapist tells me. I keep thinking about stopping seeing her because I'm tired of being reminded of the past. I don't care to remember my time in foster care, and I honestly don't understand why I keep finding myself going to the appointments.

Stopping by my favorite coffee place on the corner, I order an iced coffee hoping the caffeine will make me feel better. By the time I get to the shelter, I've downed the large cup and feel no better. Except now, my bladder is screaming at me. I rush inside, heading straight for the bathroom.

Stupid coffee.

"Good morning," Sasha greets me as I rush past her.

"Morning," I call as I slip into the bathroom. Sighing, I empty my bladder and vow never to drink that much coffee that fast again. When I'm done, I wash my hands and walk back out into the receptionist area.

"Too much coffee?" Sasha giggles.

"You know it," I admit. "I don't know when I will ever learn." I shake my head.

"We got two new surrenders this morning. One of them is a puppy," Sasha tells me. "They only had the dog for three weeks, then realized they would have to actually spend time training the dog not to pee and poop in the house."

"Ugh, why do people get dogs if they can't take care of them? At least the puppy will be easy to adopt out."

Making my first round through the shelter, I make sure all the animals have water and that their cages are clean. There isn't much I can do for all these poor creatures, but at least I can make sure they're taken care of while they're here. Make sure they're fed, warm, and get some human interaction.

Stopping at the last cage that holds the new puppy, I smile. It's some kind of shepherd mix, but its breed doesn't matter, not when it's as cute as it is.

"Yeah, you definitely won't last long, not with that face." The pup is looking at me with big, brown eyes and a wagging tail. It isn't unusual for me to talk to the animals. I don't feel bad or weird about it. Not when the truth is, I'd rather talk to them than to another human.

"Did you see him?" Sasha coo's when I head back to my desk.

Withholding an eye roll, I nod. "Yes, I saw him, and no, you cannot take him home with you. Henry would shit bricks if you brought another dog home."

Her lip curls into a frown. "Maybe I should get rid of him then? The dogs never let me down." This is an ongoing thing with Sasha, she loves Henry, and he loves her, but they're always fighting about something.

"Tell me, are you on or off again?"

"Neither."

"Right..." I shake my head.

"What about you? You find anyone to share that huge apartment with yet?" I shoot her a look that says, *really?*

"I don't date, Sasha. You know this."

"Sorry, I thought maybe you met someone the other night, and that's why you left so early. I didn't even get to ask you what happened?"

Goosebumps pebble my flesh at the reminder. "Yeah, about that, I, uhh... I left because there was this guy that wouldn't leave me alone. He followed me when I left, and then right before I was going to call 9-1-1, he disappeared."

Sasha stares at me wide-eyed. "Holy shit, are you okay? Why didn't you call me and tell me what happened?"

Truthfully, calling Sasha wasn't even something I'd think to do. All my life, I've been alone. I didn't know how to rely on someone else because it had only ever been me.

"I don't know. I just... I was thankful that I had gotten away. I'm really lucky... it could've been much worse."

The thought of being raped and beaten, and then left in a gutter somewhere makes my stomach churn. You hear about it all the time in this city, but no one ever thinks it will happen to them, not until it does.

"Not to sound like a total bitch because I do care about you and would never want anything to happen to you, but you're the luckiest person I know. I mean, the guy just disappears? That never happens, and now that I'm thinking about it, you seem to be lucky all the time."

My brow furrows in confusion. "What do you mean? I'm not lucky."

Sasha gives me a disbelieving look. "Really? You don't actually believe that, do you?" When I don't say anything, she continues, "Let's take your apartment, for example. It's in one of the safest, nicest areas of the city. The rent there is insanely low, and the waitlist for that place is like a mile long. Yet, you somehow got in, and on top of that, you got a discounted rate on your rent."

"Yeah, I still don't know how that happened either." I truly don't. All I did was submit an application and hope for the best.

"What about how you got your car? The guy just wanted it gone so badly, he gave it to you for a fraction of the cost? Then, after all of that, even brought it to you because you didn't have a way to get over there. Come on, you've got to see it too?"

"I mean, I see it, but I don't know if I would consider it luck."

Sasha rolls her eyes. "Girl, start playing the lottery because you're a good luck charm."

All I can do is shake my head and laugh at her. I'm not lucky, not really, right? As we work throughout the day, answering calls and setting the animals up to find their forever homes, I can't shake the conversation away and come to the conclusion that I truly am lucky.

I escaped death the other night, or at least something that would've been close to it. I went to college and got a nice place to live, and a car for a really good price. This job even fell into my lap, so I suppose I agree with Sasha a little, though I won't tell her that.

It'll go straight to her blonde head.

Doing our final walkthrough, I stop at the new puppy's cage. "Don't worry, buddy, you won't be here for long."

"Who are you talking to?" A voice startles me, and I jump back half a foot and grip onto my chest, my heart beating right out of it. Looking to the side, I see Shawn standing only a few feet from me.

"Jesus, Shawn, you scared me," I say, the words coming out in a rush as I try and calm myself.

Giving me a dimpled grin, he says, "Sorry, didn't mean to use my ninja skills on you."

"Next time you scare me like that, I might need to use *my* ninja skills on you. Which consists of a punch in the face." I say, smiling.

"Whoa." He puts up his hands, showing me his palms in surrender. "Easy killer. I'll try not to sneak up on you anymore."

"You better, for your own safety," I joke. Shawn has been working here for a few weeks now, and we've quickly become friends. We joke and laugh together all the time, which are two things I always welcome. Plus, it helps that he's good looking, not that I spend my day checking him out or anything. It's hard to ignore his dreamy, blue eyes, and model-like features.

"So... I was actually wondering what you're doing tonight?" he asks as we are walking back to the front.

"Tonight? Ahh..." I look at him wide-eyed. Is he trying to ask me out? "Nothing, I guess," I finally say.

"Cool, I was wondering if you wanted to grab something to eat... with me?"

"Yes," I blurt out before thinking about it. *Way to sound desperate, Dove.*

Shawn chuckles. "Okay, I guess that's a yes. Do you just want to meet there, or I can swing by your place, and we can go together?" He shoves his hands into the front pockets of his jeans. I should probably meet him somewhere, but I've always dreamt of going on a real date where the guy comes to the house and picks you up, so I push the paranoia away. Plus, it's been forever since I went on a date or was asked out on one.

I smile up at him, my belly filling with butterflies. "Yeah, that would be great."

"I'll pick you up at six. Send me a text with your address." We pause in the foyer, and when he smiles at me, my heart skips a beat.

"Uh, yeah..." I stutter. Jesus, I need to work on my skills. Shawn waves goodbye to Sasha and then winks at me before walking out. As soon as he's out of earshot, Sasha pounces.

"Oh, my god, he finally asked you out. Jesus, I never thought that was going to happen. The boy has been watching you since he started."

My cheeks start to warm. "He has not!"

Sasha nods. "Yup, and now you've gone and made his dreams come true."

"It's just a date, not like we're getting married or anything."

"*Yet...* not getting married yet."

Ignoring her, I get my stuff together and prepare for my drive home. I can't believe I have a date. A real date. Not that I'd have a fake date or something, or that I'm so ugly that no one finds me attractive, but it isn't often that guys ask me on dates. Usually, I find I have to build up the courage to do it.

"I'm so proud of you, Dove. Maybe tonight will be the night." Sasha wiggles her eyebrows.

"Shut up," I say, laughing as I get into my car.

∼

AFTER SPENDING an hour curling my hair, I move on to my makeup. I don't wear it often, mostly due to my lack of skill when it comes to putting it on. Taking my time, I apply the foundation, add some eye shadow, and only manage to stab myself twice in the eye with the mascara. After, I walk into the bedroom and start pulling every dress I own from the closet.

Yes, I know it's just a date, and we see each other every day at work, but I want Shawn to see me as more than the girl in always sees in jeans and a T-shirt. I want him to maybe wonder what's underneath. Shaking my head at the thought, I find a cute dress and decide to pair it with some dark tights and heels.

For a moment, I stand in front of the mirror in my bra and panties, trying not to look at my reflection, but like a magnet, my eyes are drawn to it. It's like the sun, you know it will hurt your eyes, but you still want to look at it.

As soon as I see myself in the mirror, my eyes find the ugly scar marring my otherwise smooth stomach. My hand raises on its own to touch the raised skin. It's an old habit I can't seem to shake. Running my fingers over that horrendous scar, I try not to let the memories of how I got it bubble up.

Instead, I worry about what Shawn might think if he gets a chance to see it. Will he think I'm disgusting? Will he ask questions? Would I be able to answer? Pushing all of those concerns aside, I grab the dress and start slipping into it.

Once dressed, I smooth my hands down the front of the dress and look at myself in the mirror.

I can't help but smile at how well put together I look. Applying a thin layer of gloss to my lips, I give myself the once over one last time and then make a beeline to the kitchen for my phone, purse, and a light jacket.

Checking the time, I bubble over with excitement, realizing he should be here soon. Sitting on the couch, I wait like a child on Christmas morning. Max greets me with a purr as he brushes against my leg, begging for attention as he always does.

Scratching the top of his head, I look down at him. "I can't believe it, Max. I've got a date." I'd hate to be that crazy cat lady who sits at home and talks to her cats, but if I don't get a roll on this whole dating train, that's the path I'm headed down.

Anxiously, I watch the clock, and my excitement slowly turns to disappointment as the minutes continue to tick by without any sign of Shawn.

Opening my text messages, I check to make sure I gave him the right address, which I did. I contemplate sending him a message, and after going back and forth over it, I decide to keep it simple and just ask if he's still coming. Maybe he had something come up? Maybe he can't figure out where I live? I try and come up with any excuse I can, but deep down, I know it's not really any of those things.

It's pitiful how long I stare at my phone, waiting for a text message to come through that never does. An ache forms in my chest after a short time, and stupidly, tears fill my eyes and slide down my cheeks. I swipe at the treacherous tears, wishing I didn't care so much.

There must be something wrong with me. I know I'm not that pretty, but I don't think I'm worthy of always being left in the cold. Every time I have a date, they either don't show, or there is never a second one even though the first goes great.

Swallowing down the pity I'm feeling, I change out of the dress and into an oversized T-shirt and then go into the bathroom and wash my face. It's obvious, he's not coming, and even more obvious, he doesn't plan to apologize for standing me up.

When I'm done, I crawl into my bed and pull the covers over my head.

What is wrong with me? Am I that repulsive? I don't want to think about it, but maybe I'm not meant to be with anyone. Maybe I'll actually become the cat lady with thirty cats, and her virginity intact. God, I hope not, but what are my other options? I can't find a guy who wants me if I can't get him to ever go on a second date, let alone a first.

After a while, I doze off, hoping tomorrow will be a better day.

4

*H*er tears kill me more than anything. I'm a bastard for doing this to her, but I can't help it. The thought of seeing her with another guy is unbearable. It's easier to make the guy disappear than let her think she'll ever have a future with him.

The organ in my chest tightens as I watch her crawl into bed on my cell phone screen. I wish I could wipe her tears away. Tell her that everything is going to be okay. That she has me forever and doesn't need anyone else.

I doubt she would welcome me with open arms into her life. If she knew the things I'd done, and continue to do, how obsessed with her I am... how closely I watch her, and how often I'm inside her house, she'd be terrified, and I never want to see her look at me with fear in her eyes.

Shoving my phone back into my pocket, I look out at the bright neon sign that's flashing back at me. I had just finished with the Shawn guy when Christian called me for a job. He asked me to swing by Venus, the mob's strip club.

Upstairs is the strip club, but downstairs they maintain a brothel. Everyone in this town is paid off, the cops, the judges, any one of importance is paid blood money to keep their mouth shut because when you fuck with the wrong people, they send me to take care of you.

Forcing myself out of the car, I make sure my gun is secure in the shoulder holster hidden beneath my jacket before I walk up to the back door. I make sure I have at least one weapon on me at all times. You never know when shit will hit the fan, and I'd rather be the one with a gun than without one.

Lifting my closed fist to the door, I knock three times in quick succession. A moment later, the door is pushed open, and Diego, Christian's right-hand, greets me. He looks more like a bear than human; huge, and muscular, with a face full of hair. His arms alone look like tree trunks, reminding me I should probably spend a little more time in the gym. Every inch of exposed skin is either tattooed or scared from the hundreds of fights he's been in.

"Zane," He says gruffly.

I nod my head to greet him. "Diego."

He gestures toward the hall. "Boss has been waiting for you. He's in his office." As if the boss would be anywhere else. Girls rush past me completely naked, but I don't even glance their way. I lost my appetite for other women years ago. I used to fuck girls that looked like Dove, but even that wasn't enough. There's only one fucking woman for me. And if I can't have her, I won't have anyone.

When I reach the door to Christian's office, I don't even knock. There's no point, not when he's expecting me. Opening the door, I find him sitting behind his desk, a glass of amber liquid placed in front of him. His face is blank as always, refusing to give away any emotion.

I've worked for the Sergio family since I was a teenager. He somehow got me out of prison even though I was supposed to spend a few more years behind bars. He saw something in me and let me work for him. Slowly, I worked my way up, and now I'm one of his most trusted men.

"You're late," he says. I want to tell him it's five fucking minutes, but I don't feel like arguing tonight.

"Do you have a job, or did you just call me in here so you could bust my balls?" I slam down into one of the seats in front of the mahogany desk.

"I like you, Zane, you don't walk in here with fright, or like a death sentence awaits on the other side, and you have a sense of humor."

He smiles or at least attempts to. It looks more like a grimace than anything. Christian is considerably older than me, and I think he lost the ability to smile before I was born. His black and gray hair is slicked back, and his face looks weathered, but that could be simply from doing this shit for years.

I shrug. "It's not like you're going to kill me. I'm the one dealing out death. Plus, I doubt if you wanted me dead, you would do it here."

He grabs his glass and takes a gulp of the liquid before setting the crystal glass back down. He stares at me intently—other men would be intimidated, but not me—and says, "First, I wanted to let you know that things with the Castro family are tense. They've been intercepting some of our drugs and undermining some other deals. If things continue the way they are, I might have a few jobs coming up for you. I'll need you to handle those more silently than normal. No one can know that I'm the one calling the hits."

"Okay." That's a far cry from my normal job because usually Christian likes everybody to know who is responsible for the deaths I deal out. He's known for being ruthless and killing for petty reasons. Once you're on his shitlist, your days are numbered. So, I won't deny that I'm a little curious, but not enough to ask any questions.

"That won't be a problem. Give me a list, and I'll get the job done."

"Besides the Castros, it seems like the Rossi Family is looking for a fight as well."

"Rossi, as in Xander Rossi?" I say, raising a skeptical eyebrow at him. Xander doesn't look for fights, and most know better than to fuck with him.

Christian frowns and takes a large gulp of his whiskey. He finishes the glass and slams it down onto the desk before grabbing the bottle and pouring himself another. "Yeah, the one and only."

I shouldn't ask, not that it matters, but I'm curious... far more curious than I should be. "How did you end up on his radar?"

He shakes his head like he's trying to banish away a bad dream. "It doesn't matter. What matters is staying off his radar for now. We can take care of him once I deal with the Castros, but until then, I need to stay on Xander's good side."

"Got it. Play nice with the Rossi family... *for now.*"

He takes another drink. "Perfect. I do have a different job I want you to do right now, and it's a bit time-sensitive."

Where the hell are all these stipulations coming from?

"You know any job you need, I can get done. Why're you dragging your feet, Christian?"

"Your next job is a woman. I'll have Diego give you the folder with all of the details, but I need her dead within three days, and I want her body brought here. The boys will take care of it."

That little tidbit of information surprises me because typically, I have my cleanup crew take care of the bodies, but I don't say shit. Women, men, doesn't matter to me. All I see is a paycheck when I look at them, not a name, a family or a future. It's easier that way.

"Zane, have you listened to a fucking word I've said?" Christian snaps.

"Of course." I swirl the amber liquid in my glass. "Are we done here?"

"Yes, but I want you to stick around for a little fun. I got a couple new girls, and every time I offer you one, you decline. You like cock, Z? 'Cause I don't care what floats your boat. I can get you a pretty boy in here too."

"Fuck no," I sneer. "Just because I don't take up your offer doesn't mean I don't like pussy." I'm pissed that he would even say such a stupid fucking thing.

"What's the problem then? You don't like my girls? Or do you have a woman waiting for you at home?" There's a dark glint in his eyes that makes me want to smash his face into a pile of mush, but I tamp down my rage. I wouldn't ever consider telling him about Dove, not in a million years, and acting on my anger, however tempting, wouldn't be worth it.

There's always someone else to think about before I make my next move.

"Why would I have a woman in my life? They're only trouble." I say, staring at him blankly, not giving away a single thing. He thinks simply because I work for him that I'll kiss his ass and take any job he tosses my way, but what he doesn't know is I'm the real boss.

He grins. "Good, then you'll take my offer tonight. I've got a girl in one of the VIP rooms willing and waiting for you. Go blow off some steam and consider it a thank you gift for all the work you're going to be doing soon."

I consider declining, so I can go check on Dove before returning to my empty apartment, but I don't want to deal with Christian questioning me anymore. Keeping Dove a secret is essential to keeping her safe. Every single thing I do is for her, well, minus the killing; that's just to keep my impulses in check.

"Fine, you know where to find me if you need me." Pushing out of the chair, I leave his office and head in the direction of the VIP rooms.

When I enter the room, it's bathed in darkness except for a red light that's placed above a leather couch. On that couch is a naked brunette waiting for me. She smiles and climbs off the couch to walk over to me as soon as I enter the room, but I lift a hand and shake my head.

I don't plan to let the girl anywhere near me, but no one needs to know that. I'll give the woman a fat tip, and she'll keep her mouth shut, and if she doesn't... well, I'll get rid of her.

"Here's how this is going to go. I'm going to give you a couple hundred dollars, and you're going to tell your boss that we fucked, and it was great. If I find out that you tell him anything else, I'll slit your throat and watch you bleed out. Do you understand?" Her big eyes grow even bigger, and she takes a step back as if she knows being too close to me is bad.

"I swear, I won't say anything else." Her voice is as shaky as her legs.

"Sit on the couch."

"I... I won't tell anyone anything... please, please don't hurt me." She starts to cry, and I damn near lose it.

Breathing through my nose, I exhale, trying to calm myself. "I'm not going to hurt you. Not unless you don't follow my directions."

The girl doesn't say anything else and wraps her arms around her middle while watching me closely. Soft cries fill the air, but they annoy me more than anything. I've seen so many men and women cry, begging, and pleading for their lives that I'm all but immune to it.

After subjecting myself to her cries for twenty minutes, I pull out my wallet and toss two crisp hundred-dollar bills at her.

"Remember what I said..." I give her one last look before leaving the room. On my way out of the strip club, Diego hands me the folder with my next hits information. I wait until I'm in the confines of my car before I open the envelope.

The picture of the target slips from my fingers and falls to my feet. I'm about to reach for it, but then I catch the name printed in black ink before me. My heart stops, and air stills in my petrified lungs. My chest is so tight, I fear it will explode as I read the name over and over again.

No! It can't be.

5

Shawn doesn't come to work the next day, nor does he answer any of my text messages. I tell myself that it probably has nothing to do with me, but that's hard to believe when everything was fine before we agreed to go on a date.

Leaving work in a flurry, I drive across down to my therapist's office. I've been thinking more and more about stopping my appointments but haven't gotten the nerve to do it yet. They've helped a lot over the years and been a great outlet for me, but if I'm ever going to move on, I need to stop living in the past.

As I walk into Sharon's office, the hairs on the back of my neck stand on end, and a sickening feeling coats the inside of my belly. It's like tar clinging to my organs. I should be used to having this kind of feeling by now. The truth is, it never gets easier, only worse.

I wait in the waiting room, which is mostly empty, minus a man reading the paper in the corner of the room. I'm not sure why, but my attention is drawn to him, and I stare for a long time. There is something about him, but I can't pinpoint it.

He doesn't pay me any attention since he's far too focused on his paper. Unable to shake the sense of familiarity, I almost wish he would look over at me, so I can see his eyes full on. There's a pounding in my head, and my body warms all over. It's the strangest thing I've ever experienced in my life.

"Dove," Sharon calls my name, breaking the connection, and gives me a warm smile.

I stand up quickly, feeling flustered for some reason. Like I just got caught doing something I shouldn't be doing.

"Hi," I say and walk into her office. Taking my usual seat across from her, I shake whatever *that* just was off and focus on my session.

Sharon is middle-aged, divorced, and has three kids. She's been my therapist since Donna adopted me when I was a teenager, and she knows everything there is to know about me.

She stares at me, her soft eyes bleeding into mine. "How have things been?"

"Fine." I lick my lips. "I, uhh... got asked on a date."

Sharon's face lights up. "That's great. Tell me about it. How did it go?"

Defeat sits heavily on my chest. Maybe I shouldn't have started our session with this. Nonetheless, I tell her, anyway. "We never went because he never showed up. I texted him to see if he was still coming, but he never messaged back, and I haven't heard from him at all." My gaze falls to the floor. "This happens to me all the time. Someone shows interest, and then I somehow mess it up. I don't even know what I do wrong. Whatever it is must be bad because I never hear from them again."

"How does that make you feel?"

I look up at Sharon and give her an *are you serious* look. "Like I'm not good enough, obviously. Or like something is wrong with me. Why would he not show up? Why would they never call?" I deflate against the couch with disappointment. "I would get it if they'd seen my scar or found out how messed up in my head I am, but they don't even get that far."

"There's nothing wrong with you, Dove. You know that. You have a history of always being let down, it's very normal for that to carry over into your adult life."

"No one has as much bad luck at dating as I do."

Sharon shakes her head. "How about a subject change. How is Donna doing?"

I smile at the mention of Donna. She adopted me when I had lost all hope; when I was sure I would never find someone to love me. I knew she would never be my *real* mom, but she was the closest thing I had to one. I love her, truly love her.

"Good, she's good. I try and talk to her once a week. The nursing home she's in keeps her busy." Words can't describe how glad I am that I got her into that nursing home. It's the nicest one in town, and I figured it would be too expensive, but as it turned out, Donna had some kind of insurance no one knew about that ended up paying for everything.

"Are you still having nightmares?"

A cold chill runs down my spine. I haven't had a nightmare in months, but that doesn't mean they're gone. Sometimes I go through spurts of being normal, and other times I'm so close to shattering that I'm in a constant state of fear, day and night. There is no glue to fix the broken pieces of a person's past. You can go to all the therapy sessions in the world, take all the anxiety pills there are, but sometimes nothing helps indefinitely. There are parts of me that will always be broken.

"No, the nightmares have been dormant." I fiddle with a loose string on my pants. "I went to a club the other night with Sasha. I've been trying to go out more, be a normal person, you know?" I say, sighing.

"That's good. I'm proud of you."

"The night was going well, and I was having a good time until I went to the bathroom and got separated from Sasha. I couldn't find her and..." My lip trembles at the memory of that night. How afraid I was, how fragile. It reminded me of my time in foster care. A time I'm so desperately trying to forget.

"It's okay, Dove, if you don't want to talk about it, we don't have to." Even though I'm not looking in her direction, I know she is smiling at me kindly. She always is.

"No, I want to talk about it." I swallow around the lump in my throat. "The feeling of someone watching me is at an all-time high, and I think it's because of what happened that night because I'm not talking about it."

"Okay, then continue."

Exhaling, I tell her everything from that night, how I felt when the guy touched me. How helpless I was as I rushed down the sidewalk and then how he randomly just disappeared.

I don't even realize that I've lifted my hand and been touching my scar through my shirt the whole time I've been talking. Quickly, I drop my arm and look at Sharon, who smiles at me knowingly.

"Your worry over someone watching you is very normal, especially with your history and everything that happened with that guy. If you see him again, I want you to call the police. I also want you to work on your breathing techniques. I know it's going to be hard, but try not to give in to those impulses of checking over your shoulder a million times."

I almost roll my eyes. *As if it's that easy.*

"I'll try to control my impulses, but as you can see, I'm not good at it."

"You still like to run your fingers over your scar?"

"Yes. It's just a nervous habit. I've been doing it more frequently the last few days," I admit. "I don't know why, but it calms me when I do it."

"Do you still not remember anything from that time? How you got that scar?"

"No. I don't remember anything that happened in that place." I've lied about it for so many years that the words pour out on their own. It's the only thing I've ever lied about in therapy. The only thing I never want to talk about. So, I've been sticking to my lie. I don't remember anything. The truth is, I could never forget.

The smell of alcohol and mold fills every room in this house. I've only been here for a few days, but it feels like much longer, every second in this place feels like an eternity. This is supposed to be a home for children, a safe place for me, and the other foster children to stay. There is nothing safe about this place.

My stomach growls so loud it hurts. I haven't eaten anything today, which is nothing out of the ordinary. I scour the kitchen for food, hoping that no one finds me. When I see the old granola bar wedged between empty cartons in the bottom of the pantry, I almost cry out in joy.

Grabbing the bar as fast as I can, I tuck it into the waistband of my jeans.

However hungry I am, I know there is someone else here who needs food more than I do.

On tiptoes, I sneak up the stairs, avoiding the steps that I know creak. I go to the room at the end of the hallway, our room. Opening the door quietly, I hope not to wake him, but he still opens his eyes as much as he can to look at me as I enter the room. They're only open a sliver, both eyes too swollen from the beating he took before I got here.

"Hey, William," I whisper. Careful not to move the mattress too much, I crawl back into the spot beside him. "Found you some food. It's not much, but it's something."

I hand him the granola bar, and he just stares at it for a long time. He's barely talked to me since I arrived, and I'm not sure if it's because he doesn't want to or simply because he is in so much pain. He looks like he would be in a terrible amount of pain. His whole face is black and blue, swollen and scratched all over.

"You need to eat too," he finally says, handing me back the bar.

"How about we share?" I ask while opening the plastic wrapper. He sighs as if he doesn't want me to fight him on this, but then he still nods.

Taking out the bar, I break a piece off and hand it to him. Then I break an even tinier piece off for me and start nibbling on it. Most people would probably take less than thirty seconds to eat this, but we take our time. Enjoying every morsel, chewing until there is nothing left. Swallowing until each bit heavily lands in our empty stomachs.

When we're done, I hide the wrapper underneath the mattress and lie down next to him. The house is eerily quiet, which is not a good thing, maybe the calm before the storm. I close my eyes and feel around between our bodies until I find his hand. I grab it and revel in the feeling of his fingers intertwined with mine. Then I say a silent prayer, hoping that no one will come into our room tonight.

6

No matter what I do, I can't stop staring at the picture from the envelope. I don't understand why Christian would want Dove dead... how did she possibly end up on his list? Is he on to me? Watching me? Watching Dove?

I've grown more and more agitated over the last twenty-four hours. It has to be because of me. I just don't see why else she could be a target, but if it is because of me, why give me the job? Is it a test? Is he making me choose between him and her? Because no matter what, I'm always going to choose Dove.

Grinding my teeth together so hard it hurts, I look at the screen of my phone that shows me her apartment. She's sitting on the couch, curled up with a book. Not the slightest idea of the danger she is in and how drastically her life is about to change.

My head hurts from thinking about all of this. No matter how much I dig through my mind, I can't seem to find a single clear-cut answer. I better get my shit together fast because I only have three days to figure everything out.

It'd taken everything in me not to kidnap her last night and take her to the safe house I've prepared for a situation like this. I always feared that it would come to this, I just never thought it would happen this way.

I'm still ready to go, but disappearing now would put my name on top of the hitlist. No one walks away from Christian Sergio. I'm not sure what the fuck I should do next.

I need a plan. I can't go to Christian and question why Dove is on the list, not without giving myself away.

I've never questioned the people on the lists he gives me because, honestly, I've never given a fuck about any of those people. But I don't just give a fuck about Dove, she is my entire fucking world. I exist because of her. If anything were to happen to her... every muscle in my body tightens, and for one brief moment, darkness overtakes me. No. I won't let anything happen to her. I'll kill them all, every single one of them.

Exiting the app, I move to my contacts and scroll through them. The way I see it, I'm going to have to grab one of Christian's men and torture them until they tell me everything they know.

I'm already going to be number one on his shitlist when he finds out in three days that Dove isn't dead. Killing one of his men isn't going to hurt me anymore than not doing the job, so I might as well fucking do it.

Hitting the green call key, I bring the phone to my ear. The phone rings three times before Billy's deep voice fills the line.

"Hey, fucker!" *Fucker? Who does he think he is talking to?*

Swallowing my dislike for the guy, I ask, "Hey, Bill, want to grab a drink?"

"You know I can never pass on a chance to have some whiskey or beer."

I've never heard a truer statement in my life. Billy is half-drunk all the time, and when he isn't drinking, he's beating his wife.

"Let's meet at Oscars in about thirty?"

"I'll be there, Zane."

I hang up the phone without a goodbye. Billy is an easy target since he is nothing but a tech guy. That's what he does for the mob. Finds out information through hacking computers and cellphones. If anyone is going to know something, it's going to be him.

Clicking back into the app on my phone, I allow myself to check on Dove one last time. She's still sitting on the couch, immersed in her book. Without thought, I find myself stroking the screen, wishing I could touch her, taste her, feel her body against mine. I want her so badly it almost kills me. *Not yet.* I tell myself.

Closing the app once more, I shove my phone into my pocket and drive in the direction of Oscars. Since the hit was placed, I've been more cautious, looking over my shoulder, carrying an extra gun. I can't risk something happening to me and then Dove being put at risk because of it. I've worked so hard to get where I am. Worked my ass off to make sure Dove had the life she deserved, and now it's all crumbling around me.

Part of me hates myself for what I'm going to have to do while the other part of me wouldn't have it any other way. Dove is the one and only person I'm ever conflicted over. I refuse to hurt her, but my obsession with her can't be sated. I want her beside me. I want to be inside her whenever and wherever I want. For the first time ever, I want to be able to let go completely, but with only her.

Pulling into the shitty bar's parking lot, I suppress the thoughts of Dove and me sharing a future together. That can't happen if I don't get the answers I need. Which means... I need to let go. As easy as flipping a light switch off and on, I let my emotions go. Getting out of the SUV, I walk across the parking lot, the rocks crunching beneath my boots.

Walking inside the bar, the sound of loud music, laughter, and glass breaking greet me. I spot Billy in the corner of the room, looking like he's already had a few too many. *Perfect*, it should make it easier to get him to talk. I don't want to waste all my time on him.

"Hey, buddy," he slurs as I walk up to the table. As soon as I take a seat, a waitress wearing a low-cut tank top appears by my side.

"Hey, handsome, what can I get you?" she asks in a sultry tone, utterly unaware of how futile her efforts of flirting are with me.

"Beer, whatever you have on tap," I say gruffly without looking at her. She must have gotten the hint because she scurries away without another word.

For the next half an hour, I engage in friendly small talk with Billy, only sneaking in innocent questions here and there. I haven't decided if I'm going to kill him yet. It all depends on how much he knows.

"I have to say, I'm surprised you called. You never just hang out, relax, or let loose, ya know?" he says with a laugh, waving his glass around, spilling half of his beer on the table.

"What can I say? I'm turning over a new leaf. Trying to be more outgoing." The lie rolls easily off my tongue. "Especially with all these jobs, Christian has lined up for me. First, he gets into it with the Castros and now with Xander Rossi. He needs to pick his battles better; he can't fight everybody at once."

"Yeah, not sure what he was thinking, stealing those guns from Rossi. He should know better than to steal from him. This isn't the first time either... he's going to get himself killed."

I nod my head as if I already knew about the guns. Knowing this might come in handy later, but for right now, all I care to find out is what he knows about Dove.

"Yeah, not sure what he was thinking. I think he is in over his head. He has me killing all these people, and I'm still trying to figure out how I'm going to get to this chick he wants. You know, the one working at the animal shelter."

"Oh, yeah, Dove," he says, and I want to smash his face against the table just for saying her name. No one should say her name, least of all him. Licking his chapped lips, I can only imagine what he's thinking about her, "Shouldn't be too hard. She's completely unprotected." He shrugs, taking another sip of his beer before burping obnoxiously loud.

What a fucking pig.

Ignoring the impulse to slug him in the face, I say, "I wonder why the hell he would want her anyway? She seems to be a nobody."

Billy snorts. "If you only knew the half of it."

His comment has me gripping onto my glass a little tighter. Doing my best to keep my face void of all emotion, I act like I'm not interested in the subject anymore and change it.

"Anyway, I could really go for some pussy right now. Wanna head over to *Venus?* Hookers are on me tonight." I grin at him. While internally thinking about all the ways I'm about to torture him.

"Fuck yeah!" He slams the glass on the table with much more enthusiasm than necessary before getting up. Staggering over to the bar, he closes out his tab. I pay for my beer, and we both head outside.

Sucking in a lungful of fresh, crisp air, I lead Billy to my car. The idiot whistles as he gets into my SUV, completely oblivious to the fact that I'm about to torture and kill his ass.

Pulling out of the parking lot, I head toward the strip club. Billy's eyes are cast down as he plays on his phone, not noticing when I make a turn, going off route. Only when I've come to a complete stop and parked at an abandoned train station does he realize something is off.

"Where the hell are we?" He looks up and around confused. When I don't say anything, he reaches for his gun. Even without him being drunk and slow, I would have seen that move coming. It's just funny that he thinks he'll actually be able to shoot me in the condition he's in. I grab the gun from his hand with ease before he even gets the chance to point it in my direction.

"Get out," I order, pointing his own gun at him. He swallows hard and gets out slowly. As soon as I open my door, he takes off running across the parking lot. *Idiot.*

Sighing, I get out and raise the gun and pull the trigger. The bullet hits him in the leg, and he goes down with a pained groan.

"You're a fucking idiot, you know that, right?" I yell as I walk over to where he's lying. He tries to crawl away from me, but there's no hope for him now. I've drawn blood now, and I'll be the one to snuff him out.

Rearing my foot back, I kick him in the ribs, he rolls over onto his back, and I point the gun at his other leg.

"Tell me everything you know about the girl! Why does Christian want her dead?"

"You know I can't—" I cut him off by pulling the trigger. The shot rings out through the air, and another bullet rips through the flesh of his leg.

"Fucking fuck!" He's squirming around on the ground in agony, trying to get away. "I don't know why he wants her!"

I'm past playing games, now I just want the truth, want the information, so I can keep Dove safe. "Don't fucking lie to me. You already told me in the bar that you know something. Tell me and die quickly.

Or I can torture you for hours. That's up to you. I've got all fucking night."

"Jesus, fuck. You can't kill me. Christian needs me, and he'll have your balls for this. I'm more useful to you alive."

"Do I look like someone who gives a fuck? At this point, you're more useful to me dead." I pull the trigger a third time. The bullet hitting him directly in his kneecap. A high-pitched scream rips from his throat, and for the next few seconds, all he does is scream. It's annoying, and I'm half tempted to shoot him in the head to make him shut up, but that wouldn't get me the information that I need.

When he is somewhat calmed down, probably because he is starting to lose a lot of blood, I ask him again, "Why does he want her dead?"

"All I know... is that..." He's fighting now to get each word out. The pain makes it hard to talk, but I don't give a shit.

"Talk!" I snarl like a dog ready to bite.

"He's been... looking for her... for a while," he groans. "For a long time."

"How long?"

"Years. Ten, maybe more."

"He has been looking for Dove for over ten years?" I have to confirm that I heard him correctly.

"Yes..."

"Why?"

"I-I don't know." He shakes his head, and I believe him. Christian's not a damn chatty man by any means, and whatever secrets he has, he keeps them close to his chest. Aiming the gun at Billy's head, I fire one last bullet, hitting him right between the eyes.

Staring down at his lifeless body for a few seconds, I try to decide if it's worth moving him. Deciding it's not, all I do is grab his wallet from his jacket and walk back to my car. I'll let the cops find him and figure something out on their own.

On the drive home, I roll down my window and throw his wallet into the river as I cross the bridge. My mind is a fucking mess as I try and connect all the dots.

Why the hell has Christian been looking for her, and why for so long? I thought Billy would be able to give me answers, but instead, he gave me more questions.

I might not have a lot of answers, but I do know one thing. I need to get Dove away from here. She's not safe anymore. Not in her own home, not at work, and definitely not anywhere in this town.

7

*Y*ou know that feeling that tells you not to do something? When your gut tightens, and your palms grow sweaty. When it feels like something bad is seconds away from taking place? That's how I feel right now. Like I shouldn't be coming home, like something terrible is going to happen. I force myself to take a calming breath and unlock the door.

It's all in your head, Dove. I mean, seriously, this is my house. My home. I have no reason to be scared. Shoving the door open, I take a hesitant step inside. The hairs on the back of my neck stand on end, and goosebumps break out across my flesh.

Slowly, I close the door behind me and reach for the light switch right beside the door. It doesn't turn on, and I reach for it again, flipping the switch off and on. The light bulb must've gone out.

Feeling through the darkness, I find my way to the lamp on the side table. I flip it on, and a second later, the room is bathed in a soft glow. Flicking my gaze around the room, I realize something is terribly off. *Max.* He's not here, and he always greets me at the door. Always...

"What the..." The words are cut off when a mammoth hand comes out of nowhere, cutting me off. A scream rips from my throat, but the sound is muffled beneath the hand that's pressed firmly against my lips.

Pulled back against a firm chest, a thick arm of muscle wraps around my middle, restraining me completely. All I feel is a hard body against my back as I'm practically carried away from the door.

Panic like I've never felt before rises up inside of me, and instantly I start to struggle, my fight or flight instincts kicking in. Those instincts do me no good when the man holding onto me is so much bigger and stronger than I am. Fighting is a waste of strength and effort, two things I'm already lacking. Tears prick my eyes and hot breath fans against my ear.

I wasn't wrong. Someone was watching me, and now he's got me. Now he's going to hurt me. Rape me and kill me. He's going to get what he wanted all along.

Kicking out my legs, the heel of my foot lands against my assailant's shin, and a grunt fills my ears. The kick isn't enough for him to release me though, so I continue fighting. I won't be a helpless victim again. I won't let him hurt me without a fight.

A million scenarios run through my head. Opening my mouth, I feel his flesh against my lips, and it hits me then what I need to do. What I should've done all along.

Biting into the meaty flesh of his palm, I sink my teeth deep like a dog and don't let go, not until he forcefully pulls his hand away.

"Fuck," he growls. The timbre of his voice is deep and frightening, and fear blankets my insides. I do my best to tamp that fear down, but it reminds me of a time when I was helpless and had no one. Putting everything I can into getting away, I let out a horrid scream, knowing this is probably my one and only chance of having someone hear me.

Instantly, his hold disappears and shock courses through me as I twist around coming face to face with my attacker. *Is this a game to him? I don't understand why he let me go, maybe to leave me feeling hopeful?*

Flattening myself against the wall, I look at him. He's tall and handsome, and for one single second, I'm stunned like a deer seconds away from death. Standing there, I stare at the man who has been following me.

The same man who was sitting in Sharon's waiting room with me hours ago.

He lifts his hands, and I flinch. "I'm not going to hurt you. I would never hurt you," he says. His words don't match his actions though, and when I look into his eyes, I see emptiness. I see someone without a conscious, without the ability to feel. It chills me to the bone. I feel like prey caught in a trap, and here right in front of me is a predator.

Taking a step to the side, I slide along the wall. My gaze flicks to the door and then back to him. If I want to get out of here alive, I'm going to have to be fast. He's definitely stronger than me, but I might be faster, especially if I can catch him off guard. I don't care if he says he's not going to hurt me. I need to get out. Get away from him.

All I can hear is my heartbeat hammering in my ears. A rush of fear ripples through me as he takes a step forward, partially blocking the front door. My throat closes, and it feels like an elephant is sitting on my chest.

Run. Escape. I internally scream at myself, but it feels like my feet have blocks of concrete attached to them. Snapping out of it, I turn on my heels and rush toward the kitchen. If I can just get a knife or something to fight him off. I toss anything and everything in my path at him, but nothing deters him, and I don't make it far before he catches me. His hand wraps around my wrist, and he tugs me backward, causing my body to collide with his chest. The air is forced from my lungs with the impact.

His strength is a reminder that I am nothing more than a fly in the fight against him. Wrapping both arms around me, almost as if he's giving me a bear hug, he picks me up and presses me to the nearest wall.

"Please, don't, please..." I start to beg.

"Shhh," he murmurs softly. The man's face is millimeters away from mine, and I can feel his harsh heartbeat through the thin material of his shirt, the clean scent of soap invading my senses.

He releases his hold on me, but I'm still trapped between him and the wall with nowhere to go. No escape. Fear wraps around my throat like a shackle. Lifting a hand to my trembling face, he cups my cheek and gently swipes away the tears. I wasn't even aware they'd started falling from my eyes.

"I would never ever hurt you. You are way too important to me,

Dove. You have to trust me, I promise everything is going to be okay."
He tries to soothe me, but not a single part of me believes him. My
mind is racing, and I have a thousand questions. Why else would he
break into my house and attack me if he wasn't going to hurt me? How
does he know my name? And most importantly, why am I important to
him? He must have the wrong person. This is all a big misunder-
standing.

I'm shaking now, consumed with fear, and my vision is blurry with
tears.

"Stop," he orders, slamming a fist into the wall beside my head. His
voice is harsh and only makes me cry harder. He seems to grow frus-
trated by my failure to listen and releases a hard sigh a moment later. "I
didn't want to have to do this to you... but you've left me no choice."

He takes a step closer, and we're so close now that we are chest to
chest. Our faces are only inches apart. My eyes are in line with his full
lips, and that's when I realize just how much taller he is. Out of the
corner of my eye, I see him reaching for something, and I know this has
to be it. The end is near, after all I've been through in my life, this is
how it's going to end.

"I'm sorry," I whimper, and even in the face of death, I'm unable to
stop the tears from coming. I want to fight, but it's as if there isn't
anything left in me.

I'm barely hanging on, barely breathing, barely here. I flinch when
he leans into me and buries his face into my hair. The action is so intimate, and when I hear him inhale sharply like he's smelling me, a
shiver skids down my spine.

"No, it's me who is sorry, Dove," he whispers against my ear a
moment before I feel a pricking sensation against my neck and something cold entering my skin.

"Don't...please..." I try and get the words I want to say out, but my
thoughts become hazy. Muddled. Up and down become the same.

Leaning away from me, his face once again comes into view, his full
lips a breath away from my own. Strangely, I find he's beautiful as he
peers down at me. Beautiful and frightening, all at the same time.

"Shhh, everything is going to be okay now. You'll always be safe in
my arms." He threads his fingers through my hair and brings our fore-

heads together. He holds my head in place, forcing me to stare into his dark, cold eyes.

I'm fading fast and find that most of my body sags against his now. My heartbeat slows, and my lips part, and I want to ask him how I'm going to be safe with him? The words never come though; my tongue is too heavy to talk.

"It's okay, don't be afraid..." His voice is the last thing I hear, and his haunting eyes the last thing I see as the world fades to complete darkness.

8

*P*art of me knows what I did to her is wrong and fucked up. But I couldn't help myself. What other choice did I have anyway? If I don't disappear with her, Christian will find her and have someone else kill her.

Having her in my arms, even with fear in her eyes was everything I thought it would be and more. Her soft body molded against mine perfectly, her sweet scent surrounded me, and feeling the rapid beat of her heart against mine was the best kind of high.

When she started crying, I snapped, her tears are a trigger to me. I hate seeing her cry, but even with her tears, I can't seem to shut off my body's reaction to her. My cock grew harder than steel, and I had to stop myself from taking from her, reminding myself that she is fragile and that if I did something, I might regret it. *No*, I would definitely regret it.

The drive to the safe house seems to take forever, and I find myself glancing between Dove's sleeping body and the road over and over again.

With every mile, we leave the city further and further behind. I stop once to switch cars. Luckily, I had parked the getaway car in a parking garage, so no one saw me as I dragged Dove's unconscious body from one vehicle to the other.

Soon enough, I'm pulling into the driveway of what looks like an ordinary farmhouse. The white picket fence has seen better days, and the siding on the house needs to be power washed. The paint on the porch is chipped, and the windows look like they haven't been cleaned in years. It looks like no one has lived here in some time, but it's not about what you see on the outside but what lurks inside.

When I bought this place, it wasn't because of the farmhouse, but because of what was underneath it. The house was built on top of an old 1960's bunker. The house itself was nothing more than a cover-up. I gutted the entire place, made it bigger, and homey, knowing that someday I may have to bring Dove here. I wanted her to be happy here, on the off chance that we ever got to a place where we could be together.

Parking, I turn the car off and sit there for a long second. Normally, I can shut off my emotions and let go completely. This is different. In order to protect Dove and ensure I don't hurt her, I can't shut down. I have to keep myself in check.

That means I have to learn to deal with the feelings I'm having right now. Which is hard as fuck because all I want to do is strip her bare and take until there's nothing left. All my sick and twisted dreams have come true, but only at the expense of Dove's life.

Remember that, asshole.

I may have finally gotten her, but I'll die before I let anyone hurt her. Things have just gotten ten times more complicated. Not only will I have to protect her from Christian, but I'll have to protect her from myself.

I walk around the SUV to the passenger side and open the door. Taking her body into my arms, I cradle her protectively against my chest. She weighs hardly anything, and I don't like it, not one fucking bit. I'll need to plump her up a bit before I consider fucking her. The last thing I want is to break her. Right then, an image of my sweet little Dove broken—her beautiful face stricken with pain—fills my mind.

I can't let that happen, ever.

The sun has just started rising, illuminating the house with an orange glow as I carry her inside. The floor creaks as I walk up the porch, unlocking the front door of the house. Gripping onto her a little tighter, I manage to punch in the code to the keypad leading downstairs. There's a loud beep, and then the door opens.

I walk inside and close it behind me before descending the stairs. The basement is expansive, with a full-sized kitchen, master bedroom, living room, a library, a gym, and a master suite with a jetted tub and a full floor to ceiling shower. When I had this place redone, I wanted to be sure that Dove would be comfortable here, especially if we have to stay for a while, which at this time looks that way.

Heading straight to the bedroom, I deposit her gently on the silk sheets and brush a few strands of dark brown hair off her face. *Angelic.* Part of me feels like this is nothing but a dream, that there's no way she's here, and mine to do with as I please.

I let my gaze move lower and stop on the exposed skin of her abdomen where her shirt has ridden up. Smooth, creamy white flesh taunts me, and I drag two knuckles over it, reveling in the warmth and pleasure it ignites deep inside me.

I've wanted this forever... for as long as I can remember. I just want her. The thick rod between my legs twitches, and I nearly chuckle. He, too, has wanted this forever, and soon enough, he'll get a taste, but for now, we'll both have to do with my hand.

Forcing myself to move away from the bed, I walk out into the living room and make my way back upstairs. Going back out to the car, I gather all the bags I packed, then I get the travel crate out of the back that has Max in it. He starts meowing as soon as he sees me.

"I'll get you out in a minute," I say, realizing then that I just talked to a cat.

I carry everything downstairs in two trips, before double and triple-checking all the locks. When I get back into the bedroom, Dove still hasn't moved. Not that I expected her too. I gave her quite a strong sedative. I wouldn't be surprised if she sleeps for the rest of the day.

Allowing myself to touch her face one last time, I cradle her cheek and press a kiss to the crown of her forehead before breaking away to take a shower.

Pulling out some clean towels, I walk into the bathroom and strip out of my clothing before turning the shower on. As soon as the room starts to fill with steam, I step beneath the spray. Leaning against the tile, I let the water beat down on my tired muscles.

My cock is still harder than steel, and my balls are aching, begging me for release. The image of her in my bed doesn't help matters and only makes me crave the warmth of her body more. Taking myself into my hand, I give the rod a hard stroke, causing a hiss of pleasure to slip past my lips. Repeating the stroke, a little harder this time, I rub my thumb over the slit at the head of my cock.

Fuck. Letting my eyes drift closed, I envision my hand as Dove's pussy, my hips thrusting forward, my cock moving in and out of her furiously, claiming her like I've always wanted to. Squeezing myself a little harder, I picture her clenching around me, her lips parted, her cheeks red, and her beautiful eyes frenzied with heat. Thrusting into my hand a little harder and faster at the image, it doesn't take long before I explode.

Ropes of sticky come leave my cock and land against the tile before the water washes it away. I barely keep myself standing upright, the orgasm rocking me straight to the core. I've lost count of how many times I've allowed my mind to wander like this, to use Dove as an image to jack off to. I've seen her naked on camera so often, I know every curve of her nude body, but I've never got the chance to feel them, never got to touch her soft skin.

It's almost too tempting now, I have her here with me, and I'm no longer forced to hold back. Soon enough, I'll be giving us both the pleasure we desperately deserve.

Finishing up my shower, I wash my body and hair and then rinse.

When I'm done, I get out and dry off before wrapping the towel around my waist. Walking back into the bedroom, my eyes immediately fall on the sleeping form on the bed. My gaze never wavers as I drop the towel and start getting dressed. Even though I just came, my dick is already stirring back to life again. *Shit*, I need to get a grip.

Trying to keep myself occupied and my mind anywhere but on Dove, I unpack the bags I brought and get everything else situated. Once done, I take a seat on the edge of the bed and stare at her. Now I just have to wait for my sleeping beauty to wake up.

9

Dove

The first thing I notice when I wake is the pain radiating through my head. It feels like someone is trying to pry my skull open. The second thing is the silky sheets my cheek is pressed against, and that alone gives me enough steam to force my heavy lids open.

For one single moment, all I am is confused, then like a freight train, the events come rushing back to me. All the confusion is shoved aside as fear and panic overtake me.

Eyes as black as night. The prick of a needle in my neck. Promises of love.

My stomach churns, and a wave of dizziness slams into me as I scan the room, my gaze darting around, looking for an exit, for *him.* When I don't see anyone, I look down at my body and find that I'm still completely clothed.

Thank god for that.

There's no soreness between my legs as I move to the edge of the bed, so I feel confident enough that he didn't rape me. Lifting my hands to my face, I feel around for any bumps or bleeding. I don't find any wounds, and I don't feel any pain besides the soreness in my neck and the splitting headache I have, so I'm thankful for that.

Overall, I seem to be fine at the moment, but that's not a complete relief because I have no clue where the hell I am or how I'll get out of here. On top of that, I don't even know where my captor is. Or if there is more than one of them.

Another wave of fear slams into me, threatening to immobilize me. There has to be more than one of them. It's just not possible that this was done alone. Who can just kidnap someone from their home and take them god knows where without anyone noticing them?

God, this is so bad, and something tells me it's not going to get any better.

Frantically, I get up and start pacing around the room. It's pretty luxurious, with a large king-sized bed and expensive-looking furniture. Two bedside lamps give the room all its light. *It still must be night.* Heavy curtains are draped over the windows. *Windows...*

Rushing across the room, I grab two fistfuls of the curtains and pull them open. I suck in a sharp breath when I see what's behind them. *Bricks.* They're just bricks. It's a sham, a damn facade. I check the other window and find the same kind of brick wall behind it. Then the third, as if that one would be any different. Still, there is a small sliver of hope that lives inside me, which is crushed as soon as I pull the last set of curtains away.

Bile rises in my throat, and I press a hand to my stomach. I think I'm going to be sick. I'm trapped... in some kind of basement. Digging my nails into the palm of my hand, I swallow down the vomit and focus my attention.

I need to find a way out.

There are two doors, both are closed, so I have no idea where they lead or what lurks behind them. Taking a deep breath, I walk over to the first one. Fear trickles slowly into my veins. Hesitantly, I reach for the doorknob, my fingers curl around the cold metal, and I turn it. Thinking the door is probably locked, I don't expect it to open, so when it does, a surprised gasp falls from my lips. I stand there shocked for all of two seconds before I walk out into the huge open space.

I'm trapped in a god damn, underground apartment, a giant one at that. My apartment would probably fit three times in this room alone. I try and act like I don't care, but this place is something else.

I stare out into the living room, where a large sectional couch, an entertainment center with a TV the size of a small theater screen is.

A dining area sits in the center of the space, with a table that seats six. A large colorful flower centerpiece ties the room together, giving it a homey feel.

The entire place leaves me feeling completely confused. It's almost like someone lives here... It's far too nice of a place for a prisoner to live in, which makes me wonder if I'm really a prisoner here or something else entirely.

The kitchen is on the other side of the room, with modern-looking cabinets and stainless-steel appliances. Then it dawns on me. There's a fully functioning kitchen, and a kitchen means knives, which I can use as a weapon. Carelessly, I rush from the bedroom and into the kitchen. My hands are shaking as I search the counters for a knife block.

Opening the drawers, my hope splinters as I only find spoons and forks, but not a single knife. Desperate, I grab a fork just to feel like I have something I could do damage with. With my free hand, I continue to open the drawers hoping maybe something will appear.

When nothing does, the panic starts to set in again. Oh, god. I'm trapped in this basement, with nothing more than a fork to protect myself with. Running a hand through my hair, I will my out of control heartbeat to slow down.

Think, Dove, think.

"Are you looking for something?" That deep voice pierces the fog around my mind, and I whirl around, raising my arm in front of me and pointing the fork in the direction of the voice. My eyes find the name-less guy that took me from my apartment. Inky black hair, and eyes the color of charcoal add to the dark vibe he's got going on.

Dragging my gaze down his body, I find he's wearing nothing more than a pair of low hanging basketball shorts. His broad, muscled chest is on display, and beads of sweat drip down it, leaving a trail behind.

Why is he sweating? Why am I staring?

I force myself to look away from his chest. I don't care what he looks like, he kidnapped me. Peering up into his eyes, I find he's staring me down, the dark orbs twinkle with a sliver of amusement when he spots the fork in my hand.

The blood in my veins turns to ice at the darkness I see in his eyes. There is no light, no good, and that scares me almost more than what's happening because if he has no conscience, no reason to care, then I'm as good as dead.

"Let me go!" I order, cutting the fork through the air like a knife.

He grins, literally grins at me like I'm an adorable kitten, instead of a woman willing to do whatever she can to get free.

"Do you truly think you can hurt me with a fork?" he says, and it feels like a taunt, which only angers me more.

"There is no thinking about it. If you don't let me go, I will stab you with this fork." I make my voice sound strong and tighten my grip on the end. My palms are sweaty, and I'm scared. So damn scared. The last time I was this scared, I was sure that creeper was going to get me, and I refuse to let something bad happen again. If I have to, I'll save myself.

He takes a threatening step toward me, and my muscles quake. My brain is telling me to run, ordering me to, but looking at the man before me, there is no way I'll get around him, and even if I do, I have no idea where I'll go.

"Put the fork down before you hurt yourself. I told you I wasn't going to hurt you, and I meant it." He speaks gently to me like I'm a child, and I stare at him with confusion. His words don't match his actions. His voice is a soft whisper and doesn't match the devil persona he's giving off. I can only assume this is some sick game to him.

"Not *yet*... you're not hurting me yet, but you will. I'm not stupid. Why else would you kidnap me and lock me in a basement? Let me go, and I won't call the police. I won't tell anyone about what happened."

"I'm sorry, but I can't do that, Dove," he says, frowning and taking another step toward me. He lifts his hand, and I flinch, taking a step back to keep the distance between us.

"Can't and won't aren't the same thing." I look over his shoulder, trying to plan out my next move. It's a mistake and one that'll cost. He moves with lightning speed toward me. *He's going to kill me.* All I can do is gasp as he grabs the wrist with the fork in it and squeezes hard enough to cause me to release it.

It falls to the floor, the sound of the metal bouncing across the tile fills the space. As if his touch burns my skin, I tug my arm out of his hold. His dark eyes narrow, and he looks at me like he wants to grab my hand again, but he refrains. *Who is he? Why does he want me?*

"Please, just let me go, please!" Panic is clawing at my insides.

Something resembling remorse flashes across his face but is soon replaced with an emotionless mask.

"Come, I'll show you around, and if you behave, I'll let you go into the library."

Library? How can he act so normal, like nothing is wrong? Like he isn't breaking the law? He has got to be out of his damn mind if he thinks I'm following him anywhere.

Lost in my thoughts, I forget he's standing here, watching me, staring like he can see deep inside my soul. An involuntary shiver ripples down my back.

"You're insane, psychotic." I cross my arms over my chest, trying to make myself appear big when I feel like a tiny mouse trapped in a trap. "I'm not going anywhere with you. I'm not staying here. Just let me go. Whatever you want, I don't have it. If it's money or something, I have none. I have nothing, you chose the wrong girl."

His lips twitch as if he wants to smile. "I've been called worse in my life, and I've most definitely chosen the right girl. I don't want your money, Dove." Taking another step, he crowds me. My heart thunders in my chest, and I bite the inside of my cheek to stop myself from crying out. The coppery tang of blood fills my cheek. He's close enough for me to touch him now, and his nearness terrifies me almost as much as his distance. When he leans into my face, I catch a whiff of sweat, soap, and just man, "All I want is you, and now I have you. Right where I want you, so relax and let me show you around your new home."

"My... my new home?" My lips tremble as I speak, and he pulls back a little, his eyes studying my face. Heat blooms in my cheeks at the inspection.

"Yes, your new home. I hope you're happy with the accommodations. I wanted to be sure you are as comfortable as possible. I even brought Max since I know you love him so much."

"M-Max?" I'm shocked. Shocked and terrified and confused. The reality of everything sinks in very slowly, and I realize then what I should've realized all along. Whoever this guy is, he's never going to let me go.

10

*M*ax must have heard us talking about him because, on cue, he appears in the kitchen. He purrs loudly as he wraps his body around the corner of the cabinet. Dove bends down to pick him up, holding him to her chest protectively. I do my best to understand her fear, but she should know better.

"If I really wanted to hurt you, I could've easily done so when you were knocked out." I point out the obvious, but it seems to fall on deaf ears.

Although the whole *I'll stab you with a fork* thing was quite adorable and turned me on a little bit. It's cute that she thinks she can fight me off, that she can escape.

"I... I can't stay here. No." She shakes her head, strands of hair fall onto her face, and she looks up at me with panic in her blue eyes. "I won't stay here. You can't make me. I... I'll scream. I'll fight you. I will not let you keep me here."

Each word is like a lash against my heart. Her words hurt me more than I expected them to. I knew she would want to escape, to fight me, but I never expected her to be so strong-willed. I realize instantly that I need to try a different approach, or I'm going to have to drug her again and tie her to the bed.

"Would it help you if I told you my name?"

Her eyes widen, and she looks shocked. "No! I don't care about your name. I don't care about any of this. I just..." She pauses and then darts forward, dropping Max in the process to run away from me. Like cats do, he lands on his feet and lets out a hiss as he scurries away.

Jesus Christ. This is turning out to be a shitshow. Now I'm going to have to do the one thing I don't want to do. Her panic is out of control, and the only thing that's going to keep her in line and make her see through the fog is fear.

I hate the idea of deceiving her like this, of threatening her, but it's my last option before drugging her again.

"I tried to be kind, tried to reason with you, but my patience is wearing thin." My voice drops and turns menacing as I chase after her. Without having a clue as to where she's going, she runs back into the bedroom, basically trapping herself. Her determination is almost comical. She tries to shut the door behind her, but I block it with my foot.

"Please..." The anguish in her voice calls to me. It begs for my protection, but there's no protecting her from me. At least not right now.

Like a trapped and wounded animal, she rushes around the bed, hiding on the other side. Ha, like a piece of furniture could protect her from me. I'll rip the fucking thing apart piece by piece. Vibrating with frustration, I try to talk myself off the ledge.

My gaze collides with hers, and the softest whimper I've ever heard escapes her lips as I prowl toward the bed. She doesn't know how dangerous this is for her. How easy it would be for me to let go and ruin everything.

There's nothing to stop me from falling off the edge, no one to hold me back.

Standing next to the bed, her eyes dart to the door and back to me again. Back and forth, they move like a bouncy ball, and without her even knowing, she's giving herself away.

I'm trained to kill, trained to see peoples' next move. She's a chessboard, and her face is giving away her next move.

Walking a little further into the room, I say, "If you don't stop running from me, you'll force my hand. You're going to make me do something I'd rather not. I'm not a monster, Dove, but I'll do what I have to, to prove my point."

"I'm not scared of you," she yells across the bed, her cheeks red. The tremble in her voice, giving away the lie.

Shaking my head, I walk around the bed. Her eyes scan the room, and with nowhere else to go, she climbs up onto it. If my next move doesn't work, I'll have to subdue her with my body.

"If you don't stop, I'll visit your friend from the shelter. Sasha...is it?" As soon as the words leave my lips, she freezes in the center of the bed. "Or maybe I'll visit Donna at the New Haven Senior Care."

My threat hangs heavy in the air as I watch Dove's face pale. She might act brave and fearless when it comes to her own safety, but she won't risk the lives of the people she loves. She doesn't know I wouldn't actually hurt them.

Not since I know how important those people are to her. Not knowing how well Donna took care of her and how good of a friend Sasha has been to her.

Fresh tears pool in her eyes, and when she blinks, they slide down her cheeks.

"Don't... don't hurt them. Please, I'll do whatever you want. Just don't hurt them."

I should feel satisfied with myself as I watch her drop down onto the mattress, her cheeks stained with sadness, but I hate that I had to go there.

"I won't hurt them unless you make me. Now, I want to show you around the house. This doesn't have to be a prison, it's all what you make of it. Will you behave now?"

She nods and hesitantly crawls off the bed, her head lowered in defeat as she comes to stand next to me.

"Now that we've gotten that out of the way. I'm Zane. I built this entire place for you. The library, gym, living room. Every inch of this place was built with you in mind."

That seems to get her attention, and she looks up from the floor and right at me.

"Why would you build this place for me? I don't even know you." I ignore her question, knowing that answering one will lead to a million more.

"Come, let me show you around." I extend my hand, and she looks at it with hesitation before placing her own in mine. Pleasure sparks deep in my gut and radiates south into my cock. Her hand is so tiny, fragile, and warm. Before I let my brain drag me in a different direction, I start the tour.

"This is the master bedroom, which we'll share together. Through that door," I point to the far-right door. "That's the bathroom. There is a huge shower, and a tub for you to soak in since I know you like your baths."

Her eyes go impossibly wide, and I can only imagine what's going on in her head right now. Tugging her out of the bedroom, I walk toward the living room. "You already know where the kitchen and dining room are. Here is the living room. I've got all your favorite movies and tv shows here." She doesn't say a thing just stares open-mouthed at the space.

"Off the living room is a short hallway, which leads to the gym and library." I point in the direction of the hall.

Turning to me, she looks up at me, her wet lashes fanning against her cheek. "W-why would you do this, and how do you know what I like and don't like?"

Part of me wants to tell her nothing, to remain silent, but eventually, she'll know the truth. Eventually, she'll find out just how important she is to me.

I tug her closer and grip her gently by the hip, loving the way she molds like clay to my will. "Because, Dove, I've been watching you. I know everything about you. What you like, what you don't like. Your favorite foods, movies, what time you wake up in the morning. I even know when you get your period and for how long it lasts."

Shock, fear, confusion, it all blends into one on her face.

"Y-you watched me?" She's trembling now, and I know it's not because she's cold.

"Yes, for a long time." I can't help but smile. Yes, she's afraid now, but soon she'll come to realize she has nothing to be afraid of, that everything I did was for her.

"W-Why?"

"I told you. Because I care for you, and I want you to be safe."

"I... I think I'm going to be sick." She lifts a hand to her mouth, and I release her, watching as she runs away from me and in the direction of the bathroom. I follow behind her and walk in to see her hunched over the toilet. Gently, I pull her hair back away from her face as she empties her stomach contents into the bowl.

"Shhh, it's okay." I soothe, using my other hand to rub up and down her back.

"It's not okay," she whispers, "none of this is okay." Her body goes rigid.

I'm tempted to tighten my hold on her hair a little bit, but I don't want to hurt her. That's the last thing I want. There will be time for the things I want later, but right now, Dove needs me. She needs my kindness.

"It might not make sense, or be okay right now, but eventually, you'll come to terms with it. Change is hard."

Pulling away, the silky strands of her hair fall through my fingers as she scurries back against the side of the tub. Wiping at her mouth with the back of her sleeve, she peers up at me with confusion.

"I don't understand. I don't know why I'm here or why I'm important to you or what any of this is. I just want to go home. Please, let me go home." Tears well in her eyes again, tugging at my heartstrings, but I banish the thoughts away.

I am her home, forever, and for always.

"This is your home now, and it will be so until I say otherwise. Now, when you're ready, you can come out and join me for dinner." I want to take her into my arms, hold her and make her forget about the fear but it's too soon. Instead, I do the only thing I can. I put some distance between us because like the old saying goes: Distance makes the heart grow fonder.

11

Zane walks out of the bathroom, leaving me alone with my thoughts, All I can do is sag against the vanity.

The things he knows about me are terrifying and completely unnatural. It's not normal to know how someone takes their coffee when you have not spent any time with that person. Nothing is normal about any of this, how can he not see how crazy this is?

I'm exhausted and afraid of what's to come. He's been watching me... and the things that he knows. I bite my lip to stifle a whimper. I have to get it together and try to escape this prison.

Forcing myself to use the breathing techniques Sharon taught me, I back away from the ledge of fear and analyze the information I have. He's not going to let me go, that much is obvious. It's clear he has an obsession of some sort with me, but he doesn't want to hurt me, or at least it seems that way right now.

Hugging my knees to my chest, I do my damnedest to try and come up with a solution, a way out, but there isn't one. There is nothing, and that leaves me feeling hopeless and ten times more afraid.

"Dove." He calls my name from a distance, and then I hear him moving around, his feet barely make any noise. A moment later, he appears in the doorway, still shirtless.

"Dinner is ready."

Shit. How long have I been sitting here?

Pushing myself up from the floor, I come to stand in front of him. A ghost of a smile appears on his lips before he turns around and walks out.

I follow him through the apartment, watching the muscles of his back move with every step he takes. I'm so mesmerized by them that I don't realize when we've made it to the dining room table until he stops abruptly, and I slam right into his back.

He spins around and grabs me by the forearms to steady me. His touch is gentle, warm, and makes me feel weird. Like he shouldn't be kind to me.

"Sorry."

"Nothing to be sorry about," he says, his voice softer now. "Sit down. You must be hungry." Now that he's mentioned it, yes, I'm starving. Though I'm not going to tell him that.

Looking at the table, I see that he's already prepared two bowls of what looks to be some kind of hearty soup. Taking a seat, I let the savory smell invade my nose, causing my stomach to growl loudly.

"All we have is canned goods right now, no meat and no fresh produce. I wanted to be here when you woke up. That's why I didn't leave to get it earlier. Since you're up now and know where everything is, I'm going to make a quick supply run after we eat."

Bringing the spoon to my mouth, I pause. "You're going to leave me here?"

"Yes, there is no need to worry. You'll be completely safe here. No one is getting in."

"Or out?"

"No, you won't be able to leave without me." He confirms what I already knew before adding. "But that's for your own protection." Like it's important, I know that or something.

"You keep saying you're trying to protect me, but you never say from who or what?"

His eye twitches, and I swear I see the cold mask of indifference fall back over his face. "Let's not talk about that now. You need to eat. I can hear your stomach from here."

Shoving the spoon into my mouth, I bite back a groan as the soup lands against my tongue. I don't care if it's canned soup it takes like heaven right now. In a matter of minutes, I have my entire bowl eaten. Zane eats slowly, watching each and every bite I take, like it's the most entertaining thing in the world.

"You're staring at me."

Zane shrugs. "I like watching you."

I swallow down the witty come back, and instead, get up and take my stuff into the kitchen. Placing the dirty dishes in the sink, I lean against the counter, trying to figure out what I'm supposed to do now.

Shoving out of the dining room chair, he walks into the kitchen, and my eyes gravitate toward him. I try not to look at his perfectly sculpted stomach, or each ab that's on display and definitely not the deep V partially hidden by his low hanging shorts.

"I'm going to clean this up, get dressed, and then leave. Do you need anything while I'm out?" he asks, and I swear I can hear the smirk in his voice.

"No." Staring down at the floor, I shake my head.

"Are you sure? This might be the last time I'll go out for a while. We need to lay low for the next few weeks."

What does that mean?

"What am I supposed to do while you're gone?"

"Whatever you want. This is your home too. Watch some tv, read a book, or take a bath." He tosses out suggestions like he didn't just kidnap me and threaten people I care about.

"Okay." I move out of the kitchen as he cleans up. Slowly, I walk into the living room and sit down on the sectional. Sinking into the leather, I wish I could enjoy it, but I'm too tense. My stomach churns, and I press a hand to it to keep the nausea inside at bay. Zane walks into the bedroom, and a moment later, returns fully dressed.

He stops directly in front of me and squats down, bringing us eye to eye. I try to avert my gaze, but trying to look anywhere else is impossible with him right in front of me. "I'm going to leave now. I'll be back before you know it. Don't do anything stupid while I'm gone. Please. I don't want to have to threaten you again, or worse, follow through on my threat."

Chewing on my bottom lip, I nod. What the hell could I possibly do anyway?

"Good." He smiles and then leans forward, pressing a kiss to my forehead. His lips burn where they touch my skin, and something strange erupts inside me. It's foreign and confusing, and I don't understand it because, in a strange way, that simple gesture is comforting to me. At the same time, it's sickening too because I shouldn't feel anything close to comfort from this man. He's my captor, not my roommate or friend.

Leaving me sitting on the couch, he walks up the stairs and pauses at the top. Leaning forward, I curiously watch as the door opens, and he walks out. Not even a second later does the door close heavily behind him. As soon as I'm alone, my chest feels heavy. I'm trapped and alone. Complete quiet blankets the room. All I can hear is the swooshing of blood in my ears and my own soft breathing.

Do something! My brain screams. He said it will be a while before he leaves again, so this might be my only chance.

~

I SPEND the next two hours looking for a way out of here while trying to find things I could possibly use as weapons. With each passing minute, my hope diminishes. My first thought was to get a weight from the gym, but of course, that was the only door that was locked. I beat my fists against the door for a while before giving up.

The fork was pretty much the best protection I could find. The second thing I found was a lamp with a heavy bottom. Taking off the shade, I do a few trial swings with it. *I can do this.* My anxiety is through the roof. I've never hurt a person before, never punched someone, never drew blood, and now I'm about to try and take out a guy bigger than me with a lamp.

A few minutes later, I hear the door at the top of the stairs open. Oh, god. With the lamp clamped tightly in my hand, I scurry across the room and hide next to the stairs. I flatten myself against the wall and say a silent prayer. My heart is pounding so loudly I fear he might hear it. Sweat forms against my palms as I adjust my grip while listening to him descend the steps.

You can do this. It's this or nothing.

His body comes into view, and I see that his arms are full of grocery bags. *Perfect.* Shutting all rational thinking down, I move out of my hiding spot and swing the lamp at his head just as he turns in my direction.

I catch him across the face instead of the back of the head like I had planned. The lamp smashing into the side of his face.

Shit! My hands tremble as I drop the lamp to the floor at the same time, he drops the grocery bags. I take an instinctive step back when he lifts a hand to his face in slow motion. When he pulls his hand away, I see red on his fingers.

Blood. He's bleeding. My lungs burn, and I freeze. The look in his eyes is murderous, rooting me in place and turning the blood in my veins to ice. All I can think is, this is it, this is where he kills me. Where he beats me and ties me to the bed. Where I die a slow, painful death.

"Fuck, I told you to be good." He's almost growling like an animal, his lip is curled as he takes a threatening step toward me.

"Please." I lift my hands to protect my face because I know what's coming. I know he's going to hurt me. Bracing for the pain, I grit my teeth and squeeze my eyes shut.

Except the pain never comes. Instead, he tenderly grabs my hands and lowers them while gently nudging me backward. In that moment, fear roots me to the floor, and I'm not sure I could scream or run away even if I wanted to. When my back collides with the wall, the air in my lungs expels, and I know I'm trapped.

I haven't known my captor long, but I already know that with him, I'm always trapped. I look anywhere but at his face. I don't want to see the cut or the bruise on his cheek. I'm not a violent person, and I hate that this situation has made me into someone I'm not.

His hand comes out of nowhere, and I flinch as he pinches my chin between two fingers, forcing me to look into his eyes. Dark black pools of nothingness reflect back at me.

If there is anything I've learned about Zane, it's that he is unreadable. Like a lake, you can't see the bottom, but you know there's something there beneath the surface. Lurking in the dark, deep waters. You just aren't sure what it is. That's Zane.

Releasing my chin, he drags his knuckles over my cheek before he cups it. The gesture is gentle, kind, and it confuses me. I'd expected his rage, his anger, fury, but kindness? No way.

"It doesn't matter what you do to me, Dove. I will never put my hands on you in any way to cause you harm. I will never hurt you." He leans into me, so close that I can feel his hot breath on my lips.

This strange heat blooms in my belly, and my gaze darts from his eyes and down to his full lips and back again. I'm riding a teeter-totter of emotions and toeing the line between what is right and wrong. This is wrong, bad. I want to kiss him, to let him consume me, to taste his venom on my lips, but I don't understand why. I'm terrified, but also curious. I shouldn't let my captor kiss me or touch me, but a very strange part of me craves him.

As if he can read my mind, his lips descend on mine. Lifting my hands, I rest them against his chest. Do I want to stop him? My brain says, push him away, but my heart tells me to hold him close. My entire body trembles at the gentle brush of his top lip over mine before his bottom lip caresses mine.

Though the kiss is soft, nothing more than a whisper, the intensity of it steals the air from my lungs. It evokes an emotion from deep within that I haven't felt for years.

Safe. Protected.

The smell of clean soap and the warmth of his body clings to me. My ribs are a cage, and my heart is a bird beating against it to break free.

Gripping onto the fabric of his shirt, I want to tug him closer, and I'm tempted to, but before I can, he's pulling away. He breaks the kiss and presses his forehead against mine while placing his hands on either side of my head against the wall.

We're both panting and out of breath. His chest rises and falls rapidly, like kissing me was running a mile uphill.

Licking my lips, the coppery tang of blood lingers on my tongue. It's both shocking and alluring. *How can I like this? It's wrong...*

"You're everything, Dove. Everything. You have no idea the things

I've done for you. The blood that's covered my hands. The darkness I've endured, but that's okay because now you're mine. You're here, and you're mine, and it was all worth it in the end."

Everything he is telling me confuses me more. Blood? Darkness? Is he telling me he's hurt people for me? I don't want to know, don't want to ask, but I know, eventually, I'll have to because deep down, I need to know.

"I'm going to put the groceries away and meet you in the bedroom. Take a shower, so we can get ready for bed."

"Bed?" I croak. That's when I remember what he said earlier when he showed me the house. He said *we'll be sharing the bedroom.* I've been so occupied with trying to escape, that I forgot about that part, or maybe I just wanted to forget it.

He wants me to sleep with him. This insane man who drugged and kidnapped me is making me sleep with him.

"Yes, bed, it's late, and you should rest since I had to give you that drug. It'll take a little while to completely wear off. Now go shower."

He puts some much-needed space between us, though it looks like it's the last thing he wants to do. In fact, he looks like he wants to ravage me, consume me, breathe me in until there's nothing left. Like watching a bad accident happen right before your eyes, you can't make yourself look away, and that's how I'm feeling right now.

When I don't move, Zane gives me a dark smirk that gets the blood pumping through my veins. "Go, now. Before I strip you bare and take what's always been mine." The muscles in his forearms tighten, and his fists clench a little tighter, and it's almost like he's holding himself back.

Always been his?

That thought gets me moving, and I scurry away from him, practically running to the bedroom. Once alone, I finally feel like I can breathe. I touch a finger to my lips where the kiss lingers and wonder why I'm feeling this way?

Something is terribly wrong with me.

12

Scrubbing a hand down my face, I ignore the raging hard-on I'm sporting between my thighs. *Fuck*, it was just a kiss, but that little touch of our lips was like a lightning bolt of pleasure zinging through me, making my entire body come alive.

My skin tingles and feels hot to the touch. I feel so incredible, I couldn't care less about my swelling face or the open cut on my cheek.

It's no surprise that she's fighting me on every corner, not that I expected anything less. That doesn't mean it doesn't bother the shit out of me though. I want her to trust me, want her to believe that I'm protecting her. That my intentions come from a good place. I mean, how can she still not see that? I guess she needs more time.

Yes, in time, she will understand. Soon enough, it will make sense to her. She will learn to trust me, see that I mean her no harm. I know she's scared and unsure, so I need to give her more time to digest everything.

This place is so quiet that I can hear the shower running through closed doors and from across the apartment. Which, of course, doesn't help my boner any. Immediately, my mind conjures up an image of Dove in the shower, naked, her skin covered in bubbles. Her delicate fingers slipping between her legs. Maybe touching her pussy at this very moment. *Shit*, this is not helping... thinking about her naked is not going to help me keep myself in check.

Looking down at my steel hard cock, I groan. Soon... *very soon*, but not today.

I make one more run upstairs to the car. When I come downstairs this time, I'm a little more careful. I wouldn't hold it against Dove if she tried to hurt me again, she's a fighter after all. She might not look like it on the outside, but she is stronger and braver than many people I've met. I doubt she's giving up so fast. She'll continue to push me, and that's not her fault. It's just not in her to give up, and I admire that about her. Her determination.

By the time I've put all the groceries and supplies away, the sound of running water has stopped, and I know she is finished with her shower. The ache in my balls has subsided a little, but having her so close, and yet so far away at the same time, makes the cravings unbearable.

Making my way back into the bedroom, I wonder if she is going to try and fight me on our sleeping arrangements. I'm sure she will. If she's trying this hard to escape, I can only imagine what she plans to do to get out of sleeping beside me.

Stepping into the room, I find her standing in front of the dresser wrapped in a fluffy white towel. The long strands of her brown hair cascade down her back while beads of water cling to her skin. I want to lick them away. Lick every inch of her body until she's completely spent and can do nothing but lay there as I take her over and over again.

Biting back a groan, I force the thought away.

"Nightgowns and Pajamas are in the second drawer, I believe," I say, making her jump a good foot off the floor as she turns around.

"I didn't hear you walk in," she whispers, staring at me with a puzzled expression as she white knuckles the towel. I wonder what she's thinking. Does she think I'm going to attack her? Rip the towel away and ravage her?

After a moment, she turns back around to face the dresser and opens the drawer, causing the thought to evaporate into the air. She pulls out a pair of flannel pajamas, and while holding onto them with a death grip, she disappears back into the bathroom. Her need for privacy is laughable. I want to tell her that there is no need to hide from me, that I've seen her naked many times over the years, but I don't think she's ready to hear that yet.

I've shared enough with her today. We have many weeks to come to discuss all of these things. While she is getting ready in the bathroom, I strip out of my clothes and slip into some sleeping pants. Usually, I sleep naked, but since I'm making a conscious effort to make Dove comfortable, I opt for clothing. She's not ready to see me naked, yet. A moment later, she reappears in the doorway. I can see her hardened nipples through the sleep shirt she's wearing and saliva pools in my mouth.

Fuck me. I used to think it was so hard to see her and only be able to watch her, but I was wrong. This is a far more difficult battle. Dropping my gaze, I take in the rest of her body. Clean, dressed, safe.

"The bathroom door doesn't lock," she says as if I didn't know that already.

"I know. None of the doors lock except the main entrance and the gym." A tense moment of silence blankets us. Pulling the covers back, I ask, "Do you need anything before we go to sleep? A drink of water?"

"I'm not sleeping with you." She lifts her chin into the air. Her defiance really is a fucking turn on, and if she didn't matter so much to me, I would snap her in two.

Turning to face her fully, I don't bother making my voice soft, there is no way she will win this fight. "You will sleep with me in this bed. This is one thing I insist on. I've waited too long for you to not sleep in the same bed with you now. So, you can either come to me on your own, or I will drag you to the bed and tie you to it. Choose, but either way, you're sleeping beside me."

Slowly she blinks as if she's not sure she heard me correctly.

"What's it going to be?" I ask, my patience slipping.

Padding over to the bed, she climbs up onto the mattress, a look of rage on her face. God, she is adorable when she's mad. She lies down at the edge of the king-sized mattress and pulls the blanket all the way up to her chin.

Her gaze stays trained on me the entire time, like I'm a big bad monster. I can see fear, anger, and curiosity swirling around in the dark depths of her ocean colored eyes. I didn't bother putting a shirt back on, and just like earlier, she stares at my bare chest when I climb into the bed, taking the spot beside her.

Her cheeks are a hue of pink, but when she realizes she's been caught, her face turns bright red.

"It's okay to look. You don't have to be shy with me."

"It's wrong. You're a monster. You kidnapped me."

Ignoring her words, I roll onto my side and pat the spot beside me. "Come here. I want to hold you."

Her lips press into a firm line, and she shakes her head. "I'm fine here."

Sighing, I reach for her, throwing an arm over her middle, I drag her toward me. "When I said sleep, I meant in my arms."

"I don't want to sleep this close to you. I want to go home." She squirms against me and rolls onto her side, facing away from me. Tightening my hold on her, I crush her back to my chest and keep her there. It takes a few minutes, but eventually, she stops struggling.

I guess it's because she feels my cock hardening and pressing against her ass while struggling. Burying my face into the back of her neck, I inhale deeply. For the first time in a very long time, calmness sweeps over me. The same calmness I felt all those years ago when Dove held my hand and told me everything was going to be okay.

Years of pain and anguish are washed away in the blink of an eye and all because I get to hold her, finally. All I feel is Dove. Her warmth surrounds me, her sweet scent tickles the hairs in my nose. And I'm reminded that this isn't a dream. This is real. The steady rhythm of my heartbeat drums in my ears and I squeeze her a little tighter.

"Goodnight, Dove," I whisper into her hair. She doesn't say anything back, but that doesn't bother me; soon enough, she will see things for what they are.

For a while, her tiny body shakes with fear, but when she realizes I'm not going to do anything, she relaxes into my arms. It doesn't take long for sleep to find me, and I hold Dove in my arms the entire night, my love for her an unbreakable prison that she will never escape.

∾

MY MUSCLES ache when I finally open my eyes. Having Dove in my bed was both heaven and hell. Heaven because I was finally holding her, finally sleeping next to her, and hell because she woke up every few hours trying to wiggle out of my grasp. Every time she fights me and tries to get away, it's like a small stab in the heart.

"Can you please let me go?" she whispers sleepily. "I have to use the bathroom."

"Sure," I murmur into her hair before reluctantly releasing her. She climbs out of bed and disappears into the bathroom as if she can't get away fast enough. Lying on the bed, I watch the door, waiting for her to reappear. My cock has made a tent in my sleep pants, and there's no point in hiding my arousal.

When the door creaks open, and her head pops out, her eyes go straight to the tent, and those plump lips of hers part on a gasp before fear flickers in her gaze.

"There isn't anything to be scared of. I'm not going to attack you. I'll wait till you're ready. I can control myself."

She makes a choking sound. "Ready?"

I smirk. "Yes, when you're ready. I'll wait till you're begging me to fuck you, then, and only then, will I touch you."

"You'll be waiting for a long time because I won't ever beg you. I didn't even want to sleep next to you. The last thing I'm going to do is have sex with you." She turns her button nose up at me as if doing so would hurt my feelings.

All I can do is let out a harsh chuckle. "Sure, sweetheart. Whatever you say. Let's go have some breakfast and then I'll show you the library. We have plenty of time to argue, but I'd prefer to do it after I have my coffee."

Dove doesn't respond, and I toss my legs over the side of the bed and stretch my arms above my head, releasing a loud groan. Looking over my shoulder, I find Dove staring at me, when she sees me watching her, she looks down to the floor.

As amusing as it is to stand here and watch her squirm with embarrassment, I really could use some coffee. "Come, let's eat breakfast."

Dove follows behind me, her feet move with little noise. Heading straight for the coffee pot, I prepare the coffee and then get to work on breakfast. I don't bother asking Dove what she wants for breakfast. I know what she likes, what she's allergic to. Her opinion when it comes to meals isn't needed because I won't ever make her something she won't eat.

Preparing eggs and bacon for us, I place a plate down in front of her and lean against the counter, taking a gulp of the steaming hot coffee. Thankfully, Dove eats without complaint, and when she's done, I take her plate and put it in the sink.

Then I gesture for her to follow me.

As we walk down the hall, past the gym and toward the library, Dove asks, "How long will I have to stay here?"

"Until it's safe, and I'm ready to leave." I stop us directly in front of the door. Her cheeks are a soft pink, and her bee-stung lips are begging to be kissed. My attraction to her is spiraling out of control. I'm going to need to get a grasp on it.

Reaching for the door handle, I twist the knob and push the door open. I revel in the audible gasp she releases at the sight. I wasn't lying when I said I built this place with her in mind. Her love for reading was front and center when I designed the bunker. In fact, she's the only constant in my mind. The only person that matters.

Walking inside, I watch her face, the way her gaze widens, and her lips part. She's both shocked and in awe. I knew she would love this room.

Turning to me, she asks, "You built this for me?"

My heart lurches in my chest because, for the first time, she's looking at me like I'm more than her captor. Some deeper feeling swirls in her eyes, and right then, I wish she could remember me. Remember that night. Remember where it all started.

13

The rest of the day is tense. I try to keep myself busy reading and watching movies, but nothing holds my interest because my mind is too exhausted trying to make sense of my situation. I still catch myself thinking that this can't be real, that I must be asleep in my bed. That any minute now, I'm going to wake up and laugh about the crazy dream I had.

Curled up in the large recliner in the library, with Max cuddled up next to me, purring away, I do my best to focus on the book I'm reading. Looking at the pages, I read the same paragraph for the third time. *This is pointless.* Zane has left me alone for the last few hours, giving me space, he said. As if that was the issue here.

When I hear approaching footsteps, my head snaps up, and I drop the book I've been trying to read for thirty minutes into my lap.

"Would you like to work out with me?" Zane asks while leaning against the door casually.

"What... how?"

He chuckles. "In the gym. Do you want to work out? There is a stationary bike, a treadmill, and a rowing machine."

"Oh..." I'm about to decline, but then I remember that there are probably heavy weights in the gym, weights I can use as weapons. "Sure, I'll come."

Looking pleased about me taking his invitation, he nods and starts to walk away. "Come, let me show you the rest of your closet. I got you some workout clothes as well."

I've been wearing these thick pajamas all day, which are comfortable as hell, and it's not like anyone will see me here, so there really isn't a reason to change, though I guess I won't be able to wear these while working out. Getting up from the recliner, I follow him through the apartment and into the bedroom.

Pulling out the drawers, he shows me what's in each one, then he walks to the large mirror that spreads from floor to ceiling. He pushes a button—I hadn't noticed—on the side of it, and the mirror slowly swings open.

"Oh, wow," I exclaim as the enormous walk-in closet comes into view. He walks inside, and I follow behind him, too curious not to.

"This side holds all of my clothes, and these two sides hold yours. Workout attire is over there." He points to the far right of the wall.

"Wow," I repeat because, really, it's the only thing I can think to say. This whole thing is so unreal. He bought all of these things for me? People don't just spend money on other people, not unless they care about them, so why did he spend all this money on me? Why did he build this fortress and bring me here? Is it because he's obsessed with me?

I snap out of it when he grabs something from his side of the closet and starts to walk out. "I'll give you a minute so you can get dressed and meet you in the gym."

All I manage is a nod, still baffled by the number of clothes and shoes he got for me. I wish I could say that I don't care about any of this, that material things don't matter to me, but that would be a lie. The sad truth is that these things do mean something to me. They mean a lot. Growing up poor, I never had pretty clothes or even *new* clothes. I was simply glad when I got clothes that would somewhat fit me and didn't have huge holes or stains on them.

Having him buy all this stuff for me, providing me with the things I need, has my stomach in knots. I've never been so conflicted in my life.

I want to hate him. I want to feel nothing besides anger toward him, but looking at what he's done for me, has my feelings and thoughts twisted, a knife piercing me in the gut.

No, I can't let him do this to me. This was probably exactly why he did this. He's trying to buy my trust, trying to make me thankful. Thankful that I have him, thankful that he got me all these things. A sour taste fills my mouth.

I can't let him win. I need to keep a clear head. No matter what he does or says, he is the enemy, and I can't forget that because the moment I do, all chances of me getting out of here will be lost. I can't get wrapped up in this game he's playing.

Searching through the clothes, I pull out some capri pants, a sports bra, and a loose-fitting T-shirt, which I switch into quickly. Then I find a pair of socks and running shoes, which, no surprise, are my exact size. Putting those on as well, the last thing I do is put my long hair up in a ponytail with a hair tie that I find in the bathroom.

As I walk to the gym, my mind wanders. I've come to the conclusion that Zane's obsession with me knows no bounds. I wonder just exactly how much he knows about me? How long has he been stalking me, watching me? I shiver at the memory of being watched—at the fear. It was him all along, it had to be, but the biggest question is, why?

I walk into the large room, holding a plethora of fitness equipment, too many to count, but my eyes land on one in particular. It's a metal bar hanging from the ceiling.

Attached to that bar is a shirtless Zane doing pull-ups. I remember having to do them in school, hating that I was so weak I could barely do a single one. Zane makes it look like it's the easiest thing in the world. Up and down, back up and down, without stopping.

His back is turned toward me, and all I can do is watch his bulging muscles flex as he repeats the motion. I'm so mesmerized, I'm frozen in place, forgetting for a moment why I'm even here.

Suddenly Zane stops. He is just hanging from the bar now, his arms extended like he is catching his breath.

"Enjoying the show?" His deep voice fills the room. Even though he is facing the other way and can't see my face redden, I look away embarrassed. Only then, as I avert my vision to the wall, do I realize that the entire left side of the gym is a giant mirror.

Shit. He caught me watching him. *Again.*

A little bit flustered and more than ashamed of myself, I walk over to the treadmill and start walking. Seeing that one wall is a mirror, ruins my plan to sneakily attack him with a weight. Even if he turns away from me, he would be able to see me coming.

It's like he thought of everything.

✑

AFTER SPENDING some time in the gym, Zane makes us dinner, and I do my best to ignore the way his muscles clench and work as he moves about the kitchen. I have to be sick, or this is really nothing more than a fucked-up dream. *That has to be it.*

I don't understand why I am drawn to him, why my treacherous body is attracted to him. It's probably because I've never been with a man. No one wanted me until now. Of course, leave it to me to attract the psycho kind.

"You've been very quiet today." He states as we sit down to eat.

"I'm trying to figure out why you want me. What's so special about me?"

Zane smiles, showing off his stupidly straight, white teeth. "You're special because you're mine, and that's all you need to know. I brought you here to protect you, and that's what I'm doing." He shoves a piece of broccoli into his mouth and starts chewing.

Frustration bubbles over inside of me. "You keep saying that, but it makes no sense. The only person I can think that I might need protection from is you."

Shock overtakes his features, and then his face goes blank. "There are far worse people out there than me. People that will kill and rape you. Sell you. Make you wish you were dead a million times over."

Wanting... no, *needing* to hurt him, I lash out. "And you know this how? Because you're one of them? Because you've done all those things and more?"

Zane's eyes zero in on me, and they are dark, punishing. The hand resting against the table closes into a tight fist. The veins in his arm bulge. Is he going to snap? Part of me hopes so. It's so hard when he's kind and caring, I really need him to be angry and cruel. I'd much rather have his fury, than kindness.

"I've been kind to you, Dove. I've done everything to make you feel at home and comfortable. I haven't hurt you. I haven't taken from you, and still, you make me out to be some evil villain."

"Evil? Isn't that what you are though? Isn't that what kidnapping and drugging someone is? I'm here against my will. It's wrong. Your obsession with me is wrong. All of this is wrong!" I shove out of my chair, my emotions spiraling out of control.

I don't make it two feet before Zane grabs me, spins me around, and has me pinned to the dinner table face down. He holds me in place, his fingers digging into the back of my neck. The weight of his body presses against me, and I feel his hard cock against my ass. Fear swirls deep in my belly, and I hold onto it. Fear and anger are what I need right now. I need this because I refuse to take his kindness.

"There is something wrong with you, and I refuse to think just because you haven't hurt me yet that you won't. You're no better than any other person who kidnaps and murders people," I scream and continue my struggle against him.

Snaking his other hand beneath me, I feel his fingers at the waistband of my capris. The air ceases in my lungs. This is what I wanted, right? Why I lashed out?

"Do you want me to hurt you, Dove? Do you want to see what happens when I let myself go? I can assure you it's not something you'll forget." Warm breath caresses my earlobe, and then I feel it. His tongue flicks against the sensitive flesh. I bite my bottom lip to keep the cry in. It feels so wrong.

When I don't respond, his grip tightens, and I let out a whimper. "Answer me. Is that what you want? Is my kindness not enough... do you need my anger too?"

"Let me up. I hate you. I don't want you to touch me or look at me!"

Zane chuckles darkly and cups my pussy. "That's not what I asked you, Dove." There is a hint of warning to his voice, and my body starts to tremble.

"I don't want this," I hiss, finally getting the words to come out.

"But you do... I can feel you, feel your warmth, the tiny wet spot on the front of your panties."

My breaths quicken, and my pulse races at a million miles per hour. *This is wrong. I don't want this. I don't want him.*

"You said you wouldn't hurt me."

"And I won't. I'm not hurting you right now, am I? I think I'm doing quite the opposite. I'm going to make you feel good. All you have to do is let me."

"Stop," I gasp, feeling his fingers gently graze my center. Pushing back against him, he leans in more, pushing more of his weight into me. Keeping me in place.

"Why? Isn't this what you wanted?" His voice is cruel, sinister. His finger rubs against my clit, back and forth, back and forth. His strokes are meticulous, and pleasure like I've never experienced before blooms deep in my core.

"Oh, god..."

The pleasure mounts.

It's dangerous. Unstoppable. It grips me by the throat and refuses to let go. My nails dig into the wood of the table. I need something to hold onto, something to keep me grounded.

"Come for me, let me feel how much you *don't* want this." Zane pants against my ear, and as if on command, my body does just that. Light flashes before my eyes, and I explode like a rocket. Shattering into a thousand pieces, my muscles tighten, my core clenches around nothing, and a muffled cry escapes my lips.

Tears sting my eyes because this is wrong, but it feels right.

As I drift back down to Earth, Zane gently removes his hand from my panties, and the weight of his body on mine disappears. I feel like mush, every muscle exhausted. Even though I don't want to, I push off the table and turn around just in time to see him shoving his finger in his mouth. His eyes fall closed, and dark, untamed pleasure overtakes his features.

"Lies. You taste like lies." His eyes flash with primal hunger. "Next time, don't provoke me. I told you I wouldn't hurt you, but I'm not a saint. Every man has his limits..." Before I can conjure up a response, he walks away, heading for the bathroom. The place I planned to run and hide.

14

I shouldn't have done that. Shouldn't have let myself go like that. I shouldn't have let what she said bother me, but like I knew she would, she's crawling underneath my skin. I'd prepared for this for a long time, for a time and place when she would be all mine, but like most things when it comes to Dove, I never expected for it to really happen. Her ill thoughts of me are the most frustrating part.

Yes, I've killed, outright murdered, and hurt people. I've done things that no one can fathom doing, but for her to compare me to the rest of the monsters that want to harm her... I just can't stand her thinking of me that way.

I've spent years protecting her, shielding her, making sure she had a nice place to live, and a good job. That no one hurt her. *If it wasn't for me.* Nails sink into the flesh of my palm. My nails. The pain brings me back to reality, but reality isn't any better than my mind.

Slamming my closed fist against the tile of the shower, I try to let go of some of the tension that's clinging to my bones. I need an outlet, but I don't have one.

Violence is a parasite, a vicious eater of all the good in you. It's also the only thing that keeps me from becoming a full-fledged serial killer, and since I have no one to hurt, and no one to destroy here, I'm going to need to control myself better. Which means I'm going to have to work through my emotions instead of shutting them off.

Sighing, I scrub my skin hard, drawing out the pain, reveling in it. I knew this wouldn't be easy, but I don't understand her need to provoke me. Does she want me to hurt her?

Something inside my chest squeezes. She was probably expecting the worst, and all I've given her is the opposite. I can imagine she's confused as fuck, but there isn't anything I can do to fix it. Not yet. I don't want to tell her the extent of the danger she's in yet. If I do, she'll want to know why and from who, and I don't have any of that information.

The more I think, the more pissed I get.

Fuck Christian for putting us in this situation. As soon as I get the chance, I'm putting a bullet right between his eyes. Hell, I'll do it anyway simply because he threatened Dove. Rinsing one last time, I shut the water off and open the shower door, grabbing a towel from the rack.

My cock is still rock hard, which is annoying as hell and only adding to my frustration. I should've beat off in the shower, but I was too angry, too caught up in my damn head.

Drying off, I toss the towel to the floor and walk into the bedroom naked. It's highly unlikely that Dove is going to seek me out. Not after what happened. She'll stay hidden in the library until it's time for bed.

Fucking shit. I run my fingers through my hair, tugging at the longer strands. Her body is ingrained in my mind. Every. Single. Inch. I can still feel her tight, little body beneath mine, my cock screaming for entrance. Her tiny pussy gushing against her panties.

I wish like hell that I could've peeled off those pants and plunged my finger deep inside of her. I'm sure I would've come right then and there, right in my fucking boxers like a teenager.

Jesus, I have to stop thinking about this. Control yourself, asshole.

Stomping over to the closet, I open the drawers and grab random clothes, putting them on in a hurry. I need to get a grip, need to calm down before I go back out there. Leaning against the rack of clothing, I wait a few minutes just standing and concentrating on nothing more than my breathing. When my heart rate returns to a semi-normal pace,

I leave the room and walk out into the living area. Like I expected, Dove isn't anywhere in sight.

Needing to cool off a little more, I walk into the kitchen and head straight for the fridge. I knew I bought that six-pack of beer for a reason.

Grabbing one, I twist the cap off and bring the bottle to my lips. I take a long pull, letting the refreshing beer cool my heated body. It doesn't take long for me to finish the first beer, and when I'm done, I toss the bottle in the garbage and grab a second, which I drink a little slower.

Easing into the leather of the couch, I sit in silence and drink my beer. After a short while, I hear the soft patter of feet coming my way. Never one to shy away from confrontation, it's hard for me to watch as Dove stops at the entrance of the living room staring at me for a good second, big, blue eyes wide with apprehension before darting to the bedroom.

Does she really think that horrible of me? I squeeze the bottle a little tighter.

The sound of the shower turning on fills the apartment, and I force myself not to think about her naked. I've made it this long without fucking her, I think I can handle a little longer.

Finishing the last of the beer, I get up and take the bottle to the trash. Standing there, I consider the fact that Dove could easily use the bottles to try and hurt me. In fact, I wouldn't put it past her, but with my watchful eye on her, it won't happen.

She got me good with the lamp, but now I know what to watch for. When I hear the shower turn off, I start to prepare an apology in my head. I don't want her to be afraid of me, so I'll apologize and make everything better.

The apology never comes though when I enter the bedroom, I find Dove completely naked, the towel at her feet. I'm only a little shocked, not fully since I've seen her like this before.

"Jesus Christ, have you ever heard of knocking!" She squeals, cheeks red with fury as she plucks the towel up off the floor. She wraps it around herself, but not before I catch a glimpse of her perky round breasts and pink, dusky nipples.

The towel blocks my view of her pussy, but I've seen it enough times to know that it's completely bare and most likely soft and warm, just like the rest of her.

"One, there is no privacy between us. Two, I've already seen you naked, so I don't know why you're hiding." That gets her attention, and those pretty blues widen with shock.

I watch her throat bob as she asks, "What do you mean, you've seen me naked?"

"Many times, yes." I know my confession is going to scare her, and it's not the apology I had planned, but there isn't any point in hiding my feelings from her.

"There is...there is something wrong with you. How did you watch me? When? How?" The questions tumble past her lips, and her knuckles turn white as she holds the towel with a death grip.

"Camera feed that I installed in your house. I will add it was for your protection entirely, but I did watch you. I also checked on you every night while you were sleeping."

Her body starts to tremble as more truths come out. "You... you were in my house? You had cameras?" She looks like she's going to pass out, and that's the last thing I need or want. If she falls, she could hurt her head. Taking a cautious step forward, I reach to steady her.

Fear flickers in her eyes, and she shakes her head in disbelief. Scurrying backward, she collides with the wall in her haste to get away from me.

Looking up at me with confusion and fear, she whispers, "What is wrong with you? Why would you watch me?"

I tell myself not to move. Not to corner her, but the truth is, I want to. I want to make sure she stays right where I want her. While I don't want to hurt her, I need her to understand that I will do anything, kill and hurt anyone to keep her with me.

"Because you're mine. I've told you this already and when I can tell you more, I will. I'm doing my best not to scare you. I don't want you to be afraid of me, Dove."

"Afraid?" A humorless laugh fills the room. "Afraid isn't the word I would use. I'm outraged, sick. I'm past afraid." Her words cut through me like a knife, but I remind myself that this is all new for her.

"You should get dressed so we can get ready for bed," I say, ignoring her outburst. "Unless you want to sleep naked, which I am more than fine with."

"Why do you do that?"

"Do what?" I cock my head to the side.

"Act like it's not a big deal. Like this entire thing isn't completely fucked up."

"Because it's not. Not for me. Now, are you going to get dressed, or am I going to have to dress you myself? I'm tired and done fighting with you for the night."

Dove wrinkles her nose in disgust at me. "If you touch me..."

All over again, she's taunting me. "Or what? I didn't bring you here to hurt you. I could've done that back in your apartment." The mask on my face cracks a little. "All of this is for you, now get dressed, and get in the bed before I do it for you. If you want to act like a child, then I will treat you like one."

"I'm not sleeping in that bed with you again. I'd rather sleep on the floor." Fear gives way to anger, and she walks right past me and into the closet. I go to the nightstand and pull out the handcuffs I stashed there. After what I just told her, and her reaction, I don't feel like being forced to strong-arm her all night. Handcuffing us together is the easiest solution, that way, even if she was able to hurt me, she'd have to lug my body around.

When she emerges from the closet and sees the cuffs in my hand, she pauses. Her eyes flick from the cold metal and back to my face again. Fear. That's all I see, and I know what she's thinking. That I'm going to take advantage of her, hurt her, but I'm not.

Before I can say anything, she whirls around and rushes out of the room.

Fucking Christ. She's halfway up the stairs when I enter the living room, and by the time I reach her, she's screaming and beating her fists on the door as if someone is on the other side coming to let her out.

Wrapping my arms around her, I pull her to my chest and hold her tightly even as she kicks and screams.

"You said you wouldn't hurt me. You lied! You're a liar!" She continues to struggle against my hold. Throwing her head back, she smashes it into the side of my face, barely missing my nose. Pain lances across my cheek, and I squeeze her a little tighter. The urge to shake some sense into her is strong.

"I'm not sleeping with you!"

"You're doing whatever I tell you to," I snap.

When we reach the bedroom, I'm exhausted, my face hurts, and I'm fed up with her bullshit. I drop her down onto the mattress, and she does her best to crawl away from me, but she's not fast enough. Grabbing her by the ankle, I drag her back toward me. Her hands claw against the sheets.

She flails against the mattress, trying to kick me, but I roll her over onto her back and force myself between her legs. Grabbing both hands, I press them into the mattress and move her arms so I can hold her wrists with one hand and handcuff her with the other.

Clicking the cuff into place, I release the wrist I cuffed and cuff the other one to my own wrist. The heat of her body seeps into mine. She feels perfect beneath me, even if she isn't willing to be there.

"Please, Zane! Please, let me go! Please! I won't tell anyone. I'll just go back to my apartment, and we can pretend like none of this happened." The way she says my name... I know it's out of fear, but I want to hear her say it again.

She's desperate to escape, to feel safe, but there is no safer place on this planet than right here with me. Tears pool in her eyes, threatening to fall. A tightness fills my chest cavity. I hate when she cries, and this time it's worse because I'm the reason for those tears.

Looking into her eyes, I lean forward and say my next word with firmness. "I'm never letting you go, and the sooner you come to terms with that, the better things will be."

"You can't keep me here. Someone will wonder what happened to me. I have a job and friends." I'm half tempted to tell her the job was given to her because of me and that I have her phone and can easily text her friends to let them know, but I don't. I'm done with this conversation now. Easing off of her, I put as much space between us as I can.

"Crawl underneath the covers," I order.

She tugs against the cuff instead of listening to me, and because I'm so fed up with her, I pick her up, hauling her against my chest and move us both the way I want on the mattress.

Once lying down, she tries to move away, but there is only so far she can go with us cuffed together.

"My wrist hurts."

My chest rises and falls rapidly, anger and lust pumping through my veins.

"Stop pulling, and it won't."

"I don't want to be cuffed to you."

"I don't want you to act out, but you continue to, so I guess neither of us got what we wanted. Now go to sleep, or I'll find something to gag you."

"You wouldn't." I can hear the shock in her voice, and because I'm an asshole and already pissed off, I feed right into her fears.

"I would, and worse yet, I would enjoy it."

I hear her gasp and can only imagine how red her cheeks are right now. Thankfully, that shuts her up, and soon silence falls over the room. She tugs against the cuff a few more times, trying to get comfortable but eventually stops moving.

Time passes slowly, but Dove soon falls asleep. Her even breaths giving her away.

Her body gravitates toward mine in the night as if her subconscious knows what her mind doesn't yet.

That she's forever safe, in my arms, in my bed, and in my heart.

15

I curl up into a tight ball. *Trying to make myself as small as I can, wishing I could just disappear altogether. William is next to me on the mattress, his hand tightly wrapped around mine. Our door is closed, but our foster parents are fighting so loudly, it sounds like they are in our room. The walls shake when someone slams a door shut somewhere inside the house. I jump at the noise, and William holds my hand a little bit tighter as if to tell me he's here.*

"It's okay, don't be scared," he whispers into the dark room. "I won't let him hurt you."

Like a warm fuzzy blanket, his words settle over me, giving me warmth and shelter, I wish I could shelter him too. I wish I could protect both of us, but we're only kids. Our foster parents are supposed to take care of us.

Heavy footfalls meet my ear. Fear trickles down my spine. Larry is coming up the stairs. Coming for us... any time he's in the room, something bad happens. My stomach tightens with worry. A moment later, the door flies open, and my worst nightmare fills the doorframe.

The light coming from the hallway is almost completely blocked out by his body, but there is a sliver of light that casts through, allowing me to see his face.

His bloodshot eyes tell me he is drunk, no surprise there. I think he's been out at the bar every day since I arrived, and when he isn't there, he's fighting with our foster mom. He sways lightly on his feet as he moves to take a step forward, an evil smile spreading across his face.

"Hey, little bird," he slurs, stepping inside the room.

I squeeze William's hand so tightly, it must hurt him, but he doesn't make a sound. He, like myself, is frozen in place, knowing what's to come.

"Come here, Dove." He motions for me to get up, but I can't move, my limbs are useless, petrified.

"No," William says, his voice stern and almost... scary. To me, anyway.

"No?" Larry, our foster father, starts laughing. "Did little Will grow some balls overnight?" He shakes his head. "I said come here, Dove. I want to spend some quality father-daughter time in the other room." He licks his lips, and my stomach churns.

"I said, no!" William growls. "You don't touch her."

"What are you gonna do about it, Willy boy?" Larry taunts. "I thought I already taught you a lesson. Obviously, I didn't beat it into your head hard enough."

Though drunk, Larry is still fast and crosses the room, coming straight for me with ease. I'm shaking so hard, all I can do is sit there and wait for the inevitable to happen. At the last second, Will lets go of my hand, and moves to stand. He's sluggish and I know it takes a monumental amount of effort for him to move.

Pain contorts his features, and I want to tell him, no, to stop, but my tongue is too heavy, the words lodged deep in my throat, refusing to come out.

"I said, don't touch her!" I've never seen or heard Will speak so violently, and a new sense of fear washes over me. What if Larry hurts him again? Just as the thought enters my mind, all hell breaks loose.

Larry lunges for me, but William intercepts. I know this isn't going to end well, not for me or for Will. Everything happens so fast. Fists start flying, landing with heavy thuds against skin and bone. Tears fill my eyes as screams and grunts erupt inside the room. I can't make out what belongs to who. All I can do is pray that Will is going to be okay. He has to be, he's the only thing keeping me together here.

My mind is in disarray from fear as I helplessly watch the scene unfold.

"You're as good as dead, boy," Larry yells and pulls something from his pocket. Then I see it. Something shiny, metal... the blade catches in the light.

He has a knife. Larry has a knife. My brain screams the warning at me. I act without thinking. Without fear. Jumping up, I throw my body between Larry and William. I don't care what the outcome is, all I know is I have to protect Will, protect him like he's protecting me.

The pain of the blade as it slices through my skin barely registers in my mind. I don't care about the physical pain because there are much worse pains. Like the pain I feel as I look at William. Seeing all the blood soaking his shirt. Blood... so much blood.

"Dove! Wake up..." I feel hands on me, warm, and firm. My eyes pop open, and the first thing I do is try and sit up.

"Calm down, it was just a dream, there is nothing to be scared of..." Zane's soft voice filters into my mind, but I'm still there. In that room with him.

I would do anything to bring him back. Anything for him to be alive today. I would have gladly taken his place. I should have been the one dead.

Pressing a hand to my stomach, I look down at my sweat-soaked body. I trace the scar there... *Blood. So much blood... William died, and it's all my fault.*

"There was blood, so much blood," I whisper. Tears prick my eyes, but I blink them away. The weight of the cuff on my wrist disappears, and then he's there, right in front of me, his dark eyes piercing mine, looking at me with nothing but kindness.

"Shhh, it's okay. I've got you," Zane whispers as he pulls me to his chest, wrapping his arms tightly around me. Holding the broken pieces of my soul together.

I know I shouldn't, that it's stupid and wrong, but I seek out his comfort. Needing it so badly, it hurts. I'm too weak to deny it.

He's nothing but a stranger, but he's all I have. Clutching onto his shirt, I pull him closer. I want to embed myself beneath his skin. Burying my face in his chest, I inhale deeply. Clean. He smells like soap and man, and very slowly, the dream recedes.

As I come down, floating like a leaf through the air, I'm reminded that the last time I felt this safe was with *him*... William.

It doesn't make sense. I shouldn't feel safe with this man. He's certifiably crazy, he drugged me, kidnapped me, and that's not even mentioning all the other things that he's done, but at this moment, I wouldn't want to be anywhere else.

There has to be something wrong with me if I'm seeking out the comfort of my captor.

After what seems like forever, he pulls back, his eyes travel down my body and land on the spot where my scar is hiding under my clothes. He must've seen me holding my stomach. I expect there to be a hunger, a lustful need in his gaze, but there isn't. All I find is a tenderness that makes my chest tighten.

"You're safe, Dove. You'll always be safe with me. Whatever your nightmare was about, it was only a dream. I'll always watch out for you." Something about those words tugs on me. It takes my sleepy brain a moment to let what he just said sink in.

You're safe. I'll always watch out for you...

"That night, when I walked home from the club, did you follow me?"

"I did."

"There was a guy at the party. I think he followed me—"

"The one in the plaid shirt?"

"Yeah. He was following me home, wasn't he?"

"He was, but I took care of him." I draw in a shaky breath, not knowing how to feel about what he just said. *Took care of him.* That's code for killing him. "He wanted to hurt you, Dove, and he would have if I hadn't been there."

I know he is right. That guy would have hurt me, but did he deserve to die because of it? I feel terrible, strangely not because he died, but because I feel very little remorse, even though it's partly my fault.

Lifting his hand, he softly touches my skin there. Even through the thin fabric of my sleep shirt, the gentle touch feels like an electric shock. Not one that would make you hurt, but one that wakes you up, makes you feel alive.

His fingers dance over the scar, and he touches it the same way I touch it when I'm nervous. Closing my eyes, I let my arms fall to my side and just let him touch me. I revel in the feel of his fingers on me. Enjoying the closeness without thinking about all the craziness between us.

For a moment, I just want to be happy and feel safe. He gently tucks me back into his side, his fingers never stop caressing my stomach, moving back and forth right over my marred skin.

"Go back to sleep," Zane coaxes, his voice deeper than usual. "It's still the middle of the night."

Exhaustion washes over me again as I settle deeper into the down feather pillow. My head feels heavy, just like the rest of my body. I shouldn't feel content in his arms. I shouldn't let him touch me like this, in an intimate but non-sexual way. I shouldn't... but I am. And that's how I fall back asleep. Content and happy, blissfully ignoring the danger I'm in. Tomorrow, I'll worry about what I've let happen. For now, I'm going to let my captor give me a belly rub, enjoying every second of it as I drift back into a dreamless sleep.

16

I hardly sleep for the rest of the night. Not because I'm not tired, but because I don't want this moment to end. It feels like a dream, one I'm going to wake up from any second. I hate that she had such a nightmare, but I fucking love the way she came to me. She let me calm her down, the way she opened up, letting me hold her, touch her. For the first time, it felt like she really believed that I was more than the guy who took her.

Lying there beside Dove, I watch her chest rise and fall for a long time. My gaze moves slowly as if I'm taking a picture of each part of her. Soft, pink, plump lips, tiny nose, beautiful high cheeks. The tiny freckle in the corner, near her lip. I don't want to ever forget these moments with her.

It doesn't take long for me to grow restless. I'm used to keeping busy, so I force myself out of bed, moving slowly, so I don't wake Dove. I have some stuff to check, and I'd rather do it when she's asleep, that way I don't risk another fight or more questions I don't have answers to.

Walking out to the kitchen, I close the bedroom door behind me and head to the coffee pot. I fill the coffee filter and push the brew button, listening to the machine work. A few minutes later, I take my steaming cup of hot coffee and walk to the library.

Setting my cup down, I kneel in front of the cabinet that holds my safe. I open the door and punch in the code, watching as the heavy safe door pops open. I pull out the laptop and phone and sit down in the recliner.

The laptop and phone itself are password protected, then there is another passcode that needs to be entered every time you connect to the internet. Having a connection built into the bunker was a pain in the ass but necessary. I need to know what's going on outside, after all.

First, I check the video surveillance for Dove's place, fast-forwarding over the feed. No one has been in there, which means no one has reported her missing yet, nor has Christian sent anyone else to kill her, which is good.

Checking my phone messages next, I find multiple calls and text messages from both Christian and Diego, asking when they can expect the girl. Neither one asks about Billy, so they must not have discovered his body yet, or they just haven't made the connection.

"Hey." Dove's sleepy voice fills the room. I look up to find her standing in the doorway, curiously eyeing the phone in my hand. Her hair is a wild mess, and she looks, well, sexy as hell.

"Good morning." I tuck the phone and laptop back into the safe.

Dove watches me as I finish locking up. "I didn't think a phone would work down here."

"It doesn't. Not cell service anyway. I do have internet down here; I can make calls through that connection." I say.

"Would you let me call Donna? Or Sasha? Just to let them know I'm okay." The pleading tone of her voice makes my chest constrict, but it also gives me a bargaining chip.

"How about this? Let's have breakfast first. I need to make sure you understand the rules and are willing to follow them. If I think you can, then I'll let you call Donna later."

"Really?" she says in a high-pitched voice as if she can't believe I just made that offer.

"Really." I watch as hope blossoms in her eyes.

Together, we walk back to the kitchen, where she takes a seat at the table, and I start to prepare breakfast.

"What was your dream about?" I ask, after a moment of silence.

"I don't remember..." She must be desperate to change the subject because immediately after, she says, "You know I can cook too."

"I know, but I like taking care of you." I glance over my shoulder at her just in time to catch the tiniest smile tugging at her lips.

"How old are you?"

"Twenty-three."

"I'm guessing you know how old I am?"

"Twenty-one," I say, matter of fact. Of course, I know that and much more.

"Is there anything you don't know about me?"

"I don't think so. I'm pretty sure I know more about you than you know about yourself."

"How is that even possible?" she asks, squirming in her seat.

"I've watched you. I see things that you don't. For example, you feel weak, and you think that you're scared of everything. In reality, you are brave and downright fearless."

She makes an adorable snorting sound and shakes her head. "If you think so. What about you. I know nothing about you. Is there anything you can tell me?"

"I grew up in foster care, like you," I say, just as the eggs and bacon get done cooking. I place everything on two plates and take a seat next to her.

She doesn't say anything to my foster care remark and just nods her head. She probably enjoys reminiscing about it just as much as I do.

"What else? Like what do you do for work... or did? I mean other than being a criminal? You must've had a job at one point, like a real job, right?"

"I've only had two jobs my entire life. One is killing people for the local mob—"

Her fork slips out of her hand, making a loud clanking noise as it hits the table. She jumps in her seat, scared by the sound, or maybe by what I just said.

"A-and the o-other?"

"Protecting you," I say softly. She lowers her head and sighs deeply. I can see the conflict in her eyes, even though they are downcast.

She stays quiet for the rest of the meal. Must be out of questions for the day. When we've both cleared our plates of food, I take them and deposit them in the sink.

"You know if I let you call Donna, you have to lie to her. You can't tell her where you are... not like you know where you are anyway."

She frowns. "I'm not stupid, I won't say anything. I just want to hear her voice and make sure she isn't worried about me."

"Okay, let's call her then." At my words, she perks up, shock takes over her face. She still doesn't believe me, probably thinks it's a trap, but it's not. "Well, come on."

Dove eagerly follows me into the library, where I reopen the safe and get everything out again. I set up a secure line and call the nursing home's number. When I hear it ringing, I hand her the phone.

I watch and listen closely as she talks to the nurse, then to Donna. As soon as she hears her adoptive mother's voice, a genuine smile spreads across her face. Dove is beautiful on any given day, but when she smiles, she literally takes my breath away.

Enjoying the view of Dove being happy and content, I let them talk for as long as she wants. After about twenty minutes, we hear the nurse in the background telling Donna it's time for her morning exercise. The two women say their goodbyes, and Dove hangs up the phone before handing it to me.

"Thank you."

"Anything for you." And I mean, *anything*.

I LET the hot water beat down on my tired skin after my afternoon workout. Steam has filled the entire bathroom by the time I wash my hair. Watching the water drain, my mind wanders to Dove. She was different today, more open to the idea of me not being the enemy. She is still guarded, but there seems to be less resentment coming from her now.

The image of her smiling, so happy when I let her call Donna, enters my mind. I love seeing her like this... lighthearted, joyful, simply happy. I want her permanently happy, to smile all day, to smile every time she sees me, to smile every time I touch her.

Groaning, I take my hardening cock in my hand and imagine her smiling, her beautiful, plump lips are wrapped around it. She sucks hard, taking me deep into her mouth. *Fuck.* I bet her mouth feels like heaven.

A hiss of pleasure escapes my lips. I want to be inside her so badly. I don't care where or how. Mouth, pussy, ass... Doesn't matter because eventually, I'll claim all of her. For now, however, only one will do. Anything but my fucking hand.

Pumping my cock harder, I think about how warm and wet her pussy will be. How tight she'll be squeezing my dick when I take her virginity. How slow I'll take her, savoring every inch that I gain inside her.

I thrust into my hand, tightening my grip as picture after picture of the things I want to do to Dove play behind my eyes like a movie. My balls tighten, and the pleasure builds. Just when I'm about to blow a fat load onto the shower tiles, I get this weird feeling. The feeling of someone watching me. I still my hand with my cock heavy in it. My eyes flutter open and connect with a pair of big blues.

I don't know who is more shocked, her, or me. She didn't just walk in here by accident, see me and walk back out. No, she is standing in the middle of the bathroom, watching me jerk off. She walked in here, knowing I was taking a shower.

Her mouth hangs open, and her eyes are so impossibly wide, I think it must hurt to put so much strain on them. It looks like she's about to say something, her lips moving slightly, but no words come out.

I would give anything to know what's going on inside her pretty little head right now. There's only a second for me to make my decision, a second before she turns and walks away.

A good man would tell her to get out, to go into the bedroom and wait, but after this morning, and all these years of being so close but yet so far away, I'm just not strong enough to. I want her, in whatever way she'll let me have her.

Opening the glass door, steam billows out. "I see you watching me. Take your clothes off and come in here."

Fear briefly flashes over her face, but something else emerges beneath. Curiosity? Need? Want? Even if she is afraid, this other emotion must win out because she reaches for the hem of her shirt.

Her movements are slow and jerky, almost unsure as she shoves her pants down and then pulls her shirt off. She stands there before me in plain panties and a bra, and I'm so wound up I could explode at the image. *Perfection.*

"Don't be shy. I've already seen you naked." I say as she hesitates, her fingers dipping into the sides of her panties. I can see her mind working, fighting with herself. Arguing about what she wants and what she thinks is right.

Maybe she won't do it? Maybe she'll turn around and run out of the bathroom? It would be the smart thing to do. The right thing.

Her eyes stay trained to my face as she shocks the hell out of me by slowly dragging her panties down her legs before kicking them away once they reach her feet.

Next is her bra, and it takes everything inside of me not to look down at that valley between her thighs. I've dreamed about this moment. Fucked my hand so many times to the image, it should be illegal. Hell, if she knew how often I've fucked her in my mind, she would be terrified.

"I..." Her cheeks turn fifty shades of pink as she slowly walks into the shower. "This is... I don't know why I'm doing this. I don't know you. You kidnapped me. You drugged me, but..." She shakes her head almost as if she too doesn't believe it.

Shame overtakes her features and I close the door before crossing the space that separates us. I can't allow her to feel this way. To question this. We were made for each other. We're two different sides of a fractured soul.

"You're doing it because you know deep down, I'm not the monster you're making me out to be. Yes, I brought you here against your will, but have I hurt you?"

"No," she answers nervously.

"And I won't. No matter what happens or what you do, I won't hurt you. I just want to make you feel good. Do you want that? Do you want me to touch you?" Her throat bobs, and her teeth sink into her bottom lip. I won't touch her, no matter how badly my fingers itch to unless she says yes.

"I've never been naked with a man or touched a..." Her naiveté only makes her more attractive as she refuses to say the word out loud.

Leaning into her body, I watch with pleasure as she shivers, tiny goosebumps pebbling her flesh. I want to taste her, suck on her tender skin, mark her. Make her mine. Forever.

"Did you forget that I know everything there is to know about you? I know that you're a virgin, that you've never let a man touch you, let alone fuck you."

Her chest rises and falls, drawing my attention to her perky breasts.

"Will you touch me?"

"Only if you want me to," I say hoarsely, running my fingers underneath the swell of her breast. "Is that what you want? For me to touch you?"

Her voice is so soft I almost don't hear her response. "Yes."

Forcing myself to breathe slowly, I lean into her and touch my lips to hers. I kiss her lazily, drawing out each caress until she's lifting her hands and placing them against my chest. Tiny nails sink into my flesh, and I knead one breast before switching to the other.

We're both panting now, and my balls ache so badly I feel like I'm going to blow at any second. I need a release, and soon.

"I want to touch you." My lips move across her jaw and down her throat. My kisses grow hungrier as I reach her throbbing pulse.

"You are..." She says innocently.

Easing back, I chuckle. "No, I mean, here..." I trail my hand down to her abdomen and run my finger over the top of her mound.

"I don't want to have sex," she blurts out as if we were going there right now. "I'm not ready for that."

"Not sex, sweetheart, just touching. Nothing else."

She looks like she might say no but then nods her head. I can tell she's nervous, but she has nothing to be nervous about. I'll make this good for her.

"Spread your legs a little." She immediately widens her stance, and my fingers move over her skin tenderly as if she's a delicate flower.

When I reach her folds, I slide a finger between them and smirk when I find her already wet for me.

Looking down at her, she's staring up at me with uncertainty.

"Relax. I won't hurt you, and if you want me to stop, I will." Fluttering my finger against her clit, I watch as her facial features do a one-eighty. There's something wild in her eyes, like a stallion that needs to be lassoed.

"You're so reactive to my touch... like you were made for me. Fuck, I want to be inside of you so bad."

"That feels..." She trails off like she can't find the word.

"Good?"

"Yes, so good." She tugs her bottom lip into her mouth, and I'm tempted to bite it just like she is, but instead, focus entirely on her pleasure. After rubbing gentle circles against her clit for a while, I move to her entrance, exhaling all the air in my lungs as I very slowly sink one digit inside of her. Heaven. Absolute fucking heaven is the only way I could describe this. Come leaks from the swollen head of my cock, and every muscle in my body tightens.

Dove clenches around my finger, and I look up into her angelic face. She's tensing up again, it's most likely nerves; still, I have to make certain.

"Am I hurting you?"

"No... I want...you." The urgency in her voice tells me she's telling the truth, plus she's drenched, soaking my fingers, she wants this.

With her pussy in my hand, I watch her face intently as I slowly pump my finger in and out of her channel, maintaining pressure against her clit.

And fuck, what I see as I watch her is what I always imagined it would be like when I touched her. Euphoric pleasure clouds her eyes. Her pupils dilate, and her mouth opens, forming a perfect O. She looks like a sex goddess.

Her arousal coats my hand, and I know she's close, so close. Curving my finger upward, I rub against the tissue at the top of her channel. At that very moment, I feel her fingers graze my cock before gripping it fully.

Holy fucking shit. I've died and gone straight to heaven. Gritting my teeth, I barely keep myself from flying off the edge with her small hand wrapped around my cock, she's stroking me slowly, her inexperience showing but I don't care.

"Come for me, sweetheart, I can feel you fluttering, building up for release. I want to feel your tightness all around me, feel you let go. Come for me..." I whisper against her lips, plunging into her a little faster, my palm slapping against her clit.

Little sex kitten noises spill from her mouth, and her nails drag across my chest, leaving behind red marks. The pain only heightens my pleasure. I'm desperate for a release, desperate to fill her with my fucking cock. But I'm beyond desperate to know what it feels like to have her fall apart. To feel her crumble in my hands.

"I'm..." She starts but doesn't finish as she slams head-first into pleasure. Her hand stops moving on my cock, and her body arches into mine as she pushes up onto her tiptoes just as her pussy starts clenching around my finger. I'm so fucking turned on, so fucking in need of release that I shatter right along with her. Lightning bolts of pleasure zing through me, heading straight into my aching balls, and like a teenager touching pussy for the first time, I come undone, ripping at the seams.

Sticky ropes of semen erupt from the head of my cock and land against Dove's thigh, marking her. Heat rips across my skin, my heart thundering in my chest, and all I can feel is her in my arms, falling apart, her pussy creaming against my hand.

After a moment, I ease out of her and smile when my eyes catch on my release that's dripping down her thigh. I'm tempted to tell her I don't usually go off that easy but decide not to. She's not experienced enough to care, and when the time for me to take her comes, I'll make sure I give her the best fucking performance ever.

"Thank you." I press a soft kiss to the crown of her forehead, waiting for us both to catch our breath.

She gives me a half-smile, her eyes heavy with post orgasm pleasure. "I didn't do anything."

Shutting off the water, I turn back toward her. "Yes, you did. You trusted me enough to let me be a part of something special, so yes, you did do something."

She shrugs. "I didn't, not really."

I help her dry off and then slip into a pair of grey sweatpants. She hurries into the closet and comes out wearing a nightgown. Her eyes are trained to the floor, almost like she's afraid to look at me. Worry knots in my gut.

She's so quiet. I don't know what I thought would happen afterward, but I didn't think she would withdrawal so much. Maybe I did hurt her, and she just doesn't want to tell me. I watched her face the entire time and felt her fall apart, but maybe I had misjudged something.

I hate feeling this way when it comes to her and refuse to bite my tongue. I have to know if I did something...

"Is everything okay?" I ask when we go to lie down for bed.

She nods but doesn't make eye contact with me. "Everything is fine. I just feel... weird, like I did something wrong. Like letting you touch me was bad."

"It wasn't bad—" I start to explain but am cut off before I can finish.

"Can we just go to bed? I don't want to talk about this anymore." Desperation coats each word, and though I want to push her to explain to me what's going on in her head, there will be other times I can do that. I don't want to fight and ruin the moment we shared, so I shut off the light and crawl into bed beside her. There is a foot of space between us, which seems strange now, after how close we were in the shower.

"Goodnight, Dove," I say.

"Night," she whispers back.

It isn't long before she falls asleep, her soft snores filling the quiet room. However, like all the nights of my life, I can't sleep and instead stare at her, watching as she finds blissful sleep.

17

The days start to blend together. Time isn't a variable when there is no clock or sunlight. Each day the walls seem to close in on me a little bit more. Sleeping, reading, and eating are what my life consists of now. At least Max isn't bothered by the isolation. He's still his purring self. I, on the other hand, have cabin fever.

I do my best to stay away from Zane, but it's a lot harder than you think. Shoved into a box, I'm forced to interact with only him, a man that has me completely baffled. Being here makes me feel lonely. There is no sun, no animals, minus Max, and nothing to do. I miss my normal, boring life more and more every day. I miss talking to people, conversation. I'm longing for that human contact you can only get outside these walls. I never realized how important that is to me, the connection to other people.

I'm in a constant battle of trying to stay away from him and trying to seek him out. So far, my brain has won, and I've managed to keep my physical urges in check, but I know damn well that that's not going to last much longer.

Ever since that night in the shower, my body tingles all over whenever our eyes meet. Stupidly, I replay what we did over and over again in my mind. His thick finger entering me, owning me. The way I spiraled out of control. How he held me through the pleasure, finishing right along with me.

Repeating to myself over and over again that he's the enemy, would be easier if my body felt the same way I did. All this confusion does is give me a never-ending headache.

I still don't know why I went into the bathroom that day. It was like my mind shut down, and my body took over. I heard the shower running, and I swear I was just going to take a quick peek. Curiosity and all. I thought to myself, it would be only fair to watch him since he watched me for so long. But then I saw him jerking off in the shower, his hand wrapped around his cock. It was mesmerizing. Even after he saw me, I didn't care. There were blocks of concrete tied to my feet, stopping me from going anywhere.

Stupid. I was stupid for letting him touch me. Stupid for craving his touch. Paging through the book, I pretend to be reading while Max snuggles into my side.

I've discovered another layer of the extensiveness that is Zane's obsession with me. It's like he knows everything, and I mean everything. It's not simple things like your favorite color or food. It's what I'm allergic to, the surgeries I've had, my work hours, and therapy schedule.

He knows things that others would never notice. Like when I touch my scar...

I try not to think about the other things he knows... like my time in foster care or that *night.* I feel a sliver of triumph because no matter how much he knows, he can't know about that night. He might have read the police report, but he doesn't know what really happened because I never told a soul.

Every once in a while, he'll share something about himself, but those moments are far, and few between and none of those things are of great significance. They're mundane things, like how he loves Italian food but hates Chinese.

I don't ask him about working with the mob, mostly because I'm afraid of what he'll tell me. Then again, it probably wouldn't be a bad idea for me to think the worst of him. It would certainly make it easier for me to hate him.

I still haven't pieced the puzzle together on where I fit into things. I don't know where and how his obsession with me began. All I know is Zane is determined to keep me here and protect me from whatever evil he feels is lurking in the outside world. Because of his kindness and the feelings he has for me, my hate and fear are becoming harder and harder to maintain.

It's impossible for me to make myself hate someone who refuses to hurt me. Yes, he's my captor, but he doesn't act like it. He treats me like a lover, he's been waiting for his whole life. Like a rare piece of glass, I'm fragile to him. Beautiful. To be put on a shelf and gazed upon. I'm none of those things though. Or at least I don't want to be.

I'm hyper-aware of his presence, and I hate it. I hate that I'm drawn to him. That my nipples harden and my core burns when he's near.

Stupid, treacherous body.

I tell myself it's because I've never had a man's attention on me before and maybe that's it, or maybe it's something else. Something I don't want to admit to. The power he has over me is terrifying. It entices me. He hasn't tried to touch me since the shower, but I know he wants to.

His gaze lingers a little longer than it should, and yeah, he might be good at hiding his emotions, but he isn't that good. The way he looks at me is how I imagine a starving man looks at a steak. Like he could devour it, consume it all in one single bite.

That single thought gets the wheel in my head spinning. What if I use his obsession with me against him? He wants me, deep down, I can see it, and feel it, so what if I try to seduce him? Maybe that's how...

"Do you want to watch a movie with me?"

A high-pitched squeal leaves my lips, and I jump about a foot off the chair. My movements cause the book in my lap to fall to the floor. "Jesus!" I press a hand to my chest to stop my heart from lurching out of it. "Maybe make some noise before you appear out of thin air."

Zane smirks, showing off two dimples. I feel my insides warming already. My hormones are out of control. He's so handsome it hurts. His body's cut from stone, his features dangerous, but alluring. If I'd seen him on the street, I wouldn't just find him attractive. I'd find him salivating.

"You need to become more aware of your surroundings. I've been standing here for five minutes now, just staring at you."

It makes sense now, how easily he watched me. He's like a ghost, or ninja, or both. And apparently, I need to pay better attention. Maybe if I had, I wouldn't be here right now.

"So, is that a yes or no?"

"Uhhh." My face heats to the temperature of the sun. "Yes, sure." I've been doing anything and everything I can to keep the distance between us.

Maybe now is the time to try and implement my plan. I don't know the first thing when it comes to seducing a man, but all I can do is try. It's my only hope. Plus, Zane knows how inexperienced I am. It's not like he'll be able to notice something is up.

Like a lost puppy, I follow him out and into the living room. I plop on the couch, letting the soft cushion and oversized pillows swallow me. Watching him put on the movie, I try to come up with a plan while also trying not to look too nervous.

By the time the movie starts, and he's settled onto the couch next to me, I've come up with nothing. My anxiety builds, stacking up like Jenga blocks. One misstep and everything could come crashing down.

"Are you okay?" Zane turns, asking me in that deep gravelly voice that reaches inside of me and refuses to let go.

I nod, afraid of what might come out of my mouth if I open it. Zane gives me a half-smile and directs his attention back to the TV.

I watch him out of the corner of my eye. He looks like he's watching the movie, but he's not. He's watching me too.

I can sense it. Feel it.

There's this fluttery feeling in my chest. Like a butterfly is tirelessly beating its wings, trying to escape.

Just do it. Make the first move. It's your only way out...

Inching closer to Zane, I wonder if he can sense how nervous I am? Gah, what am I thinking? Of course, he can. Like he said, he knows me better than I know myself, which is scary as hell, by the way.

Forcing myself to keep moving, I inch closer and closer. If I stop now, I won't move anymore, so I have to keep going. Push through the fear. Scooting closer to him, I try and keep my movements subtle, but it's a lot harder than you would think.

Ignoring the heat in my cheeks and the tension in my muscles, I keep moving until we're so close I can feel his body heat radiating into my side. Zane is huge compared to me, his body dwarfing mine, and as I attempt to cuddle into his side, I become more aware of this.

I don't know why this is so hard for me. He holds me every night, this shouldn't be any different, but it is. It's a whole lot different because he doesn't give me a choice at night. He just pulls me into his chest and holds me, whether I want to or not.

This, however, is one-hundred percent my choice. I'm initiating this. Diving head-first into dark waters. It's sink or swim time.

Trying to calm my erratic heartbeat and breathing, so Zane doesn't catch on to me, I focus on the movie and ignore the wall of muscle beside me. The tension slowly eases out of me, and I lean further into Zane until my head is resting against his arm.

I wait to see if he pulls away or even objects, but his body stays glued to mine. He's probably enjoying the nearness of my body, that I'm making an effort to be close to him all on my own. As the movie plays, I find my eyes gravitating toward the apex of his thighs.

Should I do it now? Would grabbing his penis be too on point? I don't want to come across as desperate, but honestly, I am, so does it really matter? Patience isn't really my strong point, and being here has made me even antsier.

"Are you even watching the movie?" Zane asks, catching me off guard.

"Uhh..."

"You didn't have to watch it with me just so I would hold you. Movie or not, I have no problem being close to you." I hate the way his words make me feel. Like I'm precious, a gift.

Instantly, I feel bad about deceiving him like this. He might be sick and fucked up in his head, but he really has been trying to make me feel safe and comfortable, and in a lot of ways, he has. I've never felt safer, not since Will. Zane gives me comfort, he protects me, and I know even without asking, he's done things for me. Things I could never picture.

"Oh, okay," I murmur. "I still want to watch the movie," I say, even though I haven't actually paid any attention to it.

Zane lifts his arm and motions for me to come closer. I take the invitation and cuddle into his side. He lowers his arm and drapes it over my shoulders, engulfing me in his warmth. It feels nice. Right. Like I was meant to be here.

The movie plays until the end, but I couldn't really concentrate on it. I'm in too much of an argument with myself in my head, giving myself a headache.

"Ready to go to bed?" Zane asks, turning off the TV with the remote.

"Yeah, sure..." We untangle ourselves from each other and the couch. Walking together into the bedroom, my heart is going a million miles per hour. *I can do this.*

"Are you sure you're okay? You seem tense."

"I'm fine," I say. It probably sounds as unconvincing as I feel.

Once in the bedroom, I grab my pajamas and get changed in the bathroom. I purposely leave the top buttons undone, showing off a bit more skin than I usually would.

When I get back, Zane is already sprawled out on the bed. The blanket is covering his lower half, his upper body bare. His muscular chest is on full display. My mouth starts watering, and my core tightens.

Zane raises an eyebrow when he sees me trying to walk sexy as I make my way to the bed, but he doesn't say anything. I crawl under the blanket next to him, and instead of taking our normal spooning position, I turn to face him. Draping my arm over his middle, I use his chest as a pillow.

Like this, I can hear the steady rhythm of his heartbeat, and I wonder how much faster mine is beating right now. Zane reaches over to his nightstand and switches off the light, blanketing the room in darkness.

"Goodnight, Dove."

It's now or never...

"Actually," I whisper, and let my hand trail down his stomach. Swallowing down the fear, I make it to his thigh, where I graze the rod between his legs. It's thick and hard, and suddenly I don't know if I can do this. I think I'm in over my head.

"What are you doing?" Zane's voice is like a bucket of cold water. I pull my hand away like touching him is fire.

"I-I..." Is all I can manage to get out before Zane has flipped me onto my back and has climbed on top of me.

"Don't play games with me, Dove," he says, his face so close to mine that his minty breath fans over my face. His large body looms over me, caging me in, pressing me into the mattress.

It's hard to make out his features in the dark, but I don't need to see his face to know he's angry. I can feel it like a branding iron on my skin.

"I'm not." I lie... kind of.

"You want me to fuck you? I can make that happen right now. Just say the word, and I'll rip off our clothes and slide inside of you so deeply you will never forget who you belong to. Is that what you want, Dove?"

Say yes, say yes. This is what you wanted.

I can feel his growing erection between us, long and hard, nestled between our bodies. Moisture soaks my panties, and my nipples tighten, rubbing against my shirt. My body is ready, but I...

"I don't know..." *God, I'm such a chicken.*

Leaning in even closer, he whispers into the shell of my ear, "Then don't tease me."

Just as fast as he was on top of me, he is gone. I'm still breathing heavily when he gets situated next to me. Turning us, he pulls me into his chest like he always does. I close my eyes and force myself to calm down, so I can go to sleep while wondering if I just made a huge mistake or if I barely escaped one.

18

I wake up the same way I fell asleep, with a terrible feeling in my gut. This isn't my first rodeo. I've been with women many times before, and I know Dove well enough to know she's acting out of character. This isn't her. She's sweet, naive, and so incredibly innocent. Reaching for my cock isn't something she would do... not unless... she's trying to play me. In which case, that would make perfect sense.

I don't exactly know what her goal is, but it doesn't matter. Either way, she's got it in her head that she can manipulate me. Use her body as a weapon. Ha. The thought is laughable in itself. If she were any other woman, I'd have tied her up and fucked the words right out of her mouth. Found out what she was doing with little effort, hell, I could've done it last night.

A silent rage bubbles up inside of me. She's the only person I've ever shown kindness to, and this is how I'm rewarded? We've been here for days now; she must have realized by now that I only want her to be safe. I get that she was scared in the beginning, but I've proven myself over and over again. Still, she wants to try and use me? Manipulate me? Use sex against me?

She wants to play games? Fine. I'll play along. I've been nice. I've shown compassion. Maybe I need to show her what happens when you provoke a man who is crazed with need over you. Right on cue, Dove stirs next to me.

She turns in my arms, her eyes blinking open slowly. Even though I'm angry with her, I still admire her beauty. "Is it the morning already?" She asks sleepily.

At least one of us slept well last night.

"Yes, time to rise and shine." I pull away first and start to roll off the bed when I feel her hand land against my shoulder. "Yeah?" I toss over my shoulder.

Dove is looking down at the comforter with an ashamed look. I'm tempted to tell her everything is okay, but I don't have it in me. Not right now. I'm still pissed that she would try and get me to have sex with her when we both know she's not ready.

What's her motive? Does she think I'll let her go if she does?

"I'm sorry about last night. I... I don't know what I was thinking," she mumbles shamefully, and I can see two bright spots forming on her cheeks. I wounded her last night with the way I handled things, but I had to, and I'll continue to handle them this way until she gets the point because if she pushes me too far, I'll snap, and we'll both be screwed.

"It's fine. It was a mistake. Everything is good," I say. Though my brain is screaming at me that it's not. My damn cock is permanently hard, and my balls are always aching because of her. Her sweet scent surrounds me, and her body tempts me to do sinfully bad things to it.

I want her bad enough without having her throw herself at me. I don't need to be tempted any more than I am.

"You still seem mad though." She rolls her bottom lip between her teeth. "I didn't do it to make you mad."

I tense. "No, you did it to see what I would do, but next time, I can't promise you that I'll stop myself from taking you. I've spared you this far, don't make it harder than it needs to be for me. I'm only human, and I promised myself that when the time came for me to claim your virginity, I would do so as you deserved, but you make that harder every single day."

Dove gives me a shocked look. "How do you know I haven't had sex before?"

It's too early to do this, but what the fuck, why not? It's either now or in five minutes. Turning to face her so I can see her eyes fully, I say, "Because I made sure no one would get that far. You were always going to be mine."

Her mouth pops open, and her eyes widen in shock. For a moment she just stares at me, processing the information I just gave her. "W-what do you mean?"

"You're a smart girl. You know what it means." I let her draw her own conclusions.

"You scared them away?"

I shrug, deciding not to tell her that I murdered a few of them. "I mean, you could say that, yes. I made sure they didn't come back for another date. Some I even made sure they never made it to the date to begin with." Yes, I'm a fucking asshole, but nothing and no one is going to touch or taint what's mine.

Dove is pure white snow, and I wasn't going to let some fucking asshole piss all over her. The guys she went on dates with were pigs and only wanted to get between her legs. No way was I going to watch that shit go down.

"All this time, I thought there was something wrong with me..." Sadness coats her voice, but quickly her eyes turn to fire, and she shakes her head angrily. Her statement brings my own anger down a couple of pegs. "I thought they didn't want me. That I was ugly and unlovable. I thought there was something wrong with me!"

Fuck me. Shit, I didn't expect it to turn into this. The hurt in her words, it's like a knife piercing me in the chest. Reaching for her, all I want to do is comfort her, but when my fingers graze her hand, she pulls away. She's looking at me like I've ruined her life, but doesn't she see that I've only made it better?

With a tight chest, I say, "I'm sorry, Dove. I only did it to protect you. I wasn't trying to hurt you. You aren't any of those things. You're perfect."

She moves off the bed, putting too much distance between us.

"Don't lie to me! You did it because you're selfish and didn't want me to fall in love with someone else before you had the chance to kidnap me. You wanted me alone because if you can't have me, no one can? Isn't that right?"

It takes every ounce of self-restraint I have not to grab her and throw her back onto the bed. To tie her up and keep her bound to this bed with me. Yes, everything she just said is true. No one can have her, only me. Yes, I've been selfish, and yes, I wanted her to be alone in a way. I never intended for her to feel as if she was at fault though, but there isn't anything I can do about that now. Nothing of the past matters. She's mine.

Anger fills my voice when I speak. "It wouldn't have mattered if you had found someone. I would've disposed of him and took you anyway. You're mine, don't you see that?"

Dove's tiny hands form into fists, and her body vibrates with unbridled anger. I wonder if she's going to punch me, act out on her rage?

"I'm not yours! I'm a human being with feelings. Not a pet or a *thing*. I am not, nor will I ever be yours!"

As soon as the words are out of her mouth, I'm off the bed and across the room. My heart races in my chest, and I don't think. I just react. Gripping Dove by the back of the neck, I hold her in place while staring down at her. Her body starts to tremble, and I know I'm scaring, her but maybe that's what she needs. I'm tired of her being a brat. Tired of her being ungrateful for all I've done, for us, for her.

A coldness sweeps through me. How dare she say she's not mine. She has been and always will be *mine*.

"You. Are. Mine!" I growl into her face. "I've killed for you, bled for you, sacrificed everything for you. You will be whatever I want you to be."

"I never asked you to do any of that!! I never wanted this. I never wanted you!" Just like that, I snap. My patience is gone. All I feel at this moment is anger. Burning, red hot anger. My vision blurs for a fraction of a second.

I release her nape and sink my fingers into the silky strands of hair. With a fist full of hair, I tilt her head back, forcing her to see me, really see me. Her big, blue eyes fill with fear, but I'm too far gone to give a shit. I'm done. Lifting her hands, she plants them against my chest and pushes against me, but I'm a fucking mountain and don't budge, not even an inch.

"It's never been your choice and never will be. Fight me all you want. Cry. Beg. Plead." Looking down, my eyes catch on her pulse, and I lean in, licking the sensitive skin, tasting her fear. "I'll die before you're ever free of me."

"You're hurting me," Dove whimpers, struggling against my grasp. I'm tempted to shove up her nightgown and rip her panties off of her. To teach her a lesson. If I knew I could stop there, I would. But I know I wouldn't be able to. Not even as she begs me to, so I do the last thing I want. I let her go. I release my hold on her hair and take a step back.

"I hate you!" Angry pants slip from her lips, and I can feel my own rage boiling over. I need to leave this room, get away from her.

"Hate me all you want, but that doesn't change anything. You're still mine, and you're still going to be here even when the anger passes. So, hate me. It doesn't change a damn thing."

Leaving the room, I feel like I'm drowning in my own rage. When I reach the library, I close the door behind me and sit down in one of the chairs. I hold my head in my hands for a long time, trying to get my breathing and mind back on track.

Needing to think about something else, I walk over to the safe, punch in the code and pull out the computer and phone. Dealing with some shit from the outside world should help. I set everything up and then check my email and messages. There are numerous messages from Christian, and I feel all the better about my choice of kidnapping Dove with each one that I read.

Christian: *Bring me the girl, and I'll spare you.*

Christian: *I've sent my men to find and kill both you and the girl. You're a good kid, Zane, but you don't fuck with the mob.*

Christian: *Where the fuck is the girl?*

Christian: *You're dead.*

There are at least a dozen more texts just like these. Some mentioning torture and rape if I don't give both of us up. I'm not afraid though. They'll never find Dove here. Never suspect that I've hidden her. They don't know who she is to me. Just like I don't know who Dove is to Christian, but I'll figure it out. Nothing remains a secret for long in the world we live in.

Some corrupt asshole will take the money I offer him for information. It's happened before, and it will happen again. We just need to lay low for a while, and then I can reach out to some people and get the ball rolling.

I check the surveillance on Dove's apartment. I'm not shocked to find the place completely ransacked. If she could see how her apartment looks right now, she'd be devastated, or maybe she would finally believe me that she is here for her own protection.

I've rescued her from the darkness, saved her the heartbreak. She should be thanking me instead of fighting me. Thinking about what she said angers me more, and I shut my thoughts down completely.

Locking up the computer and phone, I try to think of what to do next. I haven't had breakfast or coffee yet, but I don't think my stomach could handle either. I decide to workout. I need to get rid of this tension in my muscles. I need an outlet, and the punching bag is going to be my best chance of making it through the day.

19

I t takes me a long time to get my breathing under control after he leaves the room. My scalp tingles where he pulled my hair, and my insides twist with pure rage. I've never been this angry. Consumed by hate. All I can do is think of escaping. I'm not a person to him. I'm an obsession, an object. Something he owns and that he won't let anyone else touch.

God, I can't believe he did that. All the people he took from me... *Shawn*. I can't even imagine the sinister things he did to him, to them. Fear coils deep in my gut. He said I'll never be free of him. Tears fall from my eyes and cascade down my cheeks.

He did this for his own sick pleasure. He's not protecting me. He's keeping me. Locking me up. I won't be a victim. I won't let him control me. I'm going to get out of this, no matter what I have to do. Swiping at the tears, I force myself to get dressed.

It takes me forever to put my clothes on and even longer to walk out of the room, but when I do, Zane is nowhere to be found. I feel this strange tug on my heart at not seeing him, but I push the feeling away. He doesn't deserve anything from me, least of all, for me to care about him. He's a monster, a killer, and a criminal. He may not hurt me, but he's hurt others, and that's the same thing.

The living room is empty, as is the kitchen. I continue walking toward the hall that leads to the gym and library. I do my best not to make any noise, and when I reach the door to the gym, I spot Zane. He's doing push-ups on the floor, his complete attention on counting each up and down rep. I look to the free weights sitting a few feet away.

Now is your chance...

I know if I miss or don't knock him out that I'll be screwed. There is no coming back from this, but the other option is worse. It forces me to stay here with a man who is what real monsters are made of, and I can't do that. Wiping my clammy palms against the front of my yoga pants, I walk up to the weight rack and grab a fifteen-pound dumbbell. It should do the job. Nervously, I do my best not to trip or startle Zane as I edge closer to him.

You can do it. For one brief second, I contemplate putting the weight back and walking away. I'm not the type to hurt someone, and this is going to do some damage. It's going to rip me apart on the inside. I just don't see a way around it. It's him or me, and I have to save myself.

The muscles in my stomach tighten as I lift the weight above my head. Closing my eyes—because I can't look at this—I bring it down in an arch motion. Flinching when the heavy weight makes contact, and his body crashes to the floor with a thud. I lift the weight again, aiming for the back of his head, probably what I should've aimed for to begin with.

Except as I lift the weight above my head, Zane rolls over and pushes up onto his feet with lightning speed. Fear grips onto me, causing me to freeze. The dark shadow that casts on his face is terrifying. Zane might care about me, might be obsessed, but right now, all I see is a man who wants to hurt me. My lungs shrivel up, and my throat tightens. It feels like I'm suffocating, and he hasn't even touched me yet.

He's going to kill me.

"You just don't know when to quit, do you?" His lip curls with fury, and he tugs the weight out of my hand, tossing it to the floor behind him like it's nothing.

I'm going to die. I can feel it. He's looking at me with murder in his eyes, and I have nowhere to go, no way to escape him. I swallow down the scream building in my throat as he lunges for me, his nostrils flaring like a bull.

Lifting me, he tosses me over his shoulder. I land harshly, and it takes me about a half-second before I start pounding on his back and kicking my feet.

"Keep fighting me, Dove. It makes my cock hard feeling you struggle, and we both know how badly you want me."

"Let me go! I hate you. I hate you, and I will never let you touch me again. Never." I'm screaming the words now, my voice cracking from fear and anger.

Before I can grasp onto my bearings, Zane is doing just that, letting me go, but my relief is short-lived when I'm tossed onto the mattress like a rag doll.

His firm body blankets mine in an instant, and I try to move away, but he holds me in place, his fingers digging into the flesh at my hip. "You want me to treat you the way I treat everyone else? You don't want my kindness? Because that's all I've given you so far. You still fight me and try to escape. I'm doing all of this to protect you, but you don't see that. You don't see that the biggest monster isn't me but someone else. Why can't you see the truth?"

Like a wounded animal in the clutches of a predator, I twist my body and kick my legs, hoping to land a jab against him. Zane is skilled though and stops my assaults before they can even get started by pressing me deeper into the mattress.

My breaths are coming out in pants, and it's almost like I'm suffocating. Choking on the fear. The weight of his body is all I can feel. His hard cock is against my stomach, and I think I'm going to be sick. Bile rises in my throat.

Fight. Fight! Digging deep inside myself, I lash out. I catch him right across the face with my hand and drag my nails down across his nose and cheek, leaving deep gouges.

"Fuck!" He takes both of my wrists into one hand and pressing them to my chest. Once he has me trapped, I can hardly move, let alone breathe. When he leans into my face, all I see is the devil looking down at me.

The look in his eyes is pure violence. It promises pain, suffering, agony. This isn't the Zane I've come to know. This is the obsessed man who kills without thought, who will do anything to keep me where he wants me.

"You really shouldn't have done that, Dove."

No. This isn't happening. All of a sudden, this has gotten real. His body against mine. His rock hard cock. The searing heat bubbling between our two bodies. Hate and lust mingle together.

"Please. You don't have to do this. I'm sorry..."

"Oh, I do... I have to teach you a lesson. I need to show you what you don't want to admit. We belong together, and it's time I prove it to you."

He let's go of my wrists and starts ripping off my clothes. Fabric tears and cool air kisses my skin as my bra and shirt are ripped from my body. I'm trembling with fear, but still try to shove against his chest as hard as I can to escape. There is no point though. I can't move him. He's a steel wall, cold and impenetrable.

Snatching my wrists once more, he pins them above my head this time. With his free hand, he reaches into the drawer beside the bed and pulls out the handcuffs he used on me before. A moment later, the cool metal is fastened around my wrist, and the other end fastened to the headboard. He pulls out another pair and does the same to the other hand.

"Please..." I whimper, but even I know that the time for begging has passed. I've dug my own grave, and now I'm going to have to lie in it. "You said you would never hurt me!"

"Shut up," Zane growls as he makes quick work of my pants, pulling them down right along with my panties, leaving me completely bare to him. "You've tried to kill me. How the hell do you think you would have gotten out of here without me? You don't have the code for the door. You would have died in here!"

My whole body is shaking, my fear only intensifying as he strips out of his clothes. His very hard, very angry cock comes into view, and my fear reaches new heights. It's so big, the veins bulging out on it, visibly throbbing.

I didn't think that I would lose my virginity in such a savage way, taken from me without mercy, but there isn't anything I can do to stop him.

"Is this what you wanted?" He stares down at me. "Did you want me so angry that I take from you? That I take the choice from you, so you don't have to admit that you want this?"

"I hate you," I lie. I should, but I can't, even now. I squeeze my eyes shut and try to shut the world out.

"You try to hate me, but we both know you truly don't. You can't, we are too connected, whether you like it or not. We belong together, and I'm about to show you how much." His lips brush against mine, and I move against him on instinct, seeking out his comfort even with the threat of him hurting me.

"Open your eyes and look at me as I take you. Feel every inch of my cock as I sink deep inside you." The head of his cock brushes against my entrance, and I freeze, my entire body shutting down. I tell myself to stop feeling. Tears escape my eyes and slide down the sides of my cheeks. I can't breathe. I can't swallow. I feel cold all over, broken and scared, so scared. He's going to hurt me after he told me he wouldn't, he's going to. I don't understand why that matters so much at the moment. His words don't mean shit, not after what he's done to me, but deep down, I know that's a lie.

They mean everything...

A pained cry fills the room. It takes a moment to realize that it came from me. I made that sound. Zane's body freezes above mine, but I still don't open my eyes. I can't. I do want this, but not like this. I don't want to be a victim of his rage and anger.

I try to suck in a breath, but my chest is too tight, panic holding it prisoner like a hundred-pound weight. I feel like I'm suffocating, gasping for oxygen. My mind races at the things he's going to do to me, the savage way he's going to claim me over and over again.

"Shhh." I feel the warmth of his hand against my cold cheek. He cups it gently, swiping at the tears that still linger there. It's like he knows I need this. I know I shouldn't, that I should hate him, tell him to release me, but instead of doing those things, I seek comfort in his touch, nuzzling my face into his palm, needing it. Needing him.

"I never want to hurt you, Dove. But dammit... the way you act, it makes me want to break you down just so I can build you up again. To prove to you that you need me. But I'm not sure I could come back from that. I can't see my Dove broken in her cage. I want her to sing and fly, but I'm tired of her trying to escape."

"I can't accept this..." I whimper.

"You have to, and after today, you won't be able to fly away from me, Dove. I'm going to shackle you to me. Make you mine forever. Do you understand?"

"Zane, please..." I whimper, my breathing slowly returning to a normal pace. When I finally force my eyes open, I find Zane hovering above me. There's a softness in his eyes. I want to reach out and grab it, wrap myself up in it.

He's watching me cautiously, tenderly almost, penetrating my soul with his gaze. Before, when I looked at him, there was nothing. An empty pit of nothingness. Now, there is light in his eyes, pieces of his shine through and down at me.

A rough hand skims down the side of my body, gently stroking the tense flesh. It feels like he's taking the fear he gave me and replacing it with something else, something deeper. Leaning forward, he presses an open-mouthed kiss to my breast, his tongue sliding over the flesh makes me shiver. Every hair on my body awakens at his touch. Reaching my nipple, he takes it into his mouth, flicking the bud with his tongue.

A spark of pleasure ignites in my belly, and I have to stop myself from arching into his mouth. He sucks deeply, tugging on the hard bud before releasing it with a pop. He works the other one over in the same fashion, and I feel my arousal for him dripping down my thighs. I'm drenched, my core clenching, silently begging him to take me.

I want him. Even though I shouldn't. Even though it's wrong. I still want him, and I can't deny that. I can't lie about the strange connection we have. Nothing about Zane is normal, and after all the things he's told me, I know I should be fighting him, but I'm tired of pushing him away. I want this... need it.

"I want you, Dove, and I'm going to have you. I'm going to take what's mine, own you, seal our bodies together as one. You were meant to be mine, and it's time I claim you. Time, I make you mine so no one else can."

Every muscle in my body tenses, and I think he's going to spread me wide and plunge deep inside, but he shocks me when he moves back and peers down between my legs. Dropping down to his belly, he slides his hands under my ass and lifts me to his face. He inhales deeply, and my cheeks burn. He isn't doing what I think he is, is he?

I tug against the cuffs and try to look down at him, but in this position, I'm at his mercy. Just like he wants, needs. *Dove trapped in her golden cage.*

"You smell divine, perfect, and I can't wait to fucking taste you. I've envisioned this moment for years. Tongue fucking you. Tasting your release as you explode into my mouth." His lips trail the inside of my thigh. My muscles jump underneath the scrape of his tongue. Every touch is heightened. Hot breath fans against my entrance, and I'm not sure if I should beg him to stop or keep going. Zane doesn't give me a chance to dwell on the thought long before making the choice for me.

His lips close around the bundle of nerves hidden between my folds, and the pleasure that sparks is so intense I lift my hips and gasp his name at the same time. Strong fingers dig into my thighs as he spreads me wider, his hulking frame fitting between them as if he was always made to be there. He feasts on me without care, driven by primal need. His mouth is relentless, and all I feel is him owning me, worshipping me.

I grow wetter and wetter as he sucks, and when his tongue flicks over the bud, I explode. He rips the orgasm right out of me. I'm almost ashamed at how fast I fall apart, but my brain is too drunk on lust to think about that for long. Not when my entire body feels like it's gone to heaven. My toes curl into the mattress, and I lift my hips arching into his face.

Zane presses a kiss to my mound, and then I feel a finger at my entrance. I've barely come down from my high when he slowly slides into me and starts fucking me with that single digit. All I can do is focus on the pleasure he gives me, and when my body starts to coil tight, gearing up for a second release, he adds another finger, stretching me.

I'm consumed by him, and when I look up, our eyes connect. "Come for me, fall apart so I can fuck you the way you should be fucked. Like only I can."

The intensity in his eyes, the love and want that pours out of him. He's obsessed, but his feelings are deeper than that, and I feel that now. Feel his attraction. It's like sticking your finger into a light socket.

Scissoring the two fingers inside of me, he touches that sweet spot at the back of my channel that he touched before and I come undone. Split down the middle. My muscles tense, and like a rubber band, my body snaps. Pleasure pools in my core, and I clench down on his fingers, my channel gripping him like it never wants to let go.

"Tell me you want me... that you want my cock," Zane says as he eases his fingers out of me. My gaze flicks down to his massive cock. Come beads the tip as it bobs in the space between us. Can I do this? Take him? I'm afraid... but also spellbound with need.

I want him, need him.

"Yes, take me..."

The words have barely left my lips, and he's on me, centering himself between my legs. Hovering above me, his entire body vibrates. He's so big and warm, and I feel safe. I feel safe in my captor's arms. Snaking a hand between our bodies, he guides the crown of his cock to my entrance, and I tense. I look up at him and find him watching me.

"There is no way around this. It's going to hurt, but I promise I'll be as gentle as I can," he whispers hoarsely, and relief floods my veins.

He won't hurt me. He won't just take.

I try and relax as the head of his cock enters me, but I can't. It feels like he's taking everything from me. Pain. Pleasure. Love. Hate. My lungs tighten, and my thoughts become dizzy. It's like he's ripping me in two.

"Breathe, baby, breathe for me." Zane sounds as pained as I feel, and I realize I'm not breathing then. Sucking in a shaky breath, I half expect him to just plow into me at that moment, but he doesn't. He takes his time, savoring every inch he gains. Pain ripples through me, overtaking the pleasure.

I feel full, so full, and when he reaches the resistance of my virginity, he smiles. He actually smiles as he thrusts forward and claims it. Like a prize that can never be returned or given to another, he makes certain I will always remember him. Remember this moment. No matter what happens, I will always know who my first was.

Peppering my face with kisses, he thrust a little deeper, and I whimper when his balls press against my ass. He's all the way in... he's inside of me. His muscles strain, and a bead of sweat slides down the side of his face.

His lips find my ear, and he stills inside of me. I can't imagine the amount of self-control it's taking for him not to plunge into me over and over again.

"Fucking Christ, I can't tell you how many nights I fucked my hand thinking about your pussy. Imagining how warm and tight it would be. How it would feel to claim that one piece of you that no one else ever could again. Through all the dreaming, I never could have imagined it would feel this good. That it would be this perfect. That we would fit together so well, like two pieces of a puzzle." All I can do is whimper as I try and adjust to his cock inside of me.

His lips sear mine hungrily, and pleasure starts to build again when he moves a hand between our sweaty bodies and finds my clit. He strokes me gently, circling my bundle of nerves, playing them like an instrument until my entire body loosens, slowly becoming a melty pile of mush. When I start to lift my hips and mewl against his mouth, he pulls out and thrusts back in. His strokes are slow and precise at first, and though there is a bite of pain with each push, it's far more bearable with his finger on my clit.

"Am I hurting you?" he asks, our foreheads touching.

"No..." I gasp and arch into him, the cuffs around my wrists dig into my skin as he swivels his hips, touching something inside me. It's foreign, but it feels like heaven.

"Good. I want you to come with me."

"I don't know if I can... girls don't come their first time," I whisper.

Zane smiles. "Girls that are with guys who don't care about their pleasure don't come their first time. You're going to come, or I'll continue fucking you until you do."

The intense look in his eyes tells me he's not lying, and I become hypnotized by him as he starts fucking me, sinking deep into my flesh, taking and taking until there is nothing left. Until I'm a shell, and he is the harbor for all my happiness and misery.

Together we crest the hill of pleasure, me crashing into the wall and shattering first, forcing the orgasm right out of him. He fills me with his come, the hot ropes paint my womb, and since I'm riding the waves of pleasure, it takes me a moment to realize what we just did.

"We didn't use a condom." The words come out shaky as I interrupt the moment.

Zane lets out a harsh breath as he gently pulls out of me and undoes the cuffs. "It's okay. I'm clean, and you're on the shot."

I'm about to ask how he knows that, but I already know the answer, he knows everything. Zane takes my wrists, inspecting them for injury most likely. Once satisfied, he rubs the life back into my arms and then settles into the spot beside me. I can already feel the soreness between my legs, it feels like a dull ache hanging low in my belly. My gaze darts to his cock, which is already growing hard again. It's smeared with blood, my blood, and it makes me sick.

I gave myself to him.

"I love you, Dove," he whispers as he tugs me into his side, rubbing small circles against the small of my back. I don't say anything because there isn't anything to say. I don't love Zane. I can't allow myself to. He kidnapped me, took everything away from me, he stole my life.

I might feel safe in his arms, but he's not William. He's not going to save me. He's going to trap me and keep me forever.

20

Two days have passed since I made her mine completely and took that sweet cherry between her thighs. It's been a tense forty-eight hours. Even though fucking her was heaven, I didn't let it slip from my mind what she did before that. She submitted to me during sex beautifully, but she also tried to kill me. I hope she doesn't think I've forgotten that.

I've been keeping my distance, not because of her attacking me, but because now that I've had her, I can barely keep a leash on my inner beast. I want her again, and this time, I refuse to be gentle.

I always thought that once I had her, my obsessive need for her would be curbed. I knew it would never be gone, but I had hoped it would at least take off the edge.

Boy, was I wrong... so wrong.

Having her only intensified my cravings, the need to possess her is stronger now than it ever was. I want to own her in every way. Claim every hole on her body, every sliver of her soul. I want it all, and in return, I will give her the same. I'll give her the good, the bad, the angel, and the demon. I can't hide the dark side of me anymore. It's out for blood, and it wants Dove just as badly as I do.

"Are you hungry?" My question causing her to jump off the recliner. She still has no awareness of her surroundings. She never hears me coming, and always gets scared. I shake my head at her inability to protect herself. How could she ever think that she doesn't need me? She'd be dead in ten minutes without me.

"Yes, I'm starving, actually." The smile she gives me, though shy, is enough to make me want to bend her over the dining room table and fuck her senseless. She's under my skin, in my head, pumping through my body. She consumes me.

Reheating the leftovers from last night, I set two plates on the table and take the seat next to her.

"You've been avoiding me," she says in between bites.

"Yes," I admit. No reason to lie.

"Did I do something wrong? I mean... it was my first time. I'm not sure if it was okay for you." I almost drop my fork at her words.

"Do you seriously think I've been avoiding you because I didn't enjoy the sex?"

"Yeah. No. Maybe. I-I just didn't know," she stutters, her cheeks turning pink.

It would be easier to avoid her if the sex was bad, but it wasn't even close to bad.

"Maybe I've been avoiding you because you tried to kill me?"

Her face falls, and I can see the guilt written all over it. She stares down at the broccoli on her plate like it has all the answers. "I'm sorry about that," she whispers, still not looking at me. Her apology means the world to me, but it doesn't change what happened. She was so desperate to get away that she was prepared to kill me. I just can't forget that.

"I know you are, but that's not actually the reason I've been staying away."

She finally glances up at me, curiosity flickering across her face. "Why then?"

Did I want to tell her why? I could lie, but that wouldn't make any sense. I didn't want there to be lies between us. Clearing my throat, I answer honestly. "Because I knew you would be sore, and every time

I'm close to you, all I can think about is stripping you naked and shoving my cock into your tight cunt."

At my crude usage of words, her mouth pops open, and the hand she is holding the fork with starts to visibly shake. *Is she scared? Aroused?*

She looks up at me through her thick lashes. "I'm not sore anymore..."

I raise an eyebrow at her. Who is she trying to convince, herself or me? "Is that an invitation, Dove? Do you want me to fuck you again? Because I'm telling you right now, I was gentle with you before because it was your first time, but this time, I won't hold back. I want you too much. I've gotta have you hard and fast."

She swallows so hard I can hear it as well as see her throat work. She puts the fork down on the table next to her plate. Licking her lips, she looks around the room, clearly trying to think of a response. When she still can't seem to find the words, I clarify.

"I want to go back to the bedroom, strip you bare, and tie you up. Not because you've done anything wrong, but because I simply like having you restrained. I like being in control, and I like you being help-less and at my mercy. I want you to submit to me, to trust that I will take care of you. I want to put a blindfold on you this time, and then I want to use your body however I see fit. Do you want that?"

Another moment of silence stretches out between us before she finally has the courage to nod. That's not good enough though. I need her to tell me this is what she wants.

"Use your words, Dove." The words come out a little more sternly than I intended, but when it comes to her, I lack self-control.

"I want you to do that," she says, finally looking up at me.

"Finish eating then." I adjust my hardening cock under the table and watch as she shoves a few more pieces of food into her mouth before she gets up and dumps her plate in the sink. I don't even bother with my plate. I just take her hand and pull her into the bedroom.

"Strip!" I order while undressing myself. Dove does as I say and gets naked, surprising me with her eagerness. She has no idea what I'm about to do to her. Hell, I don't even know how far I'll go. All I know is that I have to have her. I have to make her mine, feel our bodies pressed against each other.

Once she's completely naked, she stands in the center of the room, looking at me like she's waiting for me to tell her what to do next. I won't lie, it turns me on so fucking badly that she takes my commands.

"Get on the bed," I say and watch as she climbs onto the king-sized mattress, my eyes going straight to the valley between her legs. "Lie on your back, legs spread."

A moment later, she's spread out on the bed for me like a fucking offering. Her dark hair fanning out like a halo on the pillow, her smooth, creamy skin pebbled with goosebumps, her chest rising and falling rapidly. My eyes travel down her body and land between her thighs, where her pinks pussy lips are already glistening with arousal. Fuck, she is so perfect. I don't want to break her, but I will bend her.

"Don't move." I rush into the closet and open the bottom drawer on my side. I briefly scan over its content before choosing four items. As soon as I walk back into the room, I order her to close her eyes.

Dumping the things from the drawer onto the bed, I grab the blindfold first, securing it around her eyes. Then I take the rope and start looping it around the bed frame so I can tie every one of her limbs to it. She doesn't say a word while I tie her up, and her trust in me is the most potent aphrodisiac of all. I want her to know she's always safe with me, in the bedroom, and outside of it.

Next, I take the small bottle of lube, flip the cap open, and pour some out onto my palm. Then I bring my hand between her legs. Dove sucks in a sharp breath when my fingers find her center. Gently, I rub the lube all over her pussy, down her slit, and over her tight puckered asshole. The next virgin hole I plan to claim on her.

"What are you doing?" She gasps, half tensing as I dip the tip of my pinky finger inside her ass.

"I warned you that I was going to use your body however I wanted. Every part of you is mine. This part too," I say, pushing my finger a little deeper into her ass. A groan ripples through my chest as her muscles squeeze down on my finger. "Just relax... and trust me. I'll never hurt you. Never." I remind her.

Sliding my finger in and out, I let her adjust to the size and angle before I add a second. I know it stings and probably feels foreign, but what I'm going to do is give her the best orgasm she's ever had in her life. Stretching her tight little hole, I move my fingers faster while pressing my thumb against her swollen clit at the same time.

"Oh, god..." She cries out, and I know she's close to coming, her tight, little body trembles, and her nipples become diamond hard peaks.

Using my other hand, I grab the fourth item I brought, and pour some more lube over the small-sized butt plug, making sure it's slick all around before I bring it to her ass. Easing my fingers out, I replace them with the plug.

Dove lets out a soft whimper but doesn't ask me to stop. Thank fuck, 'cause I'm not sure I could even if I wanted to.

I take in my handy work, a smile pulling at my lips when I see her tight little asshole clenching around the butt plug. Fuck, I can't wait to be inside of her. I need her now. Right now.

"Are you ready for my cock, Dove?"

"Yes," she says, almost breathlessly.

Lifting a hand, I caress her body, letting her know where I am. Having her at my mercy is doing insane things to my head. "Remember what I told you. I won't be gentle this time. I want to fuck you raw. To fuck you until you can barely walk. I want you to still feel me inside of you every time you move tomorrow."

"Mhhm..." Apparently, we are past words now.

Gripping my cock, I give it a few good pumps before I move between her legs. I lower myself until I just hover inches over her. Her hardened nipples are grazing against my chest with every breath she takes. I line myself up with the center, bringing the tip of my cock to her entrance.

I enter her in one deep thrust, bottoming out until my balls are flush against her stuffed asshole. Her whole body arches off the bed, and the room fills with the sound of her pleasured cry. The plug making her pussy even tighter, and all my restraint is gone.

Plunging into her over and over again, I fuck her hard and fast. I go so deep, I can feel the end of her channel, the head of my cock bumping into it with each thrust.

"Do you feel that?" I ask, my voice coming out rough and gravelly. "Do you feel me deep inside of you?"

"Yes... so deep," she whimpers in between thrusts. Her head is tipped back into the pillow, her slender neck exposed to me.

"Who do you belong to? Tell me, Dove."

"You... you, I belong to you."

Like a crazed animal, I rut into her, grunting on every thrust. She moans and squirms beneath me, her small body smothered by my larger one.

Sweat forms on my skin and my muscles ache, but I can't get enough. I never want to stop fucking her like this. Raw, primal, animalistic. Hard and rough.

Her orgasm slams into her out of nowhere, her pussy squeezing me so tightly. Her thighs quiver, and a silent scream forms on her lips. Her whole body tightens before relaxing back into the mattress. My cock's harder than steel, and I'm ready to fuck her next virgin hole.

"Is your ass ready for my cock?" I ask, and she moans in response.

I pull out of her, listening to her whimper at the loss. "Don't worry, I'll be back inside of you in no time."

Making quick work of the ropes on her ankles, I untie them and flip her over, leaving her wrists tied to the headboard. Her chest is pressed flat against the mattress, her cheek pressed to the pillow, her ass hanging high up in the air. Her pink pussy glistens with her juices, and I'm tempted to taste her, to lick every drop, but there's something else I want more right now.

Moving to her ass, I carefully remove the butt plug. Her ass is still tight when I push my finger inside, but it has loosened up tremendously.

Fuck, I can't wait.

Removing my finger, I replace it with the crown of my cock. I run my hands up and down her silky-smooth skin a couple of times before I start to push inside.

Dove whimpers into the mattress. "You're too big..."

"Shhh, it's going to be a tight fit, but you were made for me. Made to take my cock in every hole." I snake a hand beneath her body and gently stroke her clit. When I feel her greedy pussy getting wetter, I push into her, watching with glee as her ass swallows my dick beautifully.

She was made for me. Made to take me in every hole. Made to be worshipped and protected by me. Mine. All fucking mine.

"Fuck, Dove... you should see how well your ass takes me. Can you feel it? How your greedy ass is swallowing me... begging me for more? You like this, don't you? Like me filling your ass? Giving yourself over to me."

"Yes... Yes... God, yes," she chants into the pillow.

I thrust into her ass slowly for a couple strokes. I'm big, and I don't want to tear her, but once I know she's stretched out enough for me, I start fucking her in earnest. I pump my iron rod in and out of her just as furiously as I was fucking her pussy moments ago.

My hands dig into her hips, and I know there will be bruises. I can't be gentle with her. I need her, every fucking inch. Each thrust is rougher than the last, and the headboard makes a loud thudding against the wall as I fuck her.

My balls are so full and ready to explode. The tingle on the base of my spine tells me I'm about to come. I pick up my speed, slamming into her as fast and deep as I can. Moans, grunts, and the sound of naked flesh slapping against each other fill the room. I'm surrounded by her scent and the sweet combination of sweat and her pussy.

"Come again, Dove. Come for me as I fuck your ass hard. Squeeze my cock."

When I feel her ass clamping down on me and her release coming, I allow myself to fall over the edge with her. My orgasm is like a tidal wave, slamming into me and flooding my body with pure ecstasy. The entire contents of my balls explode into her tight little ass, ropes of sticky come filling up her no longer virgin hole.

And I keep coming, my cock filling her ass with come. My vision goes blurry, and I feel light-headed. *Fuck. Me.*

We both collapse on the bed, and it takes a moment for my muscles to start working properly again. Dove falls asleep almost immediately. Her body is worn out from the intense sex we just had. It's done the opposite to me though. I'm like an addict who just took a hit. I'm wide awake and too wound up to keep my eyes shut.

Walking into the bathroom, I grab a rag and soak it in luke-warm water. Then I clean between her thighs, remove the blindfold and untie her wrists. I cover her naked body with the blanket and tuck her in. I press a kiss to her clammy forehead before making my way to the library. Since I can't sleep, I might as well check what's going on in the outside world.

Not bothering with clothes, I walk naked through the apartment and into the library. I get out the laptop and phone from the safe and turn on both.

As expected, there are multiple calls and messages from the Sergio family. Christian has put out an official hit on me. Ten thousand for whoever brings him my head. *Cheap bastard.* Doesn't surprise me that he wouldn't put a bigger hit out. In fact, I'm a little offended.

I'm relieved to find that he didn't put out an official hit on Dove, which is interesting.

He wants her dead, but he doesn't want people to know. That reminds me of something... he wanted me to take out people from the Castro family quietly too.

Could there be a connection?

Before I can dwell on that thought for too long, another message catches my eye. It's from the nursing home Donna is at. Immediately, I get a bad feeling. I've been paying her bills because the only place she could afford was a piss poor nursing facility, and I knew there was no way Dove would allow that, nor would I. So, I took on the cost and made up some insurance program so Dove wouldn't know. The nursing home has my number, but I told them to only contact me if something was wrong.

Hitting play, I listen to the message.

"Hello, Mr. Brennan, this is Julie from the Westfield nursing home. You wanted us to call you if something happened to Mrs. Miller. I'm afraid to say she had a stroke this morning. She was rushed to the hospital and is currently in critical condition. Last I heard, she was in the ICU. I'm sure the hospital can give you more information. I'm sorry I had to do this over the phone..."

I end the recording, I've heard enough. My stomach twists, and my heart rate skyrockets. Resisting the urge to throw the damn phone across the room, I close the laptop and lock everything up.

Fuck, fuck, fuck...

What am I supposed to do now? There's a hit out on my head. Dove is still in huge danger. We can't leave the safety of the bunker... but if I don't let her go and Donna dies. Fuck, if she dies and Dove doesn't get to say goodbye, she'll hate me forever.

21

Dove

I know something is wrong before I even open my eyes. It's just a feeling lingering in the air. A feeling that something bad is going to happen. Moving my hands to Zane's side of the mattress, I find the spot empty and cold. Zane isn't next to me. My heart clenches a little, and I blink my eyes open and sit up, looking around the room.

The room is dark, the only light source coming from the bathroom. The door to it is only cracked, not letting a whole lot of light in. I almost don't see him. Zane is sitting on the edge of the bed, his elbows resting on his knees, his head in his hands like he's defeated. I know instantly that something is wrong.

"What's wrong?" I ask, my voice still wrapped up in sleep. I throw the blanket off my body and crawl over to him. As he promised, I feel an ache between my legs with every move I make, a reminder of what we did last night.

Placing my hand on his shoulder, I ask again, this time a little more urgently. "Zane, what's wrong?"

He raises his hand and places it on top of mine before he starts talking. I look down at it. The gesture so gentle and kind it's a stark reminder that he can be both kind and possessive.

"I'm sorry, Dove. I have some bad news for you." The way he's looking at me almost shatters me. He takes a deep breath like he's afraid to tell me. The guy who kills people for a living, who stalked and kidnapped me is afraid? Whatever he has to say is going to be bad, but I have to know. I have to.

"Please, tell me!" My voice comes out more demanding than I wanted it to, but I can't help it. I need to know what's wrong.

Zane sighs, his eyes filling with panic. "It's Donna... she's had a stroke, Dove."

I hear the words right away, but it's almost like they don't make it further than my ear. Somehow, my brain doesn't understand them. *What happened?* The information sinks in slowly, and seconds pass before my brain can comprehend what he is telling me, but once it does, dread consumes me.

"Donna? Donna had a stroke?" I ask as if I didn't hear him the first time. He nods, and I try to ask my next question. "Is she..."

"She is alive, but she's not doing well. The nursing home said she's in critical condition—"

"I need to see her!" I cut him off mid-sentence. "Zane, you need to let me go." I tug on his arm.

"I know... but I need to make preparations. I need to make sure it's safe for you."

"Safe for me? I don't give a shit about *my* safety. The only parent I ever had is in the hospital dying, and I need to be there! Right now!" Please let him see how important this is to me because if he doesn't... if he doesn't take me to her. "Zane, if she dies and I'm not there, I will never forgive you."

He suddenly jumps up from the bed, his large body looming over me. "You think I don't know that! You might hate me forever, but at least you'll be alive! At least I won't have to worry that someone took you from me!"

"I don't care about me," I yell back at him, my face flush. I don't care what happens to me, so long as I get to see Donna before she dies.

"I know that too, but I care. I care. Do you still not get it? You're everything to me. If something happened to you, I'd kill myself. You are the only person that matters to me, and if you die, I die with you."

Tears fill my eyes, and my lungs burn. "Zane, I have to see her. I know that I'm the most important person to you, but Donna is important to me, and she's dying right now. I need to be there with her. I need to say goodbye."

His jaw turns to steel, and he lets out a growl that's more animal than human. "Fuck, Dove, if something happens to you. They're looking for you. For both of us. I can't protect you out there. I can't make sure nothing happens to you out there." For the first time ever, I see panic fill his eyes. I see fear, real fear, and it sinks in just how much I mean to him.

I thought it was just an obsession, but it's clear it's more, deeper.

"You have to let me do this. I know you're scared. I am too, and I don't even know who it is that's trying to hurt me, but I'd rather die than not be there when she takes her last breath. Please, Zane. Please do this for me. I won't fight you anymore. I won't try to escape, just, please... Please, give me this last moment with her."

Zane looks like a statue, his entire body is rigid, every muscle clenched. Terror is all I see when I look at him. A man terrified of what may happen. If he lets me go, and if he doesn't.

Like lightning striking, he snaps out of it. "We will go, but you will remain by my side the entire time. You will not go anywhere without me. If anything happens, we will leave and come back here. I will not risk your life. If it's not safe, we won't go inside."

He's barely finished laying down the ground rules, and I'm off the bed, running into the closet to get some clothes. I'm dressed in seconds and walk back out into the bedroom to find Zane standing in the same spot. He looks to be lost in thought, and my heart sinks into my stomach. Has he changed his mind?

When he sees me, his gaze flicks over my dressed form. "Ready to go?"

"Yes, are you?"

Crossing the space separating us, he takes my cheeks into his hands and leans down, so his lips are a centimeter away from my own. "I'm ready, but I've never been more scared of something happening to you than I am right now."

"Nothing will happen," I assure him even though I don't know anything about who is after us, or why they would want to hurt us.

"You're so naive and so good. I wouldn't expect you to understand how dangerous this is. I just want you to know that if something happens to you, anything at all, I will blame myself forever, and I'll gladly put a bullet between my own eyes. You're my world, and if you're not in it, then there is nothing left for me to live for."

I feel each word slicing through my skin and piercing my heart. This man is consuming me, and while I know I shouldn't feel a single thing for him, my emotions are twisting, becoming more confusing with each day I'm here. I shouldn't want Zane, but a part of me is drawn to him, to his darkness.

"Everything is going to be okay," I say before gently pressing my lips to his. I don't know what is going to happen. What I do know is that I have to get to Donna before it's too late.

THE SUNLIGHT FEELS good against my skin after not seeing it for a while. I won't lie, I hate the reason we are leaving, but I'm happy to get some fresh air and leave the confines of that place. As it turns out, we are in the middle of nowhere, miles from the city, so even if I had escaped, it wouldn't have mattered much. The entire drive Zane white knuckles the steering wheel, his eyes darting between the rearview mirror and the windshield like someone is going to appear there.

I'm tempted to force him to tell me who is after us, and what all is going on, but I need to focus on the most important thing right now. Donna had a stroke, the one and only person to ever care for me is most likely dying, and there isn't shit I can do about it.

Guilt clings to me as we get closer to the city. Maybe I should've spent more time with her, maybe I should've tried to get her into an even better nursing home, maybe something closer. The thoughts swirl like water running down a drain.

"Everything is going to be okay. I will always protect you... love you," Zane says, breaking the silence. It's like he knows how much I need someone to lean on.

Like he can feel the despair pumping through my veins. His words don't change what's happening right now though, and they don't make the loss of Donna any easier, but they do make me feel less alone.

"My heart hurts. It feels like I'm losing a piece of my soul." I swallow around the lump of emotions in my throat. "Donna was the only person to ever care for me. She adopted me when all hope was lost. When I was sure, I would forever be stuck in the system. Someone as sweet and caring as she doesn't deserve to die, especially from a stroke." I don't know why I'm telling him this, it's not like he doesn't already know everything about Donna and me.

Zane's hand comes to rest on my thigh, his touch makes my insides tingle.

"Donna doesn't deserve this, no, but we don't get to choose how someone dies."

I turn to him. "Says the one who kills people."

He gives me a sly grin, and my entire body warms all over. "Touché."

We arrive at the hospital a few minutes later, pulling into the emergency room parking lot. Zane parks, but before I can get out, he shakes his head, ordering me to stay put for a second. We're so close, and all I want to do is go inside and see Donna. Walking around the car, he opens my door and helps me out. His fingers interlock with mine as we walk across the sidewalk and into the hospital. With each step I take, the sicker I feel. Part of me wants to scream and yell and ask why the hell this is happening, and the other part just wants to break down and cry.

I remember Zane's instructions as we reach the round circular desk, where the receptionist is. *Don't talk to anyone. Keep your eyes down. Don't draw attention.* Staring down at our joined hands like they're the most majestic thing I've ever seen, I let Zane do all the talking while pretending like I'm not interested in the conversation.

"She's in the ICU. I'll send you down there, and one of the nurses will meet with you," the receptionist says. I don't even bother commenting on the fact that she's checking Zane out, drool basically dribbling down her chin. Jealousy has no place in my heart right now.

"Thank you," Zane says with a smile, and we head in the direction of the ICU, following the signs in the hospital.

When we reach the unit, there is a set of double doors that you have to be buzzed to get into. Zane squeezes my hand tighter and turns to me.

"It's going to be hard to see her like this. Are you sure this is what you want?"

"We're here, and we're going in. I don't care what condition she's in. I need to see her." My voice cracks, and my heart splinters in my chest. Zane nods and presses the button for us to be buzzed in. A second later, the door opens, and we walk into the ICU unit. There are monitors everywhere and things that sound like alarms going off.

Zane guides us up to yet another desk, where a woman in scrubs greets us.

"Hi, we've come to see Donna Miller."

The nurse walks around the desk and comes over to us, a folder in her hand. "Come with me, and we will discuss her condition."

I can hardly breathe, and suddenly I feel dizzy. Latching onto Zane's arm, I let him guide us where we need to go. "Donna is in critical condition right now. She's on a ventilator, and her brain function is..." The nurse pauses and frowns when she sees my reaction. I'm pretty sure I look like I'm about to pass out.

"She doesn't have any brain function?" I ask, my voice breaking at the end.

"This is very common after a stroke. Her brain was without oxygen for too long. The doctors have been looking for any brain activity, any signs that she'll recover, but as of this morning, there was nothing. I'm so sorry. The doctors have done all they can at this point. I can let you see her."

The tears I was holding back break free, and I swallow down a sob as I bury my face into Zane's side. He releases my hand and wraps his arms around me, holding me a little tighter. She's gone. The one and only person I ever had is gone. Physically, she's still here, but in the sense of her really being here, her spirit, she's gone.

The nurse takes us to her room, and what I see when I step inside has the ground crumbling beneath my feet. My knees go weak, and I feel like I'm going to pass out.

Donna. My sweet mom has tubes going in and out of her body everywhere. Her body is so still she doesn't even look alive, and in a way, I guess she isn't.

"I'll leave you alone for a bit," the nurse says, dismissing herself. The room spins around me, and I press a hand to my forehead to steady myself.

"Are you okay?" Zane's gravelly voice fills my ears. He turns me to face him, his hands circle my arms, holding me in place and blocking my view of Donna.

"She's just..." A sob escapes my lips, and I press my face into his shirt, gripping onto the fabric. It's like I'm losing everything.

"It's okay. I told you this was going to be hard, and it is. But you should be allowed to say goodbye. She would want that." I nod, blubbering into his shirt. I'm a mess, a complete mess. How will I survive this?

"I'm okay. I need to do this." I speak out loud, even though the words are just for me. Zane nods and takes a step back, releasing me, though it seems it's the last thing he wants to do. With him out of the way, I stand there for a long time, just staring at her. The woman who supported me when I felt hopeless. She nurtured and watered me, turned a wilted rose into a woman. I was lost before her and found the instant we met. Now she's leaving me again, and it feels like all those times I was left behind. Never the child picked. Forever alone.

Forcing my feet to move, I walk over to the side of the bed. I take her hand in mine. It's cold and makes me shiver at the touch. Of course, she doesn't react to my touch. She doesn't squeeze my hand. Doesn't even acknowledge that I'm there. The machines she's hooked up to make her chest rise and fall.

Seeing her like this breaks my heart. I miss seeing the smile on her face and the twinkle of joy in her eyes every time I would come and visit her. Never did I think the last time I saw her awake and happy would actually be the final time I'd see her that way. I can't stop the tears from falling as I stand there holding her hand. My shoulders drop, and I bite my lip to hold back a sob.

"I miss you already, and you aren't even gone yet." I wipe my face with the back of my hand. "I'm sorry I wasn't there; that I've been so busy and haven't been able to come and visit as much. I wish we had more time. That this didn't happen."

Sniffling, I continue. "I'm so thankful that you took me in and gave me a future. I've enjoyed every minute of being with you, and I am proud to call you my mom."

Bending down, I brush the grey hairs from her forehead and press a gentle kiss there. When I pull away, I'm crying so hard I can barely see. It's like I'm losing a piece of my soul, a piece of my upbringing.

"I've got you," Zane whispers, his arms circling my waist. He pulls me back against her chest, and I turn in his arms, needing someone to hold onto.

e stay for another twenty minutes, and I hate every second of it. I hate seeing Dove hurt, and I hate that we are here, out in the open where I can't protect her. Not the way I want to, at least. After a short while, I know I have to tell her it's time.

"Dove, we need to go. It's not safe to stay here."

She pulls away from my chest and nods in understanding. With her head hung low, I watch her walk over to Donna's side once more.

She says her tearful goodbyes before turning back to me. I hold my arms open, and she falls into them, letting me lead her outside the room. Donna will be given a proper funeral, it's the least I can do, and I know it will set Dove at ease to have her funeral taken care of.

"Everything is going to be okay, Dove. I promise it won't always hurt this bad." I try to console her, but her sobbing only intensifies. I walk her past the nurses' station and down the hall. I'm so focused on Dove that I don't pay attention to our surroundings the way I should. All I can think about is getting us out of this hospital and back to the bunker.

We take the stairs down to the parking garage, and as soon as we step outside, something feels off. I pause, pulling Dove even closer.

"What's wrong?" she asks, peeking up at me through thick lashes.

"I don't know yet." I scan the area and spot two blacked-out SUVs in the same aisle we are parked. I take a step back, shoving Dove behind me as two car doors pop open. *Shit.*

Turning around, I take Dove's face into my hands and stare deeply into her eyes. "Listen to me. I need you to go back inside and find a place to hide. Hide until I come and find you, okay?" I try not to sound panicked, but this is my worst nightmare being brought to life.

"What's wrong?" She repeats, sounding more frantic this time. Tugging from my grasp, she tries to look over my shoulder.

"I'll explain everything to you later, please, just go and hide. Please, Dove," I say, feeling more desperate than I ever have before. She nods, and I release her, watching her step away from me. It hurts me physically to let her go, but I know I can't protect her if she's standing there watching me. I'm outnumbered and outgunned. I can't fight them and keep her safe at the same time. When she disappears through the door leading into the stairwell, I turn around to face whoever Christian has sent to get me.

Color me fucking shocked when I see the asshole himself walking toward me, a triumphant smile on his smug-ass weathered face. "Did you really think you could hide forever?"

I shrug. "I wasn't hiding from you. I was just taking a much-needed vacation." Maybe I can get him to talk a little bit, which will give Dove a little more time to hide.

"Do I look like a fucking idiot, Zane?" He cocks his head to the side. Each step he takes brings him closer and me closer to death.

Two men flank him, and I know he's got more men here somewhere. Christian is not stupid; he knows I could take out two guys with ease. As if they could read my mind, more car doors open, and four more men start to approach.

"Brought a lot of people just to chat," I say, forcing a grin on my lips.

"You know there is not going to be a whole lot of talking. Less talking, more killing."

"You brought a lot of people for that too. Did you forget how to hold a gun yourself?" I know provoking him is probably not my best bet right now, but fuck, I'm mad. Mad at him, mad at myself, mad at the world.

"Why shoot the gun myself when I have people that can do it for me? People like you. It's really a shame, you were one of my favorites. I guess it was my own fault for not finding the truth out sooner." He shakes his head like he still can't believe it.

"Find out what?"

"Find Dove... then find out who she is to you—"

I cut him off before he can finish. I don't want to hear him talk about my relationship with her, but I do want to know why the hell he wants her. "Why have you been looking for her for the last ten years?"

He chuckles. "So it was you who killed Billy. I knew I shouldn't have trusted that prick. Did you at least make him suffer first?"

"Am I known for delivering peaceful deaths?"

He laughs louder. "No. And that's exactly why it's going to hurt me to see you go. You could have had a long and prosperous career with me."

"Answer my question!" I growl. Two of his goons take a threatening step toward me, but Christian raises his hand, motioning for them to stay put. "Why do you want her?"

"Well, let's just say it's Castro's fault that I want her dead. But I don't want to bother you with the boring details since you are going to be busy dying. Rest assured, I'll take good care of your little Dove. I'll make sure my men have some fun with her before I kill her."

I lunge for him before his last words have left his mouth. I'm fast, but his men anticipated my move. Two of them are on me before I can even get close to Christian. I let my fist fly, hitting one of them right in the nose, bones crunching beneath my knuckles. The other one grabs my arm and twists it back painfully.

Twisting my body, I free myself and punch him in the chest in one move. The guy stumbles back but not before slugging me in the side of the head. My head is pounding, but I shake it off and try to push past him to get to Christian. When I look up, I freeze.

Christian is only a few feet away from me, his gun pointed at my chest. I hear the gun go off and I feel the hot searing pain lancing across my chest like fire moving outward. My body jerks back involuntarily as the bullet slices through my muscle and tissue.

"I guess for you, I can make an exception and pull the trigger myself, old friend," Christian says, and if I didn't know him any better, I would say he is actually a little bit remorseful for killing me. "Get the girl and bring her to me," he orders his men without looking away from me.

Anger and despair fill every fiber of my body. I want to kill him, want to kill every single one of his men, but all my body does is sag to the ground. I try to reach for my gun, but my limbs are useless. *I'm useless.* Dove is going to die. I'm going to lose everything.

"Goodbye, Zane..." Christian's voice sounds far away, but that can't be right. He was just here. I feel my eyes close, my mind fading away. No, no, no! I need to stay awake. I need to get to Dove, protect her.

I try to get up, but my body feels like it's made out of lead. My mind is whirling, and all I can think of is how much I hate Christian. How much I want to kill him right now. I used to think he was my savior, Dove's as well. He saved us both, and now he ends us both.

The memory of how it all began comes rushing forward. The beginning of the end.

"I'm not supposed to be released; you're making a mistake."

"I can't believe you're complaining about being released early. Be glad you get to leave. Mistake or not. You're no longer my problem," the prison guard says and shows me through the door.

I'm only seventeen, but for the last few months, I've done nothing but work out every day. Now I'm bigger than most kids my age, maybe that's why they deemed me mature enough for prison. I'd only spent a few weeks in juvenile detention before they shipped me off to the state penitentiary.

"Put this on." He throws a bag in front of my feet, and I quickly realize it's the clothes I wore the day they brought me in. I change out of my inmate uniform and into my old worn jeans and T-shirt.

Then it hits me. I'm about to walk out of here. Free. But I have nowhere to go. I hate to admit it, even to myself, but here I know what was coming every morning. Every day was the same, an endless cycle of structure and routines. On the outside, there is nothing but chaos.

I'll be lost.

Twenty minutes later, I'm outside, standing in a parking lot with nothing but two twenty-dollar bills in my hand. What the fuck am I supposed to do now?

I start walking down the sidewalk, not knowing what else to do. I can't just stand there. I make it about half a mile down the road when a blacked-out SUV pulls up to me. The window is being rolled down, and some guy appears on the other side.

"I don't need a ride," I bark out before he can say a word.

"You must be Zane," the guy I've never seen before says.

"How the fuck do you know my name?" I stop walking, and the car stops moving at the same time.

"I'm Christian, and I'm the one who got you released early."

"And why would you do that?" I ask suspiciously.

"Why don't you get in and we can talk about it."

"I'm not getting into that car with you to suck your cock. Go ask what happened to the last guy who tried that shit. Oh, wait, you can't, 'cause I fucking killed his ass."

The guy named Christian throws back his head and starts laughing out loud. He laughs for ten minutes straight before he can compose himself enough to talk again.

"I like you already, Zane. Don't worry, I'm not into that either. I want you to work for me... taking care of people. Just like you took care of that guy you were talking about."

"What's in it for me?"

"Anything you want. Money, power, women, drugs. Name it, and it's yours."

Maybe I should have just kept walking that day. Maybe I could have kept her safe in a different way. I guess I'll never find out. The past is the past, and there is nothing I can do to change any of that now. My eyes fall shut, and this time, I can't pry them back open. I fade in and out of consciousness, knowing deep down, that this is it. I'm going to die.

Pictures of everything I've ever loved in my life flash before my eyes, every single one an image of Dove.

23

Forcing air into my lungs, I focus on each step I take. The last thing I want to do is trip and fall or injure myself. I'm not sure who is after us, but I don't want to find out. The fear in Zane's eyes was enough for me to stop asking questions and just listen.

I should be jumping for joy right now, planning my escape, but I can't even consider that knowing that Zane is back there going through god knows what. Yes, I know I should feel different, but I can't. I just can't. My stomach churns when I think about something bad happening to him. *Shit*, I think I'm going to be sick. Gripping onto the metal railing, I stop on the stairs and gulp precious oxygen into my lungs.

It feels like an elephant is sitting on my chest. Like no matter how much air I breathe in, I'm never really catching my breath. A door opens a flight above me, and I force my feet to move, carrying me down the stairs. I don't make it but a few feet before I hear someone descending the steps. *No.* Not someone, there are two sets of footsteps. Two people.

"You can run, but you can't hide..." That voice is like nails on a chalkboard, and fear trickles down my spine at the sound. Immediately,

I start running down the steps. I need to get out of this stairwell. It's like a trap. If I stay here, I'm as good as caught. Dead.

When I get to the bottom floor, I grab the door handle and twist it open. Cold air whips through my hair as I make it outside. The door falls shut behind me and I get ready to start running down the street when I stop dead in my tracks. Two men standing a mere ten feet away, smiles that promise horrible things on their faces.

What do I do? Where do I go?

Like a trapped mouse, I look for a way out, but there isn't one. I can't go back into the stairwell. I can't go forward either.

"Give it up, baby, just come with us, and maybe we'll take it easy on you... maybe we won't kill you right away. We can always have a little fun, give you a little pleasure..."

My eyes dart around the space, there is nowhere to go. I'm trapped. Zane told me to run, to hide. I can't die like this. I won't die like this.

"Don't even think about it." If his voice didn't scare me half to death, the scar running from eye to chin on his face would.

What do I do? I feel the panic rising, bubbling over inside of me. The hairs on the back of my neck stand on end. This is bad. Something terrible is going to happen. Zane was right. He was right. The next moment, the door behind me opens and the before I can turn around a hand slams over my lips while an arm wraps around my middle.

Releasing a blood-curdling scream, I struggle with all my might, kicking my legs and flailing in his grasp. One kick must hit its mark because a second later, the guy releases me, a harsh *fuck* filling my ears. I don't think I just start running. I make it all of ten feet before I'm cut off. My lungs burn, and my muscles are tense, fear and panic overtake my body. It's fight or die, and I can't die yet.

"We told you we'd take it easy on you if you were a good girl, but of course, you couldn't come quietly... looks like we have to do things the hard way." One of the men pulls out a gun, and I open my mouth to scream, but the sound never comes. Before I can react, he's on me, the butt of his gun flashes over my vision before it connects with the side of my head. Crumpling to the ground, the entire world goes dark around me.

WHEN I COME TO, my entire body is throbbing, and my head feels like someone ran it over with a bus. Blinking my eyes open, I resist the urge to cringe at the bright light dangling above my head. *What the—* I don't finish the thought as I realize by looking down at my hands that I'm tied to a chair, my wrists bound to the arms. Flickering through my memories, I try and recollect how I got here.

Donna. Hospital. Zane. Knocked out.

"Help! Someone help!" I call out to anyone who might hear me while pulling against the ropes that bind me to the chair. I need to find Zane, need to get out of here and away from these people. A soft chuckle fills the room, and I whip my head around, looking for the person the voice belongs to, but I don't see anyone. Darkness surrounds me, except for the tiny light hanging above my head. I try and swallow down my fear, but it's suffocating me.

"Well, hello, Dove." A man appears before me, he looks like a mobster, in a nice suit. His beady eyes trail over my body, and I can feel every single movement. "It's a pleasure to finally meet you, granted it's not under the best circumstances." He motions to the rope and chair. "I'm sorry, I couldn't offer you better accommodations. I'm Christian," he says his name like I should know it.

"Where is Zane? Where am I? Why did you take me?" The questions pour out of me like an overflowing sink. I doubt this man will give me an answer, but I still ask. I have to.

"Zane?" He leans into my face, and I crane my head back to put some distance between us. The man's voice smells of liquor, and that only intensifies my fear. Tremors wrack my body, and I start to shake as if I'm cold. "Zane is dead. I left his body back in the parking garage." He pauses as if to take in my facial expression. Then his lips curl up into a tiny smirk as he watches me take in what he just told me.

Zane is dead. My chest tightens, and my heart hurts. I feel like a piece of my soul shatters. Rationally, I shouldn't care if he's dead, but for some reason, I feel connected to him. Like I've known him my entire life.

"I mean, it really is such a shame that he dies after all this time. It took you so many years to find each other again just for him to leave you..." Christian frowns, and then without warning, he reaches out and grabs me by the back of the neck, his fingers digging into the tender flesh hard enough to leave bruises.

"I... I don't... understand. What are you talking about?" Confusion swirls. "I don't know Zane. He kidnapped me, and..." The words keep coming until Christian squeezes the back of my neck so hard the words cut off, and pain consumes me.

"Don't lie to me, you little bitch. I know all about your connection to Zane. It took me long enough, but I finally figured it out."

He pulls back my head and stares directly into my eyes. He must see my genuine confusion because a moment later, he lets out a humorless laugh I feel in my bones.

"You really don't know, do you? Does the name William ring a bell?"

Now I'm even more confused. How does he know about William, and what does he have to do with anything? The information isn't adding up in my brain, or maybe I just don't care to try and add it together.

"William... he's dead. I saw him die... I was there."

"He didn't die, sweetheart. He recovered, and a few months later, he went back and killed your foster dad in cold blood. William Zane Brennen was a born killer, and that's exactly why I hired him."

Like an atomic bomb, everything around me explodes.

Zane is William.

William is Zane.

Christian shakes me by my neck, dragging me out of my own mind.

"Let me tell you the rest of the story, Dove. When I found him in prison, he was killing guys left and right, even though he was one of the youngest inmates. I found a way to get him out so he could work for me. His talent was really wasted in prison. He did well for himself too. Worked his way up, became one of my best men. Little did I know, he had been hiding the one thing I'd been looking for all along. You."

Me? What does he want with me? I can't fully wrap my head around it. Not around any of this. I have so many questions, so many, but I guess it's too late for any answer now. Zane... William is gone.

When the asshole let's go of my neck, I lull to the side, staring off into nothingness. How couldn't I see it? How did I not put one and one together? Why didn't he tell me?

Now he's gone, and I... I'm going to die. He warned me, and I didn't listen. Tears swim in my eyes.

"You know I sent him to kill you?" His menacing voice draws me back to the present, and I shiver at the darkness of it. "He took you into hiding instead. I guess I should thank him for that. Killing you would have been a waste of something good, I see that now." His eyes roam down my body, and I feel vomit rising in my throat.

"What... What is going to happen to me?" It's a stupid question to ask when you're obviously standing on the edge of death, but I have to know if that's where I'm going. If I'm going to die right now. "Are you still going to kill me?"

Christian smiles, and I feel the promise of pain in that one single look. "I was going to, but it's your lucky day because I'm feeling generous, and well, I have a much better use for you now." Before I can respond, his fist comes out of nowhere, his knuckles crashing into the side of my face. Pain lances across my face, and all I can think before everything goes black is that I should've listened to Zane.

24

Cinder blocks weigh my eyes down. I attempt to roll over but every muscle in my body tenses. It feels like I've been tossed off a ten-story building, landing flat on my back. Groaning into the air, my fingertips graze something soft, a sheet...or blanket. I don't know, but it's not cold or hard. Shifting, I realize I'm no longer on the cold concrete but somewhere else. Confusion clouds my mind.

"Shhh, the police are on their way. Everything is going to be okay. They'll find the person who shot you." A voice soothes, but that's not the effect it has on me, and instantly my eyes snap open. Frenzied, I look around the room. The smell of antiseptic assaults my senses, and I piece the puzzle together very quickly.

Hospital. I'm in the hospital. The same hospital where Christian left me in the parking garage to die. Joke's on him though, because I'm not going to die. At least not today. Pain erupts across my body, and my muscles protest as I push off the bed and stand on unsteady feet.

"Sir, you need to lie down!" The nurse rushes over to me, her eyes panicked but I pin her with a dark look that promises pain, and she stops in her tracks. I don't say shit as I walk out of the room, my body screaming at me, begging me to turn around and go lie down.

That's not an option. Dove needs me. *Fuck.* I failed her. I let him get to her. I can't imagine what he's doing to her right now. Touching her. Breaking her. She's too fragile for a man like Christian. Like thin glass, he'll shatter her with a single touch.

My heart thrashes in my chest. Revenge. I need it. I'll take it. I'll bathe in his fucking blood for touching her and if he does anything to her. If there is a single hair out of place on her head... I can't allow myself to think that.

Hobbling out of the hospital, I get a barrage of dirty looks and some shocked ones as I pass people. Looking down at my shirt, I realize the entire thing is soaked in blood. All I can do is shrug because I don't give a fuck. My side is burning with each step I take, and I'm dizzy as hell. If I'm going to be there to save Dove, to save us, then I'm going to need to find a way to get this bullet removed. As I walk—to where I have no fucking idea—I play over in my head what Christian told me.

The Castro's, the rival mob family to the Sergio's, is the reason he wants Dove dead. *But why?* Who is Dove to the Castro's? Gritting my teeth, I know exactly what I'm going to have to do and that I'm going to fucking hate every second of it. The last thing I want is to leave Dove in Christian's hands any longer than I have to, but even with the raged haze that surrounds my head, I know there isn't any way I can save her if I go in there guns blazing by myself.

I need weapons, a plan, and to get this goddamn bullet out of my side and stop the bleeding before I really do die. Which means I'll have to go to the Castro family. Sagging against a nearby wall, I squeeze my eyelids closed, and force myself to breathe through my nose. The pain in my side is nothing compared to the way my heart feels in my chest right now. Even though it's hard as hell, I force myself not to think about Dove in that instant. Shrugging out of my shirt, I take the fabric and press it against my side as hard as I can. My fist clenches and pain radiates across my skin. It feels like razor blades are slicing through my flesh, leaving deep cuts in their wake. My eyes flutter closed, and I force myself to think about anything but the pain. Shutting down is my only option right now.

Car. Weapon. Castro's. In that order. Pushing off the wall, I continue limping my way down to the car. By the time I reach the car, there is a sheen of sweat on my forehead, and my muscles are protesting with each and every step I take. Swallowing the pain down, I open the car door and slide inside. Sagging against the seat, I start up the car and lean over the center console ripping open the glove box.

Pulling out the gun that I keep there just in case, I check to see how many bullets I have and then place it down beside me. Backing out of the parking spot, the tires squeal as I take the twists and turns to get out of this labyrinth of a place.

Following the exit signs, I slam my foot against the gas pedal and drive out onto the street. The sound of a car horn pierces my ears, but I don't pay the driver any attention. I'm on a mission. Determined. I don't need directions to the Castro estate. As soon as Christian told me about his rivalry with them, I started keeping tabs on the family. Figuring out their schedules, where they live, how they spend their money and time.

Going to them might get me killed, but it's a risk I'm willing to take if there is even a chance that I'll be able to save Dove. I'll make any deal; kill anyone they want. There is nothing that I won't do, no one I won't hurt. I have to get her back. I have to save her.

No matter what happens to me, I have to make sure she survives. She is all that matters to me. If she dies, then I die.

The wound in my side pulses with its own heartbeat as I drive through the city and to the town over. My insides twist and twist until there is nothing but a knot of fear in my belly when I arrive at the gate of the Castro mansion. There is a twelve-foot wrought iron fence surrounding the place, and the fact that I'm going to have to haul my ass over that fence to get inside is not a welcoming feeling. My side is already screaming at me, might as well plunge a knife into the wound. Staring up at the fence, I cook up a plan, one that has a fifty percent chance of getting me killed. Walking up to the fence and ordering them to let me in isn't an option.

I'm going to need to cause a scene, force Matteo Castro to see me face to face. Driving a ways down the road, I pull off on a side road and stash the car in the trees. If they haven't spotted me on the security cameras yet, I'll be shocked as hell. Hobbling down the road, I force myself into a steady jog. The air outside is cold, and when it clashes with my heated skin, I shiver. I feel weak, so fucking weak, but I have to do this.

I need someone in my corner, and since Christian wants to go to war, I guess I'll be the one to bring it to his door. But first, I need to get Matteo on my side.

Reaching the edge of the fence on the property line, I gaze up at the mountain I'm going to have to climb. Exhaustion coats my insides, and I have to force myself to continue forward. *Think of Dove.* Off in the distance, something catches my eye. *Not something, someone.* Two men are headed right toward me. Beefy, muscled, and with guns strapped across their chests.

I'm in no position to fight. Hopefully, they don't kill me, because fuck, would that be a shit way for this to end.

"Either you have a death wish, or you have a fucking death wish." One of the men sneers when he gets closer. The fence is still between us, but I know that won't save me. If they wanted to kill me right now, they could.

"I need to speak to Matteo," I grit out.

The same guy who spoke moments ago lets out a bemused chuckle. "You *need* to speak to Matteo? Sorry, buddy, but that's not how this works. If the boss wants to see you, you'll know. Now get the fuck out of here." He makes a shoo motion with his hands, and if I wasn't in so much fucking pain, I'd grin.

My gun sits heavily in the waistband of my jeans, and I know as soon as I reach for it, they're going to shoot me. It's a risk I have to take though. Shooting one of them will definitely get me to Matteo. Dead or alive? Not sure.

Moving with agility I didn't even know was possible, I grab my gun and aim it at the guy that laughed at me.

"No hard feelings," I grunt as I pull the trigger. At the same time, his friend pulls a gun and shoots. The bullet rips through my shoulder and into the tender tissue. How much more blood can I lose before I die? My skin stings where the bullet lodges itself inside, and I stagger backward, my knees shaking. I can feel the ground coming into view. Who knew that the mighty would fall so hard? After all I've done, everything is crumbling to the ground. The man always killing and ending lives has finally been caught by karma.

Landing on the ground with a hard thud, all I can do is look up at the sky.

"Idiot," The guy who shot me growls as he walks over, his face coming into view. The toe of his boot collides with my ribcage and pain ricochets through my body. *Fuck.* "You got your wish. Looks like you'll be leaving via a body bag, after all."

Pain encompasses me, and I watch through heavy lids as he lifts his gun and pulls the trigger again. Another bullet sinking into my flesh, burning through muscle. Another bullet that I'd gladly take if it brings Dove back to me. Blackness and pain are all I feel as my eyes close for what I feel is going to be the very last time.

THE FIRST THING I notice when I come to is that I'm alive. *Scratch that.* I'm not alive. I've died and gone to hell. Actually, hell would be a vacation compared to what I'm dealing with right now. My entire body is like a flame, burning and pulsing, gushing gasoline on a never-ending spark of fire. Every muscle tightens as I struggle to make sense of what's going on.

"Welcome back, Zane," an unfamiliar voice says, and I twist in the direction of it. Finding nothing but darkness. It's then that I realize my wrists are handcuffed to the sides of the bed. The metal dinging with my sharp movement. Tugging on them to the point of pain, I grit my teeth as the metal digs into my skin. Slowly, everything starts to come into perspective. Looking down at my bare chest, I find I'm no longer bleeding. Each of the bullet holes that littered my chest are now clean, and the wound covered with gauze.

What the hell happened?

"You can say thank you at any time." There's that voice again, and it grates on every last fucking nerve ending. I didn't go through all this for nothing and every second that ticks by is another second that Dove could be somewhere hurting or worse...

"I need to talk to Matteo!" I growl.

"Well, it's your lucky fucking day, boy." Out of the shadows appears Matteo, the man I need to speak with. His honey-colored hair is slicked back, and his dark eyes are menacing, well, about as menacing as a small dog chewing on your ankle. "I don't really appreciate you shooting one of my men, but I suppose we're even since he took one shot, and you took three."

"Not that it matters, but I was shot when I got here. Your guy only shot me twice."

Matteo narrows his gaze, a smirk twisting his lips. "I see. Still, you deserved to be shot, showing up here and shooting one of my men. Hell, he should've killed you. I will say that I'm surprised that I finally get to meet the infamous Zane though. Hitman for the Sergio family. Did you know there is a bounty on your head?"

All I do is shrug. "I'm not here about the bounty, and if you want to hand me over to Christian, then do it. He has something of mine, and I want it back. You'd be doing me a favor anyway."

Matteo stares at me, just stares. "You know that's not how this works. Your balls must be the size of Texas if you think you can come in here and ask for my help."

At this point, I don't care about anything. All that matters is saving Dove, making sure she is safe, alive, and protected. "I'll tell you all of his secrets. Kill whoever you want. Do anything that you need. I just need some guns and manpower. That's all I'm asking for. It's not a marriage or relationship. It ain't shit. You help me. I will help you." I try not to sound as fucking weak and desperate as I feel, but I don't think there is much I can do about it at this point.

Matteo gets up from the spot he's perched on. "And why the fuck would I help you? I don't know anything about you, and the last thing I need is your help. I know the odds are stacked against you. As the hitman for the Sergio family, a family that is a rival of mine, that continues to fuck with my business, I should kill you. In fact, give me one good reason not to shoot you straight in the fucking head right now."

"I don't have one. All I have is the knowledge that Christian wanted you dead. You were next on my list. Now, if you aren't going to help me, then let me fucking go." I tug against the handcuffs again, my muscles burning with exhaustion. Matteo looks indifferent, and I wonder what the hell is going to happen next.

"What is it that he has that would tempt you to make a deal with the devil?" I swallow thickly, hating that I'm going to have to explain to him who Dove is to me. It's obvious I'll burn the entire world down for her, so there isn't any point in hiding that she is my biggest weakness. I've already exposed that myself.

"Dove. He has her. She is mine, and I want her back." I growl.

Matteo chuckles. "You want to start a war over a girl? Over some pussy, which you could get from any woman?"

"She isn't just anyone, and he's going to hurt her. I..." It kills me, rips me to fucking shreds to say my next set of words. All my life, I've vowed to be strong, to look death straight in the eyes and smile, but this isn't just about me anymore. Dove wasn't cut from the same cloth as me, and she can't handle this world. "Please, she is my entire world, and I...right now, I have nothing. I am a walking target, if I go in there to save her on my own, we're not getting out. You're my last chance..."

Matteo cocks his head to the side, drumming his fingers against his chin. "And why would he steal your precious little girlfriend?"

"Because he's been looking for her for ten years... I don't know why, but I know he plans to use her for something. He claims it's your fault that he wants her dead, but I haven't figured out the connection yet."

"Interesting...so this girl, he assumes I know her?"

I nod. "But we won't be able to figure out how or why until we get her back."

A spark of curiosity fills his eyes, and I know I've hooked him.

"Fine. I'll help, but you'll be indebted to me, Zane. Indebted till I say otherwise."

Hope springs in my chest. I don't care what it is, or what he needs me to do. I'll do it. All that matters is Dove. My sweet Dove.

"Fine, just help me find her."

25

Dove

My bones are aching, every muscle in my body is stiff. My whole body is sore, and there is a permanent crater, an ache in my chest, that's accompanied by a never-ending emptiness. I'm so exhausted, my body and mind.

I'm not sure how long I've been here or how much longer I can take this. There are no windows, and the single light bulb hanging from the ceiling is always on. Someone brings me food, but the times are not regular. I know because sometimes I'm so hungry, my stomach is rumbling, and a pit of pain fills my belly.

Of course, it's nothing compared to the pain of losing Zane... *William*. I still can't wrap my mind around it. How did I not see it before? How could I have been so blind? He wasn't the boy I thought died all those years ago, but he still made me feel safe all the same. I should have known. Now I've lost him all over again.

Wiping the tears off my cheek with the back on my hand, I stare at the same wall I've been looking at for the last few days. I've counted every brick, memorized every crack because I have nothing else to do. Nothing to keep me sane.

The room I've been kept in only holds a dirty mattress, a thin blanket, and a bucket in the corner for when no one is there to take me to the bathroom. So far, that's the only time I'm allowed out of my cell—to go to the bathroom down the hall. I know I'm in some basement, a heavily guarded basement, but that's pretty much all I know.

I still don't understand why Christian is keeping me here, why he wants me in the first place, or what he is going to do to me next. All I know is that it can't be good. The days blend together. Night and day. I'm terrified of the unknown. Of what's to come.

Pulling my knees up to my chest, I wrap my arms around them, hugging myself tightly as if that would somehow keep me from falling further apart. Letting myself sink down onto the mattress, I curl up in the fetal position.

The rusty springs beneath me dig into my side, but the pain is only minimal. Forcing it away, I close my eyes and try to pretend I'm somewhere else... anywhere else.

Funny to think how I felt like a prisoner in the apartment, Zane kept me in. The whole time I was there, I tried to get out. What I wouldn't give to be back there right now? To be locked away, safe and sound from the world. Locked away with Zane by my side.

Another sob wracks through my body, leaving me a shaking mess. A sound from outside my cell has me quieting down in an instant. I sit up straight and wipe away the tears with the back of my hand. If they come in, I don't want to look vulnerable. I'm not giving them the pleasure of seeing me cry. It's something small I'm holding on to, the one thing I'm not going to give up easily.

A key enters the lock, the mechanical of it fills my ears. The door is unlocked and opened a moment later, and one of the men who has been guarding me appears in the doorway.

"Time to come out and take a piss," he growls. "Unless you prefer to go in the bucket?"

It doesn't warrant a response. Pushing myself off the dirty mattress, I get up and walk toward him on shaky legs. He hasn't touched me, other than jerking me around by my arm when he takes me out of the cell. Which I'm thankful for, but the way he looks at me is enough to make shivers of disgust skate down my spine. Like I'm some piece of hanging meat that he'll eventually be able to take a bite of.

Creep.

He drags me down the hall and shoves me into the bathroom. I close the door behind me, grateful for the privacy. There is no window in here either, so it's not like I can go anywhere. I do my business quickly, so I have a minute to wash up, and because the last thing I want is for him to walk in on me with my pants down. I splash water on my face until he opens the door and wraps a mammoth hand around my arm, tugging me out of the closet-sized bathroom.

"Dinner will be here in a little bit. My men eat first, and you'll get the leftovers... if we have some. Unless you want to eat now? I'll let you sit on my lap, and you can eat all you want." He grins, and the look in his eyes tells me he is anything but joking. He's serious and while I'm hungry. I'm not hungry enough to take him up on that offer.

"I'll wait," I mumble.

The guy starts laughing like the whole thing is funny to him. I feel like anything but. I feel like screaming, crying, and destroying this place with my bare hands if I could.

His laughter is suddenly cut off when the sound of some commotion carries through the long hallway. I can't see anything, the brute's oversized body blocking my view, but I hear the ringing of guns off in the distance.

What the hell?

"Fucking shit!" The guy with the death grip on my upper arm growls as he starts walking faster, dragging me right along with him. He moves me like a rag doll, my legs barely making it possible for me to keep up with him.

Then something hits me. I'm not sure what it is, but I don't even think. I just react. Normally, I don't fight him, but something about this moment tells me I should. Digging my heels into the ground, I try to slow him down.

I start struggling in his hold, hoping to get away from him, but all he does is pick me up like I'm a stubborn child. He throws me into my cell, and I land on my back against the cold hard floor. My bones rattle, and the impact knocks the air out of my lungs.

The door is slammed shut before I can get back on my feet, and the guy walks away. It takes me a moment to stand up, but when I do, I rush to the door and hold my ear to it.

For the next few minutes, I hear men fighting, more guns going off, and then silence. When I don't hear anything at all for a few seconds, I realize that no matter what's happening, no matter who saves me, good or bad, I need to get out of here.

If they leave me here, I will starve to death in this cell. I can't die yet. I refuse to let my life amount to this.

"Help! I'm in here, please, help!" I yell at the top of my lungs while banging my fists against the metal door. It rattles only a little bit beneath my harsh raps. "Anyone, please! I'm begging you, please, save me!"

It feels like I've been banging on the door forever when I finally hear someone approaching. The footsteps are muffled through the door, but I know whoever it is, isn't going to be good. The door is unlocked, and I step back toward the center of the room. Even if I wanted to hide, I'd have nowhere to go.

The door swings open, and two large men curiously look into my cell.

"Who do we have here?" one of them asks, his eyes roam my body up and down like he is evaluating me. For what, I don't know, nor do I want to find out.

"Answer," the other one growls, more in disinterest than anything. "Who are you, and why are you here?"

"I-I'm no one. I work in an animal shelter. Some man kidnapped me and brought me here." I don't know why that is the first thing I reveal about myself. They don't care where I work or who I am. I can't think straight. My thoughts are swimming, and the words I grasp for seem to slip right through my fingers. "They just took me and have been holding me here since. I don't know why. I don't know who they're or what they want with me? Please, just let me go. Please." I try to make myself look as innocent and fragile as I can.

I'm desperate to escape this place, to feel sunlight on my skin, to be free. I need to find Zane. No way do I actually believe he's dead. I need to get out of this place. Away from these crazy criminals.

The two men look away from me and back at each other, engaging in some kind of silent conversation. Then the silence breaks and the one closest to me, yells down the hall, "Ivan, we've got an issue over here." I jump, startled by the darkness in his voice.

Oh god, are they going to kill me? What's going to happen next? Panic bubbles up inside of me, but neither of them makes a move toward me.

For a few moments, we all just stand there looking at each other until the man named Ivan joins the other two in the hallway.

As soon as I see him, I instinctively take another step back. It's like my body knows how dangerous this guy is. I thought the two men who opened my door were big, this Ivan guy looks like he could eat both of them for breakfast, and then me. Strangely, my eyes snag on a tattoo that is peeking out of his collar and winding up his neck. It makes him look even more intimidating, not that he needs it, his size and the harsh look on his face is enough.

Yes, they are definitely going to kill me.

"She says she works at the animal shelter; they took her and have been keeping her here. She doesn't know why," one of the men explains to this Ivan guy, who I'm assuming is their boss. Ivan stares down at me, and I try not to look like a cat that's ready to hiss and claw her way out of this room.

"Go, clear the rest of this place. I'll deal with this myself," Ivan growls, and I almost pee my pants right then.

The two men disappear from view, their heavy footfall getting further and further away, and all I can do is look at this mountain of a man filling the entire door frame and bite my tongue to stop myself from begging those other guys to come back.

"What's your name?" he asks softly, finally breaks the silence after staring at me like I'm a puzzle he can't figure out. His voice doesn't match his appearance one bit. He's like the devil but with a heavenly voice.

"Dove... Dove Miller," I stutter, trying to keep my voice even, though it doesn't seem to help.

"Look, Dove, here's what's going to happen. You're going to come with us until we can verify that you are who you say you are and that you don't know anything of importance to us. If you're telling the truth and you are no one and know nothing, then you'll be free to go... as long as you can keep your mouth shut."

"And if I don't?" I ask, even though I know I shouldn't.

Ivan looks at me blankly, there isn't a sliver of emotion in his eyes. "Let's not think about that right now."

Instantly, I feel as though I've been tossed into the ocean. I'm bleeding out. The sharks are circling in on me. Who will bite first? I should've listened to Zane. Should've believed him when he said there were far worse monsters in this world than him.

"Okay," I answer because what else am I going to say? No, just leave me here to die? That's not really an option.

Moving out of the doorway, he motions for me to exit, and just as my feet pass the threshold, he says, "If you run, I'll shoot you, and I really don't want to have to do that."

A second ago, I was tempted to run, to try and escape, but the threat in his words revealed the truth. If he had to, he really would shoot me. I choose not to run. Hopefully, it's not the biggest mistake of my life.

26

It takes me a few days to heal up, which drives me batshit crazy. My bullet wounds aren't completely healed, but they're as good as it's going to get for now. I should be out there, searching the globe for Dove, burning cities to the ground and slaughtering people, not sitting in a bed, staring at my hands, willing answers to appear out of thin air. However, I can't do a damn thing without weapons and the information that Matteo promised me.

He says he's got eyes and ears everywhere, and if Christian makes one move, he'll know about it. So far, he hasn't done squat shit because Matteo hasn't come to deliver any new information to me. I shove out of the cot and come to stand, my boots scuff against the marble floors. I hate this place. I hate that I'm stuck being someone else's little bitch, but more than anything, I'm afraid. Afraid of what's happening to Dove.

The thought of one of Christian's men putting their hands on her. It makes me murderous. Clenching my fist, I dig my nails in my palm. Rage simmers just below the surface. If I get the chance, I'll kill him, draw out his death, make him wish, plead, and beg for death.

"Knock, knock..." Matteo's voice reaches my ears, and I force myself to unclench my fist, sliding the mask of emotionlessness across my face before turning around to face the door. I've already exposed my biggest weakness, and the last thing I need is to expose my emotions further. I refuse to let him or anyone else know how close I am to losing my shit.

"I hope you have some information for me?"

Matteo doesn't look amused by the way I talk to him, but the way I see it, if he wanted to kill me, he would've done so already.

"I do, but I think it's important you realize just who it is that's calling the shots here." I withhold an eye roll. I'm not used to working with anyone, let alone someone that mirrors Christian to a T. I don't take orders. I've worked as a one-man team my entire life. Now, I'm being forced to take orders from some prick in a suit. All I want to do is find Dove, do this asshole's dirty work, and fucking leave this place behind.

"Tell me what I need to know...*please*," I grit out. Matteo smirks at me as if he enjoys seeing me grit pleasantries through my teeth. Little does he know; he'd be dead too if I didn't need him as badly as I do. I'm not about ass-kissing or becoming his best friend. I just want Dove, and I'll do whatever the fuck I have to do to get her back.

"That sounds much better... glad you cleaned up your attitude because I would've hated not sharing news about your little Dove."

Her name rolling off his tongue makes me want to slit his throat, but I withhold as a bubble of hope fills my belly.

"Where is she?" I demand and take a step toward him.

"An insider let me know that there was an ambush at one of Christian's secret compounds. We believe that's where they were holding Dove. I doubt she's still there as Xander Rossi's men were just seen leaving the place."

Xander Rossi. Fuck. More bad news. Slicing my fingers through my hair in both frustration and rage, I try and think, instead of reacting. Using my fists isn't going to help her right now. I need to think. But all I can think about is my sweet fucking Dove, how she was tossed from one cage to the next, landing now with the worse villain of all.

"What do we do?" I ask a moment later.

"*We?*" Matteo blinks, "*We* aren't doing shit. You are going to go there and check the place out, see what the hell happened, and if there is anything that was left behind. Maybe they did leave her there, who knows? I'll expect you to return though, and if you don't, well, let's just say there will be more than a bounty on your fucking head."

"I don't take orders from you." I clench my fist, ready to slug him in his arrogant face. I'm so close to losing it, to shutting down completely and going on a killing spree, that it's not even measurable at this point. And this fuckhead standing in front of me will be my first victim.

"You do if you want my help."

Like a volcano seconds from erupting, I shudder with a burning rage. Coming here was obviously a mistake. I don't know if Matteo is going to be worth all of this trouble. He's dangerous, yes, but what level, I haven't figured out yet.

"All I need is a gun and a car," I say without even looking at him.

"I can provide you with both of those things. I'm also sending two of my men with you. Can't have you trying to run off if she is there."

"Yeah, yeah, I know, I owe you, and I better return. Get it."

"I'm warning you, Zane, if you find the girl and hide her somewhere, or if you try and disappear, I will find you, and when I do…"

I look up, and most men would be cowering in fear from the look he's giving me, but I'm not most men. I'm not afraid of this fuckwad, but I am afraid of what he can do to Dove, or at the very least, what he'll try to do. Double-crossing him isn't something I want to do unless I absolutely have to. With no one in my corner and no other help, I'll have to wait for the perfect opportunity to leave.

"If she's there, I'll return with her."

His gaze hardens, almost like he's trying to see if I'll break under the pressure. Luckily, he has no clue what I'm truly capable of and the lengths I'll go to save the woman I love.

"I'm trusting you, Zane. Don't make me regret it."

I don't respond. Instead, I give him a blank look. I'm going to find Dove and kill every fucker that touched her if it's the last fucking thing that I do.

PUNCHING the GPS coordinates that Matteo gave me into the car, I rev the engine and leave his mansion—my prison—in the rearview mirror.

My muscles are tense, and I'm ready for a fight. I'm consumed with the need to find Dove. All I can do is hope and pray that Xander left her there, though the likelihood is slim. Mercy isn't something that man shows, and I doubt he would just leave a vulnerable, beautiful woman alone to fend for herself. Grinding my teeth together, I try not to think of that bastard putting his hands on my Dove. The drive is a little over an hour, and I white knuckle the steering wheel the entire way.

I see the car with Matteo's goons following me the entire time. Useless idiots. Sending them is an insult more than anything. As if I couldn't take these two out if I wanted to.

As the miles tick down, knots of fear tighten in my belly. What if they hurt her? Raped her? What if she's broken, and I can't fix her? What if it's too late? The thoughts keep coming, suffocating me with fear. I need to get a grip, to focus, but the idea of finding Dove unsafe and hurt is enough to make me sick.

I slow the car as I turn onto the road where the compound is supposed to be. Off in the distance is a ten-foot fence surrounding a house. That must be it. The organ in my chest starts to gallop, beating a little faster the closer I get.

One would think a place such as this would be guarded, but I suppose there aren't any guards left. Knowing Christian, he probably went into hiding the moment the Rossi's ambushed him. I mean, he's always had me around to fight his battles, without me, I can't imagine he's going to be picking up a gun to protect himself or rid the world of his enemies. No hiding is more his style. Turning onto the road and driving through the beat-up gate, I spot two men lying on the ground. As I pass their bodies, the bullet holes in their foreheads confirm to me what I already knew. Everyone here is dead.

Closing in on the property, the feeling of dread consumes me. There are three more bodies lying on the lawn. I park the car and kill the engine. Then, I grab my gun and climb out of the SUV. I doubt I'll need it, but I'd rather have it than not.

The car with Matteo's men pulls up behind me, and the two guys get out of the car a moment later. I try to ignore their presence completely and concentrate on finding the woman I love.

I don't know what I expected when I showed up here, but it wasn't this. Crossing the lawn, I walk around the side of the house. There are more men, more dead bodies. Reaching the side door, I don't bother opening it since it's already kicked in.

As soon as I step inside, I smell it. Death. Blood. Mayhem. It's everywhere. It coats the walls, the floor, the air. There is only one thing in my mind as I walk down the hall... please, don't let her be dead.

Ignoring the bodies, and the smells assaulting my nose, I make a quick sweep of the house, checking every room as I go. Before I go into each room, I fear that I'll find her dead inside, lying between the other bodies. But over and over again, I find the rooms empty, a short burst of relief rushing through me every time.

Not finding her dead might be a relief, but not finding anything at all intensifies my anger. I need to find a clue, anything that will help me find her.

When I find a door that leads down into a basement, my heart skips a beat. Running down the steps, I'm desperate for something, anything. Before me is a long hallway, and as I start to walk down it, I find that there are cells on both sides. The space is far too quiet to have anyone in it. Still, I can't let the hope in my chest die.

My eyes scan each cell, looking for the slightest clue. I grow more and more disappointed as each cell leaves me with nothing. Reaching the last one, my heart leaps out of my throat, and I rush into the room, grabbing the thin jacket I gave Dove the day we left the bunker. It's lying on the floor next to a dirty mattress. There is a bucket in the corner of the room where she was most likely forced to piss. The place is... it makes my stomach churn. It's hell on Earth.

This is where they kept her? On a soiled mattress, in a cold and bare room. My Dove.

She doesn't belong in a place like this. She should be safe and happy. Scanning the room one last time, I note that there is no blood, and no clothing tossed aside, other than the jacket. Both are good signs, and I'm going to hold on to them. They don't prove that they didn't hurt her, but all I can do is hope that they didn't and that she's not completely broken when I get her back.

Fisting the material in my hand, I bring it to my nose and inhale deeply. The faint smell of vanilla tickles my nose, and I suck that precious scent deep into my lungs. She's a drug to my senses, to my mind, and body.

My sweet Dove.

At least I know one thing. Her not being here means that, at the very least, she is still alive. The question now, is how do I get her back from Xander Rossi, one of the most feared mafia men in the United States?

27

Dove

Ivan is quiet as he drives us to god knows where. I'm sandwiched in the back seat between the two guys that found me in my cell. I'm afraid to move, breathe, and damn well, too scared to talk. I do my best not to think about what's going to happen next. Surely, if that Ivan man was going to kill me, he would've done it back in that cell, right?

Of course, there are worse things than death...

A million and one scenarios play out in my mind. The car jerks to a stop, and I blink out of my thoughts, realizing we've arrived wherever it is that we were going. Peering out the windshield, I see a massive compound ahead. There's a ten-foot iron fence that cages the place in. It all but says no visitors welcome.

Two guards usher us in, and Ivan drives up the long driveway, past guard towers, and some smaller buildings. I guess escaping is out of the question.

In the center of the place is a giant house, or mansion even. It looks fancy. When we get closer, I see that there is yet another fence surrounding it. The lawn is manicured, and it doesn't seem like even a single blade is out of place. The gate in front of us is manned by four men, and I shiver, wondering where the hell it is they've brought me. Prison, but nicer?

It looks *nice* but kind of deadly too. We drive through the gate that leads to the mansion and down the road until we make it to a plain-looking building. I'm shaking, and there is a sheen of sweat on my forehead. Ivan shifts the car into park and kills the engine.

Ivan steps out of the car, and both men open their doors. One of the men wraps his hand around my wrist and pulls me out of the SUV. Shocked, I let out a gasp and tug my arm from his hand. I'm so tired of people grabbing me. Tired of being tossed around like a ragdoll.

"Don't touch the girl," Ivan orders, with a look so deadly, it makes my heart quake in my chest.

"It's not like I hurt her." The unknown guy shrugs his shoulders.

Ivan ignores him completely and starts walking away. My feet scrape against the concrete as I scurry behind him. I don't want to be stuck out here with these guys by myself.

"I'm glad you decided not to run," Ivan says and I almost roll my eyes. Where am I going to run to? He walks me to the large metal door. It looks like it weighs a ton, but of course, a man of his size opens it like it's a soda can. With the door open, he motions for me to go inside.

I'm not sure if I'm walking myself to my own execution or to a chat with an old friend. Either way, I'm not letting him see how scared I am. Forcing my arms to casually hang by my side, instead of wrapping them around my torso like I want to, like I need to, I walk into the building.

"That way," Ivan says and points down the hallway. The walls are bare, and everything from floor to ceiling is a light gray color. My shoes squeak against the floor as we walk. He leads me to a room that doesn't look any different than the hall, except that it holds a table and a few chairs in the center.

"Where are we?" I ask as I step into the room, gazing over my shoulder hesitantly.

"Sit," he orders, ignoring my question. "I have my guys checking on the story you told me right now, but in the meantime, I'd like to hear the whole thing again from you, and I'd like to ask you some questions.

For instance, why were you at Christian's compound, and how long were you there?"

Sighing, I slump into the chair. I guess I'm being interrogated now.

For the next hour or so, I tell Ivan my story. I repeat the same thing three times. I tell him how they kidnapped me from the hospital. How they kept me in that cell. I tell him everything I can remember about my stay there. Every conversation I overheard. I describe every person I saw and anything else I can possibly remember, none of which gives a single clue as to why they were keeping me there in the first place.

By the time I'm nearly finished telling him the same story for the third time, my interrogation is interrupted by Ivan's phone ringing. He pulls it out of his pocket and looks at the screen before looking at me and back down again.

Ivan answers the phone with a grunt, then raises his eyebrows curiously when the person on the other side says something. I can hear a male voice coming through the receiver, but I can't make out what he is saying. I feel like a small child right now. My butt is sore, and my back is stiff from sitting on this plastic chair for so long. I'm exhausted, physically, and mentally, and all I want to do is to lie down somewhere and go to sleep.

"Got it, boss," he finally says and ends the call. "Well, this is going to be either really bad or really good for you."

Fear replaces the pain in my butt cheeks. "Huh? What does that mean?"

"The boss himself is going to come here and talk to you," Ivan explains.

Puzzled, I stare at him. "I thought you were the boss?"

"Not quite." A shiver runs down my spine at the thought of meeting the man that has the power to order a guy like Ivan around. I chew on my bottom lip nervously as we wait in silence.

A few minutes later, I hear footsteps approaching from down the hall. I instinctively sit up a little straighter, wanting to seem less like a bug that this man can squish. Wringing my hands in my lap, I watch as the door opens, and a tall man, wearing a black tailored suit, appears. He's not as large as Ivan, but his dark eyes tell me he can cause just as much damage and mayhem... maybe even more than him.

His eyes are downcast, reading something on a paper he is holding as he steps into the room. He looks angry, almost furious, like he is about to yell at me, maybe beat me or worse.

"You interrupted my family dinner, little girl," he growls, his voice dripping with annoyance and hatred... hatred for me. He throws the stack of papers on the table in front of him and looks up at me.

Dark eyes connect with mine, and for a moment, I'm so scared, I forget to breathe. Then, something weird happens. An emotion I don't understand flickers in his gaze... pity? His eyes soften, but not much, and they swirl from pitch black to stormy cloud gray.

He takes the seat next to Ivan, never taking his eyes off of me. His stare is so intense, it makes me even more uncomfortable than I already am. It's like he's inspecting me, trying to figure me out. I do my best not to squirm in my seat, but that's a little hard with two of the most intimidating men I've ever seen sitting before me.

After an awkward moment of silence, he starts talking. "Dove, is it?"

"Yes," I answer before asking, "Who are you?" I don't know where this burst of confidence comes from, but I kind of like it.

He raises one of his eyebrows and leans back in his seat as if he is just getting comfortable. Maybe I should've kept my mouth shut. Screw my newfound confidence. That shit is going to get me killed. I need to be quiet like a mouse to get myself out of this.

His lips twitch up into the tiniest smile before he introduces himself. "Xander Rossi. And you, Dove, are at my compound. I expected you to tell Ivan the truth. We did save you after all, didn't we?"

"I didn't lie," I start to defend myself, but Xander holds up his hand, shutting me up.

"You told us you were kidnapped at the hospital, but your employer reported you missing a week prior to that. There was a police report stating that your apartment was broken into, nothing of value was taken, but it was ransacked like someone was looking for something."

"My apartment?" I question as if that's my biggest issue right now. "I-I can explain."

"Explain then," Xander growls a warning in his tone, "Better make it good."

"I didn't lie. Everything I said happened... I just didn't tell you what happened before that. I didn't think it would matter." I shrug. "And I really just didn't want to talk about that part." My lips tremble as I speak, and if I didn't want to make myself look weak, I was doing a really shitty job of it.

"What happened before?" Xander asks, cocking his head to the side as if the newfound angle well help decipher what I'm saying better.

"This is probably going to sound like a lie, but I swear it's not. I was kidnapped... twice. One time from my apartment and then a second time from the hospital, but the first time it wasn't Christian. It was..." I pause, wondering if I can tell this part without starting to cry. I don't want to, but tears are already dwelling in my eyes. Blinking the tears away, I continue, "His name was Zane. He kidnapped me first, but not to hurt me. He just wanted to keep me safe."

"Zane?" Xander says his name as if he's tasting it. He and Ivan exchange a glance, then he turns back to me and asks, "Who is Zane to you?"

"We both grew up in foster care. We were in the same home at one point. A bad one." My voice breaks at the end, and I'm no longer able to hold back the tears, no matter how hard I try. The memories of that time rush forward, the memory of him. William, Zane, how I lost him twice now. Unable to look at the two men, I lower my gaze and stare at a random speck on the table instead.

"Do you know where Zane is now?" Ivan is the one who speaks this time, his voice soft.

"He is dead." I start to sob. "Christian killed him."

"I think I can put the rest together myself. Christian must have taken you to get to Zane," Xander says.

"So, you believe me?" I glance up at him, hopeful that he is going to let me go.

"I do, but you did withhold information, and that's pretty close to lying." He starts tapping his finger against the table like he is thinking about what to do with me.

Please, don't kill me... "Ivan asked you to tell him everything, and you didn't. I don't like that. How can I be sure that you aren't still keeping things from me? I don't like liars, Dove, and I've killed men for lesser things."

"I'm not! I swear. I don't know anything else." The words spill from my lips, and I slam my knee against the table, attempting to get them out.

"How old are you?" Xander asks, changing the subject abruptly.

"Twenty-one," I tell him, wondering why he cares about my age. When he doesn't say anything else, I start to worry. I chew the inside of my cheek until I taste blood.

"Please, just let me go," I beg, in a last-ditch effort.

"I can't do that," he finally says, his voice clipped. "You're going to have to stay here, for now at least, until we get everything figured out."

"What? Why?" I stand up, having the sudden need to move. Or maybe for one second, I just want to feel bigger than the two men sitting in front of me. "You can't just keep me here. I'm not an object that can be taken and passed off to another person. I'm a human."

"I can, and I will." Xander gets up as well, turning his back to me. "Put her in one of the rooms back here. Have two guys posted in front of her door at all times. No one gets in this place without my permission."

"You got it." Ivan nods, and Xander disappears from the room, the imprint he made lingers behind like a heavy fog. "Come on, I'll bring you to your room."

"You mean prison?"

"Call it what you want, but it's a whole lot nicer than the shithole Christian kept you in."

"Great," I murmur under my breath. *It's still a prison.* We leave the room, and I follow him down the hallway, knowing that there is no use in trying to run. I saw the security outside this building. I wouldn't make it ten feet out there, without someone shooting me. Escape isn't an option at this point. I'll have to make do with what's here and come up with a plan later.

When we get to the very last door at the end of the hall, he opens it and waves me inside. To my surprise, I find that he wasn't lying. It is much nicer than my last cell, and no matter how bitter I am about still being a captive, this is a huge relief.

The room is small and doesn't hold much, but there is a bed inside.

A bed with fresh sheets, a pillow, and a blanket. The second thing I notice is an attached bathroom.

Thank god.

"There is a shower in the bathroom. Towels and everything else you need should be there too. The closet has extra clothes. They're men's clothes, but they're clean."

"Thanks..." I murmur before I can stop myself. I shouldn't be thanking him for anything. Then again, I guess it could be worse. These guys might not be good guys, but they are definitely the lesser of the evils I've had to endure.

"Take a shower, get some rest. I'll have someone bring you food in a bit. You need anything else?" he asks, and I shake my head, no. With that, he closes the door behind me, leaving me in the small room. I stand there for a minute, just taking in the new situation and processing everything that has happened in the last few hours.

I'm tired, so freaking tired, I could fall asleep standing up, but the smell of my armpits is enough to wake the dead, so I definitely need to take a shower first. I start to explore the room, and just like he said, there are men's clothes in the closet and towels in the bathroom. The shower is stocked with new soap and shampoo.

Stripping out of my soiled clothes, I turn the water on hot and take the longest shower of my life. I wash my hair and rinse it three times until I feel clean enough to get out. I felt so dirty after not showering for days.

When I'm done, I dry off and slip into one of the oversized men's T-shirts, and crawl into the bed. It doesn't look like it, but after sleeping on the grimy old mattress, this seems to be the most comfortable thing ever.

It doesn't take me long to fall asleep. I feel myself drifting off the moment my head hits the pillow. My last thought is that I hope tomorrow is going to be a better day.

28

*M*atteo wasn't happy when I came back to the house without Dove in hand. In fact, he was almost more upset than me, which confused and enraged me all at once. The beast in me was beating violently against the cage that housed him, wanting so badly to break free. Part of me wanted to unleash him just to see what would happen. Dove is mine, and I'll kill him to prove it if I have to.

All I have to do is hold out a little bit longer before I can kill him and toss him aside, like the asshole he is. Until then, I have to follow his orders, at least if I want to find Dove. Which, as of right now, includes going to Damon Rossi's strip club to demand a meeting with his brother, which I'm one-hundred percent sure isn't going to happen.

"Why do I have to take Alberto with me?"

"Because I said so," Matteo says. I don't understand why he insists on his second in command coming with me to see Damon Rossi. There must be more behind it than him sending a babysitter.

"I don't care to be a part of your pissing contest with Xander Rossi. All I care about is Dove," I barely get the words out. My patience is as thin as the blade I plan to slit Matteo's throat with.

"This is part of getting her back, you want her back, you do this. Otherwise, you might as well have tied a nice little bow around her."

"Shut up!" I growl, knowing that if I didn't need this bastard right now, I would already have bashed his head in.

"I shouldn't have to tell you to be grateful that I'm even offering to help you. I could've shot you dead, after the way you marched in here," he sneers, curling his lip. "Remember, it's you who needs me... I don't need you."

I don't get a chance to respond before he walks out, the sound of the door slamming, echoes through the room. I'm exhausted, angry, and disappointed...I've never felt the way I'm feeling right now. Hopeless beyond measure. I'm doing everything I can to stay afloat, but the waves of despair keep crashing into me. I need Dove. Need her scent surrounding me, need to feel her body against mine, but above all, I just need to know that she is okay, and none of that will happen until I finally have her in my arms again.

Shoving the emotions that are threatening to overtake my psyche down, I mentally prepare myself to talk to Damon Rossi. I'm not stupid, walking in there and demanding a meeting with Xander isn't going to go well for me. The fucker will most likely laugh in my face, but I have to do this. I have to try and find out where they have Dove, and what they're doing to her. This is no longer about her just being mine.

This is about me protecting her, saving her. We were destined to be together since the night she was dropped off at my foster home, and though I'm nobody's white knight, I'll do anything to save her. *Anything.*

A NEON SIGN flashes brightly back at me as I pull into the parking lot of *Night Shift.* I've been pissed off since I left Matteo's, and I get the feeling coming here is only going to sour my mood further. I'm tired of the mafia games. I never should've left the safe house with Dove.

I know Donna was dying, and that Dove never would've forgiven me for not being able to say goodbye, but I could deal with her hate if it meant she was safe and sound, tucked into my bed every night beside me. Instead, here we are because I let my feelings for her call the shots, instead of my brain. Sighing, I turn the car off and open the driver's side door.

Climbing out of the car, I stretch my tight muscles before closing the car door. Alberto climbs out of the passenger side and follows me across the parking lot.

Here goes nothing. Maybe if I'm lucky, Damon takes mercy on me. Though that's doubtful. My boots scuff against the concrete as I walk to the front door. It seems like it takes an eternity to get there. Opening the door, I step inside, the place is surprisingly clean, and bigger than I thought it would be, based on the size of the building.

Walking up to the bar with Alberto on my heels like a dog, I'm greeted by a half-dressed woman. She looks to be a little older than Dove, her eyes glitter with excitement when they land on me. The place is mostly deserted, other than a few bar patrons. Looks like I got here before the real show started. Doesn't matter, I didn't come here to watch chicks strip. Pulling my gun out, I set it on the wooden bar, and let her make of it what she will.

She blinks slowly and gives me a grim look. "If you're looking for a fight, you've come to the wrong place. This is a strip club."

Her eyes dart to someone over in the corner of the room, and I know without a doubt, she's calling one of the bouncers over here without even saying a word.

Footsteps sound behind me, and I smirk, my blood pulses in my veins and my muscles tighten, the anticipation of a fight does crazy things to my body.

As soon as his meaty club lands on my arm, I turn on the barstool, grab it, twist it around until I hear a snap, and press it against his chest.

With my other hand, I punch him right in his ugly face, a river of red blood erupts from his nose as he stumbles backward, colliding with a nearby table. I punch him again for safe measure, and because I really want to beat the fuck out of someone. Like a piece of paper, he crumples to the ground.

Out of the corner of my eye, I catch Alberto standing a few feet away, arms crossed over his large chest. He is shaking his head at me like he is disappointed in my undiplomatic behavior. *Well, fuck you.*

"Shit!" The young girl behind the bar mutters under her breath. I turn around to face her once more and find her face ashen, the excitement in her eyes before is replaced with fear. It's a much better look for her. She has no idea the things I'm capable of doing, the things I will do if I don't get the information I want.

"I'm here to speak to Damon Rossi," I growl.

Her gaze widens, and she scurries across the bar and picks up the phone, but she never gets to call whoever it is she'd planned on calling.

"Zane Brennan. I'd say it's a pleasure to meet you, but we both know it's not." Damon Rossi's deep voice meets my ear. Whirling around, I come face to face with the asshole. He briefly turns his attention to my unwanted companion.

"Alberto, didn't expect you to show your face here," he says before pinning me with his gaze once more.

"Where is she? I know you have her here. I went to Christian's compound. She wasn't there, and I know that your brother took her with him when he left the place. I don't have to tell you what will happen if you don't give me the answers I want."

I've got a death wish fucking with the Rossi family, but I might as well be dead if I don't have Dove in my life.

"Who is *she*?" Damon cocks his head to the side like he doesn't know what the hell I'm talking about. His confused expression makes me want to smash his face like a pop can. When it comes to being an asshole, Damon is the worst of the Rossi brothers. Xander might be ruthless and heartless, but Damon is a completely different can of worms. "I don't know who it is that you're referring to."

"You do." I take a threatening step toward him.

Damon looks like a typical mobster with his perfect suit and slicked-back hair. But I know more about him than he thinks. I know he's happily married, and he has a cute little family with 2.5 kids that he would do anything to protect.

"You and your brother have someone who doesn't belong to you, and I want her back, unharmed. Otherwise, I'll be forced to take something pretty and sweet of yours."

The sly grin that was on his face just moments ago has evaporated into the air. In its place is a dark emotionless mask.

"You touch my family, and you'll wish death finds you before I do."

"Then you know how I feel right now. Dove is mine, and I know your brother has her in his possession."

Damon shrugs. "I don't know anything about a girl. But I can tell you that Xander doesn't do meetings unless it's a business deal that benefits him. So, if you don't have something to offer in exchange for this girl—if he even has her—I would get the fuck out of my club while I still have the patience to let you walk out of here."

"Where is she? I want answers!" I'm very close to my breaking point, so close I can almost taste the destruction in the air.

"And I'm telling you, get the fuck out of here before I put a bullet between your eyes." The way he's looking at me, tells me he's not lying, and I'm torn on if I should continue to push him or just walk out. When I see him reaching for his gun, I lunge for him, but fucking Alberto grabs me from behind and pulls me back.

"If you die, you're no use to anyone," Alberto growls. I shrug him off, hating to admit it, but he is right. I'm no good to Dove if I'm dead.

Staring into Damon's eyes, I hope he sees just how badly I want to hurt him. I'm restraining myself, walking a very thin rope of rage. "This isn't over. I'll be back, and when I am, you'll tell me everything I need to fucking know." Damon smirks like he doesn't believe me, and I turn my back to him. On my way out, in a fit of rage, I toss a chair over my shoulder.

I don't care if he shoots me. Let him. Matteo will come for me, eventually, because to him, I'm a pawn in his war against the Rossi's. He needs me just like I need him, even if he won't admit it. Walking back out to the SUV, it takes every ounce of self-restraint I have to continue walking and not turn around.

I want answers, and it feels like I'm giving up on Dove by not getting them. It's only been a few days, but each day that passes without her by my side worries me more. Is she eating? Showering? Are they hurting her? Is she okay?

Fuck. Getting into the car, I drive back to Matteo's mansion. When we arrive, I find the bastard sitting in his study with a glass of whiskey in his hand.

"Have a seat, gentlemen," he says. Alberto takes the seat next to his boss, but all I do is cross my arms over my broad chest and stare him down like a disapproving parent.

"I told you walking in there and demanding to speak to Xander wasn't going to work, and still you sent us. I wanted to kill that asshole so badly it took everything in me not to wipe the floor with his face."

Matteo smirks. "And you're not the first to feel that way about Damon Rossi. He takes some getting used to."

"I don't want to get used to him. I want to find Dove and leave this world behind me."

"Your debt to me isn't paid until I say so, there will be none of that."

Teeth grinding, I tell him, "You've done nothing but make me run around with my head cut off. I don't owe you shit until Dove is safe and secure in my arms."

Swirling the whiskey in his glass, he stares at the amber liquid like it holds all the answers to our problems. As if it would be that easy.

"Damon said Xander won't even consider a meeting unless we have something to offer him." Matteo looks up from the glass, a mischievous glint in his eyes.

"That's not surprising in the least bit. The man is a businessman after all, so I wouldn't expect any different." He pauses. "The best I can offer him is some territory, give him a chance to expand a little."

"You're going to give him land?" I blink, surprised that he's offering anything at all. I was so sure that when I came back here and told him that, he would tell me that this was a lost cause, and I would be forced to go into Rossi territory guns blazing but color me shocked. "Why would you do that?"

"Why do you sound so surprised?" he asks.

I shrug. "Dove isn't your concern, and all I've asked for is your men and some weapons. Yet you offer me more... why?"

Sighing, he places his glass down on the desk. "It's complicated..."

"I have time. There is something you are not telling me, and I need to know what's going on. You know damn well how dangerous it is not knowing a vital piece of information.

"This needs to stay between you and me for now," he says, shooting me a threatening look. When I nod, he continues. "The truth is, Dove is my daughter."

What the fuck did he just say?

"That's why Christian wanted her and why he searched for her for so many years. He most likely planned to use her against me in some way. I mean, that's what I would've done if he had a daughter he was looking for, and I found her first."

"Wait..." I try and comprehend what he's saying. "You're Dove's father?"

He nods. "Yes, her mother and I were in love. She was married, but it was a loveless marriage. When she found out she was pregnant, she was so happy; we both were. She had planned to run away with me. Somewhere along the way, she escaped her husband but never came to me. I thought she was dead, but as I found out later, she had Dove. Then her past caught up with her. Before I could save her, I found out her husband had killed her. Made it look like an overdose, but I know it was him. My daughter was gone by the time I found out. I'd spent years searching for her but always came up empty-handed."

This... it can't be real. Matteo can't be Dove's father. She can't possibly be a part of this fucked up dark world. She's so innocent and sweet. So perfect, and all this world does is take and break you.

"That explains why you want her now, so you can use her," I say, looking down at the floor. I can't believe that after everything, Dove's father is alive, and the leader of one of the biggest mob families. How did this happen? He's just going to hurt her, and I'm going to have to kill him if he does.

"I don't want to use her, Zane. I want a relationship with my daughter. I want her to stand beside me at the throne of the Castro family."

"She doesn't know this life. She's fragile, innocent..." I tell him.

"She is now because she doesn't know any better, but she will get used to it. It's in her blood." We stare at each other for a long moment, and I swear, I can see him moving his chess pieces around, placing them strategically. "Now, we go back to Damon and tell him the offer. She's my daughter, and I'm never leaving her behind again."

Instantly, I know this changes everything... Dove is in more danger than I ever could've imagined, and I'm not sure I can protect her from the evil that's lurking in the dark, murky waters.

29

Dove

When I wake, I feel so rested that I actually forget where I am for a moment. Then reality slams back into me. I open my eyes and stare at the bare ceiling, wondering if I'm ever going to be free again or if I'm just going to be shoved from one prison to the next.

Taking a deep breath, I stretch my arms over my head. I must still be asleep because I swear, I can smell coffee.

Freshly brewed coffee...

"Did you sleep well?" A voice startles me, and I jolt from the bed like the blanket is on fire and scan the room for any threats. My eyes collide with Xander, who is sitting in the corner of the room. He's casually leaning back in the flimsy chair like it's completely normal to watch someone while they're sleeping.

"W-what are you doing here?" I ask when I catch my breath.

"It's my compound, I can go wherever I want, this room included."

"Yeah, but does it have to be my cell?" I say before I can think.

Xander stands up suddenly, and I take a step back, my legs bumping into the side of the bed. I sit down, unsure of what else to do.

"None of this is *yours*. You should be more appreciative of how well

I've been treating you. Don't forget, Ivan could have left you there to die."

"I know..." I lower my head. I do know, but that doesn't mean I accept the situation that I'm in.

"Not many people are brave enough to talk to me like that." He walks over to my bed, and I have to crane my neck to look at him. He reaches for something on the nightstand and hands it to me. I look up and find he is extending the cup of coffee out to me.

"Thank you," I whisper, and take the cup from his hand.

"I brought you some clothes. You should be about this size if I figured right." He points to a stack of clothes next to the bed that I hadn't noticed until now.

"Oh..." Is all I can get out at the moment. Over the rim of the cup, I watch him sit back down while I take a sip of the coffee. It's so delicious, I almost moan out loud. Which leads me to my next question. "Why *are* you treating me... this way, like a friend, instead of a foe?"

He has no reason to treat me with kindness. I'm a nobody, and he is some big huge mob boss. It hasn't stopped me from thinking about the fact that he could kill me, use me, or sell me. I'm of value to him in other ways, and yet he brings me clothes and coffee.

"You remind me of someone," he explains. I think he's about to tell me more, tell me who I remind him of, but all he says is, "Zane isn't dead."

I almost drop the cup of coffee into my lap, my clammy hands just barely keep ahold of the mug. Did he just say that?

"Are you sure?" I ask. I want nothing more than to believe him, but I also don't want to get my hopes up just to be crushed again.

"He came to see my brother last night, demanding a meeting with me." Hope blooms in my chest. He's alive, and he's coming to rescue me. "He knows you're here."

"Is... is he coming? Is he coming here?" I try not to sound overly excited, but I'm giddy to see Zane, to wrap my arms around him, to be reunited with him. Never did I think I'd beg to see the man who kidnapped me and kept me hidden from the world, but here I am.

"My brother sent him away last night, he didn't know about you being here. But don't worry. I'm sure Zane will be back soon. He seemed quite determined on getting you back."

"He won't stop. He'll kill all of you. Please, just let me go to him."

"Do you know where Zane is?"

"Oh...well, no." I guess I don't. But... "Zane had security built into my apartment. Cameras and stuff. If you let me go there, maybe he'll see it?"

"You think Christian doesn't have someone watching your apartment? You really don't know anything about our world, do you?" I get the feeling the words are spoken more to himself than to me, but I answer anyway.

"I told you, I don't, and I don't care about Christian. I just want to find Zane."

"I'm not letting you go anywhere, and to be very clear, I don't know if I'll hand you over to Zane at all. Even if he comes for you. There is something about you... I can't put my finger on it. But my gut tells me to keep you here, and my gut is usually right. Maybe you're going to be useful to me later. I don't know yet. For now, drink your coffee and enjoy your stay. You might be here for a while."

And with that, he gets up and walks out of the room, leaving me alone with my suppressed anger and thoughts.

EVEN THOUGH I'M in a cell, I'm treated surprisingly well. A guard brings me food three times a day, which is actually pretty good, no that's a lie. It's delicious. It tastes like it's been prepared by a gourmet chef, which is strange since I'm being held as a captive. I don't know why I'm being treated so well here, but I'm not about to complain over my treatment.

Right after lunch, two days after arriving here, I hear someone talking on the other side of my door. Moments later, the door unlocks and swings open. Sinking down onto the edge of the mattress, I'm not sure what to expect, but it wasn't the tiny woman I'm greeted by. She enters my cell slowly, almost as if she's worried someone is going to see her.

"Hi... you must be, Dove," she whispers, a soft smile creeping onto her face. Her blonde hair is long and cascades down her back in gentle waves. She looks like an angel, pure, soft, and kind.

"Um, hi," I say awkwardly. "Yes, I'm Dove."

"I'm Ella, Xander's wife."

Xander's wife? He's married? I guess I never considered him to be the marrying type.

"Oh, ah... thanks for loaning me the clothes. You can have them back... uhhh, whenever I get to leave."

"No problem, don't worry about it. You can keep them if you like. Xander likes to spoil me. I've got more clothes than I could wear in this lifetime." Her laugh is carefree, and I can't help but feel jealous.

Not of her clothes but of her having Xander and embracing it. I was so stupid. I had it all, and I threw it all away. I fought Zane tooth and nail, instead of just enjoying the time we had together.

"Do you mind if I sit?" Ella asks, pointing to the spot beside me on the bed.

"No, please do."

She smiles and takes the seat next to me. "I'm sorry they're holding you here. I know it sucks getting caught in the middle of something that's not your fault. I thought I could at least come by and check on you, give you some company, so you're not so alone all day."

Her genuineness is almost too much. I have no clue why she is being so nice to me, but being deprived of human contact for the most part, over the last few days, has me really appreciating the gesture.

"Thank you," I say, having the odd urge to hug her as well. Since that would be a little weird, I refrain. Unable to think of anything else to ask, I blurt out, "So, how did you and Xander meet?"

She scoots up on the bed, leaning her back against the wall like she is getting comfortable.

Is she going to stay here with me?

"Believe it or not, it was a very similar situation to the way you met him. I was being held captive by his father. He was a bad man, and he was about to hurt me... Xander and his men raided the compound I was being held at. He saved me and took me home."

Now his comment about me reminding him of someone makes sense. He must have meant his wife since we were in a similar situation.

"Wow... and you just stayed here with him? Did he not give you the chance to leave?"

"I didn't want to leave." Ella smiles. "But, don't worry, he won't keep you here forever."

"Are you sure about that?"

"He has no reason to." Ella shrugs. "He's just keeping you right now until he finds the best way to..." She trails off, unable to find the right word.

"The best way to use me?" I finish for her. "I mean, you don't have to sugarcoat it. He is using me as a bargaining chip to get what he wants, isn't he?"

Ella lowers her head in shame. "I'm sorry, but yes. Yes, he is."

"Don't be sorry, it's not your fault. I just wish I could talk to Zane."

"Who is Zane?" Ella asks curiously.

"He is my... well, I don't really know what he is." *My everything.*

I spend the next ten minutes telling Ella my story. I tell her how Zane and I met in foster care and that I thought he died. We talk about him kidnapping me, and then me getting kidnapped again by Christian.

"So, what else do you do? Besides getting kidnapped on a regular basis?" Ella chuckles, and I can't help but giggle with her. For the first time in many days, I laugh, actually laugh.

We talk for a while, Ella tells me about her sister being married to Ivan and how they were pregnant at the same time. Momentarily, I forget where I am and why I'm here. Right now, it feels like it's just an old friend and me catching up.

Reality comes crashing back down on me when I hear an angry voice yelling at the guard in front of my door. A few seconds later, the door swings open, and Xander waltzes inside, wearing a mask of fury on his face.

"What the hell are you doing here?" He scowls at Ella, who seems completely unaffected by his stare. A stare that has a shiver running down my spine.

"Don't overreact. I'm fine. We were just talking." She gets up and goes to stand by his side, touching his arm tenderly. I can see the rage seeping away from his body, from across the room. His shoulders relax, and the white-knuckled fists by his sides, turn back to lax hands.

"Go back home, mouse," he tells her. She pushes up onto her tiptoes and gives him a chased kiss on the lips before heading out of the room, but not before giving me a tiny wave goodbye. As soon as she's gone, I miss her presence. It's like she's taken the warmth in the room with her.

"Put your shoes on, it's time to go," Xander orders, crossing his arms in front of him.

The news leaves me shocked. "What do you mean? Where am I going?"

"Zane and Matteo arranged a meeting with me. They want to trade you for some territory."

I should probably be offended that I'm being bargained with for a plot of land, but right this second, all I can process is that I'm finally going to get to see Zane again. I jump up from the bed and put my shoes on in a hurry.

"Why is Matteo willing to give up land for you?"

"Who?" I ask as I straighten up. "Who is Matteo?"

"One of my rivals as well as Christian's. Zane must have some valuable information he is trading... or something else? What if he has information that can hurt me in the long run?"

For a moment, I think he is going to change his mind. I can see him thinking about it, weighing his options.

"Look, Xander, you treated me well, and like you said, you did save me from Christian. I owe you, if you bring me to Zane and I find something out that could harm you or your family, I will tell you. I swear."

Xander examines me for a long minute. Just when I think he is going to lock me back in here, he disappears into the hallway but leaves the door open for me. Relief washes over me. He is still letting me go.

Hesitantly, I step outside. There are still two guards outside the door, and all three men resemble that of bouncers at a club, tall and muscular, making me feel even smaller than I am.

Looking up at the men, neither of them make eye contact with me. Without a word, Xander starts walking, the two men flanking him. I fall into step and follow them down the hall. When we get to the entrance,

I find more men waiting at the door, and even more outside. All dressed in black, weapons attached to their hips, looking like an army about to take down a city.

"Everyone knows their orders, so let's go," Xander calls out, his voice void of emotion. There are four blacked-out SUVs parked in front of the building, and at Xander's word, the men start piling into them. I stare, trying to figure out where I fit in in all of this. Do I just go to one of the SUV's and get in? As if Xander can sense my confusion, his dark gaze turns to me.

"You're coming with me," he says.

Before I can take a step, Xander's hand circles my upper arm, and he starts pulling me toward one of the cars. Excitement and anxiety over the unknown swirls deep in my gut. What's going to happen next? Am I really going to be reunited with Zane, or is this a joke?

Xander opens the back door to one of the SUV's and shoves me inside. I'm surprised to find someone already sitting in the back seat. The moment his eyes meet mine, I have this odd sense of deja vu. This man looks at me the same way Xander looked at me the first time we met. On top of that, he resembles Xander, almost to a tee. Like they could totally be—

"This is Damon, my brother," Xander says before I can finish my thought.

Forced into the middle seat, I place my hands in my lap. Xander slides in next to me, sandwiching me between him and his brother.

The car starts, and before I know it, we are driving away from the building and off the compound. An eerie silence settles over us, and I don't know where to look. The two men sitting in the front? The two men sitting on either side of me? Or just straight ahead on the road before us? Yes, I'll go with the road. It's the safer bet.

With my hands in my lap, I squeeze my shoulders together, trying to make myself as small as possible. When my eyes wander, and I look out to the side window, I catch Damon's eyes on me. Even when he sees me looking, he keeps staring at me, and I don't know how to feel about that. It's like he doesn't care that I caught him watching me, which intensifies the anxiousness that I'm already feeling.

"Xander tells me you're twenty-one?" Damon finally breaks the silence. His voice is just as dark and ominous as his brother's.

"Yes." I nod my head, not understanding why my age is being brought up, yet again.

"We're almost there," Xander announces. "Lean forward."

"Huh?" I twist around to look at him, but he is already pushing on my shoulders, forcing me to lean forward.

"Put your hands behind your back," he orders while digging for something in his pocket. My eyes catch on a pair of cable ties, only then, do I realize what he is up to.

"I won't run..."

"That's not the point. Just do it," he growls, and I slowly bring my hands to the small of my back. Every inch of my body is shaking. I'm not sure if I'm scared of him, or of what's going to happen next. Xander grips my arms and fastens the cable ties around my wrists to the point of pain. The plastic cuts into my skin, but I don't complain.

With my hands tied behind my back, I awkwardly and uncomfortably lean back against the seat. Neither of the Rossi brothers says anything to me, and once again, the car is blanketed in silence. We drive a few more minutes before pulling up to a large parking lot behind an abandoned warehouse. *Oh no... I've seen movies.*

I know the kind of shady shit that happens at abandoned warehouses, and it's nothing good. We circle the building like sharks, and I catch sight of another fleet of vehicles.

That must be Zane.

My heart starts beating faster and my throat swells. Am I really going to see him? What am I going to say? What is he going to say? Will he be mad at me? I never thought this would actually happen, so I never prepared myself for the scenario.

All my internal questions are cut off when I feel a hand on top of my head. Before I can turn to see who is touching me, the hand ruffles through my hair. Like a ten-year-old boy would do to a girl to make her mad.

"Hey! What the hell?" I whine, trying to move away from the hand.

"Can't have you looking all put together and shit. You were my prisoner after all," Xander explains. When he is done making a knotty mess of my hair, he takes the fabric of my shirt and rips it around my shoulder and down my arm. "There you go. That's better."

I look over at him, dumbfoundedly. "So, if they ask about where you kept me, should I lie? Maybe make up some dungeon?"

Xander smirks. "Smart girl, you are, though there isn't any need to make it up. There is a dungeon at my place, and as far as everybody knows, that's where you were kept."

"Got it." I nod, just as the car is put into park.

The front doors open first, the guards climb out and open the back doors. Damon is the first out. When I scoot toward his door to slip out, Xander grabs me by the arm, tugging me toward his door instead.

Sliding across the seat, he pulls me out of the car. My feet land against the concrete, and I suck in a precious breath of oxygen, almost as if I hadn't been breathing the entire drive here.

Xander doesn't give me a chance to prepare myself and starts walking toward the caravan of vehicles. Good thing he has an iron grip on my arm because the first step I take, I trip and almost faceplant. Xander pulls me up, and I fall in step beside him.

As soon as I lift up my head, I spot Zane and another man, off in the distance. My entire body locks up and my heart tightens in my chest.

He's really alive.

Our eyes connect, and even from a distance, I can see the turmoil of emotions in their depths, relief, need, and overwhelming possessiveness. Zane is mine, and I am his. I realize that now. My feet move of their own accord. My body drawn to him like a magnet. I try to run toward him, wanting to tell him that I'm okay. That everything is going to be okay. But Xander jerks me back by the arm, keeping me close to his side before I can take off.

Zane's eyes lower to where Xander's hand is. His lip curls almost as if he is snarling like an animal. The glare in his eyes is deadly, and I'm positive that it's taking every ounce of self-restraint he has, not to charge at Xander right now. The mere thought of a fight breaking out between the two of them is terrifying.

I can feel Zane's rage rolling off of him in waves. I don't know how this meeting is going to end. I just hope that after everything we've been through, that Zane and I can walk away in one piece.

30

I'm a bullet waiting to leave the chamber. My body vibrates with unchecked rage. Every fiber and cell in my body is telling me to move. Telling me to go to her, and rip Xander Rossi's hand off of her body and beat him with it for touching her. For touching what is mine and always will be mine.

Like a ticking time bomb, I force myself to stand still, to hold back. I know it's the most strategic thing to do, but that doesn't make it any easier. If he does something stupid, or if I see Dove flinch even once, I'll explode. I didn't come all this way not to leave with her, but I won't let him or anyone else hurt her.

"It's a pleasure to finally meet you, Zane." Xander's lips tip up at the sides in a smile when we're just a few feet away. "Matteo, it's been a while. I would say it's good to see you, but we both know that's a lie. If it wasn't for this agreement, I'd have my men pumping you full of lead by now."

"Same." Matteo nods, and all I can think is how fucked up these two fuckers are. I need to get Dove and get us out of here before these two end up firing their guns in some sick fight to see whose cock is bigger.

Damon, Xander's brother, is watching me. I can feel his beady eyes on my skin, burning through my flesh. "The agreement has been signed by both parties and is final. You can have the girl back. We had our fun with her. I'm pretty sure she enjoyed her stay as well."

Xander fully grins, and I clench my fist, envisioning my hand wrapping around his throat and squeezing. If he touched her, I will kill him. I'll rip him to pieces, no matter what war I'll start in doing soon. I'd kill anyone, bloody my hands in any way to protect her.

"Let her go," I say through clenched teeth, surprised that the words don't come out as an animalistic growl.

"Hand over the papers first," Xander orders like I'm one of his men. Matteo nods to Karl, one of his guys, and he starts walking toward the space between our two groups. Damon takes a few steps forward, meeting Karl and snatches the papers from him.

He looks over them quickly before motioning to Xander that it's all good. Instead of letting Dove go right away, which would be the smart thing to do, Xander pulls her closer to him, leans down, and whispers something into the shell of her ear.

That's it. He's going to die...

Taking a step forward, I'm fully prepared to wrap my hands around the fucker's neck when Matteo and one of his goons, grab me by the arms, holding me back. I shrug them off, giving both of them a look that says don't fucking touch me.

When I turn my attention back to Xander and Dove, he lets her go.

As soon as he releases her, she runs toward me, almost losing her balance with her hands tied behind her back. A moment later, her slim body slams into mine. She buries her face in my chest, and I wrap my arms around her protectively. Before I do anything, I bury my face into the crook of her neck and inhale deeply. This moment is like seeing the sun after a long cold winter. Like tasting water after a drought. It's indescribable but all the words at once.

"I missed you so much," she mumbles into my chest. "I thought you were dead."

"I missed you too," I reply, stroking a hand down her back. I want to strip her bare, look her over, and worship every inch of her body. I want to ask her what happened, if she's okay, if she is hungry, tired, or hurt, but I also just want to stand here like this, doing nothing more than holding her.

"Let's go," Matteo says, nudging me in the side. I'm tempted to tell him to fuck off, but I bite my tongue. Getting Dove away from these guys is what I need to do. Now that I have her back in my arms, protecting her and ensuring her safety is my number one priority. Nothing in this world will ever separate us again.

Matteo offers me his knife, and I take it, cutting the plastic zip ties binding her wrists. As soon as her hands are free, she wraps her arms around me. There is nothing like feeling her tiny arms wrapped around me. It's so strange that once upon a time, she tried to escape me, but now she holds me close as if I'm her savior.

I lean down and whisper into her ear. "I want nothing more than to hold you in my arms, but we really need to go."

Nodding, she pulls away, her beautiful blue eyes are filled with tears, making them seem lighter. "I'm sorry, Zane. I'm sorry I didn't listen to you. That I made you take me to the hospital. It's all my fault." Big fat tears fall from her eyes, and my heart cracks a little in my chest.

"It's okay, baby, and it's not your fault. We'll talk when we get back to Matteo's place," I tell her.

Wrapping an arm around her shoulders, I turn and guide us back to the SUV. Matteo's men swarm us like we're the president of the United States, which for once, I'm actually grateful for. When we reach the car, I open the door and lift her inside before climbing in myself. Pulling her tight to my side, I press my lips to her forehead.

This feels like a dream. And I'm waiting for the other shoe to drop. Like at any second, I'm going to wake up and realize that none of it was real. That I imagined the whole thing, and that Dove isn't really here with me.

Matteo climbs into the front seat, and one of his men takes the driver's seat. Even as the car starts to move, it still doesn't feel real.

"Where are we going?" Dove whispers, peering up at me through her wet lashes.

"Matteo's place. I have so much to tell you... but first, I need to make sure you're okay. Did they hurt you? Touch you in any way?" Bile rises in my throat as I speak. God, I don't know if I can handle this. If either of them fuckers touched her...I'll lose it. Fury overtakes every emotion I'm feeling at the moment.

"Neither of them hurt me, and I wasn't with Christian long before Xander's men found me."

Thank fuck... I was getting ready to paint the entire world red.

Sighing, I hold onto her a little tighter. "All I could think about the entire time they had you was if you were okay. If they were hurting you? If you were eating, or if you were cold? All I could think about was saving you and how I had let you down."

"No," Dove whimpers and grips onto my shirt as if I'll disappear at any second. I'm certain she is close to shattering, and things are only going to get worse from here. "It's not your fault, none of this is your fault, Zane. You tried to protect me. You warned me, and I wouldn't listen. I thought you were crazy, but if I had believed you—"

"Don't worry about that right now..."

"Hate to break up your reunion, but I believe you owe me a thank you," Matteo announces from the front seat.

Rolling my eyes, I grit my teeth as I speak my next set of words. "Thank you, Matteo." Playing nice with this guy is trying on my patience, and I'm not sure how much longer I can go before I snap and do something drastic.

"That doesn't sound like you're really grateful, but I'll let it slide since you've finally delivered on bringing my daughter back to me."

Fucking Christ. Why did he have to go and say that? I was hoping to spill the beans to Dove once we were back at the house.

"Wha-what is he talking about, Zane?" Dove blinks, but the shocked expression on her face doesn't dissipate.

Tension fills the vehicle. "Dammit, I didn't want to do this yet, Matteo."

"Why not?" He shifts in his seat. "There is no better time than the present to let my daughter know that her father isn't dead and didn't abandon her."

"You're my father?" Dove whispers so quietly I almost don't hear her. "How... how is that possible?" She looks from me and back to Matteo, and I wish, now more than ever, that I had told her no when she begged me to go see Donna one last time. Maybe if I had said no, none of this would've happened.

Matteo snickers. "Well, I'm sure I don't have to tell you where babies come from, so I'll skip that part, but you see, your mother was actually a married woman who happened to fall in love with me. When she found out she was pregnant, we had planned to run away together. However, she had a change of heart and disappeared. When I finally found her, she was dead, and you were gone. I looked everywhere for you, but every trail led me to a dead-end. I was sure I would never find you, and then Zane came to me. As soon as he told me that Christian had been looking for you for many years, I knew who you were."

Just from the way she tenses beside me, I can tell Dove isn't just shocked but uncomfortable as well.

Turning toward me as if I can shield her from the truth, she opens her mouth and asks me the one question I know will be the final nail in her coffin. "Is it true? Is he really my father?"

My throat tightens, and as badly as I want to lie, I know it won't change anything. It won't help her. Finding out Matteo is her father, was a surprise. I thought I could get help and slip away into the night with Dove, but now I know that's not possible. Matteo is going to do whatever he can to keep Dove in his life, and I'll be fighting a war I can't win if I try and keep her from him.

"Yes, he's your father," I say.

All I can do is watch with an ache in my chest as she works through the emotions, agony, fear, and confusion flicker across her beautiful features. After watching her closely for years, I can almost tell how she's going to react to a situation before she even does. It's weird, but an added plus to having stalked her for years.

"I know it's a lot to take in on such short notice, especially after everything that's happened, but I want you to know that now that I've found you, I plan to get to know you better, and be the father I never got to be," Matteo says.

Father? I choke back my laughter. I haven't known him long, but Matteo doesn't take me as the father type. He's the leader of the Castro family. All he knows how to do is order his men around and threaten people. Plus, what kind of parenting is he going to do? Dove's an adult now and doesn't need his money or protection. Not when she has me.

Dove is quiet the rest of the way back to the house, and when we arrive at the mansion, she seems a little overwhelmed. Once out of the car and inside the house, I take Dove's hand into mine. "Thank you so much for helping me find her, but I think it's time we end this charade. Her safety is my biggest priority."

Matteo stares at me, his face blank. Two of his men hover just outside the massive wooden front door. I can feel their eyes on me.

"There is no safer place for her than here, surely, you can agree, given that you were the one to put her in the situation that got her taken by Christian in the first place?"

His remark is a kick to the balls, and if it wasn't for Dove standing beside me, I'd have him pinned to the wall. Strangling the air from his lungs. Still, fighting with him on staying for the night isn't something I want to do. Not when I could be holding Dove in my arms, kissing every inch of her skin, and making up for lost time.

"Fine, we will stay for tonight," I say, pinning him with a glare.

"Great, why don't you go upstairs and get some rest? Karl will take you up." He smiles, his eyes twinkling with some unknown emotion.

I don't bother paying him another second of attention. Shifting gears, I tug Dove toward the grand staircase. Karl follows behind all the way to our room, like the guard dog he is.

Opening the door, I guide us into the room. The door shuts with a soft click, and all I can think is... *finally,* finally, we're alone.

"Do we really have to stay here? This is wrong. Something feels off." Concern is etched into her delicate face.

"Only for tonight. Tomorrow we will figure this out. Everything can wait until then because the only thing that matters to me right now is making sure you're okay and reminding you of how much you mean to me."

"I thought I lost you," Dove says. Her voice is clogged with emotion.

"You'll never lose me," I tell her, pulling her into my arms. I squeeze her tight, wanting to melt our two bodies into one.

"Why didn't you tell me?"

"Tell you what?"

"That you are William..."

I peel her away from my chest just enough so I can look at her face. "You remember?"

"Yes. How could I forget you?"

"You told the therapist that you didn't remember that time. She even said it was normal, considering what you've been through. Your mind is trying to protect you and all that shit."

"I told everyone I didn't remember because I never wanted to talk about it. Losing you hurt so bad. Saying it out loud just made it worse."

"Oh, baby." I pull her back into my embrace. "If I had known you'd remembered, I would have told you. That would have made things a whole lot easier."

For a long moment, we just stand there holding each other. Then Dove breaks the silence, whispering, "You came for me..."

"Of course." Does she doubt I would have? She should know the extent of my obsession by now. "No matter what happens, I'll always come for you. I'll always protect you. I'll move heaven and hell to make sure you're safe. You're my number one and always have been. Nothing will ever change that. I love you, Dove. Always..."

31

His words hit me like a freight train. I'm overcome with emotion. Drowning in it. I'm uncertain about nearly everything at this point, everything but Zane.

I need him. Need to feel his hands on me, to press my lips against his, to carve out a piece of my heart and give it to him. It hasn't been that long since I last saw him, but it feels like years after everything that's happened. Pushing at his chest, I make him walk backward toward the large bed. I want to lie down and curl up on top of his chest.

"Can we please just go to bed? I'm so tired."

"Whatever you want or need, we can do it."

I nod, finally feeling free, safe, and secure. I haven't felt even a sliver of safety since we left the hospital that day.

Zane starts peeling off my clothes until I'm in nothing but a pair of panties. His eyes roaming over my body as if he is inspecting every inch of it.

"No one touched you?" he asks again as if he didn't hear or believe me when I told him earlier.

"No. I promise, I'm fine." I tug on his shirt, wanting his skin to touch mine. He raises his arms, and I help him out of his shirt.

I gasp when I see the fresh bullet wounds. "You were shot!" Three times?" I knew he had been hurt, but nothing prepared me for seeing the wounds up close.

Zane chuckles. "I'm fine, Dove. I'm not that easy to kill."

"I know, but you almost died." Staring at his chest, I can't bring myself to look him in the eyes. I feel immense guilt for those three wounds. Almost as if I was the one that pulled the trigger. Had I not begged to go and see Donna...

Zane's gentle voice cuts off my train of thought, and two fingers lift my chin, forcing me to look into his eyes. "*Almost* isn't the same as did. There was no way in hell I was going to die in that parking garage, knowing that Christian had you. I was put on this earth to protect you, and I don't care if I have to die to do that, Dove. In my eyes, you're the only thing that has ever mattered." The look he's giving me right now says he's telling the truth.

"I'm sorry I didn't believe you. Sorry that I tried to escape, and tried to hurt you..."

"You were only trying to protect yourself." Zane moves his hand, his knuckles grazing against my cheek while tucking some loose strands of hair behind my ear. "I don't blame you, and that's why I never really punished or tried to hurt you. All I wanted to do was keep you safe."

The agony that coats each word reminds me that he, too, feels as if he let me down. Jesus, we're a mess.

My head starts to throb, a migraine from hell, no doubt forming there.

"We have so much to talk about, but all I want to do is crawl into bed and sleep for days."

Zane smirks, his gaze darkening as he drops his hand from my cheek. "I can think of a couple other things we can do besides sleep or talk."

Even though it's probably messed up, that's all I want right now. To be close to Zane, to solidify what we were building before everything exploded in our faces.

Reaching for his already hard cock between our bodies, I look up at him. "I want you. Inside of me. Our bodies skin to skin. I need this. Need to feel every inch of your body blanketing mine."

"Me too, baby, me too."

And that's all he says before he guides me back to the bed. My knees hit the edge of the mattress, and I fall onto my back. Zane crawls up over my body with a predatory glint in his eyes, causing me to shiver, and my nipples harden.

All my worries and fears evaporate in an instant. All that matters is Zane and me. Our bodies and hearts, becoming one.

Like fire and gasoline, we come together, igniting a fiery passion that burns hotter than the sun. Zane peppers every inch of my flesh with hot open mouth kisses, his tongue gliding over my flesh, making the muscles between my thighs clench.

"I can't even put into words how much I missed you." He kisses a path across my collarbone and down between my breasts. Lifting my hips, I try and draw him closer to the place that is aching, pulsing like it has its own heartbeat. "How afraid I was that something bad was happening to you. Since that night that you saved me, I vowed to protect you. I watched you, snuck in your apartment, killed assholes that only wanted you for sex, and guess what?"

He pulls his mouth away, but his tongue still flicks out against my diamond hard nipple, teasing me, tempting me.

"What?" I ask breathlessly, my chest heaving.

A devilish grin tugs at his lips. "I'd do it all again. Over a hundred times. Again, and again because you're mine, Dove. All mine, and the next time someone tries to take you away from me, I won't fail you. I'll kill them with my bare hands, and make you watch just to prove to you that I will never let you down again."

I nod my head, letting him know that I know and that I understand. He rewards me by sucking my nipple into his mouth, tugging on the tip hard until my back is arching off the bed, and I'm holding his head against my breast.

A ravenous need that only he can satiate tightens, swirling around inside of me, and I have to have him; need him with a desperation that is way too embarrassing to say out loud.

Releasing my nipple with a pop that reverberates through the room, he takes a step back and reaches for my hips. His fingers run along the edge of my cotton panties, and I'm half tempted to shove them down my legs and pull him forward, forcing him to take me, but

I know patience is a virtue, and Zane needs this almost more than I do.

"Has anyone touched *my* pussy?"

"No," I croak.

"Are you lying to me?" Zane cocks his head to the side as he slowly tugs the panties down my legs before tossing them over his shoulder. The cool air kisses my wet folds, and I let out a hiss at the sensation.

"No... no one has touched me. I'm yours, only yours..." I'm panting like a dog in heat. I bite my lip, watching through heavy lids as he spreads my legs, his eyes going straight to my soaked core.

"Fuck, Dove. I've missed this pretty little pussy. I've only taken you twice, but I want to bury myself balls deep inside of you and live there forever."

"Yes, please..." My core clenches in response, and I'm so turned on, so ready for him. I need him to take me right now. Take me and own me.

Zane smiles and glides his knuckles against the inside of my thigh as he trails a hand closer to my center. *Yes!*

When his fingers flutter against my swollen folds, I whimper. "You want my fat cock in there. Deep inside you, don't you?"

"Yes, now, please..." I beg helplessly.

"Good because I need you, too, right now. I need you, my Dove, and I need you hard and fast, my balls slapping against your ass, my cock pressing against the back of your channel, giving you both pleasure and pain."

"Yes, Zane. God, please, I need this." Reaching for him, my hand circles his length, and for one brief second, I forgot how large he is. How thick it is, and how full I'm going to be when he enters me.

"You'll get me..." He hisses out through clenched teeth as I squeeze his length and move my hand up and down his shaft.

A gasp escapes my lips, and I tip my head back into the pillows when he enters me with two fingers without warning. I'm so turned on and wet that the intrusion does nothing but fan the flames of arousal. He pumps in and out of me, and stars appear before my eyes.

"Fuck me. I've thought about this moment every night you were gone. Me finding you, saving you, and then worshiping your body, taking every hole over and over again. Your tight little pussy likes that, wants it. She's clenching all around me, do you hear the wet sounds she's making? Do you feel your arousal against your thighs?"

"Yes!" I tug on his cock a little hard, and his thrusts become harder, the heel of his hand presses against my clit, and the added pressure sends me skyrocketing into orgasmic lands. Shivering, my muscles tense and then snap. I clench tightly around Zane's fingers and let out a deranged whimper at the loss of them as he pulls out of me.

I'm seconds away from asking him what he's doing when his body blankets mine, and he grabs my hands and pins them above my head. *Control. Zane is all about control.* With one hand, he holds both my wrists in place, and with the other, he guides his throbbing cock to my entrance.

"Tell me you don't want this, that you don't want me, and I'll take you anyway. I'll still claim your body just as you've claimed my heart, without a single fuck given. You're mine, Dove, mine and only ever mine."

Parting my lips, a response is on the tip of my tongue, but I never say it. All that comes out is a bunch of incoherent thoughts, and pants, and begging for Zane to take me harder and faster as he enters me so deeply all I feel is him, his cock impaling me, owning me.

"Heaven, home, life. Fuck, I didn't know I wasn't breathing until I met you, Dove." Zane bows his head as his grasp on my wrist tightens. He drives into me, rutting, going as deep as he can. My body tingles, goosebumps pebble my flesh, and my nipples rub against his chiseled chest with every stroke, heightening my pleasure.

"Zane... I want..." I can barely get the words out...my thoughts are being overrun by pleasure, by pain.

"What, baby, what do you want?" Zane growls, a bead of sweat dripping down his temple.

"Touch... I want to touch you."

"Your touch makes me insane," he grunts but releases his hold on my hands. As soon as my hands are free, they're on him. He hisses at my touch and thrusts faster, his balls slapping against my ass furiously. His thirst for me is unquenchable, and I'm not sure if he'll ever be able to get enough of me.

Circling my hands around his neck, I pull him closer until his face is buried in my neck, and all I hear are his heavy breaths filling my ears. Kissing along his shoulder, I grip onto him for dear life as he fucks me like a beast. This is nothing like our first or even second time. There is something so raw and beautiful about the way he comes apart. The man who would paint the world red for me becomes melted butter in my hands, and I love it.

With the quickening pace, I find I'm sprinting to the finish line. Lifting my hips, I meet him thrust for thrust. We're two crazed lovers clawing at one another's hearts until they're a bloody mess. Who will bleed the most?

Swiveling his hips, Zane makes it impossible for me to think, or form any coherent thought as the tip of his cock grazes a spot so pleasurable inside of me, I nearly come undone in a second.

"I need you to come. I need to feel you tighten around me, to have you suck the come right out of my cock...will you do that for me?"

I don't know how he's still able to talk. Every nerve ending on my body is electrified, and like sticking a fork into a light socket, the pleasure zings through me, making my toes curl and my back arch off the bed. The gates of pleasure open, and suddenly I'm suffocating, drowning, and damn, would it be the perfect way to go.

"Oh fuck..." Zane growls, wrapping his arms around my back, holding me close to him as he continues to thrust into me while my body tries to push him out. A few more thrusts and he meets his own wave of pleasure, exploding deep inside of me, painting the walls of my womb with his sticky release.

Zane collapses against me, his arms still wrapped around mine. Our chests heave as we try and catch our breaths. Our hearts beat in sync, threatening to come out of our chests.

Sweat covers our bodies, and as the intense orgasm dissipates, everything I pushed to the back of my mind comes barreling to the front. Closing my eyes, I try and push the thoughts away.

Please, not today... I just need one day.

After a while, Zane rolls off of me. He nuzzles his nose against mine and presses a kiss to my forehead so gently I almost don't feel it. It's a stark reminder of how different he can be. How the same hands that bring death to many, also bring me immense pleasure.

"I know the last thing you want right now is to talk about the elephant in the room, but there isn't any way around this. We need to talk about Matteo being your father, and about how we are going to get out of here."

Forcing my heavy eyes open, I find that Zane is sitting on the edge of the bed, his eyes roaming over my body. There is a frantic look hidden in those depths, almost as if he thinks I'm going to disappear on him again.

"How did you get him to help you?"

"Let's just say, I'm indebted to the Castro family for a little while."

Frowning, I reach for his hand and interlace our fingers. "What do you mean, *indebted*?"

Zane's lip curls in disgust, but I know his anger and feelings aren't directed at me. "It means I do as your new-found father says until otherwise."

His response is like a slap in the face back to reality. Yes, Zane wouldn't have been able to get to me without Matteo's help, I realize that, but the last thing I want is for him to be stuck in this world, for both of us to be stuck here. I don't want to be a pawn to anyone, and I want even less for Zane to be.

Shaking my head, I try to process all the information I've learned about today. I have so many questions, so many things I need to know, but my brain is exhausted. All of this has been so tiring...finding out Matteo is my father. I don't know him.

The only thing I'm sure of when it comes to him is that he's evil. The aura he gives off tells me so. I doubt there is a merciful bone in his body. I remember what Xander whispered in my ear before he let me go.

"Don't trust Matteo."

Even without Xander's warning, I wouldn't trust him. It's just another confirmation for me not to do so. I'll be the first to admit, I'm naive to the dark world I've been thrust into, but I'm not stupid. A man like Matteo, like Xander, they're willing to step on anyone that gets in their way, and that includes me. Just because Xander didn't treat me like a true captive, doesn't mean the next time we cross paths, he won't draw blood.

My thoughts swirl and shift, and the sedated feeling I had just a short while ago is gone. In its place, anxiety has bloomed, festering like a wound that won't heal.

"I don't understand..." I whisper more to myself than Zane. "I've been in the system since, well, as long as I can remember. If he was really my father, how did he not find me? Especially since he obviously has money at his disposal."

"As far as I know, both him and Christian have been looking for you for at least a decade, if not longer. Your mom changed her name, and when she died, no one knew who you were or who your father was. You were a Jane Doe for a while, being passed around from foster home to foster home. Then someone decided to give you a name. I don't know everything, but I do know that whatever Matteo is up to is bad. I have to get you away from him."

"Xander said the same thing..."

"What do you mean, Xander said the same thing?" Zane's expression becomes intuitive.

"Xander told me not to trust Matteo. Which I mean, coming from another mobster family doesn't really mean much of anything, but given that he could've hurt me while I was being held captive and he didn't, kind of speaks volumes to me."

My eyes catch on the tightness of Zane's jaw. "They're both criminals, who would kill you the second you became useless to them."

"Are you saying you don't trust Xander?"

"Fuck, no. Why do you trust him?" The defensive tone he's giving me makes it hard for me to want to answer him honestly.

"I don't... I guess... Maybe a little." I shrug. "I mean, he didn't have to treat me the way he did. The room he kept me in was clean and quiet, and none of his men messed with me. He brought me clothes and made sure I was fed well. Although, I'm not supposed to tell anyone any of those things. Plus, I really liked his wife."

"You met his wife?" Zane looks at me like I've grown a second head.

"Yeah, she came and hung out with me. Kept me company, so I wasn't so alone."

For a moment, it seems I've rendered Zane speechless. He just looks at me with wide eyes, his expression flat.

"Wow...I'm kinda shocked. Don't get me wrong. I'm glad he treated you well, but nothing you said is something Xander would do. I wouldn't be surprised if he did this by design. Trying to keep you on his good side for some reason, but that would mean he knew who you were. Which puts you in danger and on his radar."

"Ugh, I don't know. All of this is too much. My brain needs a rest. All I know is that I don't want anything to do with Matteo, even if he is my father. I don't know him, and I don't want to get to know him either."

"And you shouldn't. Matteo might be your father, but I don't think that means much to a man like him, especially when he just found you. I don't know what he has planned, but I won't let him hurt you. Someone like him always has an agenda, and no matter what he says, you're not safe here."

Hearing him say exactly what I've been thinking this whole time, only solidifies what we need to do. We have to escape, but how if Zane is stuck under my new-found father's thumb?

Sitting up, I move a little closer to him. I can feel his come dripping out of me and onto my thighs with the movement. Gripping him by the jaw, I gently turn his face to mine. "I'm not leaving without you, Zane."

His dark gaze looks like it's a million miles away when it finally meets mine. "I was afraid you'd say that..."

32

*B*y the time morning comes, I'm in no better mood than I was when I went to sleep. The only thing I have to smile about is the fact that I have Dove in my arms when I wake up. Aside from that, I hate this place, and I hate that I'm stuck working for Matteo.

An insistent knock echoes against the wooden door.

"Tell it to go away," Dove grumbles into my chest.

"I wish I could," I reply and roll out of bed. I'm in nothing but my boxers, but I don't care. I'd open the door if I was buck ass naked.

The knocking continues even as I walk to the door. Fondly, I remember a time when I killed men for lesser things. My hands itch to do some damage to whoever is on the other side of that door. Then again, the fact that I have Dove back should give me even more of an incentive not to do something stupid. Killing one of Matteo's men or him would start a full-on war, and without anyone on my side, I'd be as good as dead, and so would Dove.

As soon as I open the door, I want to close it.

"Good morning. Matteo is requesting you have breakfast with him," Karl sneers from just outside the doorway, his beady eyes try and see into the room, but I use my body as a shield to block him.

"Tell him we'll be right down," I say before slamming the door in his face.

When I turn around, Dove is climbing out of bed, completely naked, and heading toward the bathroom. "I'm taking a shower first."

"I'll join you." I smirk and follow her, watching her ass jiggle slightly with each step. I groan as my dick stirs to life.

Dove turns on the shower and steps under the spray as soon as the water is hot enough. I lose my boxers and join her in the large double showerhead stall. Taking one of the washcloths, I soap it up and start washing Dove's body gently while she washes her hair.

"This feels nice," Dove murmurs. "I didn't want to admit it before, but I like you taking care of me."

"And I love taking care of you. I won't ever stop either."

After I've washed every inch of her beautiful body, she takes the washcloth from my hand and does the same for me. Washing me from head to toe, being extra gentle around my fresh shot wounds. My cock is rock hard by the time we rinse off, but I know Castro is waiting, and I'd like him in a good mood since I'm going to tell him we're leaving today.

We step out of the shower, and I wrap Dove up in an oversized towel before drying off myself. We get dressed quickly and head down-stairs even though Dove's long dark hair is still wet.

When we get to the bottom of the stairs, Karl meets us and takes us to the dining room. Castro is already sitting at the table. In front of him, a colorful spread of breakfast food. There are only three plates on the table, but food to feed about thirty mouths.

"Good morning," Castro greets. "Please, sit, make yourself at home."

"Why did you want us at breakfast?" I ask bluntly as I take the seat next to Matteo.

"To see my daughter for one..." Matteo curls his top lip, but he's going to have to do better than that if he wants to scare me. I've taken tougher shits than him. I've ripped out men's organs and strangled them with them.

"We're happy to have breakfast with you, but after that, I'm taking Dove away from here. She doesn't belong here, and she wants to go home."

Matteo seems confused, which is weird because I'm pretty sure I spelled it out clear as day to him. "You seem to still be under the impression that you make the rules. It's you who owes me, and as for Dove, she's a big girl and can make her own decisions—"

"I want to go home," Dove interrupts Matteo.

Castro throws back his head and laughs. "You are home now, Daughter. At last, you're home. You're the heir to the Castro empire. My only child."

Dove visibly shudders at the word *heir*. She is clearly uncomfortable, and I know she wants to speak up, but she refrains.

He must think he's so smart, that he's pulled the cloth right over my eyes by helping me save Dove, little does he know, I see right through his bullshit exterior. He doesn't want a relationship with her. He wants to use her, and I'm going to figure out in what way.

"I know you're up to something, and I don't like it. I smell bullshit."

Matteo chuckles. "I only smell bacon, my friend... speaking of, could you hand me some."

I take my fork and spear a few pieces of bacon with it, imagining I was stabbing Matteo's eyeball instead. He takes the bacon from my fork with his meaty fingers and shoves it into his mouth.

"So, you're really going to stick to the story that all you want is to have a relationship with your daughter?"

"Of course, I want more than that. I want her to be part of the family, part of the business. I want her to continue my bloodline. Marry and give me grandchildren to lead the next generation..."

The clang of a fork hitting the plate fills the room as Dove's silverware slips from her shaking hand.

"I know it's a lot to take in and get used to, but you'll be fine, child. You're my daughter, after all."

"I don't want to be part of any of this, and I definitely wouldn't want my children—if I would choose to have any—to be part of this either."

Matteo sighs heavily, his eyes gleam with danger. He is clearly annoyed with Dove's outburst. "I don't care what you want. You are my flesh and blood, and you will do what's best for the family."

"Don't fucking talk to her like that," I growl, slamming my fist onto the table. Silverware and expensive china rattle from the impact.

Matteo turns his attention to me, pinning me with a murderous gaze. "Let's be very clear, Zane, the only reason you are still here—inside of *my* house—is to make the transition for Dove easier. If you don't behave yourself, I will have you removed, and Dove will have to figure things out the hard way. Am I clear?"

My jaw hurts from grinding my teeth, and my muscles ache from exercising restraint when I give him a slight nod. He grins, and I have to look down at my plate before the last shred of my control is gone. *Motherfucker.* He'll pay for this. He. Will. Pay.

I take a deep breath and look up at Dove. I expect her to be terrified, maybe cry. Instead, she surprises the hell out of me by swallowing her emotions and putting her game face on instead.

"Maybe we got off on the wrong foot," she announces. "Like you said, I'm not used to all of this, and it will take me a while to adjust to the idea of me having a family. I've been on my own for most of my life, and Zane has been in my life the longest. If you want me to marry him and have children, then so be it."

"Oh, child." Matteo chuckles deeply. "You won't marry him, of course. You have to marry one of my men. Someone I trust."

I'm going to kill him. I don't know when and where, but he just signed his death certificate. He'll die by my hands, and it will be a painful death.

I look at Dove across the table and see the flicker of fear in her eyes. It kills me, rips a hole in my chest. I want to kill Matteo now, jam the knife next to my plate in his throat and watch him bleed out on the white tablecloth.

But I know his men would kill me after. I'd never get Dove out of here alive, and that thought is the only thing stopping me from acting on instinct.

Surprising me, yet again, Dove remains calm. "I love Zane. I don't think I can marry someone else. There must be another way."

"Love will get you killed in this business, child. I need you to marry someone that can be head of the family business, someone strong, a leader, not a hitman from one of my rivals. That's never going to happen." He pauses, and for a moment, it is painfully silent in the room, then Matteo continues, "Look, the best I can do for you is let

Zane keep working for me. He can even be your guard. Which will work out great, since I know he would die to protect you. Hell, I don't even care if you two keep fucking as long as you play the dutiful wife for everyone else to see."

I open my mouth, about to say something when I see Dove shake her head across the table. Forcing the words back down, I sit silently instead.

"Can you just give me some time? I don't know anything about this family yet. I don't even know you. Can we take this slow?"

"Of course. It's not like I'm planning on dying any time soon."

You should be, old man. Because I'm planning your death right now.

33

*A*fter breakfast, we retreat to our bedroom. Zane is quiet the entire walk back upstairs, and I feel myself imploding from the inside out. So many things just happened.

My father... if I can even call him that, told me that he wants me to marry and have children with a man of his choosing. He's made it incredibly clear that if things don't go the way he wants, if Zane tries to interfere, he'll retaliate. My mind is spinning.

He thinks he can control me, make choices for me, but he doesn't even know who I am. I'm going to have to play by his rules until I come up with a plan, but the second I figure something out, I'm gone.

When we reach the bedroom and walk inside, Zane closes the bedroom door behind us, flicking the lock into place. A gasp escapes my lips when I'm pinned to the nearest wall. Lifting my head, my gaze collides with his. Fiery rage flickers deep in those depths. I can see his pain, feel his rage as he lifts his hand, and gently strokes my cheek.

"All I could think about while we were down there was how he planned to marry you off to another man, and how I will do everything in my power to stop him from doing so." His teeth are clenched so tightly the words come out clipped. "I can't let him take you from me. I didn't do everything I've done, fight tooth and nail, barter, and beg to get you back, only to have you given to another man."

The pain and anguish in his voice feel like a dull butter knife cutting through my flesh. Placing my hands against his chest, I fist the fabric and tug him closer. "I'm not going anywhere, and I'm not marrying anyone. All he's trying to do is get you to react. You should know, I won't just do what I'm told."

A hint of a smile creeps onto his lips. "Oh, I know you don't do what you're told, but that's with me. How do I know you won't bend to his will if he threatens me, if he tries to hurt me or someone else you care about? I won't put you through that. You aren't any safer here than you were with Christian or Xander. We're leaving, and we're doing it tonight."

Swallowing around the thick knot that's formed in my throat, I ask, "Tonight?"

"Yes, tonight. We aren't staying here another night." I'm not sure we should try an escape so soon.

Part of me thinks Matteo will expect it, but part of me feels that if I tell Zane we can't leave yet, he'll think I want to stay when really I want to put as much distance between us and this house of terror as I can.

Ghosting his lips against my forehead, he pulls back and walks over to the window. He pulls the curtain back and peers outside. Slivers of sunlight enter the room but disappear when he lets the curtain fall closed. Turning back toward me, determination oozes from his pores. His gaze is hard, and I know there isn't any point in trying to sway him.

"We'll spend the day biding our time. Come nightfall, we'll leave."

"Okay." I nod. I don't tell him how nervous I am, or that I feel like something bad is going to happen. It's probably nothing. Or at least, I hope it isn't.

BY THE TIME NIGHT FALLS, I'm a nervous wreck, but Zane has shot down any of my reasonings. I tried my best to talk him out of this, but nothing has worked.

"It's time," Zane says, tugging me to the door. "Remember, stay behind me."

I nod and follow behind him as he steps out of the room. We find the hallway quiet and empty, but we both know that Matteo's guards are around here somewhere. I haven't noticed any cameras inside this place, but that doesn't mean there are none. Maybe he's just good at hiding them. We have to be fast and precise because we'll likely only get one shot at this.

On light feet, we walk down the hall, about halfway down the stairs, we catch sight of one of the guards. Luckily, he is facing away from us, so we have the element of surprise going for us. Silently and fast as lightning Zane rushes toward him.

The guard doesn't see us coming, and Zane has an arm wrapped around his throat, squeezing the life out of him before he can make a single sound.

Shocked, I watch as Zane with nothing but a void expression in his eyes, chokes the man to death. I watch as he struggles until his body slowly sags to the floor. Strangely, I know I should feel some type of remorse, feel sadness, or at least some shame watching this happen right before my eyes. The truth is, I feel neither. At this moment, I'm numb, the void of feelings is confusing, but also liberating.

When the man lies dead on the floor, Zane searches him and takes his gun, giving me the sign to keep going. My feet move on their own, following Zane to wherever he is leading us.

Tiptoeing down the stairs, we make it through the kitchen and to the backdoor. There is no noise, no talking, nothing that makes me believe someone has seen us, but not seeing any other guards raises a huge red flag. When Zane turns the door handle, and we find the door unlocked, I really start to get worried. Can we really have that much luck? *I doubt it.*

It's like we're waiting for the other shoe to drop, the only question is, when? Hesitantly, I follow him outside and into the darkness. There is no light, only the stars above to guide the way. Through the darkness, Zane finds my hand, intertwining our fingers, and together we run across the lawn to the nearest line of trees.

Fear and adrenaline pump through my veins, and we're so close to freedom I can almost taste it. We keep moving, getting further and further away from the house, but not far enough away before all hell breaks loose. Loud yelling carries across the yard and through the trees from the house, it has us both looking over our shoulders.

The once dark house is now lit up like a Christmas tree. Every room in the house has its lights on. The doors and windows are being opened, and men in troves start storming out the back door that we escaped from.

Shit. I knew it was too good to be true.

With a panicked expression, Zane turns to me. "Run!" he whisper-shouts, already pulling me away. Racing through the wooded area, low hanging limbs whip across my face, scratching my skin. The adrenaline coursing through my veins, keeps me from feeling the pain yet, but I already know it's going to come later.

We run until we get to a large wrought iron fence, built in a way that makes it impossible to climb, leaving us with only one way to go. To run along the edge of it and find an end. We don't get far before we spot a guard tower ahead. Spotlights move across the lawn, searching for us like magnifying glasses.

"Let's backtrack," Zane says, the uncertainty in his voice is hard to miss.

We spin around, ready to head back the way we came when we see them. A couple yards away, some men are walking, they're headed right toward us, the beams of light from their flashlights flicker as they close in on us.

Fear bubbles up inside of me. Now we have nowhere to go. We're surrounded, trapped like mice. Apparently, Zane isn't as worried, or maybe he is just better at hiding it because his face doesn't show an ounce of fear. Instead, he acts like we're playing a fun game, rather than one that could get us both killed.

"Hide behind that tree," he orders, pointing to a group of trees a short distance away before heading straight for the search party.

"Zane," I hiss through my teeth, but he must not hear me calling his name because, like a rocket, he's off, charging toward the group of men like a Viking.

Turning on the balls of my feet, I run in the direction he pointed.

Flattening myself against the tree, I push my back into the bark and listen to the sound of men fighting. Skin hits skin, and grunts and groans fill the brisk air, making my heart race faster with each passing second.

We aren't going to escape, there's no way.

Lights flicker over where I'm hiding, and I spot more coming our way. Do I run or stay hidden? I decide to run. Twisting around, I step away from the tree just to come to a sudden halt once more. Ice fills my veins when I see three of Matteo's men pinning Zane to the ground.

"I will fucking kill you," he growls as he struggles against them. His voice is so vicious and dark, it even terrifies me.

Through the tree branches, I can see Matteo walking across the yard. It's hard to make out his features, but even from a distance, I can make out his angry scowl.

"Find the girl! No one leaves this property until I say so." Matteo's venomous voice carries into my ears, and terror trickles down my spine. We never should've run. Looking back at Zane, something shiny catches my eye. A gun or knife. I don't know. All I know is I can't lose him. I can't risk him dying, not after I've just found him again.

My heart lurches into my throat, and even though I shouldn't, I run toward him, instead of remaining hidden.

"No! Please, don't shoot him. I'm right here," I yell over the chaos that's surrounding us.

"No! Run, Dove," Zane yells, but I refuse to escape this place without him. Matteo will kill him in an instant.

"Please, please..." I beg as one of Matteo's men points the gun at Zane while two others hold him to the ground.

I reach them at the same time my father does, the look of disappointment in his eyes would leave me feeling guilty as hell if I actually gave a shit about what he wanted or thought. Another man comes out of nowhere and circles my wrist with his hand like a shackle.

"Don't fucking touch her," Zane grits out. Even with a gun pointed at his head, his biggest concern is me. "I swear to god if you don't remove your fingers, I will cut off every fucking one of them and feed them to you."

"I think that's the least of your worries right now," Matteo sneers, frustration overtaking his features. It's hard to believe a man so cunning, so violent is my father.

"I'm sorry," I tell him, knowing and feeling that something bad is going to happen, deep down in my gut. We aren't going to get away with trying to escape. There will be consequences, grave ones. I just don't know how badly they will be yet.

"No, you're not. But you will be shortly." Matteo doesn't even look at me as he speaks. "Take them downstairs," he orders his men before turning around and walking back inside.

The men holding down Zane grab him and pull him up off the ground. While another comes and grabs me by the other arm, now I'm held on each side. They drag us back toward the house, and I've never felt more like a prisoner in my life. Fingers dig into my biceps, and I want to struggle—to kick and scream, but it would do me no good.

I'm a bird caught in a cage, my wings clipped, my spirit gone. Directing us around the side of the house, the men open a side door. They enter with Zane first and then me. Sweat beads against my forehead, and my body feels like a knot tied into a pretzel. They release both of us, and instantly, Zane is off the floor and rushing toward me. His hands move over my face, down my shoulders and arms like he's searching for injuries.

"I'm okay," I say when I see the panicky look in his chocolate brown eyes. His only fear is losing me, or someone hurting me, and my only fear is the same happening to him.

"Who will be taking the punishment for disobeying me?" My father's deep unapologetic voice pierces my ears, and in a second, Zane turns from the comforting boyfriend into a vicious guard dog. Turning to face my father, he shields my body with his.

"Hurt her, and I will kill you in the most painful of ways you can imagine." The rage and anger. It erupts out of Zane like a volcano exploding. The burning hot lava licking at my heels.

"You're talking a lot of shit for someone that's alive because I'm allowing him to be."

"You aren't allowing shit," Zane spits.

The tension grows thicker with each word that's spoken, and I have to try and diffuse the situation before Zane gets hurt or worse killed.

"Please," I beg, stepping from behind my guard dog, and instead, to the spot beside him. Matteo turns his hardened gaze to me.

"The first thing you'll learn about us Castro's is that we don't beg, not for mercy, and definitely not for forgiveness. Now, tell me, will it be you, my sweet daughter, or will it be your junkyard dog of a boyfriend that takes the punishment."

"Me!" Zane and I both say in unison. I can feel his eyes shooting daggers into me.

"How cute, you're trying to protect each other. Funny, neither of you know what you're protecting the other from."

"Whatever punishment it is, I'll take it." The words rush out of Zane's mouth, and Matteo lets out a chuckle of amused laughter.

"Here is the deal...we aren't going to play games all night as my patience for your bullshit is running thin." One of the guards hands him a long stick, that looks to be made of bamboo. *What is he going to do?* Quivering with fear, I take a step back. "I'm going to cane one of you. If Dove decides to take the punishment, she will receive one strike. If you decide to take it, you will receive ten. What's it going to be?"

"I'll do it," I say, my voice trembling. "Zane is still healing from the gunshot wounds. Let me do it. Please!"

"You will fucking not!" Zane's voice booms through the space as he shoves me backward. The anger in his voice triumphs any sound I've ever heard. Before I can object or make a move, he's tugging his shirt off and walking over to Matteo.

"Stand with your hands against the wall," he orders Zane, whose movements are now robotic, almost as if he's shut down. It feels like I'm watching this from outside my body. Lifting the cane, he continues, "This is your only warning. If you try and fight me, Dove will incur the same punishment. Do you understand?"

Zane merely nods, his head tipped forward, his chin tucked into his chest. All I see at that moment is William. Protecting me. Saving me.

"No! Please, don't do this. Please, we won't do it again, I swear." The words tumble out of my mouth as I rush toward my father, but before I reach him, an arm circles my waist and pulls me backward.

Without even looking at me, the monster of a man called my father says, "This is your first lesson, sweetheart. Sometimes, mistakes are made, and sometimes, you make a bad choice, and others pay the consequence. Learn from your mistakes."

Without warning, he brings the cane down on Zane's back. The sound is heartbreaking, and I fight with all my might against the man holding me back, but it doesn't do me any good. He just tightens his hold on me. Kicking and screaming, I watch through teary eyes as Zane takes each lash of the cane on his back as if it's nothing. As if he doesn't feel the pain at all.

His hands ball into tight fists but remain against the wall. How can he do this to him? How can he beat someone without blinking? At the fourth strike, his skin starts breaking and blood trickles down his back. My throat is raw, and my lungs burn by the time the beating is over.

As soon as the last lash is delivered, the guard releases me. Anger flows freely through my veins, overtaking the sadness that was just there. I want to hurt all of these men, destroy them, make them pay for what they've just done.

"I hate you! I hate you so much. You will never be my father. Never," I scream at Matteo as I rush to Zane, who sags to the floor in defeat. His back a bruised and bloody mess.

"Hate me all you want, Daughter, but you will learn to follow my rules and learn to obey me, or more punishments like tonight will occur."

I don't bother responding to him, and he doesn't wait for me either. Handing off the cane to one of his guards, he shoves his hands into the pockets of his sleep pants and walks up the stairs. At the top, he turns around, and his eyes are like knives driving into my still-beating heart.

"Try and escape again, and you won't like what happens, Dove."

I steal my spine and curl my lip. "You don't own me."

"Ha, but I do. I created you, which means I'm your god," he says and disappears into the house. His men slowly filter out, and I remain sitting on the cold hard ground beside Zane, listening as his breaths turn from ragged to nothing but a wheeze.

"I'm sorry, Zane. I let you down. All over again, you saved me, and I let you down." I tell him as I softly cry, the tears cling to my eyelashes, making it hard for me to see.

Out of nowhere, a hand cups me gently by the cheek, and Zane's dark gaze bleeds into mine. "You didn't let me down, birdy. I'd endure any pain and go through any beating just to make sure you don't have to. It would kill me to see you broken and hurt. I know you wanted to protect me tonight, but you don't have to. It's my job to protect you, not the other way around." And that's when it hits me. The only way we're going to make it out of this safe and sound is if I save us. Zane might hate what's to come, but I'll do anything I have to in order to protect him, the same way he's protected me.

"Maybe I don't want to be saved anymore. Maybe I need to be the one to do the saving," I reply hoarsely.

There is something so pure, so heartwarming about the way he looks at me then. Like I'm his entire world, and he is the moon forever circling around me.

"That will never happen with me by your side. I was put on this earth to protect you, and I will do so until the moment I take my last breath."

It's then that I realize Zane's love for me would always overshadow his choices. At any and all cost, he would choose to protect me. But I was done being the princess who needed protection. After watching him take a beating for me tonight, I will no longer play such a role. The future is mine, and I am going to be my own knight in shining armor.

34

*E*very muscle in my body aches, my back feels like it's been run through a shredder, but I refuse to show the amount of pain I'm in. I refuse to let Matteo or Dove see me this way. It's a weakness I cannot afford right now.

I did the right thing, taking the fallout for our failed attempt at escaping. I was stupid, careless in my planning, and I could've gotten Dove hurt in a way that I'd never be able to forgive myself for doing. Every strike of the cane, every burst of pain, was well deserved. Plus, if I had seen Dove take even one strike, it would have hurt me so much more. Maybe not physically, but mentally it would have been excruciating.

Stepping out of the shower, I dry off carefully. It's been three days, and the skin on my back is starting to scab over. Not only does it still hurt, it fucking itches now too.

The bathroom door opens slightly, and Dove's appears, looking inside like she is wondering what I'm doing in here, unsure if she is allowed to look. Instantly, my mood lightens.

"Let me help you," she whispers, stepping into the room. She takes the towel from my hand and starts carefully dabbing at my back.

I'm so enthralled by the simple gesture—by her wanting to take care of me—that the pain just falls away as if it wasn't there in the first place.

"Come, let me put some ointment on your back," Dove says, tugging me to the bedroom.

I get on the bed and lie down on my stomach. Dove gets a first aid kit from the bathroom and sits down next to me on the bed. Turning toward her, I watch with fascination as she gets out a small tube from the bag. She puts some on a piece of gauze and starts to gently cover my injured skin with a thin layer. Dove isn't even comparable to others. She's unique, in scent, style, and just overall being the woman that I love.

"That feels nice," I murmur.

"Is it not hurting still?"

"No, not right now. Your hands on me will always feel good, no matter why or how they are touching me."

"So, you do like me taking care of you?" She raises an eyebrow, challenging me.

"I do... but that doesn't mean I'll ever stop taking care of you first. You'll always be first. You deserve that," I tell her honestly.

"And what do you deserve?"

"Nothing. Not even you, but that doesn't mean I'll give you up. I will still have you. Whether I deserve you or not."

She leans down and places a soft kiss on my shoulder. "Good, because I don't want you to give me up. In return, I'll never give up on you."

I smile back at her, ready to pull her into my arms and peel every piece of clothing off her body when an annoyingly loud knocking interrupts our little bubble of momentary happiness.

"What?" I'm still completely naked, but I really don't give a shit when the door opens. I sit up and find Alberto stepping into the room.

"Fucking Christ, put some pants on," he growls, his eyes bulging out of his face before he shields his eyes with his hand.

"What do you want?" I ask, not making a move to cover up. Luckily for him, Dove is completely dressed, or I'd be gouging his eyes out right now.

"Matteo has a job for you. Get ready. And by ready, I mean fucking dressed."

"Get the fuck out!" I yell, just as he grabs the door handle and slams it shut. Turning back to face Dove, I don't miss the frown on her delicate face. She should never be sad. I want to see her smiling, always smiling.

"Don't fret, baby. I'll be back in bed with you tonight."

"I know. I just don't want anything to happen to you and..." She trails off, her cheeks tinting a soft pink.

"You what?"

"I wish I hadn't fought you so hard when we were back in the bunker at the farmhouse." Her admission warms me from the inside out. It's because of her that I haven't completely gone off the rails, why I'm taking orders from this wannabe mob boss, and why the prick is still alive. Everything I do is for her, and always will be.

"We have forever, Dove, we just have to get through this place first."

I'M COVERED from head to toe in blood. I'm not sure which is mine and which is my enemy's. All I know is that every one of those bastards is dead, the life drained right out of their bodies. Sighing, I squeeze the steering wheel a little harder. Tonight was a bloodbath, and all I want to do is get back to the house, clean myself up, and see Dove.

I can still feel her soft kisses on my skin from hours earlier. I try not to think about the fact that Matteo set me up. The fucker sent me into a fight that most men never would've gotten out of alive. Thank fuck, I'm not most men. I had years of experience, killing and shutting myself down to use nothing more than my basic instincts. There wasn't anything I couldn't handle, tonight though, that was a trap.

A dirty fucking trap, and I was going to confront Matteo the second I saw him. Pulling the SUV into the driveway, I drive to the garage, put the thing in park, and kill the engine. Giving myself a moment to cool down a little before I get out, I focus on my breathing.

Sucking air deeply into my lungs, I let it settle before blowing it out. I do this a couple more times and then finally get out. There are a few of Matteo's men posted outside. Since our attempt at escaping, he's upped security a crazy amount. Not that any of his men could take me on by themselves and survive.

"Holy shit!" one of the men says under his breath as I pass him, entering through the side door of the house. I don't respond and continue walking. Exiting the garage, I enter the house and hear voices. My bloodied boots squeak against the pure white marble floor with each step I take.

"You need to eat more. You're far too skinny, Dove," Matteo's villainess voice pierces my ears, and I walk a little faster, following the sound. Rounding the corner, I enter the dining room but come to a screeching halt when I see Dove and Matteo.

Dove's gaze immediately finds mine, and her pretty pink lips part in both terror and alarm. She seems to be shocked, and her big blues, only widen further as they take in my bloodied clothes. Words of rage form against my tongue. I'm spiraling out of control like a plane that's been shot out of the sky.

This, what I'm seeing right before my eyes, is merely the icing on top of a shittastic cupcake. I want to lash out at Dove, to be angry with her for sitting and having dinner with the enemy, but the real reason for my rage sits at the head of the table, mere feet away from me.

"Care to join us?" Matteo almost snickers, but I don't miss the surprise in his eyes. He wasn't expecting me to make it back here tonight. Fucking piece of shit, coward, can't even fight me man to man, but instead, tries to get rid of me by sending me on a death mission.

"Cut the fucking shit, Matteo, and don't act like you aren't shocked that I made it out of that fucking warehouse alive. You know as well as I do, that what you sent me to do was a suicide mission."

"And yet you stand before me."

Fucking asshole.

"Next time you want to kill me, maybe do it the less cowardly way and face me, man to fucking man." I slam a fist down onto the heavy wooden table. Dove jumps at the violent move, but she should know by now, I would never lay a finger on her pretty little body, at least not one that she didn't beg me for.

"I didn't try to kill you, Zane, and I'm actually glad that you're here. I have news that I want to share with you and Dove."

I look to Dove, who looks back at me with the same confused expression. Okay, so neither of us know what this fuckhead's next move is going to be. *Great.*

"What is your announcement?" Dove asks, her voice strong. She is not a little bird trapped in a cage anymore. Not that I mind. I'll take her any way I can get here. It's just right now, she seems fierce like a warrior, and all she's done is ask a question.

"I've decided that it's time to announce your appearance to everyone. We're going to have a special event to celebrate your return home."

My anger only intensifies at his words. He had tried to kill me and was sitting here with my girl at dinner, planning a fucking party.

"Splendid." The single word drips with sarcasm from my lips. "I'm going to go clean the blood, of the five men you sent to jump me, off my body and head to bed," I sneer and turn on my heels. My eyes catch on Dove, and her mouth pops open. She wants to say something, but I don't want to hear it. Seeing her tonight, watching her play the part of his precious little daughter, makes me want to hurt her. To set her straight and remind her just who owns her body, mind, and soul. It feels like a knife is being plunged into my chest when I drop my gaze and walk away, but I can't stand there for another second.

"Trouble in paradise already?" Matteo's voice reaches my ears just as my foot graces the first step of the staircase. I could turn around and say something to him, react to his asshole ways, but I'm too fucking exhausted to keep up the charade, so I continue up the stairs.

When I reach the bedroom, I strip out of my bloody clothes, leaving a trail behind me as I enter the bathroom. Turning the hot water on, I wait a second before stepping beneath the spray. The water feels like razor blades against my aching back, but I withstand the pain, my head hung low as I watch the clear water turn pink and rush down the drain.

The door opens, and my ears perk up at the soft footfalls. I don't turn around to look at Dove, but I can feel her in the room, watching me through the fogged-up shower stall. No matter what, I always feel her, it's truly the only thing that I allow myself the pleasure of enjoying.

Her body, her touch. Turning into the spray of the water, I wet my hair, running my fingers through the strands before taking a step back.

I'm not sure what Dove is doing, so I'm surprised when the shower door opens, and she steps in behind me.

Her small hand lands on my shoulder, her fingers gently drag down my arm, and a shiver of pleasure runs down my spine. I turn to face her, ready to ask her what the hell that shitshow downstairs was, but the words lodge in my throat when she sinks to her knees before me.

"What are you doing?" I croak, the mere image before me making my cock twitch.

"Making you feel better... taking care of you," she says, a hint of a smile on her lips. She is either nervous or excited because her chest is rising and falling rapidly while she peers up at me, through her thick lashes. I'm going to go with the second, with the way her perky nipples are hardening.

She reaches for my already stiff cock, wrapping her small soft hand around it. Pleasure shoots through my body, like a bolt of lightning, pushing the pain and the anger into the deepest corner of my mind. Placing my hand against the tiled wall, I groan. Fuck, she knows just how to make me forget.

Leaning in, she takes the head of my cock between her plump lips and runs her tongue along the bottom. My dick is so hard; veins have started pulsing over the smooth skin. I'm barely controlling myself at this point, but I don't want her to stop. I need her mouth, her touch. Looking down, I watch as she starts bobbing her head, taking me deeper and deeper into her hot wet mouth, while keeping her eyes on me.

Control. I need it. Weaving my fingers through her hair, I fist the strands and pull her head back off my cock.

"I'm going to fuck your mouth, hard and fast, and you're going to let me because you're mine to use as I please, correct?"

Licking her lips, Dove nods her head before whispering, "Yes."

Guiding her mouth back to my cock, I hold her head in place and start to fuck her mouth with slow leisurely strokes. One of her hands slips between her legs, and all I can do is grin. Such a greedy fucking girl.

"Stroke your pretty pussy while you suck on my cock, and remember who it is that owns you," I grit, my voice filled with venom. Pistoning my hips, I up my pace, the tip of my cock hits the back of her throat, and she gags around my length. Her eyes water and fear trickles into her eyes as I hold her face there, my cock deep in her throat.

"Breathe through your nose, baby, and swallow with each stroke," I demand, tightening my grip on her hair as I pull her off my cock. Saliva drips out the side of her mouth and down her chin. Damn, she looks so beautiful like this. At the mercy of my cock.

Continuing to fuck her mouth, I watch and marvel as she gags around my length a few more times before following my directions. Pleasure builds at the bottom of my spine and builds upward until there is nothing but a burning in my balls to release my load into her mouth.

"I'm coming," I groan.

"Mmmm," she whimpers around my length.

"You're going to swallow every drop, do you understand?" I warn. She merely whimpers, and seconds before I explode, I hold her face to my groin. Ropes of sticky come slip down her throat as she swallows around my cock, and I pull out of her mouth, dragging my tip over her lips before releasing her. Her eyes shimmer with tears, and her lips are swollen, and fuck, I want to be inside her pussy right now, but more than that, I want her to know who it is that owns her. Tugging her up off the floor, I drop to my knees before her and back her up against the tiled wall.

"Zane, what are you doing?" She gasps as she hits the wall, and I smile up at her before lifting her by the ass and burying my face between her legs. It doesn't take long for her to get the picture, and with my tongue flicking against her clit, her legs start to shake, her fingers sink into my hair, and she shatters into a million little pieces.

When I'm finished licking every drop of her release away from her pussy and teasing her, I set her back on her feet and stand to my full height. Then I grip her by the chin and force her to look me in the eyes.

"No matter what happens, you're mine, forever. I don't care who your father tries to marry you off to. I don't care what happens in this mansion. At the end of the day, there is only you and me. I own your fucking soul just as you own mine. Don't tempt me to prove it to you again, because next time, I won't take mercy."

Dove's big blues widen, and I see something that looks like excitement in them.

"I love you," she says softly, her eyes dropping down to my chest. I release her chin and run my fingers down her chest, stopping at the scar along her belly. Back and forth, I move my finger. That scar is what binds us together. It's what made me believe she was it for me. No one ever cared about me, not until she came along.

"I love you too," I say, letting out a sigh before kissing the tip of her nose.

The problem is, I love her too much, and that just might be what gets me killed.

35

I try not to be bothered by the loneliness I feel, trapped in this stupidly large mansion while Zane is off doing god knows what for my father. It'll be a long time before I forget the bloodied mess he showed up as the other night.

This place is a thousand times worse than the bunker. At least there, Zane and I were alone, and there wasn't a knife hanging over our heads, threatening to fall and severe our necks at any given second.

Tossing the paperback down on the mattress, I climb out of bed and exit the room. Since our attempted escape, Matteo has posted more guards near our bedroom and throughout the house. Almost as if he thinks we're stupid enough to try again. I haven't told Zane yet, and I don't know if I'm going to, but I plan to be the one to get us out of this mess.

And the easiest person to start with is the one who holds all the power: my father. Meandering down the hall, I pass a couple of guards who are posted there. They give me apprehensive looks, but don't say anything as I continue on my merry way.

Walking down the grand staircase, I run my hands along the banister. The polished wood is so shiny, I can almost see myself in it, and I wonder briefly how long the maids spend cleaning this place?

Reaching the last step, I continue my exploration of the house and head into the dining area. Yet another clean room. Huffing, I walk in the direction of Matteo's office.

A sour film coats my mouth, and it feels like I'm betraying Zane by seeking Matteo out. There isn't any way around it. If I want to convince him that I'm on his side, that I'll follow his orders, I'm going to have to act like I give a shit about him and what he says.

Tiptoeing down the hall, I grow closer to his office. Matteo's voice filters out into the hall through the partly open door. He must be on the phone with someone.

"Make sure the product is as he said and only call me if you have a problem!" The finality in his words makes me shiver. A man like Matteo has no cares, no compassion or heart. All he sees his people as —including me—are pieces on a chessboard, little does he know, he's going to become my pawn. Curling my hand into a fist, I gently lift it and bring it to the door, knocking twice before letting my hand fall back down to my side.

"Come in," he grumbles, and I force a stoic mask onto my face. *Be strong. Look the part.*

Exhaling, I walk into his office. His beady eyes flick from annoyance to shock while motioning me into the room. I take slow, hesitant steps, remembering how I told him I hated him and would never be his daughter. Look at me now, buttering up the enemy, like he didn't arrange to have the shit beat out of the man I love the other night.

"What can I do for you, my daughter?" I do my best not to look as out of my element as I truly feel.

"I want to learn more about you and the family business."

Chuckling, he leans back in his chair, a brief second passes, where neither of us says a thing. Then his lips part, and he asks, "You're serious?"

"You said I'm your only heir and that I should prepare to take over the family business, so here I am."

The chair squeaks as he leans forward, placing his elbows on the desk, clasping his hands together. "You expect me to believe that you want something to do with me after what you told me in the basement?"

I shrug. "When you hurt people I care about, you should expect me to lash out. I was hurt and understandably so, but I've come to the conclusion that you aren't ever going to let me go so I might as well stop fighting the inevitable. It's time I stepped up to the plate. You want me to marry soon and produce grandchildren. This business will be mine someday, and I have a right to know all the ins and outs."

The apprehension in his face tells me he doesn't believe me. A smile creeps onto his lips, and I swallow thickly, unsure if I can follow through with this.

Staring me in the eyes, he says, "I'm a lot of things, sweetheart, but I'm not an idiot. We can play pretend if you want, till you decide to get on the horse and ride, just know that I'm in control of everything and everyone in this house."

"I'm here and willing, now will you answer my questions and help me get to know you and the family better or should I try and escape again?" It's either the stupidest or smartest thing I've ever said.

Matteo's face becomes a blank canvas, and I try and hide the slight tremble of my body. Zane isn't here to save me this time, and talking like this is only going to help dig my grave. After a long second, he finally speaks.

"You know what will happen if you try and escape again, now come sit, and you can ask your questions."

Nodding, I walk to the front of his desk and plop my ass down in one of the leather chairs. Placing my hands in my lap, I slowly drag my eyes up to meet his dark ones.

"Before you tell me about the business, I was actually wondering if you could tell me anything about... my mother? What was she like? Why didn't she try and find you after she escaped her husband? What made you fall in love with her? Anything, really. I don't even know her name..."

Easing back into the chair, Matteo drums his fingers on the wooden desk. "Your mother was special. She was looking for love since her husband was more concerned with making a name for himself than being the man she needed. We met at a charity event. I saw her from across the room and knew I had to have her."

"So, you knew she was married when you met her, and you still approached her?"

Matteo nods. "I did, but it's very common in our world to be in a loveless marriage. Women are promised to men and seen as a joining of two families into one. It's more about power than anything. I didn't care that your mother was married. All I wanted was a taste."

The way he talks about my mother almost annoys me. Like she was nothing more than a piece of arm candy, or meat for him. I can tell from the tone in his voice and the use of the word taste, that she wasn't important to him. There is no love in his voice, only a sense of accomplishment. I don't know her, and I'll never get the chance to, but she's still my mother, and that fact alone means she deserves a little bit of respect.

Matteo must know I'm disgusted with him because he starts to talk again.

"Your mother's name was Raven. She told me she was going to leave her husband and wanted to be with me. Given that she was still married and divorces rarely happen, I wasn't sure we would ever be together. Then she told me she was pregnant with you. I promised her I would care for you and her if she actually decided to get away from her husband." He pauses, and I don't know if it's for dramatics or because he's reliving the day in his mind. "Then, one night, she did just that. News travels fast, her husband had men everywhere, searching high and low for her. My men came to me and told me that she had left her husband in the middle of the night, without a single trace. No one knew where she went. I waited for her, I thought for sure since she was pregnant that she would contact me, but she never did."

I can't help but feel a little sad inside. All my mother wanted was to be loved, and this viciously dark world took that chance from her.

"Where do you think she went? And why did she not call you?"

"I can't answer either of those questions. To be honest, at the time, I thought she was already dead. I was sure that her husband had caught her trying to escape and killed her. I figured he made up the whole *she ran away* and sent his men out on a search party so no one would look into her death."

"Then how and when did you realize I was alive, and she wasn't dead?"

Matteo's eyes twinkled with, no it couldn't be admiration, there was no way a man of his nature would feel such an emotion. "I may seem heartless, Dove, but I'm not. You are my daughter, and I do love you. At the end of the day, I still hung on to the sliver of hope that she had truly escaped. I hired a private investigator to keep looking for her. I told him I didn't care how long it took, months, or years, I didn't want him to stop looking for you two. Then, out of the blue, he called me. Told me that a woman fitting your mother's description was found dead in a hotel room. There was a mention of a child, a little girl. I tried to find you then, but you were already in the system, and no one would give me any information."

"Oh..." I nod as if I understand, but on the inside, I am nothing but suspicious. All the pieces of information he's given me just don't add up. I wasn't adopted until my teenage years.

I was in the system most of my life because no one ever claimed me as their family member. If he would've made himself known as my father, why wouldn't they have given me to him? The state would have been glad to have one less kid to take care of.

Matteo smiles, but it doesn't reach his eyes, letting me know it's fake. "I'm just grateful to have found you."

"But are you really grateful? I feel a little like a pawn to you."

"I only want the best, Dove. Marriage in our world is for power, so while you may be in a loveless marriage, you will be safe. I will not stop you from seeing Zane, that's the most kindness, I can give you. I've worked tirelessly to get the Castro name to where it is. When it's time for you and your new husband to take over, I want you ready, and so babying you isn't going to prepare you for what will come. Kindness gets no one anywhere."

"How will you choose the man I'm supposed to marry?"

"I need you to marry someone who will eventually take over the business, someone I trust. But I will also make sure he'll treat you well. I won't allow someone who is violent with women for no reason."

For no reason? I'm both scared and curious to hear what reasons are acceptable in his eyes. I doubt it will take much.

Wanting to keep him talking, I ask another question, "What kind of business will I be doing? I want to be involved, to know what it is you're *preparing* me for."

"You know, you don't have to be this involved in everyday dealings of the business. Your future husband can take all of this on."

"If I'm going to do this, I'm going to do this all the way. I know you don't know much about me yet, but I can tell you that I'm not the kind who sits at home and twirls her thumbs. I want to be involved, and I don't mind getting my hands dirty."

As soon as the words leave my mouth, I regret them. By getting my hands dirty, I meant it the way most people use the expression, of course, getting your hands dirty, means something else to someone like Matteo. I wish I could take back what I just said, but I can't without sounding weak.

Matteo rubs his chin. "Are you sure you're ready to hear this?"

Pursing my lips, I say, "Doesn't matter if I'm ready, does it? Eventually, I'll be running this ship, so there isn't any better time than the present. No point in easing into things. Might as well drop me off in the deep end and let me teach myself to swim."

A soft chuckle emits from Matteo's throat, and if I didn't know how fucked up he was, how willing he was to end mine and Zane's lives, I'd say this was a nice little bonding moment.

"No, sweet Dove, I will not drop you off in the deep end. I want our name to succeed long after I've died, so I'll ease you into things. Plus, the things you'll be dealing with may be a little bit of a shock to someone as sweet and naive as you. After all, you weren't born into this world." I don't miss the jab his words bring.

Wanting him to tell me something, anything at all, I push him again. "Then tell me something business-wise that's going on."

His expression becomes impassive, his dark brown eyes emotionless pits of nothing. How can he be my father? I just don't understand.

"I'm not sure you're ready for this."

"I'll be the judge of that," I say, crossing my arms over my chest. I try to make myself seem bigger than I am. Try not to let the sharks know that I'm a bloody piece of meat, barely staying above the water.

"Human trafficking. Right now, we're recruiting women and taking them to Mexico to our whore houses. They're used multiple times a day and are one of our number one profits outside of drugs."

Bile rises up my throat, and my stomach churns. Oh god, maybe I wasn't ready for this. I do my best to hide the disgust from my face.

"Where do you find them?"

Matteo smirks. "Find them? We don't find them, sweetheart. We pluck them right off the street. Kidnap them from clubs. People that owe us debts and cannot pay. We take their mothers, daughters, wives, sisters. No one is off-limits to us."

I've never heard anything so disgusting in my life. I thought Zane was mental when he told me there were worse men in this world, far worse than himself. I was naive to think that such people didn't exist, simply because I didn't see them. They were there though. Always watching, waiting in the dark for the perfect moment to ambush you.

"It's a lot to take in, so I think that is all I will share with you tonight. Maybe we can do this again?"

"Yeah, definitely," I say, pushing up and out of the chair. Can he see my fear? Feel my anger? Surely, he can, though I doubt he cares. He already sees me as weak, a naive little girl with no backbone. I can't wait to prove him wrong.

"Nice talk, now run along. I have work to do but be back down at seven for dinner," he orders in a stern voice, much like a father would talk to his daughter if she disobeyed him. My body reacts before my brain catches up, and I scurry from the room. Once in the hall, I'm tempted to turn around and go back into his office and tell him I'm not leaving because he told me to but because I'm going to be sick over what he told me but don't.

As soon as I get the chance to kill the man that calls himself my father, I will. And I won't mourn him, knowing I'll have taken another bad man off of this earth. I'll rescue all those women who he's taken and hurt, and I'll smile triumphantly while doing so.

Matteo Castro will die at my hands if it's the last thing I do.

36

*A*nother day of killings. I don't remember a time when murdering people was ever so tiring to me. I think my biggest problem is I'm doing it for some asshole instead of myself. As soon as I enter Matteo's house, I know something is off. Voices drift from the dining room through the hallway. One is definitely Matteo, and one is Dove's, but I don't recognize the third voice at first. Not until I get closer, at least.

Clenching my fists and grinding my teeth, I walk into the house until I get to the dining room. Matteo, Dove, and Alberto are sitting around the table like they're having a fucking Sunday family dinner. Chatting and laughing casually, completely comfortable with each other. For the first time since we got here, Dove doesn't look out of place, and I don't fucking like it one bit.

What kind of game is she playing?

"Having a good ole time, I see," I say as I step further into the room. All eyes turn to me. Neither Matteo nor Alberto are even trying to hide their annoyance by my presence anymore. Dove looks at me with a mixture of guilt and apprehension. She is up to something, hiding her plans from me, and I don't like it.

"We're having a great time," Matteo says, raising his glass of wine to me. "We were just telling Dove about summers in Italy and how I'd like to take her next year."

"I would love that father," Dove chimes in. *Father? Since when is she calling him father?*

My eyes skate to Alberto, who is looking at Dove. There is a longing in his eyes that makes me want to reach out and crush him.

"Stop staring at her!" I snarl at him.

He doesn't even seem to be shocked at my outburst, which only angers me more. Does he have a fucking death wish? I'm like a damn ticking time bomb. Wonder what happens when I explode? Oh, I know...

"She isn't yours, and I can look at her if I want to. Maybe I'll even touch her?" he threatens, and I lurch toward him. I'm ready to rip his throat out when Dove's warm hand gently covers my bloodied one. Turning my icy glare to her, she meets my ice with fire.

"Enough you two. Don't act like children." Matteo dabs at his lips with a napkin before tossing it on his nearly empty plate. "You care to join us, or would you rather eat in the kitchen with the other staff?"

I'd rather slit your throat with the knife in my boot.

"I'm afraid I lost my appetite." Turning around, I head up the stairs, not stopping until I'm inside our room.

Pacing the floor, I wait for the door to open and for her to come in at any moment. When she still isn't here after twenty minutes, I fear that I made a terrible mistake. I should've stayed downstairs. Is she in danger?

I'm just about to run back downstairs when the door opens, and Dove appears in front of me.

"What the fuck was that?" I growl as soon as she closes the door behind her.

"It was just dinner, Zane."

"Don't fucking lie to me. We both know that was more than dinner. You called him *father*! What the hell are you thinking?" I throw my hands up in the air, not knowing what to do. I want to punch the wall or better, punch Alberto, but neither would end well for me.

"I'm thinking that fighting him on everything is not going to work out. He asked me to come have dinner with them, so I went. He asked me to call him father, so I did." She folds her arms in front of her body as she defends her actions.

I huff. "Oh, great, you're playing the obedient daughter now?"

"Yes! Emphasis on *playing*. Do you think I enjoyed sitting there with them, pretending to have a great time when I know you are out there in danger?" Her eyes fill with tears, but I don't know if it's because she was really worried or just because she is so angry.

"Playing or not, you are still hiding things from me. You should have told me about your plan. You should have told me your plan, so I could have told you no."

"*So you could have told me no?*" She stares at me like she can't believe what I just said.

"You heard me. You are mine, and it's my job to protect you. If I think you are doing something stupid, I'll not allow it."

"You can't control me!" Her words slam into me like a roundhouse kick to the chest, and something deep inside of me snaps. I take a step toward her, crowding her personal space. I raise my hand and wrap my fingers around her throat. I don't squeeze hard enough to make it difficult for her to breathe, but I tighten my grip to let her know who is in charge.

"Oh, Dove, how wrong you are," I say in a low, threatening voice. "I can control you, and I think it's time that I remind you of that. Now, take your clothes off and get on the bed."

Her eyes widen and her pupils dilate. I can feel her delicate throat work as she swallows hard before her tongue darts out to wet her lips.

Just when I think she is not going to do it, she reaches from the hem of her sweater and starts pulling it up. I release her so she can pull it off all the way. She drops it on the floor next to her and continues taking her clothes off one by one.

By the time she is naked, she steps past me and toward the bed. She climbs on the mattress, giving me a perfect view of her already glistening pussy nestled between her creamy thighs. She is turned on by this. My Dove might seek her independence in her life, but in the bedroom, she likes when I command her. She likes me controlling her.

"Stay on your hands and knees," I order as I make quick work of my own clothes.

Completely naked, I climb on the bed behind her. My heavy balls and my hard as steel cock, swaying between my legs with each move.

Positioning myself between her legs, I hold onto her hip with one hand and guide my cock to her entrance with the other. As soon as my swollen mushroom head enters her tight channel, I let loose. I sink all the way into her in one hard thrust.

I don't give her time to adjust. I fuck her hard and fast, without mercy. The sound of my groans and her pleasured cries fill the room. We are so loud; I wouldn't be surprised if Matteo hears us. Good, let him.

"That's it. Moan so loudly the whole house can hear you. Let them know whose pussy this is. Let them know how hard I fuck you and how much you like it. Let everybody hear what a slut you are for me." At my dirty words, her pussy tightens, and more moisture builds between us.

"Zane," she moans my name, and I fuck her even harder, digging my fingers into her flesh as I hold onto her, wanting and needing to bruise her.

"You're mine, Dove. I do own you. I own every part of you, and I'm going to use you however I want, remember?"

"Yes," she whimpers in between thrusts. "Yes... use me. I'm yours. Do whatever you want."

"That's right," I growl. "You take my cock, however, and whenever, I want you to."

Letting go of her hip with one hand, I move my hand to her ass and start massaging her puckered asshole with my thumb while I keep fucking her. She moans in response, letting her upper body fall onto the mattress so her ass is even further open for me.

"Your greedy little asshole wants me."

Before she can answer, I push my thumb inside, letting her hole suck me in. I start pumping in and out of her ass at the same speed my cock goes in and out of her cunt.

Her orgasm slams into her, her thighs quiver, her body tenses, and her pussy and ass squeeze me so tightly, I think I might come apart right then. It takes a lot to hold my own orgasm at bay, but I don't want this to be over. I'm not done with her by a long shot.

When the last tremor of her release leaves and her body is slack, I pull out and flip her over in one swift move. Her back has barely touched the mattress when I'm back inside of her, rutting into her like a wild animal.

I hold her legs up, pushing them toward her to give me better access. "God, your cunt is so tight this way. I bet your ass will be even tighter."

She moans in response, seemingly unable to form coherent words at the moment. Her hooded eyes glance up at me with nothing but pure lust and obedience. She is submitting to me completely, and even though it might be only in the bedroom, for now, I'll gladly take it.

"Play with your tits while I fuck you," I order, and her hands move to her breast on command. She takes her nipples between her fingers and starts playing with them, tugging and pulling harder than I would dare to.

"You like when I take you rough, don't you?" She nods her head, yes, before I've finished talking. "You like being my little fuck toy, like being used?" She nods again and whimpers, taking her bottom lip between her teeth and bites down, all while still playing with her tits.

That sight drives me over the edge, my balls tighten, and pleasure overcomes me. I come so hard my vision blurs. I keep thrusting deep inside of her as I come, shoving every drop of my come inside of her.

"Fuck!" I come until my balls are so empty it hurts. Stilling, buried inside of her, I close my eyes and take a moment to just breathe.

When I pry my eyes back open, Dove is watching me. Her hands are still on her chest, but not moving anymore. I carefully pull out of her, enjoying the sight of my come dripping out of her before I release her legs. She lets them fall to either side of me. I climb over her leg and fall onto the mattress next to her.

Even feeling sated as I am right now, the thought of her keeping things from me and being friendly with the enemy is too much to ignore.

"You're playing with fire, trying to get close to Matteo. You're gonna get burned."

"And what else am I going to do? Nothing? Fight him? Try to escape? We both know how that worked out last time." Her words sting, but she isn't wrong.

"I admit, trying to escape the way we did was a mistake. It won't happen again, but you getting close to him is a mistake as well. Let me deal with him."

"How?"

I don't really want to tell her, but I realize by not telling her, I'm doing the same thing I'm mad at her for. "I'm gathering info on Matteo to hand over to Christian. He only wanted you to get to Matteo. If I can get him a better way to get to him, then we kill two birds with one stone. Dove, you need to promise me that you won't do anything foolish while I'm out doing jobs for your father. I can't stand the thought of you hanging out with him, and Alberto like you're old friends while I'm out there. Promise me..."

Turning my head, I look over to her, she stares up at the ceiling. "I promise," she mumbles in defeat.

Now I only wish I could believe her.

37

Zane's gone again. Doing another job for my father. I feel him pulling away from me, emotionally, he's shutting down. I know he still wants me, still loves me, but the games my father is playing, it's draining him. He'll do anything to protect me, anything to try and save us from this situation when the only person who can save us is me.

I know I promised Zane I'd stop pretending with Matteo, but I just can't do it. I can't let Zane take all the responsibility. We are in this together, and I can't sit back and do nothing.

He thinks what I'm doing is risky, and it is, but sometimes there are risks you have to take. A knock sounds against the heavy wood of the door, and before I say anything, the knob twists, and the door opens, a maid's head pops into the room. She can't be but a little older than me, her heart-shaped face and almond eyes make me think she could be a model if she wasn't here working for my father. I look up at her and smile. Her expression is blank, and she doesn't return the smile, but in her eyes, I can see fear.

"Your father is requesting your presence in his office," she whispers, eyes cast to the floor. I swallow around the knot that's forming in my throat.

He's been eating up a lot of my time during the day, requesting me to eat dinner with him, which conveniently happens to fall at the same time Zane walks in the door. I know it's a set-up, a way to drive a wedge between Zane and me, and in a way, it's working.

"Thank you. I'll be right down," I say, and she closes the door quietly behind her. Sighing, I force myself out of bed and run my hands through my silky brown hair in an attempt to make myself a little more presentable. Once done, I slip from the room and walk down to Matteo's office. Guards are still posted throughout the house even though Zane and I haven't made another attempt at escaping.

I'm not sure when he will ever trust me, and he's smart not to because the instant he does, I'm running with it.

Standing just outside his office, I push the door open and listen as it creaks. Matteo looks up from something on his desk and to me as I pop my head inside.

"You asked to see me?"

He waves me inside, and I stop right in front of his desk. "Yes, I want you to go with Sophia and pick out a dress for the event. I also want you to get your hair done."

My brows furrow. "What's wrong with my hair?"

"Of all the things you can fight me on, you fight me on your hair?" He lets out a chuckle. "Just get your hair done, please. It looks dull."

I'm tempted to tell him to fuck off, but that would derail my plan completely, so instead, I bite the inside of my cheek.

"When is this Sophia woman coming?"

Matteo's gaze flicks to his watch and then back up to me. "Should be here any minute now." I nod, ready to turn around and walk out. Why subject myself to his bullshit any more than I have to. "Also, pick something out that isn't too revealing but gives a tiny peek. I want people to be talking about us for weeks to come."

"Of course," I mumble and step out of the office. I go upstairs and get a pair of tennis shoes before coming back downstairs. Lingering in the foyer, I wait for this shopping lady to show her face. Just as Matteo claimed, she shows up a few minutes later. Priding myself on being someone who never judges a book by its cover, I try not to judge the woman who comes walking into the mansion like she owns the place, a sneer of disapproval on her face when she spots me waiting for her.

"Dove?"

"The one and only. You must be Sophia."

"That I am. Now, I'm not one for pleasantries, so let's get on with the shopping. We have money to spend and dresses to try on."

Well then. I follow her out to an SUV and climb into the back seat while she takes the passenger seat up front. One of Matteo's men drives and another comes as security. No one says anything to me the entire drive.

The rest of my day is spent trying on dress after dress while Sophia critiques every single one. *That one is way too short. Ugly. You look fat.* Are just some of the remarks I have had to withstand. By the time we're done, my ears are bleeding, and I feel like going back to the mansion and drowning myself in the bathtub, but that can't happen because first, I have to get my hair done. Sophia ships me off to the hairdresser, whose name is Bernarto.

"You're gorgeous, sweetheart," he purrs in my ear while running his fingers through my hair. For the first time all day, I smile.

"Thank you," I say.

"What shall we do..." He drums his fingers against his chin and takes a step back, eyeing my head. After the day I've had, I don't really care what he does. Making up his mind, he gets to work, and three hours later, my hair is colored, trimmed, and styled. Surprisingly, I feel a little better. Sophia scoffs when she sees me and rolls her eyes before typing out something on her phone. Then, all over again, we're getting into the SUV and heading back to the mansion.

When we arrive, I all but dart from the car, needing to put some distance between Sophia and me. She didn't say anything directly to hurt me, but she sure as hell didn't make today fun either. Walking through the front door, I can make out the sound of voices. They're loud and manly and carry down the hall and into the foyer.

Both I know, one belonging to Zane and the other Matteo. Tiptoeing down the hall so I can hear more of the conversation, I hold my breath when Zane starts to speak.

"Fuck! I've done everything you've asked of me. All I want in return is to know that you won't marry her off to someone. Promise me you won't do it." The anguish and despair in his voice makes me take another step forward. There is a pause, and Zane starts to talk again. "If you're doing this to hurt me, then I'll break it off with her. I won't be with her anymore, but please, don't ruin her life just to get revenge against me. Dove deserves more than that."

A chair creaks, and I know it's Matteo's. "Listen here, boy. Dove is my daughter, and because of that, I get to make the rules here. She is marrying whoever I choose, when I decide. I'm not doing anything because of you. I'm doing this because it's my right as her father."

Zane growls, and I can feel the sound in my bones. "I won't let you do this. You've hurt her enough already."

Matteo chuckles, but it isn't filled with amusement, no it's the kind of humorless laugh that makes your shiver and piss yourself.

"I'm warning you now because I know Dove is fond of you, but if you interfere in any way with the plans I have for my daughter, I will have you killed and disposed of at the bottom of the harbor. Do you understand me?"

His statement sends shockwaves rippling through me. I've always known that Matteo had the power to try and take Zane out, but part of me never thought he would. Now that I've heard the words come out of his mouth, I know he'll follow through. Just like Zane won't ever give up on protecting me, making sure that my father doesn't marry me off to some man just for the sake of it.

Zane's determined, and he'll die before he ever lets Matteo do something I don't want.

"No, I don't understand, and I never will. Dove's happiness should be your number one priority. Marrying her off to some douchebag isn't going to make her happy."

"It isn't? Are you sure about that? Are you sure it isn't you who is more worried about Dove being married? After the initial shock wore off, she hasn't voiced a single concern or complained again. Truthfully, I think the only problem is you. And we both know what must be done with problems."

Dread consumes me. I know right then and there, what has to be done and it's going to kill me. It's going to rip me to pieces, but it's the only way I can save Zane and myself. The only way I can ensure that we have even a sliver of a chance at a future together.

"Kill me, but it won't change a thing. In fact, it will only make Dove hate you more."

"I don't think so," my father says, and I'm sickened by the sureness in his voice. He doesn't know me at all, but he thinks he does, and that's my advantage in all of this. I'm playing him, and he doesn't even know it.

"By the time this is all over, you'll have made an enemy out of her." The disgust in Zane's voice can't be missed.

"We'll see," my father says.

Turning, I rush down the hall and up the stairs to our bedroom before either of them can hear or spot me. By the time I reach the room, my heart is racing out of my chest, and there are tears in my eyes. What I have to do is going to kill me, but it has to happen if my plan is going to work.

38

*M*y blood boils in my veins, burning me from the inside out like acid. Putting on the uncomfortable suit Matteo is making me wear, I wonder how I'm going to make it through the night without killing someone. I can't fucking believe I agreed to this. Going to this event as Dove's bodyguard. Of course, it's not like I have a choice. *Fuck.*

After I slip into my shoes and clip on the tie, I leave the room and head downstairs. Dove is getting ready in one of the guest rooms on the other side of the house. Matteo had a whole crew of stylists coming to get her ready. As if she needs a spec of makeup to be the most beautiful creature at this event.

Taking a seat in the foyer, I wait for Dove and Matteo to be ready.

An involuntary growl slips out when Matteo comes down first, his hair slicked back, an Armani three-piece suit covering his body.

"Down, boy." He chuckles, only infuriating me further.

Lucky for him, I'm distracted the next second when I catch sight of Dove at the top of the stairs. I'm pretty sure my heart skips a beat. No, she doesn't need an ounce of makeup to be beautiful, but it does accentuate her beauty. She starts walking down the stairs, and as cheesy as it sounds, I feel like she is an angel descending from heaven. I stand without thinking and greet her at the bottom of the stairs.

I don't care if her father sees how awestruck I am by her. She's my one and only true weakness in life.

"You look beautiful," I say as I place a kiss on her cheek. The stylist must really know what they're doing because her makeup looks perfect, and the cream-colored dress she's wearing makes her seem virginal and pure. At this rate, I know for sure now that I'll end up killing someone tonight. Not being able to go to this stupid event as her date is going to be torture at its finest, but way better than being stuck in this mansion all night without her. With heels on, her head reaches the bottom of my chin, and I kinda like her being a little taller.

Her glossy pink lips tilt up into a smile. "Thank you, and you look rather handsome yourself." She wraps her arms around my neck and leans into me. The dress she's wearing isn't form-fitting, thank god, but it's short enough to tempt those wanting to take a peek.

"It's going to take a serious amount of effort not to strangle every motherfucker that looks at you tonight," I whisper into the shell of her ear.

"Hate to break up the lovefest, but we're on a schedule," Matteo interrupts, "also, there will be none of this at the event. You're her body-guard. Nothing more than that."

Turning, I pin him with an icy glare. There's a glint in his dark gaze, and he's lucky, so fucking lucky, that I care more about Dove than ending his life.

Taking a step back from Dove, a mask slips over my face to cover up the raging inferno that's threatening to consume me. Every day, this asshole pry's away another piece of the delicate armor I've erected to help stop from losing my shit on him. My patience is thin, and I'm reaching the point of no return. Once I fall off the deep end, I'm not even sure Dove will be able to reach me. Soon, there will be nothing left. No protect, no boundary, and it's then that I will end him.

"It's time to go," Matteo says, interlocking his arm with Dove's.

She frowns at me but doesn't say anything, and even though she promised me she wouldn't, I know she's still leading him on, playing with fire, so to speak. She thinks she won't get burnt, but I know better. I've done this before a time or two.

An SUV pulls up just as we cross the threshold to outside. I tug at the uncomfortable collar constricting my neck. This is going to be the longest stretch of hours of my life. Matteo being the gentlemen he so clearly isn't, opens the rear passenger side door and helps Dove in. When she's tucked away inside the vehicle, he turns to me.

"Don't do anything fucking stupid tonight, or I'll make you regret it."

"The only stupid thing I'm doing is dealing with you."

Matteo merely smirks before clapping me on the shoulder. "You have a lot to learn, and I look forward to watching you fall to your knees and beg me for forgiveness. After all, it wasn't, but a couple days ago, you appeared in my office, begging me to relieve Dove of her family duties, am I right?"

All I can do is grit my teeth and clench my hand into a tight fist because if I make the wrong move, if I do the wrong thing, it won't just be me paying the price, it'll be Dove too. Matteo releases me and walks around the SUV without another word, climbing into the back and taking the seat beside Dove.

Forced to take the passenger side seat in the front, I climb into the SUV. As soon as I look over, I feel the need to drive my fist into the window beside me. The driver is none other than Alberto, who gives me a slimy grin as soon as I'm situated in my seat.

"You look beautiful this evening," he compliments Dove as he moves the car from park and into drive.

"She really does, doesn't she?" Matteo praises from the back seat.

"Thank you, both," Dove replies timidly, and all I can hear is the blood pumping through my veins.

"Not to ruin the good mood," Matteo says, "but I want to be very clear. The building the party is held in will be surrounded by my people if either one of you steps out, they have permission to shoot you."

Don't lash out. Think of Dove. I talk myself off the ledge slowly and peer out the window, ignoring everyone, including Dove. I can't think about her, or what we're going through right now, without wanting to slaughter. For everyone's sake, including my own, I hope no one touches her tonight because I'm not sure I'll be able to stop myself from painting the room red.

~

MISERY. That's what this party is, plain and simple misery. It takes place in a massive hall that's connected to a hotel that Matteo owns. Of course, he's invited everyone and their extended family for the homecoming of the century. It feels a little too formal for a homecoming though.

I watch from the door closets to the table Dove is sitting at. She's surrounded by Matteo's men, three on one side, while Matteo sits beside her, and another two sit beside him. She's a swan in a lake full of tar, beautiful, majestic but unable to escape her surroundings.

Our eyes collide from across the room, the heat in those blues scorch me. Her gaze lets me know the most important thing of all. That even though it seems like the world is on fire around us, she is still here, burning in the same hell right alongside me.

Dinner is served, and as her bodyguard, I watch the surroundings while she mingles and eats with her father. Jealousy is like a whip, landing against my skin every time another man takes her hand and presses a kiss to it.

MINE! She is mine. I want to scream from the heavens. Forcing myself to look away, I scan the crowd. None of the faces look familiar, and I'm thankful for that. I wouldn't be surprised if Christian sent some of his men here. Then again, maybe that was Matteo's intention, after all, to bring him out of hiding.

As my eyes pass over each face, something off to the right side of the room catches my eye. It's only a split second that I see him. I can't be too sure, but I swear Xander Rossi disappears through the door at the back of the room.

Why is he here? Has he come to take Dove again? Fear pumps through me at the speed of lightning. I'm not sure if I should say something to Matteo or not. If I can find him, maybe I can strike up a deal with him instead.

Before I can think too long on it, Matteo is shoving out of his chair and moving to the front of the room. He holds a flute of champagne in his hand and smiles out into the crowd like he isn't a shark willing to shred anyone who stands in his way.

"Good evening, and thank you so much for coming to celebrate the return of my long-lost daughter, Dove back into my life," Matteo exclaims, and the room erupts in joy. "After her mother's disappearance, I never thought I would find her, but here she is. At last, home... where she belongs."

I roll my eyes because the only other option is barfing, and I don't want to make a scene. My gaze darts between Dove, Matteo, and Alberto, who not so casually slides his hand onto the back of her chair. Dove doesn't seem aware of it, or she doesn't care, which only enrages me further.

I'm going to kill him. Murder him. Rip out his intestines and strangle him with them and cut up his body, and use it as shark bait.

As I'm envisioning this, Matteo continues talking, but I'm too far gone to care what slimy bullshit he's spewing. None of it is true anyway.

"Tonight isn't just about the return of my daughter though. It's also about the legacy of the Castro family. As we all know, I'm not getting any younger, and my daughter returning to my life just happened to come at the best time."

My brow furrows as the thoughts of Alberto's death slip from my mind. My attention is once again back on Matteo.

What is this fucker doing?

Looking back at Dove, I see that she's just as confused by his speech as I am, though she could be acting the part. With her, it's hard to tell which side she's playing and when she's playing it. The room falls quiet, and my stomach twists into tight knots. I'm bracing for whatever to come, but I don't think anything could prepare me for Matteo's next words.

"I would like to announce the joining of my daughter, Dove Castro, to my finest and most fierce second in command, Alberto Salvatore, in marriage."

My vision blurs for half a second, but the bloodthirst fog over my eyes turns to mist when I feel Alberto's eyes on me. Our gazes clash, hate and venom spewing out of me, and snaking across the floor. I will make him pay. I will make all of them pay if it's the last fucking thing that I do. A shocked gasp falls from Dove's lips, but that's the only response I get letting me know that she knew nothing of this incident. Matteo blindsided both of us.

Before anyone can see Dove's shocked face, she skews her expression and pulls her lips up into a tight smile. Like the perfect fucking couple, Alberto wraps an arm around her and tugs her into his side, his lips grazing her ear.

To anyone, they look like the perfect couple, together and in love, and that's the last straw for me. I won't sit here and watch this. I can't. I already feel the bile rising up my throat, the anger in my veins fueling my rage. I have to leave before I do something stupid.

Tugging off my tie, I toss it to the ground and exit through the doors. Anger ripples through me like a seismic wave cracking through the earth. Rounding a corner, I clench my fists and try and breathe through my nose, but nothing is helping me at this point. I've left Dove back there with Alberto and Matteo, even though I didn't want to because I just can't stomach seeing it. Watching her act as if she doesn't love me, as if that shouldn't be us getting married.

Fuck! Knocking shoulders with some asshole, I continue stalking wherever the fuck it is I'm going until he opens his mouth.

"You could say excuse me," he sneers. I almost chuckle as I turn around and stare him straight in the eyes.

Cocking my head to the side, I except the challenge reflecting in his eyes. "I could, but I don't really give a fuck."

"You need to be taught a fucking lesson on manners, don't you?" This time, I do chuckle. I laugh hard enough that my abs tighten and my belly trembles. This asshole can't be but a little older than me. He's slim, with an athletic body, but he's nothing to a killer like me, and worse yet, he's just signed his own fucking death certificate.

"Don't do this, Seth." A girl tugs on his arm, her eyes pleading.

"Maybe listen to your girlfriend," I say with a sneer, nagging him on. I want him to hit me first, to make the first move because as soon as he does, I'm going to knock his lights out.

Shrugging her off like I had hoped he would, he rolls up the sleeves of his shirt and stalks toward me. Clenching his fist at his side, he rears back and aims for my face, but being the amateur that he is, he misses his mark by a mile.

My vision turns black, and all I do is react, my movements are fluid, and I'm aware that my knuckles are colliding with skin and bone, but I don't care. Screams pierce the air, pierce through my ears, but all I see in that instant is Alberto, his arm wrapped around my girl, his lips whispering into her ear.

All I see is the woman I love slipping through my fucking fingers.

$\mathcal{M}$y father couldn't have said what I think he did. My stomach churns, and bile rises up my throat at the knowledge. I do my best to keep it together, shoving all my emotions into a tight little box that I promise to let out later.

I have to be strong in front of Matteo. I can't let him know that I've been caught off-guard by his announcement. Alberto, of course, takes full advantage, leaning into my side, wrapping his arm around me as if we're a couple, and I don't want to stab him with the steak knife in front of me. His lips are so close to my ear, I can hear every inhale and exhale that passes them. "Don't look now, but your little boyfriend looks like he wants to kill me. Should I reach for your tit, or do you think that would be pushing it?"

I can't even get the word *no* to come out of my mouth before I'm shrugging his arm off my shoulder. "There is one thing Zane will always have, and that's my love." Twisting around in my seat, I glance over my shoulder and to the spot where Zane is supposed to be standing. There's no one there. The spot is empty, and I know... I just know that something bad has happened. *Where did he go?*

Panic claws at my insides, wrapping its slimy hands around my heart.

"We will have more news to share, but just know the Castro family is strengthening its ties, and soon, we will be the strongest family this side of the Mississippi." The people around us erupt with cheers, and my father descends the steps, coming back down to the table.

Pushing from my spot, I meet him around the side of the table.

"Zane is gone. I need to go and find him." I say, leaning into his face. Matteo's features become harsh, menacing.

"No, you need to worry about your obligations to this family. Zane is no one to you. In fact, I was going to wait to tell you this till after the event, but I figure there isn't any point in elongating the heartache that will ensue."

"What are you talking about?" I bite out, afraid of what he's going to say next.

He smiles, and my heart clenches in my chest. "Look, I gave this whole Zane and you having a secret relationship a chance, but obviously neither one of you can handle it. He is a liability."

"But... I don't understand. What are you saying?"

"I'm saying if you do not get rid of Zane, I will have no choice but to get rid of him. And by that, I mean, I will kill him. I honestly planned to allow him to stick around and be by your side, but his antics have made me think twice about that. He is now more of a risk than he is an asset."

Shocked, my mouth pops open before I can snap it shut. My biggest fear is now becoming my reality, and all over again, I'm faced with losing Zane.

"I..." I don't even think my brain hasn't quite comprehended what he's said yet. "I... I love him," I whisper harshly.

Matteo leans in, a single finger tracing down the side of my cheek. "I know, sweetheart, which is why I'm giving you the chance to end things with him. Make him go away so that his death doesn't rest on your shoulders because, I promise you, if you don't make him leave, I will end him myself. The choice is yours, Daughter."

The world beneath my feet shifts, and I grab onto the nearest chair to steady myself. Zane will die if I don't make him leave, but making him leave isn't going to be easy. It will mean breaking his heart. It will mean having to lie to him. Protecting him, will ultimately end everything that we have, and still, there isn't a way around it. Matteo isn't lying, there isn't a doubt in my mind that he will kill Zane. We've been heading toward this scenario since the day he went to him to rescue me.

I have to do this because the alternative is so much worse.

"I understand," I whisper to my father.

A smile splits across his face, and he nods. "I knew you would. You're a smart girl, Dove."

Before he walks away, I grab him by the arm. "Give me at least three days, please?"

Matteo looks as if he wants to say no but then opens his mouth to speak. "Three days. I'll give you three days, but that is all my little bird."

Little bird. The nickname causes a horrible reaction in my brain. The urge to vomit is strong. The mere thought of going without Zane terrifies me. It makes the game I'm playing more intense, more real, because with Zane out of the picture, the only person I'll have to save me is myself. Forcing myself to take a couple calming breaths, I resurface, realizing that I still have to play the role of Castro's obedient daughter.

For the next two hours, I think of Zane while forcing a smile onto my lips as my father parades me around like a trophy, and Alberto is slapped on the shoulder and told what a prize he snagged. By the time the sun starts setting, my father is two sheets to the wind and in a deep conversation with an allying family.

Slipping from the dining hall, I head toward the bathroom. It's been hours since I last saw Zane, and I need to find him. Deep down, I know he wouldn't leave me here. He knows I have nothing to do with this, though that wouldn't stop him from acting out on his rage and jealousy.

Around the same time he disappeared, there was a commotion out in the garden. A man had beat the crap out of another man. Matteo's men rushed out to break up the fight, but when they arrived, the other man was already gone.

Something tells me that was Zane, and all I can do is hope that he's okay while I bide my time till I can go and find him. Walking into the bathroom, I plan to stay inside just long enough to get some of the guards off my tail, so I can start my search. Matteo's men are vigilante as hell, and getting around them has been difficult, to say the least.

Placing my hands face down on the sink, I stare at my reflection in the mirror.

Can I really do this?

I nearly lost him once before, can I be the one to push him away, to end our perfect love story? Tears sting my eyes. This isn't going to end well. Zane will see right through me, right through my lies, and deep into my soul. He'll know I'm lying, and that something else is going on. I'll have to look him right in the eyes and tell him I don't love him anymore. That I don't want him to be in my life. When that is as far from the truth as anything.

Letting him go is going to kill me, but there isn't another option.

The minutes tick by slowly, and thankfully, no one else comes into the bathroom to witness my break down. I can't possibly stay hidden in this bathroom all night. I have to find Zane and make sure he's okay, but leaving this space is subjecting myself to the mayhem beyond these four walls.

Forcing myself to leave the bathroom, I turn and walk out the door. I make it all of ten feet down the hall, my heels clacking against the exquisite floor, before a hand clamps down on my shoulder and whirls me around.

The air expels from my lungs when I'm shoved against the nearest wall, and Alberto's face comes into view.

"Hiding from me?" The whiskey on his breath tickles my nose, and I struggle against his firm grasp. His eyes are bloodshot, and I know after watching him for the last two hours, that he's had more to drink than he should have.

"No, now please, let me go," I say firmly, pushing against his chest, but pushing him is like trying to move a mountain. My movement only entices him further, and he leans in, his lips descending on mine. At the last second, I manage to turn my face, and he lands a sloppy kiss against my cheek.

"Oh, it's like that, huh? Am I not good enough for you?" His hand grabs onto my tit, squeezing painfully, and a ragged hiss passes my lips. I clench my fist and swing my arm, hitting him in the side of his head. Unfortunately, my punch doesn't have much force behind it, and since he is drunk, his pain tolerance is down. He just chuckles at my feeble attempt to hit him.

"Stop, I don't want to do anything with you until after we're married."

"Awe, why not? I know you fuck Zane." Leaning in, he drags his lips across my neck, sucking harshly.

"Stop!" I say a little louder, preparing myself to push him away, but before I can, a shadow falls over us, and Alberto is ripped away and tossed to the ground like a piece of trash.

I'm about to jump into Zane's arms, telling him how sorry I am, and that he was right about everything. Instead of lunging forward into my lover's arms, I'm frozen in place. It takes me a good second to realize it's not Zane standing in front of me but someone else entirely.

Ivan.

"I-Ivan…"

"Hello, Dove," he greets me casually as if we're two old buddies who happen to be at the same party. Peeking behind him, I notice that he is not alone. With him is a man of similar stature, who is just as scary and daunting looking as him.

"Um, hi," is the only thing I can manage to say. I'm not really sure if I should be scared or relieved to see Ivan right now. Why is he here? Surely, Matteo didn't invite him, the way he talks of the Rossi family, I'm sure he'd rather eat his own shit than dine with them.

Behind Ivan, Alberto is trying to get off the ground. He only barely manages to stand on his own, more like swaying on his feet. He opens his mouth to say something but then stops himself when recognition sets in. Oh, he definitely knows Ivan and whoever this other man is, and from the way his body is trembling, it's clear he is scared of them.

"What the fuck are you doing here?" Alberto snarls after a moment of composing himself.

The man I don't know shrugs. "Heard there was a party, figured we'd check it out. Kinda pissed we didn't get an invite."

"Cut the crap, Roman. Why are you really here?"

"Congratulations on your engagement," Ivan says, both interrupting and changing the subject. "You seem like a *lovely* couple. Do you always have to force girls, or is there actually someone who touches your dick willingly?"

"Fuck you, Ivan," Alberto slurs before storming off. How wonderful of him to leave me standing with two giant men in an otherwise empty hallway.

"You okay?" Ivan asks a moment later, his facial features softening, but only a little.

"Yes, thank you," I reply, smoothing a hand down my dress, mainly because I need something to do with my hands.

"This is my brother, Roman." He introduces the man next to him. Ah, brothers, that makes sense now. "Why the hell are you engaged to that douche?"

"It's a long story." I shake my head, not wanting to tell him the whole story right here in the middle of the hall, where anyone could hear. "Why are you here?"

"We heard Castro was making a big public announcement. Xander wanted us to check out what he was up to. Gotta admit, I wasn't expecting this."

"Yeah. Believe it or not, I wasn't expecting *this* either."

Ivan looks shocked. "Oh, wow. Well, shit. Where is Zane?"

"Around here somewhere. I'm pretty sure he got into a fight after the big announcement."

"Well, folks, I would like to stay and chat," Roman announces, "but I think we should head out before dipshit gets back with a small army because he is too scared to fight his own battles."

"Yeah, that might be a good idea," I say, looking down the hallway to see if any of my father's men have noticed I'm missing. Now would be the perfect time to disappear, but it's not worth it, not after hearing we'll be shot without warning if we try to leave the grounds.

"Take care," Ivan says before turning to walk away. I watch them leave via the exit and then head back to the party to try and find Zane. Back in the main room, I scan the crowd. Alberto is sitting next to my father at the table. He's glaring at me like he'd like to strangle me. I'm surprised he didn't tell my father about Ivan and Roman, then again, I'm sure he doesn't want me to tell my father about what he did either.

Not wanting to sit down with them again and endure more pretending, I head to the bar. As I walk through the crowd, I notice everybody staring at me as if they're sizing me up or something. Some people actually look scared when I walk by them, making space for me to walk through.

The whole thing is surreal, and I feel nothing but out of place and misunderstood. I almost turn back around and walk back to the table out of desperation when I spot Zane at the bar. Knowing that I can't make a scene, I take the seat next to him without looking over.

"Can I get a glass of water, please," I ask the bartender whose attention I catch.

"Of course. Sparkling or still?"

"Sparkling sounds great." I barely finish my order before he produces a glass and a small bottle of water in front of me. "Thank you."

"No champagne to celebrate?" Zane whispers next to me.

"Stop it. You know that I don't want this," I say in a hushed voice, so only Zane can hear me. "Do you think I'm happy about this?" I ask and take a sip of my water.

Putting his elbow on the bar top, he lets his head fall into his hand. "I know, but that doesn't make this any easier."

"I'm going to ask Matteo to take us home. There we can talk." I get up from my seat and weave through the crowd, back to our table.

Matteo and someone I don't know, are deep in conversation when I get there. So, I tap my father lightly on the shoulder to get his attention.

He stops talking and looks up to see who dares to interrupt him. "Dove, you enjoying the party?"

"It's a lovely party, thank you for planning all of this, but I'm rather tired, and I'd like to go home. Do you mind having someone take me back to the house?"

Alberto perks up next to him. "I can take you."

"I would rather have someone less drunk take me home," I insist.

"Of course, dear. Let me get someone for you." Matteo smiles and waves over some of his men. "Take my daughter home," he orders, and the men nod.

"Thank you, Father. Enjoy the rest of your night." I force out the pleasant words when all I want to do is strangle this man with my own hands. I don't care if he is my father or if we share blood. This man is pure evil, and I'll do whatever it takes to stop him.

I follow the two men out of the main room and to the front door. By the time we make it to the car, Zane has caught up to us. We drive back to Matteo's mansion in silence, not wanting to talk in front of the men, but I know this silence will be over once we are alone.

We park right in front of the house. I get out as soon as the car comes to a standstill. Zane follows me inside the house just as my father's men do. But unlike Zane, the men stay downstairs.

When we are finally inside the containment of our room, we both sigh deeply.

"I can't do this, Dove. I can't watch you with them, with some other guy... even if you are pretending. It's like my worst nightmare playing out in front of me. I love you too much. I can't stand this. I'm scared, Dove. *Scared!* I don't even remember the last time I experienced that feeling, but I am now. I'm scared of losing you, losing us."

"I know..." My voice is raw with emotion, I'm feeling everything he just said. "I hate this too, but if I need to gain Matteo's trust. I need him to give me freedom so we can get away. If we try again now, he'll kill you, and lock me up."

Zane growls in annoyance, knowing that I'm right. Frustration and anger come off of him in waves, and I know if I don't calm him down, he is going to punch the wall or something.

"Can we just lie down so you can hold me? Please, I just need you to hold me," I whine.

Zane nods and starts taking off his clothes before helping me out of my dress. Together we crawl into bed and under the blanket. He pulls me to his chest, and I snuggle up to him as close as I can. I don't know how long I can have him like this, and for tonight, I don't want to think about this either. I let his warmth engulf me, let his unique scent calm me, and the steady beat of his heart lull me to sleep.

40

Something terrible is going to happen. I can feel it. Dove is acting stranger than usual. After the event the other night, I poured my heart out to her, confessing my biggest fears, and instead of bringing us closer, she seemed to be pushing us further apart. She is shutting down, and I feel helpless against it. I wasn't lying when I told her I was scared. I'm scared shitless. I feel like I'm fighting a battle I can't win. I feel like I'm watching her getting sucked into this world. Something I've been trying so hard to avoid.

I need to do something, change my tactics, so I can stop this. I need to stop this before all is lost. Before my Dove is tainted by Matteo even more.

She is not only pulling away from me mentally but physically as well. Yesterday she spent most of the day in Matteo's personal library, preferring to read a book than spend time with me. This morning after breakfast, she disappeared into the library yet again.

Tired of waiting around for her, I leave the room and head toward the library. Every guard I pass looks up at me, their watchful eyes examine me and my mood.

When I enter the grand room, filled from top to bottom with books, I find Dove curled up on a chair by the window. A book laying on her lap. Her head snaps up when she notices me walking in. I'm surprised to find her eyes puffy and red like she's been crying.

"What's wrong?" I shoot the two guards posted at the door, an accusing glare. They better not have touched her. "Did someone hurt you?"

"No, come sit." She sniffs. "I need to talk to you."

Hesitantly, I take the seat across from her. I know whatever she is about to tell me is not going to be good. I mentally prepare myself to hear what she has to say, but the truth is, nothing could have prepared me for what she says.

"You need to leave, Zane." A semi-truck could have hit me, and I would feel less wounded. "You can't stay here any longer. This..." She motions between us. "Whatever this is, it's not working. We need to end this now before it gets any further."

"*Any further?*" There is no further. We are already at the end. I've loved her for years, and she loves me back. "We are meant to be together."

"No, we are not. I'm meant to be here. I'm meant to carry on the Castro name, and you don't fit in here, at all." I know she is playing. She doesn't mean this, she can't mean this, but hearing the words come out of her mouth, regardless of their truthfulness, hurts like hell.

"Just stop, Dove! I can't listen to this shit. You and I both know that's not true," I growl. "Drop the act, I don't care who is in the fucking room. Just stop!"

"This isn't an act. I want you to leave, Zane. I need to do this. I need to marry Alberto, and you need to go your own way."

I want to cover my ears with my hands, so I don't have to listen to this or cover her mouth so she can't get another word out. Either way, I can't listen to this any longer.

"I'm not going anywhere," I growl, ready to destroy something. Getting up from my seat, I start pacing around. "And I'm not letting you marry some fuckhead just because some guy tells you to."

Twisting to fully face me, the words that come out of her mouth next cut me straight to the core. "I don't want you, Zane. I don't want to be with you, and the more you push me to do something I don't want to do, the more I'll push back. I want you to leave and not come back. I want you to forget about me and move on. I don't want to be with you. I'm not in love with you." Her expression is skewed, but her eyes tell me she is lying.

"You're lying, you love me. I've protected you your whole life. You need me just as much as I need you."

"I never asked you for any of that. I didn't even know you were there most of that time!" I turn away from her, but she gets up from her seat and gets in front of me, so I have to look at her face. "Maybe I needed you before, but that's because I thought you were all I had. I thought all my family was dead, but my father is alive, and he loves me. I don't need you anymore."

"Shut up," I yell, stepping closer. Close enough to where she has to lift her head to look into my face.

"Just go, Zane. Don't make this even harder than it already is. Just go..."

"I will never leave you. Never!" I grab her upper arm and hold her in front of me. I want to shake some sense into her. I want to make her understand, see how wrong this is.

"Let go of me," Dove demands, her voice on edge, but that only makes me hold onto her tighter. I feel like if I don't, she might disappear forever, slip away, and never return to me.

"Take your hand off of her," one of the guards growls.

Turning to him, I snap, "She is mine, I touch her wherever and however I want."

"I'm not yours!" Dove yells and shrugs out of my hold. Just when I thought this whole situation couldn't get any worse, Dove says something that will haunt me for a very long time. "I don't know how much clearer I can make it. I don't want or need you. I don't love you, and I want you to leave and never come back." Before I can respond, she drives in the final nail. "Guards, please make him leave the house and don't let him come back."

"Dove! You can't be serious?"

She backs away from me, moving out of reach. I try to take a step forward, reaching out my arms to her, but the two guards are already on me, pulling me back. I start to fight them, throwing punches at anything and everything I can reach. More men pile into the library, trying their best to get me under control.

I've lost count of how many men are fighting me, five or six... All I know is that I can't let them win, I can't let this happen. If I leave now, Dove will be all alone. I won't be able to protect her from the outside.

I'm vaguely aware of Dove's voice in the background, asking them not to hurt me. I almost laugh in the midst of all of this. They could throw acid on me, and it wouldn't hurt as bad as the pain she is putting me through herself.

By the time the men have managed to shove me out of the room, my arms are worn out, and my muscles sore. I'm still healing from my last injuries, and I'm not at my strongest, but I can't just give up either. So, I keep fighting them, even when everything hurts, even when my chest aches so much I think it might have cracked wide open. Even then, I keep fighting because right now, that's the only thing I have left.

41

Zane's face as the guards forced him off the property, still haunts me and it's been days. The despair, the burning rage, and the way he yelled my name, telling me I didn't mean it. I can still feel the sadness. It's suffocating. I carried his heart in my hands. He gave me the one thing he'd never give anyone else, and I took it and crushed it. No matter what I do, I can't forget. I can't unfeel the pain I've caused.

In my father's presence, I play the perfect daughter, a smile painted on my lips at all times. But behind closed doors, within the four walls of my room, I'm a blubbering mess, it's like I've lost a piece of myself by letting him go.

Pressing the heels of my palms into my eyes, I will the tears away. I have to get it together. I have to. There is no other way to do this. It was either let him go or watch him die, and I'd rather have him hate me for a short time, thinking that I really didn't want him, than to never have a future together.

Sucking a sharp breath into my lungs, I nearly jump off the bed when a knock echoes through the room.

Shit! I can't let anyone see me like this. Matteo is expecting it, waiting, watching in the shadows for me to slip up. At the first sign of weakness, he's going to pounce, so it's better not to give him a reason to jump at all. Taking another calm breath, I clear my throat and then speak.

"Yes?"

The knob twists, and the door opens. Laura, one of the maids, pops her head into the room, and I almost sigh in relief. *Thank god.* Since my father found out about me kicking Zane to the curb, he's been pushing Alberto and I together more.

He's even moved the wedding date up, and since I don't plan to marry Alberto, I'll have to make good on the next step in my plan soon.

"Ms. Castro, I'm sorry to interrupt you, but your father wanted me to let you know that the stylist will be here soon to prepare you for the engagement dinner."

"Oh, yes. Thank you, send them up whenever they arrive." I give her a smile, which she returns before slipping out of the room and closing the door quietly. Given my fake breakup with Zane, my emotions have been on edge and my mind, of course, elsewhere, so much so that I nearly forgot that the engagement party was today.

Matteo invited everyone far and wide and decided that having it here at the house was the best choice. It would give everyone a chance to see how rich and powerful we were. At least, that's what he told me. I agreed mainly because disagreeing wasn't an option. I finally have him on my side and eating right out of the palm of my hand. He's already been more lenient with me. Letting me walk around the house, spend the day in the library, even letting me walk outside in the garden on my own.

I won't mess this up. I didn't hurt Zane for nothing. I did this for him, for us. Now, I just have to figure out how to escape... the wheels in my head start turning. Tonight. I'll make my move tonight. Matteo will be too focused on the guests to notice if I go missing, plus, with all the traffic in and out of this place, I'll have enough of a distraction.

My lips turn up into a sly smile. My heart may be broken, but it won't be forever. I'll make this right.

∼

Two hours of hair and makeup later, and I'm finally getting into the strapless red piece that Matteo picked out for today. It's tight and shows off my breasts and slim waist. I can barely breathe in the damn thing. Looking in the mirror at my reflection, I'm tempted to take it off. I hate it, hate it so much because all it's going to do is draw unwanted attention. I don't want everyone staring at me, watching me, whispering about me as I pass by them. My snowy-white skin looks even paler, and though my hair and makeup is pure perfection, the rest of me just looks blah. Then there's the fact that Zane isn't here tonight. I'm lost without him, like a broken compass that doesn't know its way.

All the thoughts swirl and weigh heavily on my shoulders. Grabbing onto the marble counter just to have something to hang onto, I count back from ten in my mind. By the time I reach zero, I'm a sliver less likely to have a full-on mental breakdown. The door to the bedroom creaks open, and I step out of the bathroom just in time to see Matteo walking into my room, his dark hair is slicked back, and the suit he wears clings to his body like a second skin. He looks every bit as evil as I know he is.

"My dear, you look so beautiful." He reaches for my hand and brings it to his lips, pressing a kiss to the skin. I do my best not to tug from his grasp.

"Thank you, you look great as well."

Dropping my hand, he smiles, his eyes twinkling with appreciation. "I wanted to let you know that I'm very proud of you. I didn't think you would do it, but like always, you surprise me."

He's referring to my breakup with Zane. Great, now he wants to talk about it.

"It had to happen, it was him or my obligation to the family, and I wasn't going to choose some man over you. You're the only family I have, and the last thing I want to be is a disappointment." I bat my eyes for effect and watch as the mask on his face melts away like a chocolate bar sitting on steaming hot pavement.

"You could never disappoint me. You have Castro blood running through your veins. It's not in us to do such a thing." I almost snort at his response but suppress it at the last second, and instead, cover it up with a massive smile.

"Shall we get to the party?" I ask in an overly excited tone.

"We shall." He smiles down at me, and I try not to sink deeper into the uneasiness that's pooling around my feet. As we descend the stairs, people cheer, and I realize then that the festivities have already started. My eyes collide with Alberto's dark ones. He's waiting at the end of the stairs for us. I can see the desire rolling off of him in waves.

He thinks he has a chance, a shot at being with me. He doesn't know shit. My father passes me off to him, and I take his arm in mine, ignoring the churning in my gut that his touch brings. Matteo dismisses me and starts chatting with two men that look to be of some importance.

"You look absolutely divine," Alberto murmurs into the shell of my ear as he guides me through the maze of people. I recognize a few faces from the previous welcome home party, but none of the names from that night stuck, so all over again, I feel lost in a sea of unknown faces. It's even worse this time because Zane isn't here.

My chest tightens at the thought of him, and it feels like someone is using my heart as a damn stress ball.

"Look how excited everyone is to see us together." Alberto tightens his hold on me, almost as if he's trying to show everyone how possessive he is. "I can't wait to make you my wife and solidify our stronghold over the west. No one will think to try and fight us."

I don't dare tell him the only thing he's going to be looking forward to is his death because then that would ruin the surprise. Smiling up at him because there are so many wandering eyes, and I need to continue to play the part, I let him walk me through the double French doors and outside. The garden has been transformed into a party area with a buffet, tables, and chairs.

The space is decorated with fresh cut roses, tea lights, and string lights that hang above the entire area. They twinkle like stars and give the place a more intimate and elegant feel. It's beautiful, breathtaking, and I kind of hate that Matteo put something as great as this together. A man as evil as him, shouldn't be allowed to come up with such beautiful things.

Alberto and I take our seats at the head table, a flute of wine is shoved into my hands, and I take tiny sips of it as I'm forced to endure small talk with my father's guests.

"I can't wait to fuck you raw," Alberto leans over halfway through the dinner and whispers into my ear.

I feel disgust slither through me and all the way to the tips of my toes. This is the worst part of playing this game. Making those around you assume that you care and are interested.

"I can't wait either," I say, placing a hand on his thigh beneath the table. His eyes flash with primal hunger, and I know all I'm doing is taunting the beast inside the cage.

The night drags on and on, and after some time, Alberto disappears, maybe he's screwing someone else, or maybe he's talking with some of Matteo's men. I don't know. I should probably be worried, considering that he's been gone awhile, and this is our engagement party, but I'm not. If anything, I'm thankful for his absence.

It's one less person I have to pretend that I give a fuck to. Some guests linger, but many leave after dinner, which is exactly what I'm planning to do right now. If I'm going to escape, it has to be tonight. Since Matteo is busy smoking cigars and drinking bourbon with his buddies, he won't even realize that I've slipped away.

I'll never get a more perfect moment than this evening. As I glance down at my half-eaten plate of food, my eyes catch on the shiny knife blade. *Weapon.* You need a weapon, Dove, my brain screams. Lifting my eyes, I look around suspiciously to see if anyone is watching me before I grab the knife and tuck it blade side down into the side of my dress, beneath my armpit. No one should see it there, and I'll be able to make it up to the room without incident.

Pushing away from the table, I meander back into the house and toward the grand staircase. My foot has just barely touched the bottom step when a hand wraps around my arm and tugs me backward. Turning to face the owner of said hand, a gasp catches in my throat.

"Where are you going, Ms. Castro?" One of Matteo's guards asks. He's smiling, but his smile doesn't reach his eyes, he looks more like a tiger smiling at its prey.

"To my room. Is that okay, or would you like to interrupt my father and his colleagues to see if he would be okay with that?" I pin him with a glare, trying not to show my fear or trembling lips and tug my arm out of his grasp. His fake smile slips away, and he looks a little mortified, his cheeks turning crimson, probably because he's never been talked to like that by a woman before.

"Go on," he says without another word, and I force myself to walk up the steps, instead of running like I want to. With my heart racing out of my chest, I reach the top step and bound down the hall, almost falling over my own feet in the process. Reaching the door, I twist the knob and push it open. Slipping inside, I close the door, and the darkness of the room surrounds me. I sigh, but that sigh is soon swallowed by an almost scream when the bedroom light comes on, and Alberto's hulking frame comes into view.

"Hello, my soon to be bride," he murmurs. I swallow the fear of being alone with him down and force air into my lungs.

All you're doing is acting... give an Oscar-worthy performance.

Crossing the space between us, I sashay my hips and smile at him while batting my eyes as if I'm interested. I don't know the first thing about being seductive, but I'm pretty sure my attempt is working because Alberto's smile widens as he gets up from the bed. His jacket has already been removed, the white button up shirt he's wearing is pulled out and wrinkled. His hands move to his dress slacks, undoing his belt, we meet in the middle of the room.

Everything about this feels wrong, but I can't stop now.

"I came up here to tell you that I planned to fuck you tonight, but it looks like you were thinking the same thing I was." The edge of his voice is as sharp as the knife blade I'm hiding in the side of my dress. If I can get close enough, maybe I can stab him without him ever seeing it coming.

"Of course, why don't you help me out of my dress," I purr and twist around, giving him my back. It's a daring move, one that could be dangerous if I'm not careful.

"It'd be my honor," he growls, his hot whiskey breath fans over the back of my neck, and I shiver with fear knowing that it's all or nothing now. I'm either going to end up on my back, making the biggest mistake of my life, or with blood on my hands.

His fingers grip the tiny zipper at my side and start to tug down. At the same time, I drop the tiny little clutch I was holding in my hands to the floor as a distraction.

As I had hoped, Alberto leans down to grab it, and that's when I make my move. Pulling out the knife, I grip the handle in my clammy hand and twist around to face him just as he's coming to stand at his full height.

I don't think, all I do is act as I swing the blade through the air, and diagonally across his throat. Blood sprays like a water sprinkler from his neck, and the lustful haze in his eyes slowly turns to panic. He reaches for me, but I take a step back, bumping against the edge of the bed. Dropping the knife, it lands on the floor, and a second later, so does Alberto.

Adrenaline rushes through my veins, and all I can do is stare, my hands shaking, watching as the life drains out of him.

I killed someone. Something must be wrong with me because I don't feel anything, not a single thing. Actually, I take that back, I feel relieved, free, a bird that's going to escape her golden cage. An idea pops into my head, and I step over his body and start to go through his pockets. Keys jingle inside his dress pants. *Bingo.* Fishing them out, I stare at the key fob to his car. That's my ticket out of this place. They'll never think twice if I drive out of here in his car.

I pick up the knife from the floor and take it into the bathroom with me. I put the knife down long enough to strip out of my blood-soaked dress. Then I pick the knife back up and get in the shower. Holding on to the smooth silver handle of the steak knife while standing under the spray, I watch as the water turns from red to pink, and then clear.

When I'm clean of all the blood, I get out of the shower, dry off and hurry back into my room. I pull on a pair of leggings, sports bra, T-shirt, and a pair of tennis shoes.

Tucking the knife into the waistband of my leggings, I go to the bedroom door. Opening it a crack, I listen for anyone that may be close by, especially guards. Matteo may have lessened them in the days since Zane left, but there is still a heavy presence, especially tonight.

Stepping into the hall, I lock the door and close it firmly behind me. It's now or never. At the end of the hall is a laundry shoot that leads into the laundry room, which is just off the maids' quarters. I know this because I had accidentally walked down there one day while checking out the mansion. Opening the wooden door that hides the shoot, I look down into the dark tunnel.

My heart clatters in my chest, but I know I have to do this. Climbing into the shoot, I grip the edge of the door, my fingers biting into the wood a second before I let go. I can't breathe, can't see, and all I want to do is scream as I slide through the dark on my belly.

All too soon, the ride is over, and I land in a heap of clothes and sheets, the air expelling from my chest upon landing.

I can't believe I just did that.

Climbing out of the pile, I scurry to my feet and look around the room for the nearest exit. When I spot the door and walk to it, all I can do is hope and pray that it's unlocked. I reach for the brass doorknob and wrap my fingers around the cold metal. My heart pounding out of my chest in anticipation. It turns, and I push the door open. I sigh in relief when the brisk fresh air blows through my hair.

For a few seconds, I just stand there, breathing in and calming myself before I poke my head out carefully. Looking left and right, I don't see any guards. I slowly walk outside and close the door behind me. Almost... I've almost made it.

With the key heavy in my pocket, I sneak around the house, staying as close to the wall and in the shadows as I can. Most cars are parked on the lawn in the front yard, and that is where I'm heading.

When I get to the edge of the makeshift parking lot, I take out the key fob and hit the unlock button. Like a beacon in the dark, headlights start to flash a few rows down, and I weave through the cars to get to them.

I climb into the luxury car and push the key into the ignition with a shaking hand. It turns, and the car roars to life. I buckle up quickly before putting the car in drive and pulling out of the spot.

Heading for the main gate, I let possible scenarios of the next ten minutes run through my mind. If everything goes according to plan, the guards will just wave me through, thinking that I'm Alberto. If they see that it's not him and try to stop me, I will hit the gas and hope for the best. Worst case scenario, they shoot at the car and kill me... I don't want to think about that. No, that's not going to happen. I will make it out of here.

I approach the gate, and as hoped, as soon as they see the car, one of them motions to open the gate. It isn't until I'm only a few feet away that he can look into the windshield and realize that it's not Alberto driving the car.

Pushing my foot down all the way, the engine revs up, and the car jolts to the front. Both guards pull their guns just as I speed past them. I hear the shots; I feel something hitting the car, but I keep driving. My eyes are wide open, I don't think I even blinked the last few minutes. My blood pumps through my veins furiously as the car accelerates even further. I look down at the speedometer, which reads ninety-eight miles per hour. This is the fastest I've ever driven, but it's still not fast enough.

Looking in the rearview mirror, I don't see anyone following me yet. I caught them by surprise. Good. That gives me a head start. I have no doubt that they will come after me.

I don't take my foot off the pedal. All I can think about is getting away.

I will get away. I will be free, and I will be back in Zane's arms.

42

Zane

*L*ooking up, I squint my eyes at the bright neon letters reading *Nightshift*. I don't know how exactly I ended up here, or why I'm here at all. Sure as hell, isn't because of the naked women dancing on the stage. Even after Dove ripped my heart out and trampled it, she is still the only one for me. I can't even think of another woman.

Maybe because it's the only place I know I can keep drinking without getting jumped by Christian's guys. They wouldn't dare set a foot into Damon Rossi's strip club.

My head is swimming, my mind clouded from the enormous amount of alcohol I've already consumed. Still, I want more. I want to drown myself in it just to make the pain go away.

Stepping inside, the smell of cigars, expensive liquor, and cheap perfume hits me. I'm barely inside when a half-naked woman greets me with fuck me eyes and pouty lips.

"Not interested," I slur, brushing her off before pushing past her. She says something, but I ignore her, heading straight to the bar instead. I take a seat and wave the waitress over. Quickly, I realize that I saw her last time I was here.

"Here to see Damon again?" she yells over the music.

"Not today. Just pour me a whiskey."

"Whiskey coming right up," she chirps, way to happily for my taste. It's almost like she enjoys working here. *Who the fuck likes working in a strip club?*

A few moments later, I have a large glass of amber liquid shoved in front of me. I murmur a thanks before I grab the glass and bring it to my libs. Taking a huge gulp, I let the alcohol burn down my throat, enjoying the way the warmth spreads out through my insides when it settles in my stomach.

My vision is already blurry as I look around. My gaze catches on two men on the other side of the bar. They're watching one of the strippers doing her dance routine on stage with hungry eyes. A little bit too hungry for an innocent show like this.

When the song is over, and the girl walks off the stage after collecting her money off the ground, the two guys look like they're about to jump her. She gives them a smile as she walks by, and that seems to be enough of an invite for them to grab her and pull her between them.

Even with the music blaring over the speakers loudly, I can hear her squeal in surprise, followed by her asking them to let her go. Her resistance doesn't seem to bother either of the guys, since they just move in closer, caging her in between their bodies.

Slamming my glass against the countertop, I get off my seat and walk around the L-shaped bar quickly. Grabbing the first guy by the back of the neck, I pull him off the girl. He tries to twist in my hold while swinging at me, but I've already got my arm around his neck, holding him in a chokehold.

Before I can get this guy unconscious, his friend grabs the bar stool and lifts it in the air, swinging it at my head. Normally, I could have seen that move coming from a mile away, but in my current state, everything is fucked up.

I'm fucked up...

The hardwood lands with a crack against the side of my head that's so hard, I'm surprised I don't black out right then. I do, however, see stars. Releasing the guy, I stumble back and try to gather my bearings, but before I can do that, I'm being hit again, this time a meaty fist cuts across my face.

A woman's scream pierces my ears as fists of fury rain down on me, clobbering every inch of my face. Pain is a welcomed feeling though. It blends with the pain that Dove caused me. I'm so gone now, I don't think I could even bring my arms up to protect my face even if I wanted to. All I can do now is exist at this moment, and let the pain rule my life. The light inside my head flickers in and out, and I know it's coming.

One more punch and the light goes out.

Darkness surrounds me, but I welcome it.

Only in my dreams can I be beside Dove again.

~

WHEN I COME to it feels like I've been hit by a truck before sliding down the side of a mountain face first. My face is throbbing so much so, I swear I can feel my heartbeat in the side of my head.

What the fuck happened?

The memories flicker through my mind like an old movie reel with some scenes missing, the film ripped apart. Dove... drinking... the bar... a fight. Either, I drank way more than I thought, or I got hit in the head pretty hard. On second thought, I'm sure it's a combination of those two.

I pry my eyes open slowly, immediately thankful that there is not much light in this room. Blinking, I try to make sense of where I am. The room is bare, brick walls surround me, and it doesn't take long for me to realize I'm in a cell.

Fucking hell.

Sitting up, I'm forced to close my eyes yet again, as the entire room starts spinning. When I open my eyes this time, I see the iron bars, confirming that, indeed, I'm in a cell. There is nothing inside but a cot that is creaking beneath me with every move.

I look around the cell, scanning every inch before I get up. The only thing I find is a water bottle sitting next to my cot. I grab it, unscrew the cap and start drinking. My parched mouth welcomes the cool water. I don't stop until the entire bottle is gone. Still, I feel more thirst. Damn, I'm dehydrated. Of course, that's the least of my worries right now.

My first thought is Christian found me, but he would have probably killed me right away. Castro is my second thought, but why would he want me locked up? No, both of them would have either killed me right away, or I would have woken up to being tortured.

I push myself up to stand on unsteady feet. Swaying slightly, I walk to the iron bars so I can look up and down the hallway. At the far end, I see a man posted. As soon as he catches sight of me, he turns and starts to walk away from me.

"Hey, asshole!" I yell after him. Instead of getting a reaction out of him, I make my ears hurt. The sound echoes through the hallway, only intensifying my headache. *Ugh.*

Walking back to my cot, I sit down and try to gather my thoughts. Where the fuck am I, and how did I get here? Most importantly, how the hell will I get out of here?

A few minutes later, I hear someone approaching. Getting myself ready for a fight, I get up on my feet and let my hands form fists beside me. Every muscle in my body is tense when I see none other than Xander Rossi appear on the other side of the cell door.

"Good morning, Zane. Sobered up enough to behave?"

I'm so shocked at seeing him, that I'm speechless, but I'm even more shocked when he reaches in his pocket and fishes out a key to unlock the cell door. The door swings open, and he takes a step to the side, motioning for me to come out.

"Is this a joke?" I say, my voice raspy like I smoked a pack of cigarettes last night.

"Not at all. Let's go, we have a lot to discuss."

Hesitantly, I walk past him while anticipating an attack any moment now. He has to be joking. What could he possibly want with me? If he thinks I have some dirt on Christian or Matteo, he's going to be wildly disappointed.

He makes me walk ahead of him, down the hallway and up a flight of stairs. When we get to a second hallway, and I don't know which way to turn, he takes the lead and lets me walk behind him. I don't miss that huge display of trust, him turning his back on me like that. He's showing me that he trusts me, probably expecting me to trust him in return. The question is, why?

I'm shocked yet again when we turn the corner and go through another door. Looking around confused, I wonder if I'm still sleeping, and this is a dream because now I'm standing in a foyer of a mansion... I assume the Rossi mansion.

"Why am I here?"

"Let's go sit down. I had my cook prepare some breakfast for you. I'll explain everything while you eat."

He leads me through the house and into a huge dining room. As he said, an array of breakfast food is spread out on the table. Part of me wants to refuse the food. I still don't trust him, I have no reason to, but given my current state, sustenance will greatly benefit me.

We both take a seat. Xander pours himself a coffee, and the smell of freshly brewed coffee invades my senses. He pours me a cup as well, without asking if I even want one.

"Talk," I order while taking up a fork and start eating the omelet in front of me.

I glance over at Xander, who is raising an eyebrow at me, clearly surprised by my lack of fear of him. After a moment, he starts talking anyway.

"As soon as I saw Dove, I couldn't believe the resemblance she had to someone I know. I figured they had to be related in some way. I started digging when she was here, but I hit one dead end after the next. After I let Dove go, I kept looking. There was something about her that I was missing, and I couldn't let it go."

Where the fuck is he going with this story?

He pauses to grab something from the inside of his suit jacket and places it in front of me. My gaze falls onto the old photograph, and for a split second, I think it's Dove looking back at me, but I quickly realize that the woman in the picture is a little bit older than Dove, her hair just a little bit lighter and her lips just a tad bit less full.

"Who is that?"

"My mother," Xander says, and I almost drop my fork. "My first thought was that Dove had to be my mother's daughter, but when Dove told me her age, it became an impossible scenario. Dove is twenty-one, and my mother died twenty-two years ago... or so we thought."

"What do you mean?" I almost don't want to ask. If Dove is not only related to Castro but also to Rossi, she'll be forever caught between the two families.

"Like I said, I couldn't let it go. So, after Dove left, I took her toothbrush and had her DNA tested, matched against mine. The test results confirmed that Dove is my sister."

"Wow..." I don't really know what else to say to that. "So... what does that mean for Dove?" *From the frying pan into the fryer?* Fuck, she will never be able to live a normal life.

"It means that I'm going to help you get her away from Castro. We're going to take him down and protect her at all costs. She is my family, and I protect what's mine."

At least one thing we can agree one.

43

I can't believe that worked. I'm free at last, and I did it all on my own. Matteo's men never caught up to me. I had too much of a head start. It takes forever for my heart to return to a steady beat and even longer for me to stop peering over my shoulder.

For the last couple hours or so, I've been driving around without a destination in mind, too focused on simply getting away. Now that I'm certain I've lost them, I need to find a place to go, and I need to find Zane. But how?

He doesn't have a phone. I have no idea where he is staying or how I could get a hold of him. I could go back to the bunker if only I had a clue as to where it is. *Shit.* I hit the steering wheel with my hand. I should have thought of this before, but I was so busy playing the role of an obedient daughter that I didn't think my plan through to the end.

The only place I can think to go is my apartment. Maybe he still checks the surveillance there? It's a small chance, but that's all I've got right now. At the very least, I can go and leave a note for him and hope that maybe that's where he goes, once news breaks out that I escaped.

Taking the next turn, I drive deeper into the city, taking the long way to my apartment. I'm still on high alert, looking into the rearview mirror constantly, and scanning my surroundings for threats the entire time.

When my apartment building finally comes into view, a mixture of relief and fear washes over me. What if he had the same idea? Maybe he left me a note, or maybe, just maybe he is there waiting for me? I can only hope. I park two blocks down, not wanting to leave the car in front of my building. It'll draw attention, and that's the last thing I need right.

Getting out of the car, I walk down the sidewalk with my hand on my waistband, where the knife is hidden underneath. When I get to the front door, I raise my hand to ring my neighbor's doorbell, hoping that someone is still awake and will let me in. But before I can push the small round button, the door flies open.

I reach for my knife, ready to protect myself, but quickly realize that it's only the couple from the floor above me.

"Oh, hi," Susan greets me in surprise. "We were worried about you."

"Nothing to worry about." I force a smile. "I'm fine just staying with a friend."

"I'm sorry about the break-in," James, her husband, says, "we called the cops when we heard the commotion downstairs, but when they got here, the burglars were already gone."

"I'm just glad I wasn't home," I say, my tone honest.

"Well, let us know if you need anything. We're heading out for a late-night pizza run."

"Thank you, I will." We say our goodbyes, and I move past them and into the hallway. Walking up to the apartment, my hands shake. When I reach the door, I find that it's slightly ajar. It's probably been that way since Christian's men came and kicked it in. *Assholes.* I wonder if they found my stash of cash, or if they were too concerned about finding me to care? Probably the latter. Guess we're about to find out.

The door creaks as I push it open, and my mouth pops open as I take in the chaos that is my apartment. Every single item is flipped over, all my belongings tossed around the room like an f-5 tornado went through it.

It's just belongings... I tell myself as I step over pieces of broken furniture. I killed someone today. I can handle seeing my apartment ransacked.

Closing the door behind me, I ignore the destruction beneath my feet and walk into the bathroom. I have to focus on the now. What I need to survive, to find Zane. Which leads me to the entire reason I came back here. *Money.*

Opening the medicine cabinet, I scan the bottles, which, surprisingly, haven't been touched. Finding the bottle I'm looking for, I pop the cap, and smile when I see the cash rolled together inside. I used to laugh whenever I'd hide money in here, thinking how ludicrous this was, but look who's laughing now. Sliding my fingers inside, I tug the money out and squeeze it in my clammy hand. I drop the bottle into the sink and close the cabinet.

I don't want to stay anywhere too long right now, not with just having escaped Matteo. Leaving the bathroom, I walk to the bedroom, my shoes crunching against the floor. The room is destroyed just like the rest of the house, but I make do, finding some clothes and a backpack to shove them in. Tossing everything inside, I sling the pack over my shoulder and walk out. In the kitchen, I find an envelope from a bill on the floor and a pen sitting on the counter.

Part of me had hoped like hell that Zane would be here when I walked through the door, but he wasn't, and that's okay. I'll find him, and we will be reunited again. On the off chance, he does happen to stop by here, I write a note, letting him know I've escaped and that I'll come back here in a few days. Leaving the note on the counter, I walk to the door.

I should probably get rid of the car. Now that I have some cash, I can take the bus or a cab. I start walking down the sidewalk with every intention of passing Alberto's car, but when I spot two black SUVs coming around the corner, I freeze. Yes, it's just an SUV, but it's the speed that it's coming around the corner. Danger zings through the air, and my gut tells me to run.

The first SUV speeds up, and now I'm certain whoever is driving is coming from me. Springing into action, I rush around the car while unlocking it with the key fob. As fast as I can, I slide into the driver's seat and start the car. The engine roars to life, and I'm barely able to pull out of the parking spot before they're catching up with me.

The street is filled with the sounds of tires squealing and cars speeding away. Driving like a Nascar driver, I punch the gas, zooming away from them. Every fiber in my body tenses when I look in the rearview mirror and see that they're right on my tail.

They could be Matteo's men, or Christian's. The least scariest possibility is that they're Xander's, I couldn't see them chasing after me though, not like these cars are. Turning down an alleyway, I drive through two trash cans and make a sharp left back out onto a street. Headlights flash behind me, and I know they're still there.

Slamming on the gas, I weave through traffic, nearly hitting three cars in the process as I try to get away from them. If they catch me, I'm trapped. It doesn't matter whose men they are. I'll be a pawn on one of their chess boards when all I want is to be free. Taking another sharp left, I peer over my shoulder and see only one SUV.

Where did the other... The thought gets lodged in my head and scatters like puzzle pieces shoved off a table when out of nowhere, the second SUV comes barreling down a side street. Its headlights are blinding, and I squint, trying to figure out what they're doing. It only takes a second to realize they're heading straight for me. The nose of their car slams into the rear of mine. My teeth clatter together as the impact sends the car into a tailspin.

Tires squeal, and headlights flash in front of the car, making me dizzy. All I can think is to run. With sweaty palms, I reach for the door handle and shove it open. I don't think about where I'm going, only that I have to get away.

My lungs burn and my heart thunders in my chest. It's almost the only thing I hear as I dash from the car and out into the street. Crazed, I pause for one second and look over my shoulder just as the sound of car doors opening meets my ears.

"Get the girl, but don't kill her. I want to be the one to do that."

I know that voice. *Christian.* Shit. I didn't escape one crazy-ass mob family to be tossed into another. Forcing my feet to move, I start running down the sidewalk. I make it all of ten feet before a muscled body plows me into the ground with the force of a wrecking ball. The air expels from my lungs, and my hands scrape against the concrete as I try and break my fall. Twisting in the assholes grasp, I drag my nails down and across his face. A hiss passes his lips, but he doesn't release me.

"Feisty. I like it." The bastard sinks his fingers into my skin with bruising force. "Keep fighting me. I love it when they do." The weight of his body disappears, and just when I think I might have a chance of escaping, he yanks me up off the cold ground and starts dragging me back toward the cars.

"No, please...please, let me go," I resort to begging because I know what happens if I get shoved into one of those cars.

"I got her boss," the bastard dragging me behind him announces proudly. In a few steps, we're at the SUV. The door opens, and no matter how much I struggle against the hulk of a man, I'm picked up and placed into the backseat of the vehicle, beside one of the most villainous men I've ever met, next to Matteo.

The door is slammed shut, and it feels like I'm being encased in my own coffin.

"We meet again," Christian says, his voice drips with anger, rage that is suffocating. It's like trying to breathe underwater.

"Let me go," I order. Like a cat, I claw at the door of the SUV, tugging at the handle, but the door won't open. The vehicle starts to move, and no matter how much I will myself not to cry, I can't hold back the avalanche of tears.

"Why would I do that when I just got you back?"

"So, you gonna put me in a cell again?"

"No, Dove, you're coming with me to my place this time. I'll let you stay in my room if you behave." He smirks, and I have to force the bile rising in my throat back down.

"What do you want from me? I have nothing of yours... Zane is... we aren't together, and I don't know where he is, and Matteo wants me dead if you think he cares about me, you're wrong." I look up at the man through thick lashes, tears clinging, no matter how hard I try to blink them away.

A sadistic grin pulls at his lips. "That's the problem, Dove. You think you have nothing, but really you have everything, and by the end of this, I'll take it all from you."

Confusion seeps into my pores, but before I can try and piece anything together, Christian produces a needle and stabs it into the side of my neck, pressing the syringe down and injecting me with some unknown drug.

"Night, night, little bird, when you wake up, all will be different."

44

"*I*f you keep pacing like that, you're gonna leave scuff marks on my carpet," Xander growls from his desk, annoyance lacing his words. That makes two of us. I've had enough of mob bosses telling me what to do.

"If your men would hurry up and find her, I wouldn't have a reason to pace." I pin him with a stare that's sure to get me killed. I still don't trust Xander, and I'm not sure what his real intentions are, but right now, he is helping me, so I need to really rein in my anger.

"They'll find her," he snaps before returning his attention back to his laptop. I have no doubt that they will find her, but I fear that it's going to be too late by the time they do, and I don't want to imagine the condition she'll be in by then.

"I just can't wait around any longer. I'm going to go look for her myself."

"I already told you, it's best to stay here until we know what's going on. My informant gave me too little information to act right now," Xander explains again as if I didn't hear him the first ten times. Apparently, Xander managed to get one of Matteo's men on his payroll. That guy called an hour ago, saying that there was an incident at the mansion. Alberto is dead, and Dove has disappeared. Whether she escaped or was taken is still not clear.

Fuck, I hope she escaped. If not, I'm burning down the world until I find her.

"At least check the surveillance in Dove's apartment again. If she got away, she would go there, I know it."

"It's still pulled up on my computer. If she goes there—" He pauses mid-sentence, his eyes fixed on the computer screen. "She just walked in..."

I'm across the room and around Xander's desk in two seconds flat. My eyes fall onto the computer screen and catch sight of Dove... my Dove, walking into her ransacked apartment. Through the grainy screen, she doesn't appear to be hurt or really even frightened. In fact, she looks strong, like a queen. Her gaze scans the ground, looking over her destroyed belongings before moving up and right into the camera. She doesn't know where I hid the cameras, but somehow, she manages to look straight into it.

It's like she's staring at me, beckoning me to come for her.

I'm coming, baby...

"Ivan and his team are outside and ready to go. I'll stay here and continue checking surveillance. Go!" Xander commands, and for once, I have no problem taking his order.

Without saying a word, I'm out of his office and running toward the front door. I almost take the handle off while opening it. When I make it to the front steps, I realize Xander wasn't lying. Ivan is standing in front of a fleet of cars, seemingly only waiting for me to get in. He doesn't have to wait long, because the next instant, I'm shoving into the passenger seat.

Ivan jogs around to the driver's seat, and we are off before either of us can buckle up.

The ride to her apartment seems to take forever, even though Ivan seems to have his foot to the pedal most of the drive, it still feels like forever. Even if we were going a thousand miles per hour, it wouldn't be fast enough when it comes to Dove.

"She just left the apartment," Xander says over the car speaker.

"We're almost there," Ivan says as if he knows how anxious I'm feeling. Grinding my teeth, I hope and pray that we'll catch her before she leaves. These last couple of days have been pure torture, and even if I am angry at her for pushing me away, I still want to hold her in my arms just to know that she is okay.

A few minutes later, we pull up outside her apartment. I open the door and jump out of the car before we come to a complete stop. Looking around, I wish nothing more than to see her. I scan the entire area, up and down the street, but she's nowhere in sight... gone.

She's gone.

I fucking missed her.

~

Looking down at the envelope in my hand, I read over the note for the hundredth time.

Zane, I escaped Matteo. Will be back in a few days.

I love you, Dove.

Refusing to return to Xander's place, I meander back outside, I sit in the car and wait. I told Ivan he could leave, but he insisted on staying, mumbling something about how I might need him. Two more SUVs stayed as well, parked only a few spots behind us. I look out onto the street, watching every car that drives by and every person that walks out onto the street.

If I have to, I'll stay here until she shows back up. Either way, I'm not moving until we figure out where the hell she is.

Xander has been trying to figure out where she went, calling in favors left and right while we wait around uselessly. When the phone finally rings, and Xander's name flashes over the screen, I almost give up hope that he has some new information and is instead ordering us to return to the mansion, but that's not what comes out of his mouth.

"Christian has her. There was some type of chase, and now they're transporting her to his place. I'm sending more men your way, but it's going to be a good twenty minutes before they get there, and I'm not sure she has that long."

"We're going there now," Ivan says as the SUV roars to life. I clench my hands into tight fists at the thought of a fight. Why is he taking her to his place? What the fuck is going on?

My heart beats in my ears, and all I can think about is rearranging Christian's face, and wrapping my arms around Dove. Making sure she's safe and secure. Clenching my jaw, I try not to think about what might be happening to her. I can't believe this is happening again. I should have killed him when I had the chance. If they've hurt her in any way, they'll be wishing for death by the time I'm done with them.

"I'm guessing you know where to go?"

"Yes, head east." I continue giving Ivan directions until we arrive at Christian's private mansion. It's not as heavily guarded as Xander's place, but it does have its own security. Luckily, I know that security system well, and if I'm lucky, he was stupid enough not to change my code to get in.

"Is there a back way in?" Ivan asks.

"No, but you can pull up to the gate and try to enter my code. It's 891384."

Ivan drives up to the code pad and punches in the numbers. I hold my breath as he pushes the enter button, and I don't breathe until the green light blinks, and the gate starts to creak open. I suck in a ragged breath as Ivan drives through the gate and toward the house.

"I can't believe he didn't change the code." Ivan shakes his head.

I snort and say, "I can. He's too confident, and that's exactly what's going to get him killed... tonight." I half expect Ivan to tell me not to do it, that Xander wants to bring him in and torture him, but to my surprise, he only nods as if he was expecting me to say that.

"Xander told me to kill him if you didn't want to do it in front of Dove. I know you don't trust him yet, but I can tell you, he's nothing like Matteo. He actually loves his family, and now that Dove is a part of that, he'll spare her any type of pain that he can," Ivan says as we pull up in front of the mansion.

"Then let's go inside, get her, and kill the bastard who's trying to hurt her," I say while opening my door with my gun in my hand.

As soon as we're out of the car, a handful of Christian's men pour out of the house, guns raised. I stay close to the car, using it as a shield while I raise my own gun and start shooting. The first bullet hits my target right between the eyes, his body crumbling to the ground. The second one hits another guy in the arm, but Ivan gets him in the side of the head without even blinking. The other two men retreat into the house but fail to close the door. *Idiots.* Not that a closed door is going to stop me from getting to Dove. I'll rip this fucking place down to the floorboards to find her.

More shots are fired, some by us, some by Christian's men, but everybody is keeping themselves covered. I know I need to act fast; I don't have time for a fucking standoff with these idiots. Taking the risk because a bullet to the chest is nothing compared to the pain Dove will endure if we wait any longer, I push off the car and spring up to the front of the house. A guard sticks his head out the door in a failed attempt to survey the area. Without thinking twice, I lift my gun and pull the trigger while running toward him.

He falls back against the door and then crumbles down to the ground just as I get to the door. The last guard lunges for me, fear trickling into his features as if he knows the fate he's about to be delivered. Expecting it, I greet him with a punch to the chest, knocking the air from his lungs. A gasp slips from his lips, and before he can recover, I press the muzzle of my gun to his stomach and pull the trigger. Like a tiger, I move through the foyer and toward the kitchen.

A scream pierces the air and bounces off the walls of the house, and like a beacon, I'm drawn to it. Dove needs me, she fucking needs me, and I'll be damned if I fail her again. Turning, I walk back toward the hall, where I hear a whimper instead of a scream this time. I'll rip his heart out of his chest if he hurts her.

Uncontrolled, and like an animal hunting its prey, I move deeper into the hall. I can sense Ivan behind me, his movements mimic mine, but he doesn't intervene or try and stop me.

"Time to go, princess." Christian's smug voice pierces through the heavy fog around my head, and I hide slip into the room, hiding behind the door. When I peer back around the corner, Christian is tugging Dove down the hall with him. I only catch a glimpse of her face; her cheeks are stained with tears. "Your little knight thought he could save you, but all he did was damn you. You should thank me for killing you and putting you out of your misery."

Dove's cries are muffled, but I can feel her pain, taste her fear on the tip of my tongue. I have to stop them before they get to an exit and get outside. Christian wasn't prepared for us to show up here, and so we have the element of surprise right now, but I'm sure he's called more men in, and they'll be here soon.

Too bad Christian will be dead before that happens. Tiptoeing in the direction he went, I lift my gun, watching as he tugs Dove by her arm toward a door. She struggles in his grasp, and as she fights him, her gaze swings toward me. Panic. Fear. Adoration. Love. Each emotion reflects back at me.

Shaking my head, I release myself from her trance. The door opens, and I lift my gun, firing two shots into Christian's back.

I don't think, I pounce like a thief in the night, rushing toward them. Christian releases Dove at the last second, and before I can grasp what is taking place, he shoves her toward the open door. Fear like I've never felt before, pulses through me with its own heartbeat as I watch her disappear into the dark space. I hear every stair she hits, my heart cracking inside my chest, and as Christian turns to face me, a sadistic smile on his lips and a gun in his hand, I lift my own and shoot him in the head at point-blank range.

Shock flickers in his eyes, and then blood and brain matter explode everywhere, painting the hall in death. Christian's stare becomes vacant and reflects back at me. He crumbles to the ground, landing in a heap at my feet. I step over his body and rush down the stairs, my hands shaking, and my body vibrating with fear as I reach Dove.

She is lying on her side, her arms cradling her head. I kneel next to her on the floor, not sure if I should pick her up or if that would hurt her more. I gently grab her arms and pull them away from her face, so I can get a better look at her. Brushing the sweat-slicked hair from her face, her eyes flutter open and find mine in an instant.

"Are you okay?" I ask, my voice raw with emotion.

"My head hurts, but I'm okay... are you? Are you okay?" Her eyes move over the front of my shirt before she reaches for me, her hands fisting the material in her hands.

"I'm fine, sweetheart," I murmur against her forehead as I pluck her off the floor and cradle her frail body in my arms. I'm not sure what kind of injuries she has, but I need to get her out of here. More of Christian's men could arrive at any second, and I'm not going to fall into that trap. Racing up the steps, I meet Ivan's dark stare at the top.

"Is she okay?" he asks gruffly, his eyes flicking over her face.

"I don't know. He shoved her down the stairs, and she's complaining that her head hurts. She's not bleeding, but I need to get her to Xander's and have the doctor check her over before I can be sure."

Ivan nods, and I walk out of the house, carrying the woman I'd die a million times over for. No one will ever hurt her again, not while I'm still breathing.

45

*W*ho knew that your life could fall apart and come back together so fast in one day? Zane pulls me tight to his side and kisses the side of my face. I feel his heartbeat in his lips.

Taste the fear in the air. His arms are like steel bars wrapped around me, and I've never been happier in my life to be confined to a space, because I know I'm the safest I'll ever be while in his arms. A shiver rips through me, and goosebumps pebble my flesh. This could've been really bad, terribly bad, but because of Zane, Ivan, and the rest of Xander's men, I'm safe. I don't know what Zane had to do to get Xander and Ivan to help us, but right now, I don't care enough to ask. I'm sure I'll find out sooner rather than later.

Everything is going to be okay now.

I've survived Christian and escaped Matteo; the worst is behind us.

"I'm pissed at you for forcing me to leave you unprotected. If anything happened to you, I wouldn't have been able to forgive myself," Zane growls into my ear like an animal, crushing me to his chest.

"I'm okay. No one hurt me," I reassure, shifting in his arms, so I'm facing him. I cling to him like a second skin, letting the warmth of his body seep into mine.

"You took a pretty good tumble down the stairs. That's not nothing, and the only reason it wasn't worse than that is because we got to you in time. Imagine if we had been five minutes later?" Zane's fear has never been so real to me. I always knew he was worried, but I'd never seen real fear on his face for me until tonight when he rescued me.

"I know... I know, but you weren't, and I'm okay. Everything is okay. I love you, and I'm sorry, so sorry." Tears fill my eyes and slip down my cheeks. Zane wipes them away with his thumb, and I stare up at him through blurred vision, waiting for him to say something.

I won't ever tell him, but I was so afraid, afraid that I would never see him again, never get to tell him how sorry I was for pushing him away, for trying to save us both.

"I accept your apology, Dove, but we aren't done talking about this, not by a long shot. I could've lost you today, and I know what you did was to protect me, but it's my job to protect you. My job," he snarls, and I feel his anger, his fear rolling off of him and slamming into me. "Did anyone touch you? Alberto? Christian?"

"No one touched me. I wouldn't let them." Burying my face in his shirt, I inhale his unique scent of soap, and manliness, trying to calm myself. *I'm alive. I'm safe.* I repeat the same words over and over again to myself. Zane holds me so tightly it's hard to breathe, but I wouldn't trade it for the world.

I stay like this cradled in his arms, my head against his chest, the sound of his heartbeat in my ear until the SUV comes to a rolling stop. Lifting my head, I discover we've been brought to Xander's mansion.

All I can do is hold my breath and wait for something bad to happen. It's a battle of mobs at this rate, and Zane and I are the only two pawns left on the chessboard.

The doors to the SUV open, and I slide across the leather seat with Zane at my back, his hand wrapped around my wrist like he's afraid I'll run away or something.

Coming to stand outside the vehicle, I marvel at the huge wooden door before us. It's massive and intimidating, just like Xander Rossi. I suppose I shouldn't expect any less from such a man. Zane tugs me to his side, giving me a look that I can't quite read.

The door creaks loudly as it opens, and Xander's impassive face comes into view. Instead of looking at me like I'm a bug he needs to squish, he gives me a warm smile, it's almost cheery if you could picture a man who kills people for a living being jolly. It actually looks more like a shark smiling at you with all of its pointy teeth on display.

"Welcome home, baby sister."

The air in my lungs stills, and I'm positive my ears have deceived me. He didn't just say that, right? *Sister?* He has to be on drugs or something.

"Ssss-sister?" I barely get the single word past my lips.

"Yes. Come in, please, have a drink, sit down, and we can talk. You've had a tiring day, Dove, and I don't want to exhaust you further. The doctor is already on his way to check you over, but while we wait for him, we can talk."

My mouth refuses to work. Whatever words I'd prepared myself to say, sink deep into the back of my mind. Zane holds me tightly to his side as he gives Xander a weary look before guiding us into the mansion.

This has to be a trap. No way am I this man's sister. I don't have to know all that he's done to know that he's a man of power and evil. He might have treated me nice while I was here, but I've heard enough stories. He's the head of a notorious and ruthless crime family, after all. It's not like he's Santa Claus.

Zane guides me into the house and through the massive foyer, and I'm in awe of the beauty of the house. Ella isn't just a sweet person but also has excellent taste in decorations.

I try not to think about how fucked up that is as Zane moves us into a small seating area off the dining room. There's a floor to ceiling book-shelf on one side of the room and a leather sofa and two chairs centered around a small wooden table on the other. Two huge windows make the room feel bigger than it is.

Zane navigates us to the sofa while Xander takes the chair across from us.

"Would you like anything to drink?" Xander asks.

"Water," I croak. I'm not sure what's going on. He called me his sister, but that can't be right. Matteo never talked about me having any other siblings.

Xander disappears from the room and returns with a glass of water a moment later. He hands it to me, and I take a sip before placing it on the table in front of me.

"I'm sure you have a lot of questions, but I'll tell you what I know first, and then you can ask me anything that you want to okay?" Though Xander's voice still toes the line on menacing, there is a softness to it.

"When Ivan brought you here last time, you looked so familiar to me, but in a way that didn't make sense. You looked a lot like my mother, and I couldn't figure out why. I asked your age for a reason. My mother supposedly died twenty-two years ago, so when you told me you were twenty-one, I didn't think it could be true. Still, something in my gut told me to keep digging, thinking we might be related in a different way. Distant cousins at the very least. Instead, I found out that our mother didn't die when I thought she did. She left when she discovered she was pregnant with you."

I try to swallow, but the salvia in my mouth feels like concrete. A sense of Deja vu sets in. I've been here before, rescued from Christian, then being told I have some long-lost relatives. It didn't work out for me last time, so no surprise that I'm not happy about this new development. For now, I keep my thoughts to myself and listen instead of speaking.

"Our mother had you without any prenatal care, and by herself. There is no record of you ever being born, and you were never given a birth certificate. Police found you in a hotel room crying when you were about two, our mother dead from a drug overdose."

My hand tightens in Zane's, and I feel like I'm going to be sick. I have two brothers, maybe more I haven't met yet. All of them seem to be part of the mafia. On top of that, I have a father who is part of the mafia but not the same family.

My mother had an affair, ran away, and gave birth to me, god knows where, before deciding, later on, it was too hard to love and care for me. At this point, I truly do feel as broken as I look. Unwanted and unloved. It's the story of my life.

I don't even realize I'm crying until I feel the wetness against my cheeks. I look from the ground and over to Zane, hoping he didn't know. He knows everything about me, surely, he knew about this. Still, a tiny piece of me hopes he didn't know. When our eyes clash, I know instantly that he did, and like a plane, I nosedive right into the ground.

"I didn't know until a few days ago," Zane whispers, trying to reassure me. It's like I'm being cornered, all my fears and worries bombarding me at once.

"There's more," Xander says in a monotone voice.

"What more could there be?" I whisper though I had hoped the words would come out stronger. I feel weak and broken inside. It's strange because I knew most of the story. It's harsh to know I spent my entire life in foster care when I had family, a family that is wealthy, and that I could've been living with. Even if they are ruthless criminals, family is family, right?

"After you left, I sent your toothbrush in for a DNA sample. You just looked too similar to my mother for me to let it go. The test result confirmed my suspicions, that we are related but even more shocking, turns out you aren't just our half-sister, but our full-blooded sister..." Red hot rage pulses through my veins in an instant.

"So, wait... both of your parents are my parents? Which means..."

"Matteo was lying to you the whole time," Xander says before I can. "You are not related to him."

"Why would he lie to me?" I growl, asking no one in particular. "Not that I am disappointed about having no connection to him." Matter of fact, I'm a little relieved.

"Because he's a fucking prick," Zane replies.

"Actually, he might not have known he was lying. I think our mother did have an affair with him, but she was pregnant at the time, so he doesn't know you're not his daughter. He assumed, and since our mother was trying to escape our father, it makes sense."

I'm sinking in all the secrets I've been told, drowning a slow and painful death. I start to shiver, my thoughts swirl as I think of all the things I did, how I betrayed Zane. Yes, I did it to save him, but I didn't have to butter up to Matteo. I didn't have to... guilt makes my chest cave in. I can't breathe. I try and suck air into my lungs, but it feels like I'm choking.

"This is a lot to take in," I whisper just as the sound of a knock fills the room. Everyone looks up to the door, where a man with a stethoscope around his neck and a bag in his hand stands.

"Ah, Doc, please, come in," Xander greets, and the doctor steps in. "I need you to check her out. Make sure she is fine," he orders.

The doctor nods and approaches me. For the next few minutes, he gives me a good checkup. Feeling for breaks, taking my vitals, and asking me a bunch of questions, all under the watchful eyes of Zane and Xander.

At the end, he tells me what I expected. Besides a bump on my head and a few bruises on my body, I'm fine. He leaves a few minutes later, and I am once more alone with Zane and my brand new brother.

The doctor was a brief distraction, but now I'm hit with the reality of my new life once more.

"Can you give us a little bit," Zane says, turning me in his arms.

Xander nods and walks out of the room. As soon as he's gone, Zane pulls me onto his lap and wraps his arms around me. He holds all my broken pieces together, holds me together.

"I'm sorry. I'm so sorry, Zane," I sob into his shirt, feeling so torn and tattered.

"Don't be sorry, baby... You did what you thought was right, and that's how we both made it out of that situation alive. Matteo will pay for deceiving us, pay for trying to rip us apart. Pay for hurting you. You're mine, Dove. Mine to protect, to cherish, to keep. Mine until I breathe my last breath."

"I'm just confused. I don't know what to think, what to feel. First Matteo tells me I'm his daughter, now I'm suddenly Xander's sister... I just don't know how to take any of this."

"Let's go upstairs so we can talk."

Pulling away, I look him in the eyes, those dark eyes of his still give nothing away, but I know deep in their depths there is love and adoration for me that can never be rivaled by another.

"I'm sorry I hurt you... I never meant to push you away. Matteo told me if I didn't get you to leave, he would kill you, and I couldn't let you die." More tears fall, blurring my vision completely now, and I know I'm on the verge of a full-fledged panic attack.

"Shhh, you can make it up to me. Like I told you, Dove. I will never leave you. You could stab me in the heart, shoot me in the head, lie, or cheat, and I still wouldn't leave. Your crazy matches my crazy, and I'm never going to give you up."

His confession only makes me sob harder, and even if I wanted to, I couldn't object as he picks me up like I weigh nothing and carries me back out into the foyer and up a grand staircase. My vision is too blurry to make anything out, but I tell myself I can check out my surroundings tomorrow.

Zane opens a door and walks inside, closing it behind him with his foot. He deposits me onto the bed and takes the spot beside me.

"Now, let me hold you. I miss the way you smell and the way you feel in my arms. I need you like an addict needs their next fix, Dove, and I'm not sure I'm strong enough to deny myself what I want from you right now. So, please, roll over and stop looking at me like I'm a knight when really I'm the devil waiting to crack you open and feast on your soul."

"You're not the devil, Zane. You're the sun, and the moon, and every star in my galaxy. Without you, there would be no me. I'm sorry I hurt you. I'm sorry all of this happened." I know I already apologized, but I feel like I need to say it a few more times for it to sink in.

I roll away from him, wondering if he can see the shame and sadness in my face. Wrapping an arm around my middle, he holds me possessively, like there is no way to escape him, not like I would try anymore.

"I just want a normal life..." I whisper, more to myself.

His lips trail against the back of my neck, and I shiver in his arms.

"Normal will come, my sweet, Dove. But not until we paint the city red and take over Matteo's empire. Now sleep, you'll need it for what I have prepared for you."

"What's that?" I murmur half asleep.

"You'll see, tomorrow. I need to remind you who you belong to." A tiny shiver of excitement runs through me as I remember the last time he showed me that I'm his. I remember how good he made me feel, how he tied me down and made my body sing. How he coaxed orgasm after orgasm out of me.

I need this. Need him. All of him.

The dark and the light, the good and the bad. I need it all. I need his body against mine. Need his darkness like I need my next breath. If there is anything I've learned from this last month, it's that the only constant in my life has been Zane. My stalker, and me, his obsession.

46

Zane

A knock sounds against the door, and I roll over with a groan, remembering that Dove is still hurt. The doctor assured me that she had nothing but a little bump on her head. He gave me some pain pills to give her but said that she was lucky to walk away with nothing more than a bump. Rolling out of bed, I tug on a pair of boxers from the floor and walk over to the door. Opening it, I'm greeted by Ivan's emotionless face. The dude reminds me more of myself every day.

"Xander wants you and Dove to meet him downstairs for a meeting, whenever you are ready. Damon is here too," he says and then turns around and walks back down the stairs.

Closing the door, I turn my attention back to Dove. She is curled up in the bed, looking broken. The last few weeks have taken a toll on her. Her wings clipped. Her beautiful face puffy from all the tears she shed last night.

She'll learn to fly again soon, but it won't be without me by her side. Rage and lust swirl together and burn like a raging inferno through my veins. I want to punish her. No. *I need to.* I need to remind her that she belongs to me and that it's us together or nothing.

Reaching for her, I stroke her face gently like she's made of the finest glass. She stretches like a kitten, lifting her arms above her head. Her blue eyes open, and I'm struck by their beauty. My obsession, my unwilling captive. She's forever tied to me. Cupping her cheek, I lean in until our lips are almost touching. I allow myself to feel every emotion that I've repressed in the last couple of weeks. Hate. Anger. Pain. Betrayal.

My touch is gentle, even though it shouldn't be. I could never hurt Dove, no matter what she did to me. I could never hurt her as she's hurt me.

"I want you to know that even though I love you, I want to hurt you. I want to make you bleed the way you made my heart bleed when you forced me to leave you with Matteo," I say, my voice quivering with emotion. I'd never been angrier and scared all at once. The memory of her forcing me to leave, telling the guards to toss me out is all I can see in my mind.

I was scared shitless for days, worried sick knowing that if something happened to her within the walls of that mansion, there was nothing I could do. I was forced to leave her unprotected, and I wouldn't ever do that again.

Shocked by my confession, Dove's pretty mouth pops open. I know she's been through so much, everything she endured and discovered about her history. I know I should let her heal, give her more time, but I can't stop myself from punishing her. Physically hurting her isn't an option, but there are worse ways to make someone feel the pain they've inflicted on you.

"I want you naked and spread out for me."

Understanding blankets her face, and her pink tongues dart out, wetting her bottom lip. I want to taste her lips, bite, and suck on them, but I can't. Not yet. Pulling my hand away, I watch as she slowly slips out of her clothes, a cami, and pair of cotton panties, discarding them on the floor. My eyes roam over the length of her body, looking for any inflictions, cuts, wounds. Aside from a few bruises on her arms, I see nothing that worries me.

Pressing a hand to her chest, I gently push her back onto the mattress. She doesn't say anything but watches me like a timid mouse that's been caught in a trap. Pushing her legs apart, I drag my gaze lower, over her tiny tummy, and her hips before reaching the top of her mound.

Her creamy smooth thighs come into view, and I bite back a groan. They're unblemished, and as I lean in, I inhale her sweet scent into my nostrils.

The smell of her sex zings right through me and into my cock, slamming into me like a lightning bolt. Like a dog with a bone, I'm salivating, wanting to take a bite out of her pink pussy. *One taste. One lick. One drop of her sweet nectar on my tongue.*

That's all I need, but because I know I'll take more, so much more than that, I rein myself in. Using every ounce of discipline I have left, I pull away.

"Do you have any idea how much it hurt me to be pushed away by you? To watch you do as Matteo said, to hang on his every word." I pause and trail a finger down over her thigh, stopping at her knee. She shivers, and I'm unsure if it's from fear or something more. I hate that I enjoy her fear, hate that it makes my cock harder than steel. "I watched you play with Alberto, taunting him, leading him astray..."

"I didn't... I wouldn't. I'm sorry," she eventually huffs.

My lips turn up at the sides, "No, you aren't. Not yet, but you will be soon."

"What are you going to do to me?" she asks after a second, her heart beating against her ribs like a bird trapped in a cage.

"Whatever I want," I reply darkly. I'm too frenzied with need to prepare her, and so I hope like hell she's already wet because the last thing I want to do is hurt her, then again, she hurt me. Ripped my fucking heart out of my chest. Granted, she did it to protect me, this I understand, but who protects her if something happens to me?

"Zane," she whimpers, knowing what's coming. I'll be cruel to her, but I'll make sure she feels my love with each hard stroke. I'll give her pain and let the pleasure soothe the ache.

"Shh, you only speak if it's to tell me to stop. Do you understand?" I bark out.

Her gaze widens with shock and arousal, but she doesn't object. Instead, she nods her head in understanding.

"Play with your tits, get yourself nice and wet because I don't have the patience for that right now."

Dove's chest starts to rise and fall rapidly, but her eyes glaze over with lust. She likes when I tell her what to do, when I fuck her with purpose. Rolling her hardened nipples between her thumb and pointer finger, her lips part and her hips roll, seeking out my cock. I leave her this way, craving and wanting for a minute while I watch. She bites her bottom lip to stifle the whimper, trying to escape her pouty lips. I want my cock between those lips. I want to watch her swallow my length, to choke on it, to be so helpless and fragile.

Shoving my boxers down, I let my swollen cock free and kick away the fabric at my feet.

"Come here," I order, fisting my cock in my hand. Dove's timid gaze moves from my cock and up my body, stopping at my eyes. "I want you on your knees," I say.

Grabbing a pillow from the bed, I toss it on the floor at my feet. Dove's movements are sluggish, and I can see how aroused she is for me, her sweet cream coats the insides of her thighs, and my gaze is drawn to it.

I want to lick it, feast on her, to wring every drop of pleasure out of her.

This isn't about her... I remind myself, which is really fucking hard when the only thing I care about is her. Pleasing her. Making sure she's safe. Loving her. I breathe for her.

Dove sinks down onto the pillow and eyes me cautiously.

"Open that pretty mouth of yours. The same mouth that slayed me with such hateful words. I'm going to fuck it, fuck your mouth, throat, and then your pussy." I've never been so blunt with her before, so vile, but it feels good. It makes me feel free. I'm not sure what I'll do if she objects, but thankfully, she doesn't.

I bring the tip of my cock to her open lips. She flicks her tongue against the tip, and I let out a grunt. Fuck, that feels like heaven. Running my fingers through her hair, I stroke her head before sinking my fingers deep into the dark strands, wrapping them around my fist. I tug her head back and make sure she knows who's in charge.

"Open your mouth real wide, I'm going to fuck it."

It's the only warning I give her before I thrust my hips forward, shoving my cock deep into her mouth. Her tiny nails sink into my thighs, and she whimpers around my length. Pulling out a little, I slam back in and watch as her eyes water and the tears stream down the side of her face. Again, I hold myself there for a moment before pulling back out and doing it all over again. She gags around my length, and the sound only heightens my pleasure.

"You look so fucking pretty with my cock stuffed in your mouth," I say, wanting her to know that while I am punishing her, I still love her so fucking much.

Dove's mouth is so warm, so fucking perfect. I pull out again, and saliva dribbles out the sides of her mouth. I half expected her to tell me to stop by now, but Dove is stronger now than she was back in that bunker. She's a queen.

Moaning around my cock, I swear the sound goes straight through me. Repeating the process again, I continue fucking her mouth until the pleasure in my balls becomes too much, and I'm afraid I'll blow. I'm going to fill up her tight little pussy with my come.

Pulling all the way out of her, I grab her by the chin and stare into her crystal blues.

"Get on the bed on your hands and knees," I order, and she scurries from the floor and onto the bed. Climbing onto the bed, I situate myself behind her, pressing down on the small of her back. She's at the perfect angle, her pink folds glisten in the morning light.

"You come when I tell you to," I growl and line up my cock with her entrance. Thrusting my hips forward, I slip deep inside of her channel, my home. She's snug, tightly squeezing me like a vice.

"So deep," she pants into the sheets, and I slap her ass hard for talking outside the rules.

"Don't talk unless it's to tell me to stop."

Those are the last words I say for a while as I fuck her hard and fast, showing her just how much it hurt me to lose her. Imprinting my soul on hers, I fuck her like an animal, rutting deep. Every time she gets close to orgasming, I pull out. She whimpers at the loss, and when I push back into her, we repeat it all over again.

"Zane," she pleads, and it's the one time I let her get away with talking.

The need in her voice is too much for me. I can feel her gripping me, her tight cunt getting ready to pulse around me. I've been fucking her for ten minutes now, beads of sweat drip down my body, my grip on her hips is bruising, the force of my thrusts harsh, but I can't seem to get enough of her. I can't seem to get her to feel all of my pain. Withholding her orgasm is killing me as badly as it's killing her.

"Please, Zane, please. I'm sorry. I'm sorry..." She starts to sob, like actual crying, and it's the last shred. I can't take hurting either of us anymore. Slamming hard into her one last time, I grind my hips against her ass, feeling everything as she explodes all around me. We both come together, my hot come fills her channel, and I can feel it dripping down my cock and onto my balls.

Fuck, I've never come so much or so hard before.

Gently, I pull out of Dove and collapse onto the mattress beside her. I tug her into my side and stroke her sweaty face with my hand. It takes me forever to catch my breath, but when I do, I roll, so we are facing each other.

"Was I too rough?" I ask a tinge of guilt in my voice.

"No. I'll be sore, but you taught your lesson." The little smile she gives me is enough to make the guilt disappear.

"I love you, Dove. I love you so fucking much, and no one is going to come between us again. I'll kill anyone who tries, anyone who even thinks about it. You're mine, and I am yours. Say it," I urge, needing to hear her say the words.

"I am yours," she whispers, and I've never heard truer words in my life.

47

I feel the way Zane fucked me in every step I take, and I'm pretty sure that was his intention. I took away his power when I forced him to leave, and I needed to show him that I placed that control back into his hands. I know he needed this as much as I needed it myself.

The way he used me was terrifying. Like I was nothing to him, but at the same time, invigorating because, in the end, I held all the power. If I told him to stop, he would have. I could feel his anger slipping away, the pain crumbling little by little.

After lying in bed for a few minutes, we get into the shower together, where Zane takes his time helping me wash my hair and body. His hands are gentle as he moves the washcloth over my skin and down between my legs. I gasp at the contact; my folds still sensitive.

Zane's expression fills with concern. "Are you sure I didn't hurt you?"

"I'm sure. I'm just really sensitive." I give him a sincere smile, and we finish together in the shower without any more worrying questions. As soon as we're done, Zane gets out, grabs a towel, and wraps it around me. It's fluffy and smells clean and fresh.

Slinging a towel around his own waist, we walk back into the bedroom together. I sit on the edge of the bed while Zane walks over to the dresser and starts rifling through it. I can't help but stare as his well-defined muscles clench and flex as he moves.

Those perfectly sculpted abs and the bulge of his biceps cause a heat to coil low in my belly. I shouldn't be staring. I really shouldn't, but...

"Xander's wife gave me some clothes for you to wear if you want to come and look through the drawers," Zane says, his voice interrupting my thoughts. My cheeks heat, and I can't imagine how I look right now.

"Oh, okay, yeah..." I mumble and walk over to the dresser. I find some clothes and pull them on, feeling a little less exposed now that I'm dressed. Drying my hair with the towel, Zane watches me curiously.

"You know what happens next, right?" he asks, as I drop the towel to the floor.

"Yes, now that Christian is dead, Matteo is next."

"Are you okay with that?"

My brow furrows. "Why wouldn't I be? I told you, I don't care about him, Zane. I was only playing along to protect you. He told me he'd kill you if I didn't make you disappear, and so I decided I'd rather have you angry with me than never have a chance to see you alive again. Who will protect me if you're not here?" I whisper as I cross the space between us and cup his cheeks. I lean in and press my lips against his.

They're warm and firm, and when I feel his tongue pressing against the seam of my lips, I open up to him. Our tongues duel for a short while, each stroke of his tongue, stoking the warm coil of pleasure inside my belly. I know Xander is waiting for us, but he can wait a few more minutes.

Zane's hands circle my waist and he tugs me forward...I'm seconds away from ditching my clothes and climbing on top of him when a knock on the door interrupts us.

Of course, Zane pulls away with a groan, a tiny smug grin pulling at his lips.

"We should probably go. I think we've left your brothers waiting long enough."

My brothers. It's so strange to think that yesterday I had no siblings, and today I have two brothers. Giving my hips a gentle squeeze, Zane moves me out of the way so he can get to the door. Tugging it open, I'm shocked to see Xander standing on the other side.

"Sorry to interrupt your reunion, but we need to discuss Matteo as soon as possible. Now that Christian is dead, word will travel fast."

"We'll be down in a minute," Zane confirms, and Xander nods.

Sticking to his word, we walk downstairs and into the massive dining room, where Xander, Damon, and Ivan are sitting. They're talking casually like they aren't plotting to murder someone tomorrow.

It's hard not to outright gawk at all the fancy features, like the huge open kitchen off to the right of the dining room, or the chandelier with ten thousand shiny diamonds reflecting back at me. Zane takes a seat at the table, and I take the spot next to him. A maid pops her head out of the kitchen and meanders over to us with a kind smile.

"Can I get you anything?" she asks.

"No, I can get it..." I start, but Xander clears his throat, cutting me off.

"That's not how this works, Dove. The help is here to help. That's what we pay them for. If you want something to drink or eat, Matilda can get it for you." His words are clipped and cold.

I feel like a small child who's being scolded, and I'm reminded of my stay at Matteo's mansion, and I dislike greatly that he called this lovely woman *the help*.

"I'll just have a coffee. Cream and sugar, please," I say through gritted teeth before taking a seat. Zane takes the one next to me and slides his hand over mine.

"The Sergio family is crumbling apart without Christian, and Castro is running around like a chicken with his head cut off, trying to take over whatever territory he can. Greedy bastard he is. Plus, Alberto being dead leaves him spread thin. Now is the perfect time to strike, to take him down once and for all," Xander explains while Damon and Ivan nod in agreement.

"Matteo tried to marry me off and threatened to kill Zane if I didn't do his bidding. I'm all for taking him down as fast as possible."

"Good, because we might need your help—"

"Whoa, whoa," Zane interjects. "You are not involving her in this!

This was not part of the agreement. I told you I would help, but we never talked about her."

"I won't force her if she doesn't want to. I'm simply offering her the chance to help."

"She declines," Zane growls without even asking for my opinion. "She doesn't belong here in this world, and she's definitely not going anywhere near Matteo again."

"Let me ask you a question," Xander says cunningly, a sinister smile spreading out across his face. "What exactly happened to Alberto? How did you escape Matteo?"

"It doesn't matter," Zane snaps, and I just now realize that he hasn't asked yet and that I haven't told anyone either. Does Zane know I killed him? Does Xander suspect it? He must, he wouldn't have said anything, otherwise.

"You've been awfully quiet, Dove," Damon says. Speaking for the first time, a hint of amusement in his voice now. He looks identical to Xander but maybe a bit younger, and just a tiny bit less scarry.

"I... I killed Alberto," I blurt out. All eyes fall on me. Xander and Damon seem prideful, while Zane is shocked, his mouth hanging open.

"You killed him?" I watch his Adam's apple bob as he swallows.

Something in my chest swells. "Yes. I found him in my room during the engagement party, he wanted sex, I didn't. So, I slit his throat before stealing his car keys and making my escape to the apartment. I waited a little while, stole his keys, and escaped and went to my apartment." A tinge of guilt echoes through me. "I'm sorry, I didn't tell you. You never asked, and well, we never got the chance to talk about it."

"See, she's not as weak as she seems." Xander pins Zane with a glare, crossing his arms over his chest. "In fact, she's more of a Rossi than I expected her to be."

For some stupid reason, I smile.

"That doesn't mean she is going to run headfirst into danger right after I get her out of the crossfires," Zane yells. "You are not forcing her into this like Matteo did."

Xander's gaze turns murderous, and his hands curl into tight fists on the table. "Don't compare me to him," he says in a tone that has the small hairs on my neck standing on end. "I already told you, it's her choice." He turns to me. "If you want to leave, you are more than welcome to walk away right now. I won't hold it against you, and if you ever need anything, I will be here for you. I am simply giving you the opportunity to help."

"I'll help; however, I can. If you need me to do something, I will. I'm not afraid."

"The hell you will." Zane slams his fist down on the table, making the glasses jump.

"If she wants to help, then she can. We wouldn't let anything happen to her. I get your concern, but she escaped without you, she can handle this." Damon says this time, and I know even without looking at Zane that he's pissed, a vibrating wall of rage. I understand his fear, his anger, but I don't want to be seen as a delicate little flower. I saved myself once, and I'll do it again, except this time, I'll have an army of men beside me.

"What's the plan?" Ivan questions his eyes on Xander.

Xander rubs at his chin. "We use Dove to draw him out. Make him think that she's coming back to him, or better yet, put her out in the open. Make him think that she's unprotected. Then before he gets her, we end him."

"Basically, we just fool him," Ivan says.

"Basically," Damon replies. "It's really simple and safe, and nothing will happen to Dove. She is family, our sister. That fucker won't get his hands on her again." Damon's words are directed at Zane, who is still silently sulking beside me.

"When are we going to do this?" I ask.

"Tomorrow. That'll give us time to come up with a detailed plan. I have a few men tailing him now. We'll place Dove somewhere he can find her and pull her out before anything happens." Xander smiles and slaps a hand on the table. Ivan grunts, Damon nods, and Zane grabs my hand and pushes away from the table.

He practically drags me back up to our room. The door slams shut behind us, and Zane twists around and punches the heavy wood.

"What the fuck happened to you wanting a normal life? He gave you a way out! All you had to do was tell him, no, and we could be on our fucking way out of here. We could leave this all behind us. Ride off into the sunset, happy and together." Pausing for a moment, he shakes his head before muttering, "What were you thinking?"

Anger surges through me, but there is also understanding. I get why he's upset. He just got me back, and now I'm putting myself in harm's way again, but I can't let Matteo slip through our fingers.

"I was thinking that I'm tired of feeling weak and helpless. I want to take Matteo down. He hurt you, hurt us, and I want to make him pay for that." My words stun him into silence, and then I see the anger drain from his body. He sighs deeply, almost as if he is defeated by my response. Then he's on me, his lips pressing against mine, his hands in my hair. He's kissing me like he hates me, like he loves me. Like I'm his reason to live.

Then in an instant, he's pulling away, his forehead comes to rest against mine, and he peers deeply into my eyes. This moment is so intimate, so precious, I almost hold my breath.

"I almost lost you once. The thought of losing you again..." Zane's hot breath fans against my face. "I don't want to risk it. If he were to get to you. If he did hurt you..." The fear in his eyes ripples through me. I can feel it, taste it. It's real, beyond real, and it makes my knees buckle. Zane afraid is terrifying.

"Nothing... nothing is going to happen to me. I trust Xander, and Damon. I trust Ivan, but above all, I trust you. I trust that you won't let anything happen."

"I can't... I can't be sure, and that kills me. It rips me apart. If you die... When Christian shoved you down the stairs..." He exhales. "You don't understand... if you die... I die. There is no me without you."

Snaking my arms around his neck, I tug him closer. "There is no me without you, Zane, and tomorrow we will get Matteo and be free of this cage. We will be free to do whatever we want. I have you to protect me, and you've never let me down."

The look in Zane's eyes tells me he doesn't believe me, but that's okay... I believe, and that's all that matters.

"I'm afraid, so fucking scared, Dove."

"Don't be. I'm not going anywhere."

48

"I don't like this," I growl into the room as I walk back and forth along the wall. We're all staying away from the window as a precaution. We snuck into the building early this morning before the first filters of sunlight showed in the sky. Our hopes were that no one would suspect us being here. Matteo needs to assume that Dove is here alone.

"So you mentioned," Xander says, his voice laced with annoyance. "She's going to be fine. Ivan is shadowing her. She'll be here any minute."

"She better be. If that door doesn't open in the next ten minutes, I'm leaving..." I barely get the words out when the sound of a key being inserted in the lock fills the room. The doorknob turns, and the door swings open.

I suck in a ragged breath of relief when I see Dove stepping into her apartment. She's beaming, a megawatt smile on her face. "I told you I would be fine."

"This isn't over yet, Dove. You making it here was only half the battle. You are not safe yet," I grumble before pulling her into my arms. She buries her face in the crook of my neck, inhaling while wrapping her slender arms around my waist.

"Just stop worrying," she mumbles.

"I'll stop worrying when Matteo is dead." And that's the truth. As soon as I see the life drain from Matteo's eyes, I'll be free of the fear that strangles my heart when it comes to Dove.

"Now we wait," Damon says as he sinks down onto Dove's couch. I get the feeling he's the most impatient of the two brothers.

We get comfortable on the love seat while Xander sits next to his brother. For a while, we just sit there in an uncomfortable silence. Dove cuddles into my side and plays with the hem of my shirt, either because she is nervous or bored. Honestly, I don't know which one it is, and I don't really care. I just want Matteo to get here so we can end the fucker's life, and I can take Dove back to Xander's.

"Is there any food in this place?" Damon groans as he stretches.

"Can't go five minutes without eating?" Xander scoffs, and Damon scowls at him. For a minute, I'm taken aback by how normal these two seem. Apart from the expensive suits they are wearing, they act like nothing more than two bickering brothers. For the first time, I could actually imagine Dove being their family.

I let that thought run through my head, testing out different scenarios. I've spent the last few days with Xander, and I have to admit, he is not what I expected. He is feared by the other families for being ruthless, and I have no doubt that he is when he has to be, but within his inner circle, he is different than both Christian and Matteo. He treats his family, including the women, with respect, which is unheard of in our world.

"Fine, I'll starve to death, I guess," Damon grumbles, and Dove starts giggling.

"I can find something for you to eat," she says and starts to get up.

"Don't fall for his whining," Xander quips. "He is just being a drama queen. Sit," he orders. "I'd rather you tell us more about you. Like how you grew up, for example."

Dove falls back into the cushion and sighs deeply. I know she doesn't want to talk about that time of her life since it was shitty before she was adopted by Donna.

"I didn't have much of a childhood," say says, shrugging. "I was bounced from one foster home to the next. None of which were great, but I guess it could have been worse. Then Zane and I got put in the same home. That's how we met. The guy hurt him, beat him up badly, and then he tried to hurt me... but Zane wouldn't let it happen." She pauses and looks up at me, her eyes filled with tears, adoration, and love.

"After that, Donna adopted me, and she was great. She showed me what a loving home felt like. We didn't have much money, but it was enough. I definitely didn't grow up like you in a mansion..." I don't think she meant it in a condescending way, but maybe she is just a tad jealous.

"Believe me, Dove. You didn't miss anything growing up at our *mansion*," Xander says, emphasizing the last word.

"I'm sorry, I didn't mean it like that."

"It's fine. I just don't want you to think you would've had a better life growing up with us because I can assure you that you wouldn't have. Our father was a sadistic prick, and our mother was a helpless victim who couldn't protect herself or her children. Leaving with you, even though you weren't given much of a life, was the kindest thing she could've done." The corners of his mouth tug up into a ghost of a smile. And even though it is a tiny gesture, it's genuine, and I believe him.

"You're right. I wouldn't be half the person I am today if it weren't for my upbringing. Still, it would have been nice growing up with brothers."

Both Damon and Xander look away, their faces fall almost as if they are ashamed of something. I don't understand their expressions until Xander opens his mouth to explain.

"I'm going to be honest with you, Dove. Until I found Ella, I wasn't much different from our father." He sucks in a ragged breath. "There's a reason the other families fear me. I've always had a reputation of being cruel and ruthless, and that reputation was earned in ways I'm not proud of. There is blood on my hands, lots of it, and though the blood can be washed away, I'll never forget the things that I've done." Regret clings to each word he says, and I understand what he's feeling, the emotions rolling through him. It's because of Dove that I didn't fall off the edge, that I didn't let go completely.

"I'm sure you just did what you had to—"

"No!" Xander cuts her off. "Don't try to sugarcoat it. I hurt and killed people for fun. I wasn't any better than him. Even Damon didn't talk to me for years. Trust me, you can be glad we didn't meet until now. You wouldn't have liked the brother you discovered then."

Of course, I heard the rumors about Xander Rossi, I just didn't realize how much truth they held or how much he had changed.

"I'm still glad I found you," Dove exclaims. "Well, I guess you found me."

"We're glad we found you too. Family is everything to us," Damon interjects. "And now you're part of it."

"I'm not gonna lie, I was scared of you guys, since you know... you basically kidnapped and held me prisoner. Honestly, I still don't know how I feel about everything. I don't know much about you yet, but I hope, maybe we can get to know each other. If you really do want me to be part of your family."

"We do, and you already are part of the family," Damon points out.

Family. The word resonates within me. I never considered having a family with Dove, my obsession with her has always been enough for me. I'm not sure I could ever share her, even with a child of our own, but I know someday, Dove will want kids, and all that matters to me is making her happy. Seeing her smile and laugh.

I want to replace all the bad in her life with good because she deserves it. The day I met her, the kindness she showed me without even knowing who I was or how I got my injuries. It speaks volumes about the person she is. She's an angel, sent from heaven to rescue me.

Xander's phone buzzes, interrupting the moment. "We've got movement outside, two SUV's, blacked out," he says, reading from the screen, then shoves off the chair. His eyes darkening as he adjusts his suit. "It's showtime, boys."

I nod and unglue myself from Dove. I place my hand in hers and pull her to a standing position. I'm nervous as hell about this, but I know Dove can handle it. She's strong, and plus, I'm only a few feet away. Matteo won't even have a chance to touch her.

"I love you," she whispers, wrapping her arms around my middle, "everything is going to be fine. This ends today." When she pulls away, I feel like I'm letting go of a piece of my heart.

Everything is going to be okay... I tell myself as I move into place. Xander and Damon take their spots closest to the door, and I hide in the kitchen. Dove remains standing in the center of the living room. She gives me a reassuring smile, but I won't trust that she's okay until Matteo is dead at my feet.

Silence blankets the room. I pull my gun, preparing to shoot if needs be. The plan is for Dove to lure Matteo into the living room. We'll deal with his men, but the person we want most is him. My heart beats into my throat. There's a knock at the door. Loud and booming.

My gaze flashes between the door and Dove.

God, please... I've never prayed for everything to go right in my life, but I'm praying to whatever god there is above right now that this goes just as planned.

Dove walks to the door, places her hand on the brass knob, but doesn't turn yet. "Who is it?" she asks.

"It's your father. Open up. We need to talk," he demands, his gruff voice filters through the thick wood. "Open up before I kick the door in."

"Are you here to hurt me?"

"*Hurt you?* I've never been prouder. You killed one of my most feared men, escaped my men as well as Christian's. You impressed me, Dove. You are truly my daughter. Now, open up so we can talk about your future like civilized people."

I know he is full of shit, but that's all part of the plan. Dove turns the doorknob and pulls the door open. She backs up into the room, and Matteo steps in, gun in hand.

"You stupid fucking bitch," he growls, pointing his gun at her chest.

Everything happens so fast. I lunge at Dove while Xander and Damon lunge at Matteo, taking him by surprise. A gun goes off, the deafening sound echoes through the small apartment, and my heart comes to a dead standstill.

The next moment, my body crashes into Dove's much smaller one. I tackle her down to the ground, protecting her with my body and hoping that she wasn't hit. Another gunshot goes off, and my ears ring from the sound.

I tilt my head to look at Xander and Damon to find them pushing off the ground while Matteo's body remains motionless on the floor.

"Is she okay?" Xander asks. I shift my weight off Dove to get a look at her. She turns her head and opens her eyes, glancing around with a franticness that matches my own.

"I'm okay. Is he...?"

"Yes, he is dead," Damon confirms. "We need to get out of here before more of his men show up. We just declared war with another family."

"And I'd do it again to protect my family." Xander smiles. I look down at Matteo's lifeless body. It's not how I wanted him to die, but at least he's dead. I wanted to draw things out, make him feel every ounce of pain he made me feel.

"You okay?" Dove's voice pulls me out of the rabbit hole I'm headed down.

"I'm fine. Just glad he's gone."

"Me too," she whispers. I walk us out of her apartment, thankful that the only person that died today was the person who we intended to kill.

49

*A*fter dinner, we retreat upstairs to our room. Zane is quiet, as am I. Once we're alone, the door, closed and locked behind us, he's on me. His lips find mine in a punishing kiss, it's teeth and biting, and his fingers sink into my hair, tugging, needing me closer, needing to become one with me. I fist his T-shirt in my hands, feeling the same intense heat forming between our bodies. There are too many pieces of fabric between us.

We're both panting, our chests rising and falling rapidly. I know he's not done with me yet, not by a long shot. Pulling away, I stare deeply into a pair of brown eyes that are my world. I wish I knew what he was thinking.

Loving Zane is like watching your heart beat outside your body. It's dangerous, consuming, and frightening. It's knowing that at any moment, the one thing you hold dearest could be taken from you. I've endured so much; we've endured so much.

"I need you, Dove. Naked, on your back with your beautiful legs spread wide, showing me that pretty pussy." Each word drips with desire and has my insides turning to mush while sending a zing of red-hot heat down my spine.

When it comes to sex, I'll never tire of listening to him tell me what to do. It turns me on more to be ordered around, to be at his mercy. Following his orders, I tug off my clothes as fast as I can while also trying to look sexy as I do it. Which is harder than it looks.

As soon as I'm naked, I crawl onto the bed, arching my back to give him a view of my pink slit. A deep groan fills the room, and I smile, knowing how much he too wants this.

Rolling over, I lie down on my back against the mattress and let my legs fall apart, spreading them wide, just as he asked. Zane takes his time taking his clothes off, and I enjoy every minute of it. There's something different about this moment, something special. I feel free as if there isn't any weight or fear resting on my shoulders.

My thoughts take a nosedive and become lustful when Zane's cock comes into view. I bite my lip, muffling a moan as I stare at the hard rod in all its glory. It's thick with veins wrapped all around it. He strokes himself a couple of times, and I salivate at the pre-come that beads the tip.

"You want my cock?" Zane asks, crawling up onto the bed. Parting my lips, I go to answer him, but he leans into me and nips at my bottom lip, making me groan. "Is that a yes?" He smiles against my mouth, and I kind of want to punch him, but kind of want to kiss him.

"I don't want it. I *need* it." I emphasize the need because it really does feel like a need. My core is throbbing, pulsing with a heat that I know only Zane can satiate. I'm wet enough that he could fuck me right now, but the dark look in his eyes tells me I'm in for anything but a quick pounding. No, he's going to savior me, drink me like a fine wine, devour me from the inside out. Pulling back, he stares down at me.

"It's time for me to worship your body the way a queen's body should be worshiped."

I plan to ask him in what way he's going to do that, but the words stick to the roof of my mouth when he drops to his stomach between my legs and grips me by the ass, bringing my pussy to his face. Hot breath fans against my center, and I push up onto my elbows, hungry for a view of this man feasting on me.

Which doesn't last long when he starts licking my clit like it's an ice cream cone. I slide my fingers through his hair, tugging at the soft strands, urging him forward. Each hard lick is a step toward an orgasm.

I can feel myself getting closer and closer, and just when I'm sure he's going to let me fall into the abyss, he pulls away and enters me with two fingers.

Clamping down on him, I lift my hips and bite my lip, holding back the whimper of pleasure that threatens to escape. Sweat beads against my forehead, strands of hair sticking to my face. My chest heaves and my nipples harden.

I need this. I need him.

"Don't be shy... tell me how it feels... tell me what you need, baby," Zane rasps against my folds, his own desire clear in his voice.

"You... I want you." I gasp as he curves his fingers upward, almost as if he is dragging the orgasm right out of me.

"Fuck, Dove, come on my face. Let me taste you, squeeze my fingers..." He goes from licking to sucking my clit hard, and I explode, igniting into a raging inferno of pleasure. Tilting my head back into the pillows, I whimper beneath his touch, my thighs trembling, my heart racing.

My core clenches as if it has its own heartbeat, and my release gushes out and onto his face. I should be embarrassed at how fast I came apart, but I become melted chocolate in this man's hands. Eyes wide open, I stare up at the ceiling.

I haven't even come down from my high yet, and he's withdrawing his fingers. Whimpering, I want to tell him to come back, to do it all over again, but he moves to the spot beside me, resting against the headboard.

"Come here. I want you to ride me," Zane orders gruffly.

Slowly, I get my jellied body to move. As I sit up, I reach for the thick cock between his legs and lean forward, sucking the mushroom-shaped crown between my lips.

Instantly, Zane's fingers sink into my hair, tugging at the strands harshly. Each tug sends a jolt of pleasure straight to my core.

"Fucking, fuck..."

I look up at him, his cock in my mouth, and I see how vulnerable, how bare, he looks. This is Zane, the dark, psychotic criminal that would slaughter, destroy, and rip the world apart for me, and he is all mine. I'll never give him up. *Never.*

Releasing his cock, I toss a leg over his hip and straddle him. My hands move to his shoulders to steady myself while his hands move to my hips, holding me in place. My slickness slides over his hard abs, and I lift myself, guiding the head of his cock to my entrance.

Our gazes collide and stay that way as I sink down on his length, impaling myself. I can feel him deep, so deep. Feel us becoming one single eternity.

The air sizzles as our bodies come together, and our breaths mingle as we both pause, relishing in the tremors of pleasure that wrack our bodies.

"I love you," I say, sighing as I start to move up and down at a torturous pace.

"I love you more," Zane groans, and his head tips back against the headboard. He watches me through hooded eyes, his fingers digging into my hips, not guiding, but anchoring me. I love the way he's looking at me right now, like I'm his heaven, the moon, and the stars in the sky. Like I'm his everything.

"Fuck, I've never seen anything so beautiful..."

"Me either," I say, letting out a gasp as his hips flex up and the head of his cock brushes against my g-spot. I'm full, so full. I can't tell where he starts and where I end. Grinding against him, I move back and forth like a wave against the beach.

Releasing my hips, his hands roam my body, mapping out each inch of flesh, touching parts of my soul. We're frenzied, gasoline and fire, lightning and thunder, and we'll burn the world around us to the ground.

"I'm close," I whimper, tipping my head back, placing my hands against his firm chest as I ride him. He lets me take from him until I shatter like glass into a million pieces, and then he rolls us, taking from me, fucking me like an animal in heat.

Each stroke is raw and steals my breath a little more than the last. By the time Zane comes, we're both sticky with sweat, our breaths ragged, and our hearts thundering in our chests. Zane rolls off of me and pulls me into his side, our combined scents fill my nostrils while the warmth of his body seeps into mine.

I never want to leave this bed.

"There is no me without you. There is only us," Zane whispers into my hair.

"Us. Forever. For always," I croak and let my heavy eyes fall closed, knowing that tomorrow we have nothing to fear. There is no one to hide from, no one to watch for. There is only the future, and it looks a whole lot brighter now.

EPILOGUE

Family becomes everything when you've never had it before. A year ago, I was all alone, living on my own, with only one person who I thought cared about me. Lonely didn't even begin to cover what I felt. One year later, and I've got a whole new family. Xander and Damon have taken me in as if years didn't separate us. They have families of their own, and I cannot wait to share mine and Zane's happy news with them.

Zane and I got married in a tiny little ceremony three months ago. Xander walked me down the aisle and gave me away while my nieces threw rose petals along the way.

Being married isn't much different to dating. Zane is still as possessive as ever, not letting me out of his sight unless he absolutely has to.

Tonight we're doing our weekly Sunday dinner. Xander and Ella, Damon and Keira, and Ivan and Violet are here tonight.

Since getting to know my brothers, I've heard their stories of how they came to know their wives. I've also met their children and been told countless stories about how ruthless a father we shared.

They also shared some memories of our mother, the few nice ones they had anyway. I've come to terms with the fact that my mother was doing what she thought was best, that she did love me, but that she couldn't handle a life on the run. It seems her life was ruined long before I came along, and even though she tried to run from it, in the end, she just couldn't get away from her own demons.

Quinton rushes through the dining room, his baby sister hot on his heels, their squeals of joy cut through my thoughts. Xander reaches down and takes his daughter, Gia, into his arms.

She whines and pushes against him, trying to get away and to her brother, but he squeezes her a little tighter and peppers her adorable face with kisses before releasing her again. I can't believe that's going to be Zane and me soon.

"How is married life? I feel like I haven't seen you guys in ages," Violets asks, giving me a wink as she bounces her daughter on her knee.

"Yeah, I know. Zane has basically tied me to the bed," I joke, well half-joke, since what I've said is partially true. Every night before bed, we make love. Sometimes it's sweet, and other times, it's raw and consuming. There is nothing in this world like the love he gives and shows me.

"I mean, it's not like you're lying." Zane smirks and tugs me closer to him.

"Men." Violet shakes her head. "I swear, they can never get enough. I told Ivan I need at least two years without getting pregnant again."

I look over at Ivan, who is smiling like a fool. His love for Violet and his kids is profound. It's crazy to think that she was once his prisoner. Then again, looking back on mine and Zane's love story, we kind of came from the same thing.

"Doubt Ivan is going to let that happen," Damon says, chuckling.

"Yeah, me too." Violet rolls her eyes.

"When are you and Zane going to have a baby?" Keira, Damon's wife asks, taking a sip of her wine. Her question makes my cheeks flame, and suddenly, I feel everyone's eyes on me.

"Well, we actually had news to share with you all."

"Oh, my gosh, yes!" Ella basically jumps out of her chair. "You're pregnant, aren't you?"

I nod, unable to contain the smile that appears on my lips. "It's still early, but there is definitely a little peanut in there."

"Yes, mine," Zane growls into my ear, his teeth nipping my lobe in a possessive way. I swear, since discovering we're having a baby, he's become even more possessive and controlling.

He's currently working for Xander as a hitman. After we killed Matteo, we took over most of his territory. Xander asked me if I wanted to be in charge of it, but truthfully, I didn't have any idea what I was doing, so I told him he could run it.

"I'm happy for you, Sister," Xander exclaims, his eyes twinkling with joy. "We're building an empire of little Rossi's."

"We sure are." Ella giggles, looking up at her husband.

"What's that supposed to mean?" Violet narrows her gaze at her sister as if she can read her thoughts. Ella bites her bottom lip and looks like she's going to explode with happiness.

"Well, we would never want to ruin this moment for Dove and Zane because we're so very happy for you, but Xander and I are expecting again as well."

"I'm so happy for you two!" I say, taking a sip of my orange juice. I'm beyond happy. I feel safe, secure, and protected, but above all, I feel loved. I feel as if I've finally found my home.

Xander snickers. "There is nothing quite as delicious looking as my wife's belly, swollen with our child." Ella's face turns red as a tomato, and she shakes her head, dismissing his teasing.

Xander's phone starts ringing, and he curses when he looks at the name on the screen before hitting the green answer key.

"What can I do for you, Luke?" he barks into the phone.

All the men around the table sit up a little straighter, waiting for an order most likely. Luke says something, and Xander starts shaking his head.

"Okay, make sure you have someone on her at all times. We don't need any issues with the police, and I don't want to have to kill someone so young. Report back to me in a week and let me know how things go. If she talks before then, bring her in."

Luke says something else, and then Xander hangs up the phone. I'm tempted to ask what is going on but keep my lips pressed firmly together. It sounds like someone saw something they shouldn't have.

"That didn't sound good," Damon says.

"It wasn't good, but if anyone can keep people in line, it's Luke. Everything will be fine. I'm sure of it," he assures Damon, and dinner carries on. After we eat and say our goodbyes, Zane and I head back to our little cottage that's just outside the Rossi estate.

We walk into the house, and Zane reaches for me, tugging me into his arms. I crash into his chest, giggling. Max greets us at the door, curling his body around and between our legs.

While I was Christian's prisoner, Zane picked him up and brought him to the shelter I used to work at. They kept him for me, while we were dealing with all of this. I picked him up as soon as I could. Max purrs, but I'm too consumed by my husband to give the cat any attention right now.

Since he started working for Xander, his muscles seem even more firm, his abs more defined, and because my sex drive is through the roof, I find myself tracing those abs every night. Also, grinding against them.

"I never thought we would be here. Married and having children. My plan was always to let you live your life, to let you be happy. Never in my wildest dreams did I expect to be the man you'd choose to spend your life with."

I roll my eyes. "As if you would've let me pick anyone else."

He gives me a boyish grin. "Touché. Though truthfully, I would've eventually had to let you go. I knew someday you'd find someone."

"Yeah, that someone was you," I snort.

Zane's face turns serious, but I can feel the bulge of his cock in his jeans, pressing against my front, begging to be unleashed.

"I'm being serious here." He cups me by the cheeks. "I can't believe you're mine. My wife, and soon to be the mother of our child."

"Well, believe it. I'm yours today, tomorrow, and forever. Even back at the bunker, I knew that I wanted you. I was afraid to admit it, but I think I loved you then."

"Could've fooled me, unless love is shown by hitting someone in the head with a weight." I slap him playfully on the chest, loving that we can be so carefree now that there isn't anything to fear.

"It's the only way I could think of to escape."

Grinding his groin into my center, my thoughts swirl, turning from playful to lustful in an instant. I'm ready to climb him like a tree.

"You didn't escape then, and you won't now. You're my obsession, my heart, and my reason to breathe." His lips find mine, and I swear the world falls away. There is only him and me, the darkness of our past, a distant memory.

Sometimes the love your life is right in front of you.

Other times, he's hiding right outside your window, watching you sleep.

~

Thank you *for reading the Obsession Duet!!!*

Check out our MUST READ New Release Savage Beginnings and keep reading for a sneak peek.

YOU DON'T WANT TO MISS THIS!

And if you are curious about Xander, Damon, Ivan, and Roman, you can read their stories in the
Rossi Crime Family Series!

SAVAGE BEGINNINGS SNEAK PEEK

CHAPTER ONE
Elena

Slipping into my nightgown, I sit down on the edge of the bed and finish drying my dark hair while humming some pop song I heard on the radio earlier.

I've asked my father numerous times for a cell phone or laptop, but he swears it's for my own protection that I have neither, so the radio is all I've got. Dropping the towel, a shiver skates down my spine when my long wet hair brushes over my shoulder.

Bending down, I reach for the towel. Before my fingers even touch it, a deafening knock booms through the room. It's so loud and unexpected that a tiny shriek passes my lips.

Who the hell is that?

I glance at the clock on the wall and realize it's after eleven. My father never calls for me this late, and besides him, who could it be? No one, that's who. Since my mom's death two years ago, my dad is the only person I have left. I have no other family and no friends, thanks to my father's overbearing nature.

I wasn't even allowed to go to school because he deemed it too *dangerous* for his little girl. Everything I've ever learned was taught to me through homeschooling. Covering my chest with one arm, I open the door and find Richi, one of my father's personal guards, on the other side.

"Miss Elena, your father wants to see you in his study." There is a strange look on his face, a mixture of fear and remorse. He's never looked at me in such a way. Seeing how uncomfortable he appears to be makes me suspicious.

"Now?" I ask, still a little shocked, given the time. "Is something wrong?"

"Just come with me, please."

Oh no, something is wrong. I can already feel it, something is definitely going on.

"Okay, let me get dressed real quick."

"I'm afraid there is no time for that," a deep, penetrating voice comes from behind the door, filling my ears. Opening the door a little wider so I can see who that voice belongs to, I almost gasp. There's a man in a suit, a man I've never seen before, standing beside Richi.

In the dim light, it's hard to make out the man, but from what I can see, he looks down-right sinister. His gaze pierces mine, and his lips press into a thin line, impatience rolling off of him in waves.

Now I'm really worried, why is a man I've never seen or met before inside our estate, much less outside my bedroom door.

"What's going on?" I try to hide the panic from my voice, but even I can hear how nervous I am.

"Just come downstairs, Miss, enough with the questions," the unknown man orders, and I know there is no sense in arguing. When you're told to do something, you do it, that's what my father always said. If my father has asked for me, then surely this is safe.

Crossing my arms over my chest, I step out into the hallway and grit my teeth at the cold that kisses my bare feet. Goosebumps spread out across my skin as I walk between the two men, wearing nothing but some panties and a thin nightgown. I really wish they would have let me put some clothes on. This is no way to greet my father or any visitors.

The walk to my father's study seems to drag on, but when we reach the heavy wooden door, it doesn't feel long enough. I don't know what's going on yet, but I do know it's not good, and I'm not ready for it. My gut tightens with the unknown. I've had enough heartache in the last few years to last me a lifetime.

Looking up at the door, I don't bother knocking, knowing that my father is expecting me. Reaching for the knob, I pause for one more second, mentally preparing for whatever awaits me on the other side. I'm not sure why, but I glance back at Richi and the unknown guy. Both look at me with blank expressions, which is nothing new to me. My father's men are all trained to look at me like that. No emotions. Feelings get you killed.

Sucking in one last breath, I push the door open and take a step inside.

As soon as I catch a glimpse of what's beyond the door, I want to retreat from the room. It's a reflex, really.

Since I was a little girl, my father had trained me, told me to never listen to him, and his associates talk. To never listen to anything regarding his business. So, when I see him and three men in his office, I have this deep primal instinct to go in the opposite direction.

I shouldn't be here. I can't be here. My fingers tremble against the brass doorknob.

"Elena, come in," my father says, his tone clipped.

He is all business at this point, and even as badly as I would like to run from the room and seek shelter in my bedroom, I know better than to disobey my father, especially in front of his associates.

On shaky legs, I walk further into the office, my arms still tightly wrapped around my chest as if I'm giving myself a hug.

"Take a seat, we have some matters to discuss," he explains without looking at me. I hate how emotionless he sounds and looks, even more so than usual.

Two men I don't know are standing off to the side while a third man is sitting at the desk opposite my father. All I can see is his back from the position I'm standing in, his broad shoulders and thick arms rest against the arm of the chair as he casually leans backward.

Averting my gaze, I keep my eyes trained ahead until I'm at his desk, then I sit down in the free chair, hating how my short nightgown rides up my thighs, exposing even more of my skin. I feel naked and wish now more than ever that I had fought harder to change my clothes.

"Elena, do you remember Mr. Moretti?" My father motions to the man beside me. "Julian Moretti."

Moretti? The name sounds familiar, but I can't pinpoint it right away.

As I glance over to the man in question, my heart thunders in my chest, trying to put a face to the name. Immediately, our eyes lock, his icy blue stare penetrates me like a sharp dagger... just as they did the first time we met.

I remember it well, and I know the exact date because the first time I met this man was at my mother's funeral.

Just as most men I know, he too wears a mask of indifference. His eyes are blank, a carefully constructed wall placed around him, refusing to let anyone see the man beneath.

"You were at my mother's funeral." I simply state.

"Yes."

His voice is deep and smooth, not matching the rest of him. Everything else about him seems rough and jagged. His jaw sharp, his cheekbones angular, and his lips pressed firmly into a tight line. He's handsome in a devilish way, he could even be a model I'm sure. I can tell that he's older than me as he has this air of maturity about him, but I'm not sure how old since he has no fine lines around his eyes, only a permanent scowl between them.

I wonder if this man has smiled a day in his life.

"Elena." My father draws my attention back to him. "I need you to sign right here."

He pushes a piece of paper across the mahogany desk and passes me a pen.

"What is this?" I look down at the document but can't make out any of the words.

"Just sign it," my father orders, his tone harsh. Cruelty isn't something my father has ever shown me, and I can see he's struggling even right now with how to act. He's never been a great father, but that's because of his absence and overbearing nature, not because he is unkind to me. Whatever this is about is weighing heavily on him.

Dragging the paper closer to myself, I grip the pen between my clammy fingers and start to sign my name at the bottom. The room is silent, and I can hear the pen gliding across the paper. I'm not even halfway through signing my name when my hand freezes. My eyes dart from the document before me and up to my father, then back again.

That can't be right.

With the ink pen hovering over the paper, I reread the first few lines of the document.

Ownership Contract

This agreement confirms that as of today, Elena Romero will belong fully and without further stipulation to Julian Moretti in exchange for ten million dollars...

"What is this?" I question with fervor, dropping the pen as I pull back from the desk.

A knife twists in my chest, the edge digging deeper with every breath I take.

This can't be what I think it is.

"Don't question me. Just sign the damn document," my father growls, slamming his fist down on the desk, and for the first time, he looks up at me. The coldness that reflects back at me makes me shiver. I've never seen him like this, and I don't understand why he's selling me to this man. Julian Moretti.

"I..." My bottom lip trembles and I bite it to stop it. "You can't do this... You can't *sell* me. I'm not signing this." Tears blur my eyes at the betrayal that consumes me. I want to scream, to fight this with all my might, but I feel helpless. There isn't a single person in this room that will help me.

The words have barely passed my lips when Moretti leans over and grabs my hand, engulfing his much larger one with my small one. Heat encompasses my hand, and it's like being burned by fire. I try to pull away, but he only tightens his grip as he forces the pen between my fingers and my hand back to the paper.

"Please... don't do this. You don't want me." I try and tug my hand away with all my might, my hand throbbing as he tightens his grip.

"But I do, Elena." He speaks into the shell of my ear.

With bruising force, he presses the pen to the paper and guides my hand, forcing me to write the rest of my name. A sob breaks free from my lips, and big fat tears of weakness fall from my eyes. The man who now owns me smiles like the devil and releases my hand with ease, placing it down against the paper.

"Father... please?" I pull my hand from the document and press it to my chest.

"The contract is complete," my father says on a sigh, leaning back in his chair. "She is now yours, do with her as you please."

That statement has me blinking back tears.

"Please, don't do this," I whimper, looking up at my father, pleading with him.

How could he just sign me away to someone I don't even know? Sell me for money? It's like I don't even know him. Like he's not my father at all.

"It's business, sweetie, don't take it personal." He shrugs and looks away from me, giving Moretti a get out of here gesture.

My mouth pops open, and I'm shocked, completely shocked. Where is my loving, caring father? The man who taught me how to ride a bike, the man who used to read me stories at bedtime, who held me when my mother died? He wasn't always the perfect father, but I never expected him to do this.

"You can't do this!" I hiss pushing up from my chair while slamming my fists down on his desk, but it does nothing but cause my hand to throb with pain.

He doesn't see me, doesn't care.

"Don't worry, Romero. I'll take good care of her... I mean... I'll break her in gently," Julian says darkly to my father. It's like looking at a shark and expecting it not to bite you. The only difference is this man isn't just going to bite me, he's going to devour me, slowly, piece by piece.

Julian stands, smoothing his hands down his suit. My heart skips a beat, and my eyes dart over my shoulder. I want to bolt for the door, but know I won't make it. Before I can devise an escape plan, his strong arm is circling my waist. He tugs me back against his hard chest and guides me toward the door.

I whimper like a wounded animal knowing the worst is yet to come. I've been sold to the devil, my body, mind, and life bound by an unbreakable contract.

~

CHAPTER TWO
Julian

Wrapping one thick arm around her waist, I pull her from her father's office, ignoring her tears and small whimpers. There will be many more in the following days.

"You don't want me..."

Her words ring in my ear. Oh, how wrong she is. I more than want her... in fact, I've wanted her for a very long time. *Years.* And now, I finally have her and her father exactly where I want them. I've been watching, waiting, planning to take Romero down for the last five years. The moment he killed my mother, taking from me the one and only person who ever mattered, I've been plotting his downfall.

It wasn't until Lilian Romero's funeral that I knew exactly how I was going to get my revenge. Romero fell off the wagon after his wife's death, his gambling problem multiplying into the millions. He thought he had time to pay his debts, he was comfortable and being comfortable left you vulnerable.

He didn't have shit now—nothing but her.

Now, I finally have her, my prize. My Elena. A dark raven-haired beauty that would soon become my wife. As if she can hear me thinking her name, she shoves at my arm, her nails sinking into the flesh as she struggles to get away from me.

Oh, Elena, there is no getting away now.

Releasing her for a fraction of a second, I grab her by the waist and lift her up, tossing her over my shoulder with ease. The nightgown she's wearing rides up with the movement, giving me a side view of her perfectly shaped ass and a glimpse of her satin panties that hide her virgin pussy. *That too will soon be mine.*

Markus, my second in command and the closest thing I have to a friend, walks ahead of me while Lucca, one of my best and most brutal enforcers, covers my back. We can't be too careful in this place. I did just steal Romero's daughter, after all. And a contract won't matter if I'm dead.

I carry her all the way out to the car while she spends the entire time pounding her little fists against my back. She doesn't actually think she has a chance of escaping me, does she?

When we reach the sleek black SUV, Marcus opens the door. Turning around, his eyes fall on Elena, who is still struggling like a cat on my shoulder, her ass cheeks jiggling beside my face. Rage fills my veins, and I forget for a moment that Markus is my ally.

"Look at her again, and I'll gouge your fucking eyes out."

Most men cower in fear when I make a threat like that because everyone knows that when I make a threat, it's not just a threat, it's a promise. Markus is not most men, though, he takes in my words and gives me a respectful nod. If I didn't know him better, I could have sworn his lips twitched up into a smile.

Fucker.

I put her down on her feet but grab her arm before she can make a run for it. Her feistiness only makes me want her more. She covers her chest with her free arm, trying to hide her tits covered only by the thin material. She's beautifully naive, and the fact that she's even trying to maintain an ounce of modesty in this situation proves that.

I give her a quick once over. Her soft shapely legs that I picture wrapped around my waist are on full display, her small body shaking like a leaf either from cold or fear... maybe both. She's short, shorter than I remember her being, and fragile, so very breakable. My gaze moves over her delicate throat, which bobs as she swallows.

Her heart-shaped face is red, and her green eyes are puffy from crying. That raven hair of hers is a tangled damp mess. Still, she is the most beautiful woman I've ever seen. Beautiful and all-fucking-mine.

"Get in," I order.

She merely shakes her head. I stare down at her, knowing full well

I'll never be able to hurt her like I've hurt others who disobey me, she is the only person who will ever have my mercy. Though there are other ways of disciplining her.

Pinching her chin gently between two fingers, I force her not only to hear the words I'm saying but also for her to see me speak them.

"Do it, or I do it for you, and believe me, you don't want me to do it."

Her emerald eyes widen with fear, and she must be able to hear the threat in my voice because her body starts shaking furiously. Pulling away, she reluctantly climbs into the car, sliding across the backseat, going to the spot furthest away. There is ample room between us, and I decide to let her have this small space, giving her a sense of control since I just took most of that away from her. I should probably feel bad about how I ripped her from her father's hands, uprooted her without warning from the only home she's ever known.

A good man would feel terrible, but the truth is I'm too selfish to feel any remorse. All I feel is a sense of accomplishment. I've waited for a long time, watching as the Romero family struggled to stay afloat.

"Where are we going?" Elena surprises me with her meek voice, and I look over at her. She's all doe eyes and innocence. Breaking her will be a crushing blow to her father.

"Home."

She wraps her slender arms around her torso like she is hugging herself before turning away from me again to stare out of the window. Her small body trembles, and I can make out goosebumps on her creamy smooth skin.

"Turn up the heat, Markus."

"Got it, boss."

For the rest of the drive home, we sit silently—only the engine's sound and the occasional sob filling the cab.

By the time we pull to the compound, I'm sweating profusely under my three-piece suit. Markus must have turned up the heat to well over a hundred degrees. As soon as Markus opens the door, I slip out of the car.

The fresh air cools me, and I inhale a harsh breath into my lungs. Turning around, I'm prepared for a fight, or at least a struggle and am pleasantly surprised to find Elena sitting on the edge of the seat waiting to get out.

Maybe this won't be as hard as I had assumed it would be.

Eyes cast down, she wrings her hands in her lap nervously. Sliding off the seat, her small feet press against the gravel, and I contemplate picking her up to carry her inside when she winces at the contact. I love how fragile she is and how much I know she'll need me to make it through everything I have in store for her. When I'm done with her, she will rely on me for every single thing she wants or needs.

Obviously, I'm far too trusting because she slips past me like a small mouse. Breaking off into a dead run, she dashes past the car and down the driveway. I'm not worried, though, since there isn't anywhere for her to go.

She doesn't make it far before one of my men grabs her, tugging her by the arm a little too roughly. I grit my teeth, my jaw clenching as I bite back the need to tell him to get his fucking hands off of her. Anger zings through me when he tugs her again, and she loses her balance falling onto the ground, scraping her knees and legs in the process.

"Let go of me!" She screams, sobs ripping from her lungs in quick succession as she pulls against Roger's hold, trying to break free. The strap of her nightgown slips off her shoulder in the process, and she almost flashes a tit at my men.

Fuck no. No one gets to see what is mine.

Walking over to her, I gesture for Roger to let her go, and he does almost as quickly as he grabbed her, retreating two steps back. I'll deal with him later. Right now, I need to get her inside and put her in some different clothes. My men have seen enough of her already.

Looking down at her exposed legs, I see scratches from where she fell, so I'll need to make sure she isn't actually hurt. Reaching down, I grab her by the hips, feeling the heat of her skin beneath my hands and toss her over my shoulder like I did earlier.

A growl forms in my throat as I become aware of how she barely weighs anything.

She doesn't even fight me and rests motionless on my shoulder as I carry her into the house, through the foyer, and up the stairs to the bedroom we will share. Pushing the heavy wooden door open, my shoes slap against the tile as I walk across the room and deposit her on my bed... *our* bed. The moment her butt hits the mattress, she looks up and scoots backward until her back is pressed against the headboard.

Big green eyes brim with fear. I could tell her she is safe here, that nothing bad will happen to her. But that would be a lie. She isn't safe yet, especially not from me.

"Stay here, get comfortable. I'll be back soon," I tell her as I slowly walk back toward the door. I've got blood to spill before I can tend to my new toy.

Looking at my beautiful prize one last time, I close the door and lock it behind me.

I let the anger that I was swallowing down boil up to the surface as I make my way through the mansion and toward the front door.

Stepping outside, I find Edwardo guarding the porch. He turns to look at me, his hand reaching for his gun before he recognizes it's me.

"Is Roger still out here?"

"Yes, boss. He is doing a round over the west lawn. Is everything okay?"

"It will be..." I snap before walking off and into the night.

One-Click Savage Beginnings NOW!

ABOUT THE AUTHORS

J.L. Beck and C. Hallman are an international bestselling author duo who write contemporary and dark romance.

For a list of all of our books, updates and freebies visit our website.

www.bleedingheartromance.com

ALSO BY THE AUTHORS

<u>DARK ROMANCE</u>

The Blackthorn Elite
Hating You
Breaking You
Hurting You
Regretting You

The Obsession Duet
Cruel Obsession
Deadly Obsession

The Rossi Crime Family
Protect Me
Keep Me
Guard Me
Tame Me
Remember Me

The Moretti Crime Family
Savage Beginnings
Violent Beginnings

The King Crime Family
Indebted
Inevitable

<u>STANDALONES</u>

Their Captive

Runaway Bride

His Gift

Convict Me

Two Strangers

Printed in Great Britain
by Amazon

82223696R00198